D1298324

LIVING IT UP

LIVING IT UP

*A Guide to the
Named
Apartment Houses
of New York*

THOMAS E. NORTON
&
JERRY E. PATTERSON

ATHENEUM   *NEW YORK*
1984

PHOTOGRAPHIC CREDITS

Museum of the City of New York (Wurts Collection): pp. 42, 46, 54, 88, 94, 99, 123, 158, 172, 175, 200, 213, 231, 266, 303, 309

New York Public Library: pages 39 (Borough President of Manhattan, 44 (George L. Balgue), 50, 53, 62 (A. E. Sproul), 147 (George L. Balgue), 162, 185 (Joseph Smith), 204, 210 (Price Studios), 211 (F. S. Lincoln), 218 (New York *Sun*), 249 (Joseph Smith), 285 (Samuel Gottscho), 301 (George L. Balgue), 308 (Underwood & Underwood), 317, 341, 353 (both illustrations; bottom by John Adams Davis), 354, 369 (Borough President of Manhattan), 386

Nancy Phelan: pages 52, 73, 75, 79 (top), 98, 102, 115, 117, 133, 150, 157, 160, 180, 186, 195, 214, 237, 248, 253, 256, 275, 283, 318, 337, 361, 365, 377.

Real Estate Data, Inc.: pages 40, 71, 79 (bottom), 80, 90, 103, 104, 130, 138, 148, 167, 174, 228, 247, 273, 304, 339, 340.

St. James's Enterprises, Inc.: pages 298, 299

Sotheby Parke Bernet: page 226

The Trump Organization: pages 334, 335, 336

Zuberry Associates: page 152

Library of Congress Cataloging in Publication Data

Norton, Thomas E.
    Living it up.

    Includes index.
    1. Apartment houses—New York (N.Y.)—History.
2. Apartment houses—New York (N.Y.)—Directories.
I. Patterson, Jerry E.   II.   Title.
HD7287.6.U5N67   1984   333.33'8   83–45508
ISBN 0-689-11436-2

Published simultaneously in Canada by McClelland and Stewart Ltd.
Composition by P&M Typesetting Inc., Waterbury, Connecticut
Manufactured by Halliday Lithograph, West Hanover, Massachusetts
Designed by Kathleen Carey
First Edition

CONTENTS

I   *Introduction: The New York City Apartment House*   3

II   *The Named Buildings of New York: An Inventory*   29

III   *Nooks and Crannies: Named Residential Enclaves*   375

IV   *Names Writ in Water: Demolished Buildings*   381

V   *Walking Tours*   389

VI   *Geographical Index*   403

Acknowledgments   451

I

Introduction:
The New York City
Apartment House

NEARLY a million New Yorkers rejoiced at the end of the Civil War. Although far from the scene of battle, New York had experienced great difficulties during the war years. In 1863 the terrible draft riots had caused widespread unrest and had devastated sections of the city. More than one hundred thousand men from New York had served in the war, but the city was regarded by many in the North, especially in the early days of the war, as sympathetic to the South, with which the city had traditionally done a large amount of business. After the war unemployment was rife, as discharged soldiers were unable to find jobs. Inflation was also a serious problem.

Nevertheless, New York City, then only Manhattan, had grown considerably. In the 1860s the population had risen to 942,000 from 813,000. Part of this growth was natural increase, but a large part was immigration from abroad. New York was the great American port of entry: over a million alien immigrants arrived in New York in the second half of the decade.

This large population, the greatest of any American city, was badly distributed, or rather not distributed at all. Only the lower portion of the island was built up; the center of population was 14th Street and Fourth Avenue. The nine hundred thousand inhabitants—and an estimated forty thousand horses—were jammed into the lower five miles of Manhattan Island, not by choice but by inadequate housing and lack of transportation. New York was then the manufacturing and shipping center of the

United States, and in addition to residences the lower part of the island was occupied by stables, factories, shipyards, slaughterhouses, and warehouses. The superintendent of buildings wrote in 1872 that a little over half the space on the island of Manhattan was in use.

Fifth Avenue had already assumed its special position as the thoroughfare of fashion, but there was little building above 59th Street. Real estate speculators—prominent among them was the Astor family—were alert to the possibilities of upper Manhattan and were holding the lots at what were regarded as extravagantly high prices.

The Randel Plan of 1807–1811 had surveyed Manhattan from 14th Street to the end of the island and laid out streets and avenues in that vast area. It was a gridiron establishing the characteristic New York City lot—twenty-five feet by one hundred feet without an alley—and dictating the future growth of the city. But the New York of the 1870s barely stretched to 59th Street. Central Park was under construction, and its drives and bridle paths were almost completed; but the cross streets on either side had not yet been graded or paved, and the area between the park and the Hudson and East rivers was occupied mainly by squatters.

At a distance from the city were the villages of Greenwich, Yorkville, Harlem, Manhattanville, Bloomingdale, and a few others. Because transportation was poor, these villages were difficult to reach: a trip to Harlem, for example, took most of a day.

The West Side of the city, which within a few years was to be the great growth area, was being laid out into streets, avenues, and public places in the late 1860s. The circle at 59th Street and Eighth Avenue—not named for Columbus until 1892—was opened in 1867; Grand Army Plaza, west of Fifth Avenue between 58th and 59th streets, was opened in 1870.

Between the city and the villages were rocky open spaces occupied by squatters who put up shanties made of any handy material and lived surrounded by their goats and pigs. On the West Side above 59th Street were market gardens tended by the Germans who formed a large proportion of what was then called the suburban population. Other than a scattering of restaurants and beer gardens and a few decaying old mansions and farms, there was no regular settlement.

A writer to a newspaper in 1866 commented indignantly: "Several hundred thousand persons—rich and poor, male and female, wise and simple—earn their living by personal effort in that narrow corner of this island which lies south of Grand Street. We cannot live here, for most of this area is needed for stores, banks, offices, factories, workshops, etc., and it is inconvenient to live across the arms of the sea on either hand. We want to live uptown."

Since the city had not been consolidated with its suburbs, Manhattan really could only grow "uptown," to the north. Unlike some cities in Europe, especially Paris and Vienna, New York had no benevolent aristocracy to order the lines of new growth, nor was there autocratic development. The city government lacked jurisdiction over the surrounding areas across the rivers.

The *Evening Post* noted in 1867 that New York was destined to remain the center of commerce for the American continent, but then went on to list its objectionable features: "New York is the most inconveniently arranged commercial city in the world. . . . Its laborers are badly lodged, and in every way disaccommodated; the means of going from one part of the city to the others so badly contrived that a considerable part of the working population . . . spend a sixth part on their working days on the street cars or omnibuses, and the upper part of the island is made almost useless to persons engaged in daily business of any kind in the city."

Public transportation lagged badly behind the growth of population. There was an odd reluctance to better the transportation system or even to decide how it was to be bettered. Just as the Civil War was ending, a bill to permit the Metropolitan Railway Company to build an underground road in New York City was passed by the state legislature but vetoed by the governor.

In 1864 there were still only twelve omnibus lines, all operating below 50th Street and attempting, not very successfully, to carry sixty-one million passengers a year. Elevated railroads had been invented, but their use came only slowly: the Greenwich Street El was opened in 1868 but ran only from the Battery to 30th Street. In 1871 the builders of the Ninth Avenue El, with self-propelled steam locomotives, began to lay tracks above 30th Street. In 1878 the Third Avenue and Sixth Avenue els began operations. None of these developments reached very far up the island. When Commodore Cornelius Vanderbilt placed his Grand Central Station on 42nd Street, wags suggested that it should be called End of the World station. The citizenry was organizing mass meetings on the problems of "rapid transit," as it was already called. By and large, in the period just after the Civil War, New Yorkers still had to live close to their jobs, which were concentrated in the oldest downtown part of Manhattan.

Individual New York families had a limited choice of places to live, dictated, as always, by their economic standing: the majority lived either in private houses or in tenements. Although the two types of dwelling were physically mingled in most parts of the city, socially and economically the lines between the two were sharply, not to say rigidly, drawn, and they were simple: families of any economic or social substance had houses, owned or rented; the poor lived in tenements, always rented, usually from a nonresident owner, and, almost without exception, crowded and appallingly unsanitary. In a city in which by 1850 the foreign-born were in the majority, "Native Americans," as they were called, occupied the houses, and the immigrants the tenements.

But at the upper end of the New York scale of life, there were hotels with permanent residents and boarding houses and rooming houses of varying degrees of expense and comfort for those who did not want to do their own housekeeping. A surprising number of families lived in hotels; this practice continued until very recently in New York, as well as in other American cities. The vast Tremont Hotel in Boston is said to have been the first American hotel to offer accommodations for permanent guests, a plan adopted in the 1830s. Meals were included in the price of a room, the first example of what came to be known as the American plan.

Private houses varied in size, elegance, and age. The great upper Fifth Avenue mansions had not yet been built; the most lavish houses in the city were still clustered below 23rd Street. Few houses at any period in New York history have had a very long life span, but at the time of the Civil War there were still standing a good many houses built fifty or sixty years earlier. New houses were being built of brownstone or pressed brick decorated with brownstone—what Edith Wharton called "the universal chocolate-colored coating of the most hideous stone ever quarried." Thousands of brownstones were erected between 1850 and 1880, and they still exist in great numbers.

A tenement was, and is, defined by law as "any house or part of a house occupied or arranged to be occupied by three or more families living independently of each other and doing their own cooking on the premises." Although the word has become a synonym for slum, tenements, which began to be built in the 1850s, were multiple dwellings for—as was then said—"the laboring classes."

The housing problems of New York City were neither unrecognized nor ignored. The population was doubling every twenty years. Buildings that would accommodate more families than private houses and yet not be squalid tenements were badly needed for the middle class, but no one seemed to be able to develop them.

On 2 June 1857 Calvert Vaux, a young architect who had just come to live and work in New York, addressed a meeting of the newly formed American Institute of Architects held at New York University. The date is of great importance in the history of housing in New York. Vaux proposed to the attentive professionals "the adaptation of houses *à la française* to this country." He noted that in New York City multiple dwellings with separate apartments for several families were confined to tenements, and that no family of any standing would live in a tenement.

Vaux gave specific recommendations: the new buildings should have no more than four floors: in pre-elevator days prospective tenants regarded the higher floors as undesirable and well-to-do people ordinarily lived on the first or second floors. The apartments should face the street and the entrance and staircase should be attractive and inviting.

The young architect advanced at an opportune time an idea that was not actually new. Apartment houses were known even in the ancient world. Archeological remains of ancient civilizations provide strong evidence that apartmentlike multiple dwellings existed in cities when there was a large enough population of workers and merchants. By the third century B.C. there were multiple-family dwellings in Rome, and by the time of the empire these apartment houses had become quite common. Known to the Romans as *insulae* (islands), these four- or five-story dwellings would today be called tenements or single-room-occupancy lodging houses. They were often owned by speculators and were prone to fire and collapse.

The rise of populations in walled European cities in later centuries caused the haphazard development of multiple dwellings to continue. When the large urban convents and monasteries were secularized, they were often made into apartments, as were royal palaces at times. Au-

thorities were constantly bemoaning the abysmal conditions under which the poor lived, piled higgledy-piggledy
into makeshift wood or brick dwellings reaching five or
more stories—the poorest condemned to the upper stories
without heat or water.

Apartment dwelling became chic in France—by neces-
sity—when Louis XIV decreed that the nobility spend
much of its time with him in residence at Versailles,
where *appartements* were allocated on the basis of rank and
favor. The duc de Saint-Simon described his own suite of
rooms there in 1713 as consisting of an interior room, an
anteroom, two bedrooms, and a drawing room, all with
fireplaces and privies. In the reign of Louis XV an advertisement in a Paris newspaper offered an apartment of ten
rooms including a library and bedrooms with closets. People were already willing to put up with less room in a
building shared with other families in order to enjoy the
privacy and the luxuries now available to a growing middle class.

This was the pattern in Paris and other continental cities. Only in London were more or less luxurious multiple-
unit dwellings not in favor. The private house remained
the norm for the middle class, although the poor lived in
hovels crowded together in slums.

By the mid-nineteenth century, as the need for encir-
cling fortifications decreased in the cities of continental
Europe, and as the urban population continued to grow,
the old walls were torn down in Paris, Madrid, Vienna,
and elsewhere, and new boulevards, lined with grand public buildings and apartment houses specifically designed as
such, took their place.

In 1852, when Louis-Napoléon became emperor of the
French, he found the overgrown medieval city of Paris
lacking in the grandeur he desired for his capital. Sanitary
and housing conditions were abominable. Travel across the
city ranged from nightmarish to impossible, and many
Parisians never strayed out of their immediate neighborhood. Water of uncertain quality was supplied by untrust-
worthy pumps; the resultant diseases gave Paris the highest death rate in all of France.

Napoléon III had the vision and the architectural aspirations to create a new Paris, and he found the perfect
helpmate in Georges Haussmann, whom he appointed as
his prefect of the Seine with broad powers to transform
Paris into a modern metropolis. In a remarkably short
time avenues were cut through from one end of the city to

another; a reliable water supply via an aqueduct system took shape; tree-lined boulevards rather than fortifications encircled the old part of town; streets were paved; public transport developed; and large apartment houses were erected throughout Paris.

An ingenious system was devised to pay for all this grandiose development without raising taxes and incurring the wrath of the populace: the central government and local authorities issued revenue bonds purchased largely by insurance companies which then, with subsidies and tax abatements, erected income-producing apartment houses. In many respects it was an early government-subsidized slum clearance program designed to produce housing for the middle class.

Typically these apartments were six or seven stories high, with a large entrance, flanked on the ground floor by shops, leading to an inner court. Interior staircases led up to suites of rooms. The most expensive and commodious apartments were located on the first floor, and the meanest and cheapest at the top.

In 1857 George Lucas, an American art dealer resident in Paris, took an apartment on the sixth floor of an old building. Only a few years later, forced to vacate owing to Haussmann's redevelopment of the area, Lucas moved to a fifth-floor apartment in a new building; and a decade later, his fortunes much improved, he took a spacious suite on the fourth floor, consisting of a living room, dining room, kitchen, two bedrooms with fireplaces, and a bathroom.

In a similar but slightly later development in the capital of the Austro-Hungarian Empire, the old ramparts surrounding the inner city of Vienna were pulled down, a decent water supply was assured, and palatial public and residential buildings were erected on the Ringstrasse, the broad, tree-lined boulevard that replaced the old walls and became *the* address for Vienna's *nouveaux riches.* Conveniently situated near the new opera house, the university, the parliament, city hall, theaters, and museums, these newly erected apartment buildings occupied the spaces not reserved for monumental public buildings.

The typical Viennese apartment building was modeled after an aristocratic palace except that, as in Paris, the ground floor was usually commercial. Such a building for the bourgeoisie was referred to as a *Mietpalast* (rent palace) in contrast to the lower-class tenement called a *Mietkaserne* (rent barracks). The former usually had an imposing lobby, spacious suites of public and private rooms, large interior courts, and the latest in amenities. It became the typical dwelling of the upper-middle classes, who vicariously shared a sense of grandeur unobtainable in a small house. Thus, although Paris pioneered in apartment building, the buildings of Vienna were probably more widely copied by the architects of New York's great apartment houses built circa 1900.

These European developments, primarily those of Second Empire Paris, were the direct inspiration of Calvert Vaux's talk to the architects. His thoughts were printed in the popular magazine the *Crayon* and in *Harper's Weekly* ("Parisian Buildings for City Residents"). His friend Richard Morris Hunt, then well embarked on his architectural career, was especially impressed and spread the idea of "French flats." Vaux himself and his partner, Frederick Law Olmsted, won the contract to design Central Park in 1858, and both men went on to careers as landscape architects. The Civil War impeded new construction in New York, but exactly ten years after Vaux's talk Hunt built the first French flats in New York.

The Stuyvesant Building at 142 East 18th Street, near Third Avenue, the first New York apartment house by most reckoning, was commissioned by Rutherfurd Stuyvesant, designed by Hunt, and built in 1869–70. Rutherfurd Stuyvesant had turned his name around in order to inherit the property of his mother's family, which included the site of the building. He had met Hunt in France and, like him, was impressed by the Parisian solution to housing for the middle and upper classes in an ever more crowded city.

The Stuyvesant apartments were in two separate structures, each with a tile-decorated lobby and its own staircase. The first four stories each held four suites; the fifth floor had four studios for artists. One of the first-floor apartments had nine rooms, one had seven rooms, and two had four rooms. Above were seven-room apartments and six-room studios.

True to its French origins, the Stuyvesant had a concierge, who occupied quarters on the ground floor. Communication from the ground floor to the apartments above was by means of a speaking tube. The tenants, of course, had their own staffs of servants.

The problem facing Hunt and his patron was how to attract the right sort of tenant to this radically new type of home, that is, one shared with others. Stuyvesant solved that problem in large part by filling the house with his Knickerbocker friends and successful writers and artists. The *Real Estate Record* warned, "this business of renting suites of rooms will never become popular in New York, until it is first rendered fashionable by well-to-do people." The editorial writer thought that the middle-class head of a family, defined as a man who could pay an annual rent of $800 to $1,500, preferred to commute from a suburban village, and recommended that, instead of building flats, New York investors extend the steam railroad system.

The Stuyvesant, and the apartment buildings that followed it, soon became socially acceptable and, almost from the first, were profitable for their owners. The researches of Hunt's biographer Paul Baker have shown that the Stuyvesant cost $165,858.62 to build. In 1870–71 gross income was $24,091.98, less $5,781.27 in repairs, "bringing a net income of $18,310.71, an excellent return on the initial investment."

Richard Morris Hunt was the architect of Stevens House, an enormous building on West 27th Street running from Fifth Avenue to Broadway. The Haight House on the corner of Fifth Avenue and 15th Street attracted a somewhat bohemian crowd and became known as a "chosen refuge of artistic and literary people."

It was a step forward when the new buildings began to be called apartment houses, which implied that they were permanent residences and not places for transients. While the poorest citizens were only too accustomed to sharing their premises with other people (and, until a surprisingly late date, with livestock), many upper-class and even middle-class New Yorkers continued to have difficulty in adjusting to apartment life.

Competition among builders, the growth of the city, the spread of the cooperative movement, and soaring real estate values, all forced the gradual replacement of the private dwelling by the apartment house as the typical habitation for the New Yorker, except at the Four Hundred level of wealth—after all, splendid mansions were still being built along Fifth and Madison avenues and in the adjoining side streets well into the twentieth century.

Such now demolished buildings as the *Stevens House**
(ca. 1870), the Knickerbocker (1880), Jardine (1871), the *Grosvenor* (1873), the *Albany* (1876), the *Spanish Flats*

---

*Buildings appearing in italics are described in Parts II, III, or IV.

(1882), the *Hoffman Arms* (1875), and the *Rembrandt* (1882), plus such extant examples as *The Gramercy* (1883), the *Chelsea Hotel* (1884), *The Dakota* (1884), and *The Osborne* (1885), all helped to make apartment-house living not only respectable but in many ways far more desirable for the bulk of middle-class New Yorkers.

In 1872, only three years after the completion of the Stuyvesant, James D. McCabe, Jr., discussing "what it costs to live in New York" in his revealing book *Lights and Shadows of New York,* informed his readers of a significant recent development: "Of late years, a new style of living has been introduced. The city now contains a number of houses located in unexceptional neighborhoods, and built in first-class style, which are rented in flats, or suites of apartments, as in the Parisian houses."

The spread of apartment houses in Manhattan after 1870 was due not only to increased acceptance of this form of "Parisian" living but to technological advances that made possible the building of miles of apartment blocks in the last two decades of the century.

One invention made it possible for the city to grow, literally, upwards. The elevator had been used for freight transport since the middle of the century. Improvements, such as speed governors to slow downward progress, eventually made the invention suitable for transporting people. The first passenger elevator in a residential building in New York was that installed in the Fifth Avenue Hotel on 23 August 1859.

The importance of the elevator in the growth of New York City and in the way of life adopted by most of its residents can hardly be overstressed. In 1888 a city official said, "American architecture as an independent school began its existence with the invention and adaptation of the elevator."

Improvements in lighting came at about the same time. Houses, as well as shops and streets, had been lighted by gas since the 1820s, when the city chartered the New York Gas Light Company, which laid pipes and manufactured gas, first from oil and rosin, then from soft coal. The earliest apartments in the city were lighted by gas, by that time greatly improved and usually made with water. It was not until the late 1880s that the use of electricity became common in residences. The station opened by Thomas A. Edison in Pearl Street in 1881–82 was the first central electric light power plant in the world. The rich adopted electricity in their homes almost immediately, but gas lighting lingered in many buildings until World War I.

The first flats were heated by coal or wood-burning fireplaces and by iron stoves, which had begun to supplant fireplaces for heating as well as cooking. Central heating was slowly being introduced; furnaces using hot water and steam heat were available, at least to the rich, from the Civil War on.

Only five telephones were in use in the city in 1877, but by the following year there were enough subscribers to warrant publication of the first directory, and in 1879 the first telephone exchange was opened.

A thread of aristocratic, or at least socially prominent, names runs through the first fifty years in the history of New York's apartment house developers. Apartment house ownership got off to an auspicious start with Rutherfurd Stuyvesant, and he was followed by other worthies. Paran Stevens, who built the *Stevens* House in 1870, is perhaps best known today through his wife, the ambitious New York hostess Mrs. Paran Stevens (born Marietta Reed of Lowell, Massachusetts), who served as the prototype for Mrs. Lemuel Struthers in Edith Wharton's New York novel *The Age of Innocence.*

Just a few years later uptown's most luxurious apartment hotel was erected by Samuel Verplanck Hoffman at the corner of Madison Avenue and East 59th Street. The *Hoffman Arms,* as it was called, set a new standard for comfort and convenience and had the distinction of being owned by the Reverend Eugene Augustus Hoffman, dean of General Theological Seminary and reputedly the richest clergyman in the United States. It was demolished in the early 1930s.

The developer of *The Dakota* was Edward S. Clark, heir to the Singer Sewing Machine fortune, who was willing to gamble his wealth and good name on what was called Clark's Folly—an apartment house of unrivaled luxury (it was ranked among the most expensive nongovernmental buildings ever erected in the city when completed in 1884) amid the shanties, goats, and unpaved roads of the Upper West Side.

Twenty years later William Waldorf Astor joined in this Upper West Side boom when he built the *Belnord* and *Apthorp* apartment houses. His cousin Vincent Astor built *Astor Court,* also on the Upper West Side.

In the interim such prominent civic and commercial leaders as George A. Hearn (*The Ardea,* ca. 1895), W. E. D.

Stokes (*The Ansonia,* 1904), and Don José de Navarro, the
Spanish consul in New York and husband of the famous
actress Mary Anderson (the *Spanish Flats,* 1882), may be
mentioned as typifying this thread of enlightened self-in-
terest through real estate development, a thread revived in
more recent times by Aristotle Onassis *(Olympic Tower).*

Right on the heels of the nonprofessional real estate developers came those whose main source of income was derived from such activity. Interestingly enough, architects
were often closely involved. For example, the Jardine was
built by and named for the senior partner of the architectural firm Jardine, Kent & Jardine. In 1890 the *Graham*
at Madison Avenue and East 89th Street was built by architect Thomas Graham; it was the first apartment hotel
on the far Upper East Side.

Perhaps the most memorable of these builder-architects
was Gaetan Ajello *(Eton Hall, Peter Minuit),* who worked
with the Paterno and Campagna families, major developers of the Upper West Side and Morningside Heights.

Joseph Paterno (1881–1939), in partnership with his
brother Charles, developed more than one hundred apartment houses in Manhattan. He was a patron of Columbia's
Casa Italiana and was responsible for some of the most
strikingly impressive apartments ever built in New York
(Colosseum, Castle Village).

Of course, most developers were not particularly inter-
ested in the city beautiful or in altruism, and their structures were erected for profit only. However, the volatile
nature of Manhattan real estate left as many of them bankrupt as it did wealthy.

At the same time that the more affluent, middle-class
respectable New Yorkers were turning to the apartment as
the solution to their housing problems, the much more
serious problems of those at the lower end of the economic
scale were receiving attention as well, and the solutions
offered to the poor were not radically different from those
offered to the well-off.

As early as the mid-1830s a multiple-family building
for poor tenants was erected at the end of Water Street, in
what is now Corlear's Hook Park, by one James Allaire.
This was probably New York's first tenement.

Other tenements were soon built to cope with the slum
population whose ranks were being swelled by mass immigration. In 1851 a benevolent Quaker, Silas Wood,
built a large tenement which he called Gotham Court.

Although it was designed to be an improvement over existing housing, Gotham Court soon turned into a wretched slum, called by its tenants Swipes' Alley, Hell's Kitchen, or Murderers' Row. In 1896, after all attempts to clean it up had failed, Gotham Court was torn down by the city.

The Workingman's Home Association, appalled at the conditions revealed by the investigation of the quasi-governmental Association for Improving the Condition of the Poor, built the first so-called model tenement in 1855 at Mott and Elizabeth streets.

Among the model tenements for poor workers sponsored by private philanthropy were the buildings put up by the Phipps family in East 31st Street (1906; demolished) and West 63rd Street (1907–11; sold in 1961; slated for demolition); a twelve-story complex at First Avenue and East 72nd Street (1882; demolished 1960) sponsored by the Astor family; and the model tenements organized by the nonprofit City & Suburban Homes Company at First Avenue and East 64th Street (1900–1915) and at York Avenue and 79th Street (ca. 1900), and *The Cherokee* on East 77th Street designed by Henry Atterbury Smith. The Rockefeller interests were responsible for *Dunbar Apartments* in Harlem.

By 1930 private interests had put up some ten thousand or so units of model tenement housing. But with the depression, a mass inflow of unemployed moving to the city, and a deteriorating stock of old-law tenements, government came to assume a far greater role in providing better housing for the poor. Although the Phipps family, for example, is still involved in workers' housing, by and large the role of private philanthropy has been completely superseded by government at the local, state, and federal levels. From the *First Houses* (1936) and all subsequent slum clearance, Title I, Mitchell-Lama, and other housing projects, to *Ruppert Towers* and *Taino Towers*, the building of apartments for working people and the poor has continued—with government funding—along with the building of apartments by private enterprise for the middle and upper classes.

By around 1885 several distinct types of apartments had emerged, based on the varying needs—and funds—of groups of tenants and owners. In contrast to the situation at mid-century, when private homes, hotels, and rooming houses had been the only options available to middle-class people, the possibilities for housing now included studios, bachelor flats, apartment hotels, housekeeping apartments, and cooperatives.

Studios. A long tradition of special housing for creative people—especially painters—exists in New York. In the late nineteenth century many successful painters maintained in-town studio/residences even though much of the time they were out sketching in the countryside. In New York were to be found the National Academy, the Art Union, the dealers, the auction rooms, the patrons, so it behooved artists to remain visible in the city.

Richard Morris Hunt was the architect for one of the first buildings designed especially for artists, the Studio Building on West 10th Street. James B. Johnson, a rich art patron, commissioned the building from him in 1857. It contained working spaces for painters, rudimentary living quarters, and a central exhibition gallery. Emphasis was on *working* space. The building was a great success from the start, and the artists' response to communal living must have helped the architect in his design for the Stuyvesant apartments a decade later.

Soon studios were built uptown, the emphasis always being on large working space with good, preferably north, light, and separate living quarters. Often this took the form of a duplex arrangement, and studio apartments, especially those in the West Fifties and Sixties—such as the *Holbein Studios* on West 55th Street—became chic dwelling places for young couples with artistic or bohemian leanings, even if the working spaces were used far more for entertaining than for creating masterpieces. Often there were dining facilities within the studio building (artists were not expected to cook!), and some of these buildings became quite elaborate. *The Gainsborough* (1908) on Central Park South and the studio buildings of West 67th Street (1907) are surviving examples of the form. The idea of special working-living buildings for artists has persisted: the most notable recent example is *Westbeth* (1969).

Bachelor flats. In the nineteenth century unmarried gentlemen were thought to require special living arrangements and so bachelor flats were built for them. The typical suite contained a sitting room, a bedroom, a tiny manservant's room, and perhaps a small kitchen, in short, just enough space and facilities to allow a gentleman who had no family to live simply, comfortably, and well, to entertain intimate groups of friends, and, in general, to

lead a carefree life. An important early example of a building designed for bachelors is *The Wilbraham*.

In many cases bachelor accommodations were provided
on separate floors of otherwise family-oriented apartment
houses (*The Gramercy*, for example), but there were also
literally dozens of buildings specifically designed as bachelor apartments. As late as 1906 the architects Schwartz
& Gross built bachelor apartments at 225-229 West 69th
Street. Even later a number of buildings were designed for
single women, occasionally called bachelorettes (*Beekman
Towers*).

Apartment hotels. In the fall of 1883, discussing the
plans for the proposed Fifth Avenue Plaza Apartments at
59th Street, the *Real Estate Record* wondered if each suite
of rooms should have a kitchen. Each building ought to
have no more than one cooking range. "The smells are a
nuisance," the *Record* declared, "and so are the multiplic-
ity of cooks. . . . All apartments should have a restaurant
at which meals may be taken, and it is predicted that
suites with kitchens will be in disfavor a few years hence."

The prediction proved wrong, but for a number of years
most, if not all, cooperative apartments and many rental
apartments (*The Dakota*, for example) featured restaurants
and certain other features of a hotel in their plans. In the
rental sphere these eventually emerged as a distinct type
called apartment hotels and were most prevalent in Midtown and on the Upper West Side, where many still exist.
The former hotel dining rooms of the *Oliver Cromwell* and
the *Olcott* on West 72nd Street have been turned into commercial restaurants open to the public.

Apartment hotels were considered especially ideal
homes for the families of entertainers, merchants, and
professionals who did not have the time or inclination to
settle permanently by buying a house or cooperative apartment or taking a long lease. These families tended to
avoid predominantly transient hotels, where some of the
guests might not be so "respectable" (respectability preoc-
cupied nineteenth-century Americans). People were also
anxious to reduce long journeys on the elevated roads by
living close to work.

Apartment hotels proliferated in part because of a quirk
in the building laws. In 1891 it was noted that most new
hotels were called apartment hotels. "The law restricts the
height of large flats," the *Real Estate Record* remarked,
"but not of hotels. Consequently, anyone wishing to erect

a building that is really an apartment house calls it by the name of an apartment hotel."

Eventually high labor costs, among other things, brought about the demise of the apartment hotel in its original form. Many of the still-existing buildings have been transformed into regular apartment houses without hotel services. However, within the past few years many of the new super-luxury rentals and condominiums have adopted some other "hotel" services as amenities for their residents. Prominent among these services are the concierge who can speak several languages and is expected to "perform miracles"; the message-answering desk; valet cleaning services; telex; maid service—in short, just about everything *except* the in-house dining facility, which now seems hopelessly outmoded in a city of some thousands of restaurants of all types.

Housekeeping apartments. Self-contained units with full kitchens and dining rooms, plus—especially in the early days—accommodations for live-in servants, were originally called housekeeping apartments and are the predecessors of what are now called simply apartments. In the nineteenth century, with gas lamps, coal cookstoves, and little or no central heating, such housekeeping apartments were difficult to manage, but with advances in domestic technology they became commonplace.

The floor plans of housekeeping apartments gradually improved, allowing more light and air and easier passage within the flat. Each generation of builders roundly condemned the floor plans of their predecessors, but, in fact, each new development in the layout of the typical apartment reflected the changing times, so that in the middle twentieth century, for example, apartment design reflects the decrease in the size of families and the increase in the number of people living alone, the streamlining of cooking and cleaning, and the trend toward a generally less formal way of life and a consequent decrease in spaciousness.

Cooperatives. Several of the best and most attractive of the early apartment houses were built by cooperative societies and were a direct outgrowth of the movement for "cooperation" that was so powerful in Europe and the United States in the last third of the nineteenth century. Cooperation was the non-profit-making management of an economic venture, for the mutual benefit of the members. Credit unions, burial societies, food cooperatives, and cooperative housing were typically such ventures.

The philosophical foundations of the movement can be

traced to Charles Fourier (1772–1837), who advocated social organization based on cooperative effort rather than individualism. He espoused the idea of the phalanx, a community of 1,620 persons living and working together. The most famous American example of the Fourierist phalange was Brook Farm in Massachusetts (1841–47).

The cooperative society was also promoted in the writings of Robert Owen, the Welsh social reformer, and his son Robert Dale Owen, who founded the communal settlement in New Harmony, Indiana (1825). The economist Henry George, author of *Progress and Poverty* and candidate for mayor of New York in 1886 and 1897, was another advocate of cooperative organization.

Among the followers of George was a remarkable and still largely uncelebrated man, the architect Philip G. Hubert, who founded the cooperative apartment movement in New York. Born in France in 1830, Hubert emigrated to the United States. In 1880 he organized the Hubert Home Club, which was dedicated to building cooperative apartments for the benefit of the tenant-owners. Apparently the first such apartment house was the *Rembrandt,* built in 1882 at 140 West 57th Street, just east of where Carnegie Hall stands today. Now demolished, the Rembrandt was followed by another Home Club apartment at 121 Madison Avenue (still standing but converted to offices); the ten-story building was at the time of its erection the tallest apartment house ever built.

In 1882 the *Real Estate Record* discussed the new cooperative movement: "Instead of purchasing a house, the cooperator buys an apartment which may cost him anywhere from $10,000 to $50,000. The taxes, insurance, expenses of lighting and heating, janitor and elevator boy are assessed at an equitable rate upon all the cooperators."

Several of these cooperative buildings, including Hubert's *Chelsea* (1885), had dining facilities, since the cooperative effort was, philosophically, not limited to just sharing a common roof. The dwellers in a cooperative apartment looked upon themselves as quasi-utopian pioneers of a new era in human society. In 1888 Edward Bellamy's enormously popular novel *Looking Backward,* set in Boston in the year 2000, expounded a crime-free, poverty-free, prejudice-free society organized communally. People lived in large apartment structures where the cooking was done at a central kitchen and meals were taken in communal dining halls. Other domestic chores were to be organized differently, too, according to Bellamy. As the

Bostonian of 2000 philosophizes, "A very important cause of former poverty was the vast waste of labor and materials which resulted from domestic washing and cooking, and the performing separately of innumerable other tasks to which we apply the cooperative plan."

Shortly after 1900, however, the cooperative movement lost its momentum, at least as far as apartments went. The *Chelsea* and others were converted to offices, rental flats, or hotels, and P. G. Hubert left New York for southern California, where he ended his days.

Of the early cooperatives, only *The Gramercy* (1883) retains its original form of ownership. Most of the present cooperatives came into existence because the original landlords wished to get out from under unprofitable properties (during the thirties and fifties) or to make a big profit (in the seventies and eighties).

In most other parts of the United States the condominium is the usual method of organizing a multiple dwelling on a not-for-profit basis. Each tenant is the owner of his/her own apartment and can come and go, buy or sell, rent or reside, at will. In a cooperative arrangement the tenant resides in—but does not own—his or her own apartment; the tenant owns shares in the cooperative association proportional to the size of the unit and holds a proprietary lease on the discrete physical space of the suite of rooms. The board of directors of the association may lay down rules of conduct and restrictions on financing, buying, and selling and may assess the shareholders for communal expenses.

The differences in the two types of ownership are not only important in practice; they also underscore the contrasting philosophy, outlook, and enabling legislation behind the two patterns. New York's first cooperatives date from the 1880s, the condominiums only from the 1960s. Historically and philosophically, today's cooperative apartment dwellers are descendants of the Fourierists, Owenites, Bellamyites, and other utopians of the nineteenth century. The ability of the board to turn down an applicant for the purchase of a Sutton Place cooperative apartment is rooted in the idea that the owner-associates in a cooperative building are members of a self-selected and self-governing group organized for communal living.

By 1890 patterns of apartment types and apartment living had been established in New York. Many of those patterns are unchanged today. Finding the apartment one wants and can afford has always been a problem. In 1890 William Dean Howells moved with his family from Boston to New York to take over the editorship of a magazine. He depicted the trials of finding a place to live in Manhattan in a thinly veiled fiction called *A Hazard of New Fortunes*. The Marches—Howells's fictional couple—investigated residential hotels and former mansions cut up into small flats without elevators or steam heat, two features they had especially set their hearts on. "Flatting advertisements took them to numbers of huge apartment houses chiefly distinguished from tenement houses by the absence of fire escapes on their facades." Along the way they encountered buildings named Esmeralda, Wagram, Palmyra, and Asteroid. They ended up in an apartment building called the Xenophon (its twin was the Thucidides). It was really beyond their means and lacked some of the services they wanted, but it was the best they could get, and like New Yorkers before and since, they settled for it.

The fashionableness of apartment living had made such searches only too common in real life. The shortage of apartments lasted until the first decade of the new century when some four thousand new apartment buildings were constructed in Manhattan.

When returning doughboys were welcomed back to New York City after the Great War of 1914–1918, Manhattan—since 1898 only a borough of the consolidated city—had a population of 2,284,103 (1920) spread out over virtually the entire island, and almost all of those inhabitants were living in apartments that had been built between 1880 and 1910.

A postwar depression caused a temporary lull in building, but in the mid-1920s a boom period of construction began in Manhattan. Great changes were evident in the manner of building and in the style of the suites themselves. Standards of comfort, technological improvements, and new approaches to apartment living brought about dramatic changes in heights, layouts, and amenities. In the era of the skyscraper office building the "modern" apartment house came into its own.

People all over the world who learned about New York City from Hollywood films now saw an apartment above Manhattan's skyline, with a white baby grand piano at one end, as the ultimate in modern living. For the first time the apartment, temporarily at least, replaced the little house with a white picket fence as the American dream.

Many of these grand apartments of the twenties and early thirties were built on Fifth and Park avenues, Sutton and Beekman places. However, the boom produced imposing structures in all parts of town, including Chelsea *(London Terrace)*, Murray Hill *(Towne House)*, Midtown *(Tudor City)*, and the Upper West Side *(Beresford)*. In some neighborhoods, like Greenwich Village, the arrival of these behemoths was not welcomed by the local residents. Edmund Wilson wrote in 1927: "There have been erected on lower Fifth Avenue two monstrous apartment houses—one just south of the Brevoort Hotel [this is the One Fifth Avenue building] and the other between Tenth and Eleventh Streets. They loom over the Village like mountains, and they have suddenly changed its proportions. . . . The whole Village seems now merely a base for these cubic apartment buildings. Such good quality as still lingered here along with the low roofs of the provincial town has thus been rendered insignificant; it is impossible to get away from these huge coarse and swollen mounds— blunt, clumsy, bleaching the sunlight with their dismal, pale yellow sides, and stamping down both the old formal square and the newer Bohemian refuge."

After the giddy prosperity and massive building boom of the twenties came the depression of the thirties. Many buildings planned in the twenties did not actually get under way until after the crash of 1929, so that their luxurious appointments often seem to jar with their completion date *(River House,* for example). But by 1933 the full impact of the financial crisis could be seen in the fact that no new apartments were begun in that year. Building by private investors stopped, and larger apartments were split into smaller units. Private philanthropy could no longer cope with the massive unemployment and attendant demand for housing, foods, jobs, and help in general. For the first time in the United States housing was provided by the government (at the local, state, and federal levels). The era of public housing had begun.

In New York City the first such project was called the *First Houses* (1935). In a slum area of the Lower East Side, tenements were torn down or rehabilitated and new buildings erected, using Works Progress Administration labor. This was the first project of the newly formed New York City Housing Authority, and the first of what would turn out to be one of the most ambitious building programs in the history of the world.

When World War II came to an end, New York was a crowded city with a shortage of apartments and a population largely rendered stationary by rent control. Originally imposed during the war to prevent rent gouging, rent control has remained in effect, with modifications, in New York City for more than forty years. While in 1940 seventy new buildings containing 4,850 apartments had been completed, in the years 1943–45 there were no completions at all. Shortages of building materials prevented new construction; those shortages continued for some time after the end of the war.

Although between 1940 and 1950 the population of Manhattan increased very slightly (to 1,960,101 from 1,889,924), returning army personnel could find no place to live. At the same time many veterans were seeking a single-family house in the suburbs. The years after the war were the time in which vast tract house settlements were built on Long Island and in New Jersey, and tens of thousands of middle-class families moved from New York City.

Within the city there was a movement to equal the attractions of suburbia by building relatively low rise housing in the form of "villages," which served the dual purpose of reclaiming large portions of slum areas and furnishing new housing for veterans. The most famous examples are *Stuyvesant Town* and *Peter Cooper Village* (both 1947). The idea of calling such enclaves villages dates back at least to *Knickerbocker Village* of 1934.

Public housing and government-assisted housing constituted larger proportions of the housing stock than ever before in American history. "Projects" arose in many parts of Manhattan, especially the Lower East Side (*Alfred E. Smith Houses,* 1952), Harlem (*St. Nicholas Houses,* 1954), and the West Side (*Frederick Douglass Houses,* 1958). Similar large private developments were publicly assisted, such as the Mitchell-Lama projects (named for two members of the New York State legislature who wrote the program), among them *Park West Village* (1957) and *Lenox Terrace* (1957). Throughout the sixties and seventies more of these projects were built, many of them on an even larger scale. The extremely controversial *Taino Towers* (1977) may have marked the end of this phase of Manhattan housing. Even with no further building, however, the projects completed are of staggering size. In 1983 the New York City Housing Authority was the landlord of over 600,000 people in 265 projects.

As a corollary of government assistance, entire neighborhoods were bulldozed and reconstructed. The largest of
these schemes was the West Side Urban Renewal plan.
Between 1958 and 1983 nearly 600 buildings were
demolished in the twenty-block area bounded by Central
Park West, Amsterdam Avenue, West 87th Street, and
West 97th Street. They were replaced by 130 new properties containing 5,400 apartments. This new construction
was accompanied by restoration of older buildings in the
area.

During the sixties private construction tended to build
high-rise apartment buildings along the avenues of the
Upper East Side. These buildings contained what were
generally known as luxury apartments, although by the
standards of the twenties and thirties they were hardly
luxurious. The Upper East Side came to be considered the
most fashionable part of Manhattan. Gone were the days
when the Astor estate could say "no one of any standing
will *ever* live on the East Side." The tearing down of the
elevated tracks in the 1950s gave the signal for a massive
redevelopment of the area lying between East 59th and
East 96th streets. For the first time there was widespread
construction of fifteen-to-twenty-story apartment buildings. Advertisements and brochures for these buildings
put great emphasis on the views. The apartments were
higher but noticeably smaller than those built before the
war. Prospective tenants were single people, older couples
who moved back to the city after their children were
grown, or companies that rented apartments for their em-
ployees' use. In the seventies well-to-do foreigners became
an important market for these luxury apartments.

At the same time that the Upper East Side was becoming fashionable and crowded—by the eighties it had become one of the most densely populated places in the
world, with seventy-five hundred people per square
mile—parts of New York were decaying. Neighborhoods
have always risen and fallen throughout New York's history, but in the seventies and eighties processes became
both speedier and more violent. The West Side lost thousands of residents to the suburbs, and its housing stock,
particularly along Broadway, began to decay, although it
never experienced the abandonment, vandalism, and arson
suffered in the Bronx. In the Tompkins Square area east
of Avenue A and in Central Harlem there were acres of
abandoned or derelict buildings and a shrinking population, and marginal neighborhoods in many parts of the island developed pockets of decay.

The late seventies and early eighties were times of re-
discovery: neighborhoods that had not been residential for
a century, such as the financial district and Tribeca, saw
large-scale conversions of commercial buildings to residential apartments. Not only business buildings were transformed: by the eighties well-to-do New Yorkers were living in former police stations, fire halls, schools, synagogues,
and churches.

A century after the Stuyvesant opened its doors, New
York is a city of apartment dwellers on a scale unknown
anywhere else in the United States. A small number of
single-family private houses remain; their number is not
growing, but neither is it decreasing, since most are now
protected by landmarking or historic district laws. The
kind of housing that has decreased, and continues to decrease, is the tenement. Thousands have been torn down
to clear space for public housing and urban renewal; others
have been renovated or combined to make new apartment
buildings.

Apartment buildings cover the island of Manhattan
from the Battery to Marble Hill. They are of every size,
from two apartments to a thousand, from two stories to
forty, from one room to twenty. And they are in every
state of maintenance, from the derelict to the shiny new.
Several of the most famous buildings have celebrated their
centenary, and hundreds of buildings now occupied are
eighty to ninety years old. At the same time buildings
now under construction or planned are larger, more luxurious, and, especially, taller than before. New Yorkers,
more than ever, are living it up.

II

*The Named Buildings
of New York:
An Inventory*

THE names of Manhattan's apartment buildings, like the city itself, are inconsistent, surprising, and sometimes enigmatic. The nearly two thousand names in the inventory that follows do not readily lend themselves to analysis, but a few remarks can be made.

On the whole, names have been given to buildings to help rent them: they have been selling points. From the beginning they gave distinction to a building. At first, from the 1870s to the 1890s, names were needed because apartment houses were a new phenomenon in New York. Later, as blocks of apartments went up in previously undeveloped areas of the city, owners vied for tenants, and an elegant name, or one easily recalled, was thought to help fill the apartments. Certain exceptions have stood out: very few buildings on Fifth or Park avenues or Sutton Place have names. There the street address confers sufficient distinction in the minds of New Yorkers. In most parts of the city, however, names have been needed. Perhaps the chief fascination in studying them is to detect the varying appeal of names aimed at prospective renters during the last century.

New York has always been known as the city of immigrants, a city with strong and persistent enclaves of nationalities. In many ways immigration is the chief fact of New York's history. The island of Manhattan has been, and still is, the point of arrival for millions. Fifth Avenue has more ethnic parades than any other main thoroughfare in the world. Yet ethnicity is not much reflected in the names of Manhattan's apartment buildings.

The first Americans are fairly well represented: a number of buildings have Indian names, *Iroquois, Manhasset,* and *Seneca* among them.

Of the large, older immigrant groups, three are hardly represented at all: the Irish, the Germans, and the Jews. The two principal groups of the present, the Caribbeans and the blacks, are represented only in public housing, where they share the names with New York City geography, historical allusions, and politicians, social workers, and holders of government office.

The only Italian and Spanish names are those that predate mass immigration, reflecting the strong pre-1900 romantic view of southern Europe *(San Remo, Goya, Palermo).* There is a liberal sprinkling of French names because France has always seemed elegant to Americans. *Versailles, Trianon,* and *Palais Royal* are names of apartment houses circa 1900, while *Le Triomphe* and *Le Premier* are names given to buildings put up circa 1980. German names exist, for the most part, on the buildings erected by Germans and named after their owners.

The names that are most easily recognizable as New York are usually geographical *(Gracie, Sutton, Gramercy)* or datable to the period of the Hudson-Fulton celebration of 1909 when there was a revival of interest in New York's Dutch heritage *(Hendrik Hudson, Peter Minuit, Knickerbocker).*

Not too many notable Americans have buildings named for them. Washington Irving, a great New Yorker, has more buildings named for him than anyone else, but there is no Whitman or Melville, also native sons. Mayors and other politicians have been honored more by public housing than privately built apartment houses. George Washington, Ulysses S. Grant, and William T. Sherman, who lived in New York City only for brief periods of their lives, are more commemorated than American leaders born and brought up here—Theodore Roosevelt, for example. Considering how important the entertainment industry has been to New York City, there are very few buildings named for actors, opera singers, musicians, or playwrights. The few that do exist include the *Mansfield* and the *Edwin Forrest.*

American, English, and Scottish novels account for a large proportion of apartment names: Sir Walter Scott's *Kenilworth* and the other Waverley novels head the list. *Ramona, Graustark, St. Elmo,* all turn-of-the-century bestsellers, gave their names to buildings. Alexandre Dumas is well represented by *Monte Cristo, Athos,* and *Porthos.*

By far the largest single cluster of names is that of saints. Leaving aside those taken from literature and those that are really geographical *(St. Tropez, Santa Monica)*, there are still a lot of saints' names used for apartment buildings. Most of these are in the Columbia University–St. John the Divine neighborhood and the City University–Convent Avenue area, but some, like *St. Regis* and *St. Mary,* are found in other parts of town and no doubt reflect how heavily Roman Catholic the population of New York City used to be.

Classical and mythological names are quite a generous group—*Athena, Zenobia,* and *Hyperion,* for example.

Many buildings bear the names of their builder and/or developer or his family *(Osborne, Alwyn Court, King Model Houses)*. Although documentation is usually lacking, the innumerable feminine names *(Paula, Rose, Hortense)* probably honored the owner's relations. Apartment houses, incidentally, appear to be thought of as feminine, like ships.

The numerous conversions from commercial or other uses to apartments in recent years often retain their original name *(Piano Factory, American Thread Building, Armory)*, perhaps commemorating the 1970s chic of high tech.

The states that have apartment buildings named for them are almost all west of the Mississippi and at the time of naming were often only territories *(Nevada, Idaho, Dakota)*. These vast Western expanses were romantic to New Yorkers because of the wealth that flowed eastward from them.

On the whole, New York City, judging by its apartment house names, is an Anglo-Saxon kingdom with Scottish possessions. From the beginning builders have leaned toward names like *Chatsworth* and *Carlton* and *Glenn Cairn;* today they are still calling buildings *Dorchester* and *Regency*. The British-inspired name is the most persistent trend in the naming of Manhattan's apartment buildings.

Some apartment house names have been lost. Often the names appeared on the early brochures and the original canopies, but as the apartments filled up and turned over, the canopies were replaced, and the names very often faded away with the original owners and staff. Occasionally, on the other hand, the name, the building, the address, and the tenants converged in such a way that the name took hold and aged with the building. The *Osborne,* the *Dakota,* the *Majestic, Tudor City, River House,* and *Olympic Tower* are

examples of buildings that are as well-known by name today as when they were built.

   Buildings in the inventory are those that were standing
in 1983, even if in an abandoned or derelict state, and not
converted to nonresidential use. A listing of some notable
buildings now demolished follows as an appendix.
   All the buildings are listed by name. Most names were
given by the original builder, but some were added later
by a new owner. A few buildings converted into apartment houses do not use their earlier name: those names are
placed in brackets: [*St. Joseph's Hospital*], for example.
When the former name has been retained, no brackets are
used: thus, *American Thread Building.*
   If a name was never officially given, but the building
has long been referred to by it, it is treated as a nickname
and placed within quotation marks: as in *"Rockefeller
Apartments."*
   Names have been gathered from:
   • the buildings themselves
   • real estate brochures, newspaper clippings, periodi-
     cals, and other archival material
   • maps, especially those found in Stokes, *Iconography of
     Manhattan Island,* and the publications of the Bromley
     and Sanborn & Co. firms.
   Named residential buildings excluded from the inventory are dormitories, nursing homes, hostels, convents,
and the like.
   Within each entry the following information has been
provided, if available:
   • name
   • street address—the number is sometimes missing or
     approximated because it is not to be seen on the
     building itself
   • architect, builder, date of construction, architectural
     style
   • remarks on condition, special features, tenants
   • derivation or definition of the name, unless obvious or
     unavailable

ABBEY TOWERS   *4411 Broadway*
                                    (northwest corner West 189th Street)

   Medieval motifs, including turrets and battlements, adorn
this seven-story apartment building of the 1920s.

ABELARD   *1885 Adam Clayton Powell, Jr., Boulevard*

   A twin to the *Arcadia*.
   Peter Abelard (1079–ca. 1142) was the French philosopher
and theologian who fell in love with his pupil Héloïse, thereby
incurring the wrath of her uncle and guardian (and his boss)
Fulbert, Canon of the Cathedral of Notre Dame in Paris who
had Peter castrated (and fired). Peter Abelard was condemned as
a heretic and died on his way to Rome, but his body was given
to Héloïse (who had become prioress of a convent); she was buried beside him.

ABINGDON

*Abingdon Square, which is formed by the junction of Eighth
Avenue and Hudson Street (Ninth Avenue), and the following
apartment houses take their name from Willoughby Bertie, fourth
Earl of Abingdon (1740–99), who married Charlotte Warren,
daughter of Sir Peter Warren, who owned the land in the eighteenth century. Abingdon supported the American colonists during
the Revolution and even published a book defending their cause.*

ABINGDON   *2071 Fifth Avenue*

   A six-story turn-of-the-century building of brick and limestone.

ABINGDON ARMS   *557 West 148th Street*

   A six-story tan brick building with an elaborate porch; circa
1900.

ABINGDON COURT   *75 Bank Street*

   The name is over the marble entrance of this six-story late-
1930s building.

ACKERLY, THE   *241 West 101st Street*

   A nice old redbrick building with stone decoration, a fire escape, and a mansard roof. The name is written in a banderole
over the door.

ADA   *501 West 173rd Street*
                                    (northwest corner Amsterdam Avenue)

A six-story brick building.

ADAMS, THE   *2 East 86th Street*
                                      (southeast corner Fifth Avenue)

This twenty-three-story apartment hotel of 1927 is still a
wonderfully luxurious building with its classical detail and
oversize windows looking out to Central Park.
    Whether the name refers to the American political family, or
to Robert and James Adam, English architects and brothers, is
unknown.

ADAM'S TOWER   *351 East 84th Street*

A huge set-back high rise with a Spartan entrance. We've all
heard of Adam's rib and Adam's apple, but Adam's tower?

ADELAIDE   *194–198 Manhattan Avenue*
                                   (northeast corner West 108th Street)

Six stories with iron balconies on many windows; turn-of-
the-century.
    The name was also used for an 1887 apartment house at 635
Park Avenue, now demolished and replaced by another structure.

ADMASTON   *251 West 89th Street*
                                         (northwest corner Broadway)

A twelve-story early-1920s building with a stone entrance.

ADORA   *76–78 Carmine Street*

A six-story 1920s apartment house with touches of the Italian Renaissance. A restaurant on the ground floor called Chez
Vous advertises Italian cuisine.
    "Adora" probably refers to the name—given or pet—of the
builder's wife.

ADRIAN   *58 West 72nd Street*
                                    (southeast corner Columbus Avenue)

This undistinguished building of circa 1900 has six stories;
now painted gray. A door in the Art Deco style marks the entrance on West 72nd Street.

ADRIATIC   *523 West 152nd Street*

Twin to the *Highland.*
    The Adriatic Sea is an arm of the Mediterranean between It-
aly and the Balkan Peninsula.

[ADVERTISING CLUB]   *23 Park Avenue*

This splendid palace, designed for J. Hampden Robb in 1898, was the home in more recent times of New York's Advertising Club; it was converted to cooperative apartments in the 1970s.

AIDA ARMS   *445 West 153rd Street*

A 1920s building of seven stories; named for Verdi's highly successful and continuously popular opera written on an Egyptian theme in 1871 to celebrate the opening of the Suez Canal. It was first performed in New York in 1873.

AIMÉE   *505 West 135th Street*

Five-story stone apartment house of circa 1900, part of an unusually large group of named buildings on the block (see Geographical Index).

The name means "beloved" in French.

ALABAMA   *550 Riverside Drive*
(northeast corner Tiemann Place)

A six-story white-brick building with basement and three bays; circa 1900. The cornices have been removed, but a sculptured lion still guards the door.

ALAMAC HOTEL   *160 West 71st Street*
(southeast corner Broadway)

Built in 1925, this twenty-one-story building has over six hundred rooms. In 1933 rates were $2.50 per night and up, and the hotel advertised itself as a place "where there is action and something doing," and invited guests to "visit the roof!"

ALAMEDA   *255 West 84th Street*
(northwest corner Broadway)

The entrance of this thirteen-story white-brick building has been modernized, but the old name is still visible.

An alameda is a public walk. The word derives from the Spanish.

ALAMO, THE   *55 East 93rd Street*

This rather sleek (for the period) turn-of-the-century six-story apartment house has a handsome entrance flanked by pairs of twin columns. The *Alamo* has recently been converted to a condominium.

Its namesake is the famous Spanish mission in San Antonio, Texas, where some one hundred eighty Texans died defending it against the Mexican army in 1836 during the Texas Revolution.

Directly across the street from the *Alamo* condominium is the
stately Goodby Lowe mansion, once the home of show-business
impresario Billy Rose, now a rehabilitation center for St.
Luke's-Roosevelt Hospital.

ALBEA   *325 West 93rd Street*

A six-story redbrick building of circa 1900. The first two
floors have been modernized with a new facing and green-
painted decoration that jars with the upper floors.

ALBERNI   *500 West 150th Street*

An undistinguished five-story building with a high stoop.

ALBERT   *202 West 81st Street*

Five stories with moated basement. This turn-of-the-century
redbrick building has an arched doorway. The first two floors
are of rusticated stone.
Several New York buildings are named for Queen Victoria;
Albert (1819–61) was her prince consort.

ALBERT COURT   *309 West 93rd Street*

This seven-story building is decorated with bare-breasted
caryatid figures on the upper floors. Built circa 1900, but recently renovated.

[ALBERT HOTEL]   *23 East 10th Street*

This brick and stone neo-Federal building was once a fabled
hotel, but a period of decline led to its closing, and it is now
an apartment house. So dismal was the hotel's reputation that
the name is now almost completely obscured by the canopy
which says, simply, "23 East 10th Street."
Next door, at 25 East 10th Street, the name on the canopy
is *Arbert Chambers,* even though the chiseled stone above says,
more honestly, *Albert Chambers.* The building at 25 East 10th
Street is older than the corner structure, possibly dating to the
time of the original H. J. Hardenbergh structure of 1883.

ALDEN, THE   *225 Central Park West*
                                      (southwest corner West 82nd Street)

Built in the 1920s at a cost of $2 million. The nineteen-
story building was designed by Emery Roth for Bing & Bing.

ALDEN, JOHN, THE   *44 West 10th Street*

When built in the 1920s, this nine-story building contained
on each floor four suites of four rooms and one of three rooms.
Rooms for servants were available on the top floor.
The advertisements at the time of renting stressed the Washington Square location: "In no part of our city has the quaint

old-fashioned and aristocratic atmosphere been so well preserved as in the Washington Square section. The encroachments of commerce and industry, which have invaded many of our most desirable residential thoroughfares, have not entered here."

On the same block as the *Priscilla* and the *Standish*. The reference is to Henry W. Longfellow's long poem of Pilgrim days, *The Courtship of Miles Standish*.

ALEXANDER HAMILTON

Alexander Hamilton (1755–1804) was one of the most prominent New Yorkers of his day and has left his mark on many New York institutions and place names. The city was his home from 1772, when he enrolled in King's College (now Columbia), until his death. Two important institutions he founded are still flourishing: the New York Post, *which began publication 16 November 1801, and the* Bank of New York, *which opened in June 1784.*

Hamilton's country home was "The Grange," which stood on the present-day south side of West 143rd Street between Amsterdam and Convent avenues. The house still exists, but it has been moved a few blocks downtown to 287 Convent Avenue, between West 141st and 142nd streets.
[*See also* Hamilton.]

ALEXANDER HAMILTON APARTMENTS
581 West 161st Street
(northeast corner Broadway)

A six-story white-brick building built in 1906; designed by the firm of Neville & Bagge.

ALEXANDRIA   *250 West 103rd Street*

An early-1920s redbrick building of fourteen stories.
Cities and towns named Alexandria, originally honoring Alexander the Great, are found from Egypt to Kentucky.

ALFREDOS CASINOS   *1364 York Avenue (Casinos)*
1366 York Avenue (Alfredos)

These two identical old tenements (ca. 1890) between 72nd and 73rd streets have emblazoned on their separate pediments

this enigmatic combination of words. Perhaps the buildings recall the period when the neighborhood was the site of Jones
Wood, a park and picnic grounds on the East River that had
been developed during the nineteenth century on the site of the
Jones family farm. (For a time it was a serious rival to the Central Park as *the* New York City recreation area.)

ALGONAC COURT   *165–175 Audubon Avenue*

Built in 1906 by Henri Foucheaux, architect, and Frank T.
Kee, builder, this six-story building advertised apartments of
four to six rooms at a very moderate (even then) $480 to $780
annual rent. The nice porch entrance on Audubon still exists.

ALIMAR   *925 West End Avenue*
(northwest corner West 105th Street)

A seven-story building with balconied windows and a new
cornice, circa 1901. Janes & Leo were the architects. The decoration is very elaborate, with initial *A* on cartouches and lion
heads.

ALLEN HOUSE   *340 East 51st Street*

A typical redbrick 1970s building.

ALLENDALE, THE   *808 West End Avenue*
(northeast corner West 99th Street)

A well-maintained turn-of-the-century building of twelve
stories plus basement and tower, with entrance through an open
court on West 99th Street.
Allendale is the name of towns in South Carolina and New
Jersey.

ALLERTON HOTEL FOR WOMEN
130 East 57th Street

A charming 1920s brick building; one of the few remaining
single-sex residential hotels.

ALLSTON COURT   *531 West 149th Street*

A five-story white-brick building with basement; circa 1900.
Washington Allston (1779–1843) was a noted American
artist.

ALMSCOURT   *1356 Madison Avenue*
(between East 95th and East 96th streets)

A six-story apartment house in buff brick, separated from its
twin, the *Woodbury,* by a small courtyard; circa 1900.

ALPINE   *125 Second Avenue*

Seven stories; white brick with brownstone trim. Across the street at 128 Second Avenue is a six-story twin called *Florence.*

ALTAMONTE HALL   *606 West 113th Street*

A six-story turn-of-the-century building with granite columns at the entrance.

ALVENA   *14–16 West 127th Street*

A six-story redbrick building; circa 1900.

Alwyn Court *photographed in June 1918. The view is north along the east side of Seventh Avenue. Across West 56th Street is the Lisbon Apartments, part of the memorable* Spanish Flats *complex, demolished in the 1920s. That site is now occupied by the New York Athletic Club. The columned entrance to Alwyn Court is long gone, as is the elaborate iron railing.*

ALWYN COURT   *180 West 58th Street*

One of the most lavishly ornamented apartment houses in the city—and perhaps in the world—Alwyn Court was built circa 1908 by the Hedden Construction Company, one of whose directors was Alwyn Ball, Jr.

The architects were Harde & Short. The original schedule of rents ranged from $6,500 to $22,000 per year, for suites that were as small as fourteen rooms with five baths, or as large as thirty-four rooms with nine baths—all replete with rich paneling, marble chimneypieces, fitted closets, and the like.

The effects of the depression on the market for luxury apartments were so pronounced that in 1938 Alwyn Court was gutted and made over into a building with seventy-five apartments of three, four, and five rooms.

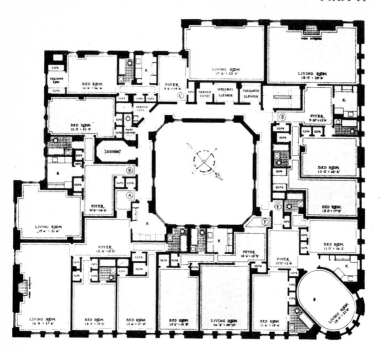

Alwyn Court. *Plan of a typical floor of the building after its remodeling in 1938, when many of the large suites were broken up into small units. Note the central open court and the room with curved walls.*

In recent years the building has been restored, cleaned, and co-oped; a trompe l'oeil mural painted by Richard Haas on the walls of its interior court captures some of the sculptured terracotta grandeur of the Alwyn Court's facade. The original entrance, now blocked up, bears the name of the apartment in block letters flanked by crowned salamanders, the emblem of Francis I, king of France, in the sixteenth century, who brought Italian Renaissance architecture and arts to his country.

The salamander, which appears in profusion on the French Renaissance exterior of Alwyn Court, was revered by the ancients, who believed it could live in fire.

AMAGANSETT
744 St. Nicholas Avenue
(between West 146th and West 147th streets)

A rather handsome building with nicely detailed windows and no visible fire escapes; circa 1900. The name is written in gold script over the door.

The Amagansett were an Indian tribe of Long Island that gave its name to a village at the eastern end of the island.

AMALGAMATED–HILLMAN HOUSES
500–550 Grand Street

Companion housing developments sponsored by the Amalgamated Clothing Workers Union, of which Sidney Hillman was president.

The original *Amalgamated Dwellings* were built circa 1930, and the *Hillman Houses* in 1951.

AMBASSADOR, THE
1393 Madison Avenue
(southeast corner East 97th Street)

Built circa 1906 by Neville & Bagge, this center-court building now has a new entrance.

AMBASSADOR EAST
330 East 46th Street

This white-brick building is so named because it's handy to the United Nations.

AMBASSADOR HOUSE
445 East 77th Street

A modest redbrick structure built in 1958, before the big apartment boom of the far East Side.

AMBASSADOR TERRACE
242 East 60th Street

A small gray "brownstone" with a new entrance and a somewhat pretentious name considering its size.

AMELE HALL
536 West 111th Street

Contiguous to and similar to the *Romana*.

AMERICAN
68 West 117th Street
(southeast corner Lenox Avenue)

A six-story building of yellow and salmon brick with limestone trim; now abandoned.

AMERICAN THREAD BUILDING
260 West Broadway

This eleven-story structure designed by W. B. Tubby was built for the New York Wool Exchange in 1894–96; the site had been residential—and exclusive—until the march of industry changed the complexion of the neighborhood, known as St. John's Park.

The building's entrance is at the corner of Beach Street and West Broadway.

The building was converted to residential use in 1982, with living units priced at $210,000 to $310,000. In terms of its amenities (which include hookup to a computer terminal), the American Thread Building (so named for the owner after the Wool Exchange failed) is Tribeca's most luxurious apartment.

AMHERST, THE
401 East 74th Street

A redbrick apartment house built in 1963, one of several put up by the Sachar firm during the sixties—all with a deadening sameness.

The name evokes the New England college named for Lord Jeffrey Amherst (1717–1797), victorious leader of the British troops during the French and Indian War.

AMIDON
233 West 83rd Street
(northwest corner Broadway)

Designed by the architect E. L. Angell in 1892 for James Rufus Amidon whose surname is written in gold on the glass fanlight of this good-sized seven-story building. The Broadway side has highly decorated windows and balconies. The pediment has been removed.

There were originally seven suites of seven rooms with a bath. The lobby is of marble and onyx.

AMITY
2 East 128th Street

A five-story building of brownstone with basement, bayed windows, and a handsome porch; circa 1900.

Amsterdam Apartment House

AMSTERDAM
175 West 81st Street
(northeast corner Amsterdam Avenue)

A five-story turn-of-the-century building with an arched entrance similar to those of its next three neighbors. Rusticated ground floor. [See also *New Amsterdam.*]

AMSTERDAM HOUSE
1060 Amsterdam Avenue
(northwest corner West 112th Street)

A thirteen-story white-brick nursing home built in 1976 by Kennerley, Slomanson & Smith. Across the street from the Cathedral Church of St. John the Divine.

AMSTERDAM HOUSES (NYC Housing Authority)
205 West 61st Street

Named for the avenue on which it's located, this complex of 1,084 apartments was built in 1948. Since then, the neighborhood has emerged as tony Lincoln Center—undreamed of when the project was erected as part of a slum-clearance effort.

AMSTERDAM HOUSES ADDITION (NYC Housing Authority)
240 West 65th Street

The unusual architecture of this 1974 building, which has triangular bay windows, was designed by Oppenheimer, Brady & Lehrecke.

AMSTERDAM TOWERS
*201 West 77th Street
(northwest corner Amsterdam Avenue)*

A sixteen-story variegated brick building of the 1920s, with a handsomely decorated entrance.

AMY
*100 West 86th Street
(southwest corner Columbus Avenue)*

A narrow five-story building of circa 1900.

ANDREW JACKSON
*720 Riverside Drive
(northeast corner West 149th Street)*

A seven-story building with a recessed circular fire escape and an open-court entrance; circa 1920.

Andrew Jackson was the seventh president of the United States (1829–37).

ANGELA
401–403 West 47th Street

An old corner building of nineteenth-century vintage whose name, like so many other apartment names, is a feminine given name and may refer to a member of the original builder's or owner's family.

ANGELA PLAZA
9–15 Adrian Avenue

A Marble Hill building of the 1920s; six stories and a new entrance.

ANNADALE
385 Fort Washington Avenue

A six-story redbrick building of circa 1890; sister to the *Belle Court* at 395.

The name was probably coined after the village of Annandale-on-Hudson in Dutchess County, New York, or the community of Annadale on Staten Island.

ANNAPOLIS   *634 West 135th Street*

A twin to the *West Point,* next door.

Ansonia, *photographed in the 1930s, showing the monument to Giuseppe Verdi in Verdi Square, formed by the intersection of Amsterdam Avenue and Broadway. Now surrounded by mature trees, the Verdi monument is difficult to see most of the year. Verdi Square, during the 1960s, was known as "Needle Park."*

ANSONIA, THE   *2107 Broadway*
(between West 73rd and West 74th streets)

All the glamour of the Upper West Side is captured in *The Ansonia,* a startlingly exuberant pile of gables, turrets, mansard roofs, arches, bays, and balconies situated at a bend in Broadway; its outline may be seen for many blocks, north and south.

Built in 1902 by W. E. D. Stokes, a rich and well-connected New Yorker, *The Ansonia* was probably named for Stokes's brother Anson Phelps Stokes (the family business and yacht were also given the name). Ansonia, Connecticut, was the company town for their enterprises. The architects Graves & Duboy successfully managed to combine the glamorous appearance of a hotel in Nice with the needs of permanent residents.

Because of its thick walls, *The Ansonia* early on became a favored residence for musicians and singers, among them Caruso, Toscanini, Chaliapin, Melchior, Stravinsky, Pinza, and Pons. Babe Ruth, Sol Hurok, Flo Ziegfeld (who lived with his wife in one apartment, while his mistress occupied an identical flat on another floor), Elmer Rice, and Theodore Dreiser also lived at the *Ansonia.*

In 1908 five rooms with one bath rented for $1,800 a year; thirteen rooms with four baths, $5,000 a year. In 1983 studio apartments rented for $800 per month, and two-bedroom apartments from $1,650 per month.

Two shrines of the sexual revolution were located in *The Ansonia.* In the 1950s and 1960s *The Ansonia* went into a period of decline and the famous (or infamous) Continental Baths opened in the cellar. It was here that Bette Midler made her mark, and trendy New Yorkers joined the boys in towels to hear the latest darling of the entertainment world perform there. A few years later the baths closed and a sex club named Plato's Retreat opened.

Under new ownership, *The Ansonia* has been cleaned up; apartments have been remodeled, and many of the older rent-controlled tenants have departed.

ANTLERS, THE   *603 West 111th Street*

An eight-story turn-of-the-century building with a handsome lion decoration over the door and gated entrance.

The Antlers Hotel in Colorado Springs was one of this country's poshest resort hotels at the time this apartment house was put up.

ANTOINETTE   *7 East 35th Street*

A recent construction or rehabilitation directly across the street from B. Altman's department store.

APTHORP APARTMENTS, THE   *2207 Broadway*
(between West 78th and West 79th streets)

Charles W. Clinton (1838–1910) and William Hamilton Russell (1854–1907) were the architects for this grand apartment house, built in 1908 for William Waldorf Astor.

Twelve stories high, originally with ten huge apartments to a floor (many apartments have since been cut up into smaller units), *The Apthorp* is distinguished by a splendid arched entrance with a wrought-iron gate, leading to an enormous central open court which provides light and air to the apartments and serves as a quiet oasis away from the bustle of Broadway.

The name is taken from the old Apthorp farm, part of which was conveyed to Mr. Apthorp's daughter and her husband, J. C. Vandenheuvel. The Vandenheuvel mansion, built in 1792, stood at the northwest corner of the block occupied by the present apartment building. It became Burnham's Hotel in 1833 and was torn down in 1905.

The Apthorp mansion of 1764 stood at a site bounded by the present Columbus and Amsterdam avenues and West 90th and West 91st streets.

Apthorp Apartments. *The main entrance at 2207 Broadway.*

AQUAVISTA   *460 Riverside Drive*

A tan-brick building of twelve stories, with balconies; circa 1900.

The water being viewed is the Hudson, which the building faces.

AQUITANIA   *545 West 164th Street*
                          (northwest corner St. Nicholas Avenue)

A six-story building with an elevator and large apartments, built circa 1905, and initially known as the Dolwood.

The original brochure proclaimed it "a distinct and notable addition to Washington Heights' list of high-class apartment houses . . . with an unobstructed view of the surrounding country as far as the eye can reach. . . ."

Aquitania is the Latin form of the word Aquitaine, a large province of southwest France. The kings of France and England struggled for its possession during the Hundred Years War (1337–1453), with France successful in adding it to the royal domain.

ARCADE   *122–128 West 116th Street*

Abandoned.

A R C A D I A   *1893 Adam Clayton Powell, Jr., Boulevard*
(southeast corner West 115th Street)

Six stories, with porch entrance and stone balconies on some windows; circa 1900.

Arcadia: an idyllic land of pastoral nature, akin to "paradise." *"Et in Arcadia ego"* (I, too, have been in Paradise) was a saying of Bartollomeo Schidoni's (1560–1616) used by Poussin as the central motto of his famous painting *Arcadian Shepherds.*

A twin to the *Abelard.*

A R C H I V E S   B U I L D I N G   *641 Washington Street*
(between Christopher and Barrow streets)

This enormous red-brick pile has dominated the West Village for almost a century, whether as U.S. Appraisers' stores (its original purpose), as post office, as storage place for archives, or just plain empty (as it is in 1984 and has been for years).

The *Archives Building*—as it is usually called—was begun in 1891 by Willoughby J. Edbrooke, whose inspiration for the massive barrel vaultings of the lower stories was probably Louis Sullivan's Marshall Field Warehouse in Chicago (1889).

Following Edbrooke's death, the construction of the upper floors was supervised by other architects. The structure was completed in 1899; its ten stories and huge area made it when built one of the largest buildings in terms of square footage ever erected: there are 500,000 square feet of floor space!

The size and location of the building have long made it a potential for conversion into residential apartments. In the early 1980s a conversion plan was announced calling for space for community groups, restaurants, commercial tenants, and hundreds of apartments clustered around a central atrium. At the time of writing that plan has been stalled, but the building retains its potential for conversion into one of Manhattan's largest apartment houses.

A R D E A ,   T H E   *31–33 West 12th Street*

This well-maintained brick and brownstone apartment house was built for George A. Hearn, merchant and art collector, by the firm of J. B. Snook circa 1895–1900.

The ardea is a type of heron.

A R D E L L E ,   T H E   *527 Riverside Drive*

Radcliff & Kelley were the architects for this 1910 twelve-story building near Grant's Tomb.

A R D E N   T O W E R S   *31–41 Sherman Avenue*
(southwest corner Arden Street)

A six-story dirty white building with an arched entrance; circa 1920s.

Although its name contains echoes of the Forest of Arden in

Shakespeare's *As You Like It*, Arden Street was named for the
New York butcher Jacob Arden, who was an active patriot during the American Revolution and a large landowner in this part
of Washington Heights.

ARDSLEIGH   720–722 *West 180th Street*

A well-kept five-story building with stone floral decoration.

ARDSLEY, THE   320 *Central Park West*
(southwest corner West 92nd Street)

Emery Roth was the architect of this 1931 Art Deco building. Its outside is enriched with reliefs in various forms.

This *Ardsley* replaced a ten-story structure called *Ardsley Hall*
which had an early-Renaissance exterior. A 1901 brochure described an "entertainment suite" and billiard room as among the
hotel's attractions. The building, it stated, had "all the service
and accommodations of the best hotels with none of the license
granted them."

ARDSLEY HOUSE HOTEL, THE
29 *West 12th Street*

Only five stories tall, this may originally have been an 1870s
brownstone town house.

ARLINGTON   229 *West 101st Street*
(northwest corner Broadway)

Three bays, with a columned entrance on West 101st Street;
early twentieth century.

Arlington is the name of many counties, towns, and villages
in the United States. Best known is the Virginia property once
owned by both George Washington and Robert E. Lee and now
the site of the National Cemetery.

ARLINGTON   506–508 *West 113th Street*

A twin to the *Stanford* at 502–504. A redbrick six-story
turn-of-the-century building with recessed fire escapes and nice
wrought-iron fences.

ARLINGTON   100 *West 114th Street*
(southwest corner Lenox Avenue)

A five-story orange-brick building with a modernized
entrance.

ARLINGTON, THE   29–31 *West 119th Street*

A twin to the *Rappahannock*, which also takes its name from
Virginia geography.

ARMIDALE   *870 Riverside Drive*
(southeast corner West 160th Street)

A huge stone entrance marks the front of this six-story building of circa 1900. Now in poor shape.

Armidale is a town in New South Wales, Australia.

ARMORY, THE   *529 West 42nd Street*

A 1980s conversion of an old U.S. Army Reserve building. Concierge, electronic security devices, terraces, and oak floors have been promised to buyers of co-ops in a part of town that has been, according to an advertisement, "tamed into the freshest, most energetic neighborhood in all of New York."

ARMSTEAD, THE   *245 West 104th Street*
(northwest corner Broadway)

A fifteen-story building of the 1920s. The site was formerly occupied by an apartment building called the Dunlap.

ARNOLD COURT   *480–490 Audubon Avenue*
(northwest corner West 189th Street)

A plain six-story building of the 1900s with an open court.

ASCOT HOUSE   *120 East 89th Street*

A 1930s six-story building at Lexington Avenue. The name is probably taken from the racetrack near London, where English and international notables gather for a week of racing each June.

An apartment house called Santa Rosa originally occupied the site.

ASHFIELD   *305 West 55th Street*

An old but well-preserved building. Ashfield, an old English family name, might refer in this case to the New York family who owned land in Manhattan in the late seventeenth century. These Ashfields are recorded as having purchased from Dutch owners a tract that had previously been granted to freed slaves.

ASHTON, THE   *26 East 93rd Street*

An undistinguished ten-story building of the early twentieth century that appears to have had some of its upper decoration removed.

Thomas Ashton was sheriff of the county of New York in the seventeenth century.

ASTEN HOUSE   *515 East 79th Street*

This white-brick high-rise co-op of 1982 takes its name from the Asten family who owned farmland in the area during the eighteenth century.

ASTOR

The Astor dynasty has been called the Landlords of New York. No other family has such a history—extending over five generations—of ownership of land on Manhattan Island. The first of the line, John Jacob Astor, founded his fortune on the fur trade in the late eighteenth century, but he invested his profits in Manhattan land. His first lots, on the Bowery and Elizabeth Street, were purchased in 1789. In 1803 he bought from Aaron Burr 241 lots lying between Spring and West Houston streets, and Varick and Greenwich streets. By 1848 he owned 470 lots, a huge proportion in a city that then lay below 23rd Street. Most of these lots were placed out on twenty-one-year lease, as Astor did not like to build. The lessee built, and when the lease expired, the improvements belonged to Astor. Astor is recorded as saying, "Could I begin life again, knowing what I know now, and had money to invest, I would buy every foot of land on the Island of Manhattan."

William B. Astor, John Jacob's son, left over 700 pieces of real estate in Manhattan, most of them slum property on the Lower East Side, which was immensely profitable. At his death in 1890 his estate, valued at more than $200 million, was split

John Jacob Astor I

among his descendants, some of whom were the English Astors, owners of the London Times, Hever Castle, *and* Cliveden, *who in 1900 received an income of $6 million a year from their Manhattan properties.*

Vincent Astor, of the fifth generation of the family, sold about $40 million of family properties, but he was also a heavy buyer of Manhattan real estate and built Astor Court *on Broadway and developed East End Avenue. The English Astors had to sell much of their property to pay heavy British taxes between the world wars, but they remained major New York property owners. When Vincent Astor died in 1958, his estate, estimated to be over $100 million, went to the Astor Foundation, which has devoted most of its income to projects in the city that made the Astor family rich.*

ASTOR APARTMENTS   *305 West 45th Street*

When this six-story building constructed around an open court was built circa 1900, the architects, Tracy and Swarthwout, won first prize for excellence of design awarded by the New York chapter of the American Institute of Architects. This redbrick building is well maintained today.

The Astor Estate owned the land on which the apartment house was built. The Astor Theatre was only a few blocks away, on West 45th and Broadway.

ASTOR APARTMENTS   *2141–2157 Broadway*
                             245 West 75th Street

Built circa 1905 by Clinton & Russell for William Waldorf Astor. Renovated and well maintained.

ASTOR COURT   *205 West 89th Street*
                        204–210 West 90th Street

Charles A. Platt was the architect of this enormous West Side building which occupies the entire blockfront along Broadway between West 89th and West 90th streets. A cartouche on the Broadway side bears the date 1915. The twelve-story building is grouped around a central courtyard.

ATELIER BUILDING   *33 West 67th Street*

A fourteen-story building of 1903 by Pollard & Steinman, architects, originally one of a row of artists' studios, or *ateliers,* on West 67th Street. Among the illustrious tenants have been the artist James Montgomery Flagg (Uncle Sam Wants You!); Walter and Louise Arensberg, patrons of modern art in the 1920s; and Marcel Duchamp, the artist, who lived here for a brief time.

ATHOS, THE   *152–154 West 118th Street*

A twin to the *Porthos.* Now in very poor condition.

ATRIUM, THE   *321 East 69th Street*

A small balconied building, even more restrained than its next-door neighbor, the *Premier.*

Atrium Apartments. *This view up toward the glass roof of the interior courtyard displays the main feature of the renamed Mills Hotel. Originally the central court was open to the sky.*

ATRIUM APARTMENTS, THE   *160 Bleecker Street*

In 1976 the wretched welfare hotel known as the Greenwich was closed down and skillfully converted to a successful apartment house christened *The Atrium* because of its glassed-over central courtyard that provides light and space for interior balconies.

The building was originally the *Mills House No. 1,* erected in 1896 by Darius Ogden Mills, merchant, banker, and philanthropist, as a hostelry for poor gentlemen; its 1,500 small rooms were rented out for twenty cents a night. Among the patrons was Theodore Dreiser, when he was down on his luck.

The architect was Ernest Flagg; his (originally open) atrium still looks good, and the dignified facade looks down majestically on the tawdry attractions of Bleecker Street.

ATRIUM EAST, THE   *153 East 32nd Street*

Formerly a commercial loft or stable.

AUCHMUTZ   *332–334 East 67th Street*

The name appears on the cornice of this circa-1900 walk-up. Its next-door neighbor—which has no name—bears the date 1906.

AUDUBON

Although he is usually pictured tramping the frontier, the great American ornithologist John James Audubon (1785–1851) spent much of his life, including his last twenty years, in New York City and has left his name on an avenue, buildings, theaters, shops. In 1841 he bought the property known as Audubon Park in the West 150s. He and his wife, Lucy Bakewell Audubon, lived at Minniesland, a house on a triangular plot at West 156th Street and the Hudson River. The house was not torn down until December 1931.

The Audubon family gradually sold off its property in the neighborhood. Between 1908 and 1923 the section known as Audubon Terrace became the home of five important institutions: the American Geographical Society, the Hispanic Society of America, the Museum of the American Indian, the American Numismatic Society, and the American Academy of Arts and Letters. They were built in the area bounded by West 155th and West 156th streets, Broadway, and Audubon Terrace, primarily as a benefaction of Archer M. Huntington of the railroad fortune.

Audubon Cottage. *"Minniesland," beneath Riverside Drive at West 155th Street about 1925.*

AUDUBON
*2321–2339 Adam Clayton
Powell, Jr., Boulevard
(between West 136th and West 137th streets)*

A restored building with new cornices and windows and both new and old rustication on the ground floor; originally The Bedford when it was built circa 1885.

Five granite columns, which must have flanked the original entrance, have been removed and are now freestanding at the front of the building.

AUDUBON APARTMENTS (NYC Housing Authority)
1909 Amsterdam Avenue

This state-sponsored project of 168 apartments was built in 1962.

AUDUBON COURT
2–4 St. Nicholas Place

This vintage building, which retains a hint of its former magnificence, dates from 1904 and was designed by Neville & Bagge on the central-court plan.

Audubon Park Apartments, *with the initials "AP" above the entrance.*

AUDUBON PARK APARTMENTS *3750 Broadway*
(southeast corner West 156th Street)

A six-story white-brick building erected in 1905; Schwartz & Gross and B. N. Marcus, architects. Entwined monogram *AP* over the entrance.

AUGHER VILLA *614 West 184th Street*

An 1880s–1890s five-story redbrick structure with basement and Ionic columns at entrance.

AUGUSTA *25 West 106th Street*
(northeast corner Manhattan Avenue)

A five-story building, now derelict, circa 1900.

AURORA APARTMENTS *328 West 15th Street*

A small 1880s redbrick building.
Aurora was the Roman goddess of the dawn.

AVALON *533 West 112th Street*

A plain white-brick and limestone seven-story building with central court.
Avalon in Celtic mythology is the Island of the Blessed, to which the souls of great heroes, such as King Arthur, go after death.

AVALON HALL *227 Riverside Drive*
(southeast corner West 95th Street)

A circa-1900 building with seven stories and rounded corners. The ground floor has been repainted green.

AVON *166 West 122nd Street*
(southeast corner Adam Clayton Powell, Jr., Boulevard)

A five-story 1880s redbrick building with a granite entrance.
The Avon is a river in central England much celebrated by William Shakespeare; it flows through his native town Stratford-on-Avon. Around the corner from this building is located, most appropriately, the *Shakespeare*. [See also *Stratford*.]

AVON HOUSE *340 East 74th Street*

A twelve-story apartment building of 1957.

A Y L S M E R E   *60 West 76th Street*
(southeast corner Columbus Avenue)

Turn-of-the-century seven-story building with four columns
at the entrance, fire escapes, and elaborately columned windows
on floors two and four.

A Z E L O F F   T O W E R S   *141 East 3rd Street*

Twelve-story 1930s brick with an exceptionally nice Art
Deco entrance; an oasis of well-maintained civility in an area of
bombed-out wrecks. Presumably Mr. Azeloff was the builder of
this apartment house.

B A L D W I N ,   T H E   *46 West 96th Street*

A six-story redbrick building; very plain, except for the lion
masks that decorate the windows.

B A M F O R D   *333 East 56th Street*

An eighteen-story rental building of 1982.
Samuel Bamford (1788–1872) was a British weaver, poet,
and radical.

B A N C R O F T ,   T H E   *40 West 72nd Street*

A fifteen-story building of the 1920s with arched windows
on the second floor, balconies, and heraldic decoration on the
facade.

B A N C R O F T   A P A R T M E N T S ,   T H E
509 West 121st Street

A truly spendid eclectic building erected in 1911 by Emery
Roth. Eight stories of tan brick and limestone, with bronze bay
windows, H-shaped, and with roof of Spanish tiles. The entrance court has four doors and five columns, each crowned with
an urn. Art Nouveau doors, two bronze lamps on pedestals.
The building was originally called *The Sethlow Bachelor Apartments,* in honor of Seth Low (1850–1916), president of Columbia University and, briefly (1901–1903) mayor of New York.

B A N Z E R   *338 East 67th Street*

An old-style apartment house with fire escapes; the name is
probably that of the original owner.

B A R B I Z O N   *140 East 63rd Street*

Built in 1927 as a residential hotel for women (Grace Kelly
and Candice Bergen lived here), this handsome brick building
with "Gothic" touches was bought in 1980 by developers who
have done a top-to-bottom renovation.

It is supposed to reopen as a combined 360-room hotel and condominium of four apartments. The huge sign on the building during the cleaning and restoration proclaimed the advent of an "Island of Civilization."

The name refers to the forest and village outside Paris where Corot, Rousseau, Millet, and Diaz painted during the mid-nineteenth century, giving rise to the term "Barbizon School" for the works of these, and allied masters, widely collected at the turn of this century by American millionaires.

BARIEFORD   *49 Claremont Avenue*
                                  (southwest corner West 119th Street)

Built in 1907; George F. Pelham, architect; Robert Ferguson & Sons, owners and builders. The apartments have four to seven rooms.

BARNARD COURT   *15 Claremont Avenue*

A nine-story turn-of-the-century white-brick building with open court entrance. It takes its name from the college across the street.

BARNEY COURT   *240 Audubon Avenue*
                                  (northwest corner West 177th Street)

A six-story 1920s building.

BARRINGTON   *209 West 81st Street*

A nine-story 1920s building of dark brick.

Great Barrington in the Berkshires of Massachusetts was a well-known resort in the nineteenth and early twentieth centuries.

BARUCH HOUSES   *100 Columbia Street*
(NYC Housing Authority)

Named for Simon Baruch (1840–1921), father of Bernard M. Baruch; a pioneer physician, public health official, and noted philanthropist. He advocated hydrotherapy and was appointed a member of the Saratoga Commission after the spa was purchased by New York State.

Located on the Lower East Side, *Baruch Houses* were built in 1959 and have a resident population exceeding sixty-five hundred.

BAVARIA, THE   *40 St. Nicholas Place*

An early-twentieth-century apartment house named for Germany's ancient kingdom of Bavaria, now a state of the Federal Republic of Germany.

BAYARD HOUSE   *203 East 72nd Street*

Four stories with a bland neo-Federal brick facade matching the savings bank next door actually forms the entrance to a tower rising twenty more floors on 73rd Street. Ada Louise Huxtable was not pleased with the results when she reviewed the transformation in the *New York Times*.

Bayard is the name of a venerable New York Huguenot family founded by Nicholas Bayard, who was a nephew of Peter Stuyvesant and secretary of the Dutch Province of New Netherland. His difficulties under English rule did not prevent him from prospering and amassing large landholdings on Manhattan Island.

BEACON   *2130 Broadway*
(northeast corner West 75th Street)

Built as the Beacon Hotel in 1928—at a cost of $7 million—by the Chanin group. This multipurpose building of twenty-five floors still houses on its ground floor one of New York's last great movie palaces, the Beacon Theater, now more often used for live performances.

BEACON HALL   *618 West 142nd Street*

This six-story apartment house proclaims its name from a sculptured banderole above the entrance.

BEACONSFIELD APARTMENTS, THE
587 Riverside Drive
(southeast corner West 136th Street)

Built in 1906; Schwartz & Gross, architects. A central-court plan with lots of long halls; six stories of red brick. Now lacks its cornice.

Earl of Beaconsfield was the title bestowed on the British statesman Benjamin Disraeli (1804–81) in 1876; it derives from a town in Buckinghamshire.

BEATRICE   *529 West 145th Street*

A five-story circa-1900 building with porch. Identical to the *Leondra*.

BEAU RIVAGE   *316 West 94th Street*

A six-story building of circa 1900; now painted rose-red. The "beautiful shore" is that of the nearby Hudson River.

BEAUCAIRE, THE   *25 East 9th Street*
26 East 10th Street

This block-long Spanish-style extravaganza on University Place announced in 1927 that it was "designed to express the

finest type American residence—the apartment house. It is in a
healthy spot—just two blocks from Washington Square, in perhaps the most interesting residential section of the city. . . .
Kitchens are equipped beyond the imagination of the average
person. . . . Smaller apartments have built-in Murphy-door
beds." Sugarman and Berger were the architects.

The name was undoubtedly inspired by Booth Tarkington's
story (1900), play (1901), and film (1925; 1946 remake with
Bob Hope) *Monsieur Beaucaire,* a comedy about a French duke,
disguised as a barber, in eighteenth-century Bath.

BEAUMONT   *730 Riverside Drive*
                    (northwest corner West 150th Street)

Late-Renaissance Revival with touches of Art Deco; 1920s.
The doorway has fine ironwork, and the balconies have roundels
of birds.

Beaumont, which means "fair mountain" in French, is the
name of a number of towns in both France and the United
States.

BEAUMONT, THE   *300 West 61st Street*
                    (southeast corner Columbus Avenue)

A 1970s redbrick high rise with offices on the first five
floors; the upper floors are for residential use. There is a small
plaza in front.

The name is taken from Vivian Beaumont, whose gift built
the theater in Lincoln Center at the southeast corner of West
65th Street and Amsterdam Avenue.

BEAUX ARTS APARTMENTS *307 East 44th Street*
                    310 East 44th Street

This matched pair of striking Art Deco buildings, erected in
1931, was designed by Raymond Hood, architect of the nearby
Daily News Building and several of the Rockefeller Center
buildings.

The two buildings, each one seventeen stories tall and containing more than six hundred apartments, form an attractive
grouping with their facades of contrasting dark and light stone
and brickwork.

In the late 1960s, during the heyday of United Nations ex-
pansionism in the neighborhood, the buildings were threatened
with demolition, but the development plan was scaled down,
the apartments survived, and in 1973 the two were sold for
$8.1 million to a group headed by Daniel Brodsky.

The buildings owe their name to the nearby Beaux Arts Institute of Design (adjoining 310 East 44th Street) designed by
Fred Hirons in 1928 and adorned with a glittering mosaic depicting Athens, Paris, and Rome. Alas, the building is now
used as a TV studio!

Lee Mortimer, author of *New York Confidential,* a sensational exposé of a seamier side of New York City written in the fifties, lived in the *Beaux Arts Apartments.*

BEDFORD, THE

165 *West 82nd Street*
(northeast corner Amsterdam Avenue)

A smallish redbrick buiding of only four stories; built circa 1880.

Duke of Bedford is the principal title of the Russell family, most famous in real estate history as owners of a large section of London centering around Russell Square in Bloomsbury.

BEDFORD

515 *West 143rd Street*

A rather severe six-story building of the early twentieth century; similar to others in a row extending from 505 to 529 West 143rd.

BEDFORD

168 *West 86th Street*

A fourteen-story white-brick building of the 1920s.

[BEECHWOOD]

125 *East 24th Street*

Now the St. Francis Residence for Men; the name *BE——WOOD* is still visible over the portico of this late-nineteenth-century building.

BEEKMAN

The name is that of an old New York family and has been especially associated with the area of 50th Street and the East River, where the James Beekman mansion Mount Pleasant stood until 1874. The site of the mansion—which served as the headquarters of General Charles Clinton and Sir William Howe during the British occupation of New York City—is now occupied by Public School 15 (used now as a community center). Nearby is the place where Nathan Hale is said to have been tried and executed, and slightly to the west, at what is now Second Avenue, was one of Manhattan's "kissing bridges."

William Beekman, the patriarch of this wealthy family, arrived in New Amsterdam with Peter Stuyvesant in 1647.

BEEKMAN, THE   *575 Park Avenue*

A 1920s–1930s residential hotel of the *palazzo* type.

BEEKMAN EAST   *330 East 49th Street*

Despite its name, this 1960s building is *west* of Beekman Place.

BEEKMAN HILL HOUSE   *425 East 51st Street*

A 1930s redbrick neo-Georgian building.

BEEKMAN MANSION APARTMENTS
                                439 East 51st Street

A beautifully detailed building; designed by Van Wart & Wien circa 1924. The main entrance, which overlooks Beekman Place, has a coat of arms in its Gothic-arched doorway.

BEEKMAN STUDIOS   *230 East 50th Street*

An eleven-story cooperative apartment building of the 1920s; brick and limestone, with huge casement windows.

BEEKMAN TERRACE   *455 East 51st Street*

A 1920s building in English Gothic style at the end of the street. The architects were Treanor & Fatic with J. E. R. Carpenter.

BEEKMAN TOWER   *9 Mitchell Place*

Mitchell Place (for Judge William Mitchell, the nineteenth-century New York jurist) is East 49th Street between First Avenue and Beekman Place. *Beekman Tower* is an apartment hotel in the high Art Deco style of 1928 (the work of architect John Mead Howells). Originally the Panhellenic Hotel, a residence for women belonging to Greek-letter sororities, the building later became a cooperative apartment hotel, but its rooftop cocktail lounge is still a popular rendezvous.

Because of its outstanding Art Deco architecture, the building has been proposed for landmark status.

BEEKMAN TOWNHOUSE   *166 East 63rd Street*
                        (southwest corner Third Avenue)

A twenty-story 1960s apartment building.

BELLA VISTA   *572 West 173rd Street*
                        (southeast corner St. Nicholas Avenue)

A nondescript five-story building; circa 1900.

Bellaire Apartment Hotel, *photographed circa 1920. This later became the* Hotel 14 *and is now used for offices. The Copacabana night-club, famous since the 1930s, is on the first floor.*

[BELLAIRE APARTMENT HOTEL]
14 East 60th Street

An eleven-story building of circa 1890, with bayed windows; later known as the *Hotel 14*. At the ground-floor level is the entrance to the once-famous nightclub, the Copacabana, now a disco-restaurant. No longer residential.

BELLE COURT
395 Fort Washington Avenue
(southwest corner West 178th Street)

Twin to the *Annadale*.

BELLECLAIR
250 West 77th Street
(southwest corner Broadway)

A ten-story turn-of-the-century building with extremely elaborate decoration and mansard roof; the first apartment house designed by Emery Roth. On the West 77th Street side there is an open court entrance.

BELLEFONTE, THE
514–518 West 143rd Street

Built in 1906; the work of Glasses & Ebert, architects, and T. J. McGuire Construction Co. The six-story redbrick and limestone building has a columned entrance. The plan is center court, with a long vestibule and a large reception hall.

BELLGUARD, THE   *216 West 89th Street*
                          (southeast corner Broadway)

A twelve-story redbrick building of the 1920s.

BELLMORE   *600 West 133rd Street*
                          (southwest corner Broadway)

A six-story white-brick building with basement; circa 1900. Partially abandoned.

BELLROSE   *220 West 113th Street*

A six-story building with fire escape; perhaps of the 1920s.

BELNORD, THE   *225 West 86th Street*

Built in 1909 on a virgin plot of land that runs from Broadway to Amsterdam Avenue, and from West 86th to West 87th streets, *The Belnord* was designed by Hill and Hobart Weekes for the George A. Fuller Construction Company.

With a heavily rusticated base, this building in the Italian Renaissance style has a large central open court similar to that of *The Apthorp.*

There were originally 175 apartments of seven to eleven rooms, and a 1926 promotional piece proclaimed *The Belnord* to be "the largest and most complete apartment house in New York City."

The Belnord was two-thirds rented before its completion. The decor was in the Louis XIV style. Tenants could choose their own wallpaper. Each apartment had a wall safe and a refrigerator that made its own ice. A vacuum-cleaning system was built in.

In recent years there has been a running battle between the tenants (among whom are the Nobel Prize–winning writer Isaac Bashevis Singer) and the owner.

Unlike so many others of the "great" West Side buildings, *The Belnord* is not a cooperative and is not in a very good state of repair.

BELVEDERE   *319 West 48th Street*

A large sixteen-story building of the 1920s on the edge of the theater district.

The name is from the Italian word for beautiful sight or view.

BELVEDERE, THE   *400 West 150th Street*
                          (southwest corner Edgecombe Avenue)

A fine turn-of-the-century corner building; six stories, with basement entrance on side street. Now decaying.

BENDOR COURT   *339–345 West 55th Street*

A nine-story 1920s building with an open-court entrance.

Bend Or, one of the most famous English racehorses of the nineteenth century, won the Derby in 1879. The name comes from heraldry.

BEN NEVIS   *382 Wadsworth Avenue*

A twin to *Traud Hall.*

Ben Nevis in Scotland is, at 4,406 feet, the highest mountain in Great Britain.

BENJAMIN FRANKLIN   *222 West 77th Street*
                              (southeast corner Broadway)

A large brick and stone building of twelve stories, with modernized entrance. This was originally called the *Wellsmore.*

Named for Benjamin Franklin (1706–1790), American statesman, scientist, diplomat, and philosopher. One of his last acts was to sign a memorial to Congress requesting the abolition of slavery in the United States.

BENNETT COURT   *44–54 Bennett Avenue*

A six-story 1920s building.

Bennett Avenue was named for James Gordon Bennett (1795–1872), founder of the *New York Herald* (later the *Herald-Tribune*), whose country place was in the vicinity.

BERESFORD, THE   *1 and 7 West 81st Street*
                                   211 Central Park West
            (northwest corner West 81st Street and Central Park West)

An enormous apartment house built in 1929, at a cost of $10 million on the site previously occupied by the Hotel Beresford. The architect was Emery Roth and the builder was the HRH Construction Company.

Three towers (two of which conceal water tanks) make the outline of *The Beresford* one of the most distinctive in New York City—especially at night when they are lighted with beacons.

Extremely large and comfortable apartments surround an open inner courtyard, and the appointments of the lobbies exemplify the luxurious ambience intended by the builders and maintained by the present cooperative tenants.

BERKELEY HOUSE   *120 Central Park South*
                               (between Sixth and Seventh avenues)

H. I. Feldman was the architect for this building of twenty stories and penthouse. Many apartments have dropped living rooms.

The name is on the elaborate marquee entrance, next to the Ritz-Carlton Hotel.

BERKSHIRE   *540 West 112th Street*

A six-story redbrick building of the early twentieth century. Berkshire is the name of counties in England and Massachusetts.

BERLIN   *123–125 West 116th Street*

Abandoned.

BERNICE   *100 West 117th Street*
(southwest corner Lenox Avenue)

This once rather grand six-story brick building is now abandoned.

BERNICE   *543 West 148th Street*

A nineteenth-century brownstone building with four columns at the entrance.

BERTHA   *515 West 111th Street*

A six-story building of 1903, with porch entrance similar to that of the neighboring *Clara Court*.

BERTHA   *16 West 125th Street*

A five-story brick and brownstone building; circa 1900. The name is inscribed in a pretty decorative panel above the door.

To the west are the Sorrento and the Amalfi, formerly residential, now commercial buildings.

BERTRAM   *519 West 135th Street*

Abandoned.

{BERWIND MANSION}   *2 East 64th Street*

The brick and stone mansion of coal magnate E. J. Berwind was built in 1893 and has recently been converted to cooperative apartments.

The architect was Nathan Clark Mellen, who designed many of the "cottages" at Newport, Rhode Island, including Berwind's grand house "The Elms"—now open to the public.

BETA HOUSE   *401 East 77th Street*

A redbrick 1970s apartment house.

Beta is the second letter of the Greek alphabet and is also related to the second letter of the Hebrew alphabet, which, appropriately enough, also means "house."

BETA NORTH   *171–175 East 89th Street*

An eight-story redbrick 1970s apartment house with balconies and sliding glass doors; pleasant.

Another in the Beta group.

BETA SOUTH   *151 Lexington Avenue*

A midblock semisliver 1970s building, taller than the surrounding brownstones.

BETA II   *359 East 62nd Street*

Redbrick; circa 1980.

BETHUNE HOUSE (NYC Housing Authority)
1945 Amsterdam Avenue

This building at West 156th Street dates from 1967 and honors the memory of Mary McLeod Bethune (1875–1955), a noted black educator. Born in South Carolina, the seventeenth child of former slave parents, she attended Scotta Seminary in Concord, South Carolina, and the Moody Bible Institute. Mrs. Bethune established the National Council of Negro Women. She held a high federal position during World War II and was awarded many medals and honors.

BETTINA TOWER   *228 East 86th Street*

This fourteen-story redbrick building of the 1980s is on the site of the Norfolk, a late-nineteenth-century apartment house.

Bettina was the name taken by Elizabeth, Countess von Arnim (1785–1859), the protégée of Goethe, and is thus highly appropriate for a building on what was once the main thoroughfare of New York's German community.

Studio apartments rented for $810 and up per month in 1983.

BEULAH   *601–605–611 West 157th Street*
(northeast corner Amsterdam Avenue)

A six-story limestone and brick building with basement and three elaborate entrances, each decorated with lanterns by the doors; circa 1900. Little corbels ornament the windows.

BEVERLY   *265 West 81st Street*

The name is still visible on this turn-of-the-century eight-story redbrick building. An unusual iron balcony runs around the top.

BEVERWYCK   *39–41 West 27th Street*

This handsome seven-story nineteenth-century building has a heavily rusticated ground floor and a grand entrance, now badly repainted. At the moment it houses the Senton Hotel, a single-room-occupancy establishment.

Beverwyck was the original Dutch name of the town that the English renamed Albany.

BIERMAN COURT   *440 East 6th Street*

An early-twentieth-century brick building. The ground floor is now mostly sealed up and covered with graffiti in charming Day-Glo colors.

The name presumably honors the original owner.

BILTMORE PLAZA, THE   *155 East 29th Street*

A buff and white brick tower with a nice arched entrance, circa 1980.

George Vanderbilt, an heir of the railroad family, made up the name Biltmore for his house and gardens at Asheville, North Carolina. The house, which stood on a 106,000-acre estate, is generally considered the largest domestic building ever erected in this country.

The famous hotel on Madison Avenue between East 43rd and East 44th streets was named after the Vanderbilt estate and was formerly the property of the New York Central Railroad, the Vanderbilt line. It was converted into an office building in 1981.

BINDERY, THE   *324 Pearl Street*

A five-story former office building converted into a condominium in the 1980s.

The name bespeaks its original function in an area that is currently undergoing a revival.

BLACKBURN   *444 West 58th Street*

A six-story brownstone with interesting balconies of wrought iron with floral designs, circa 1880.

Forms a pair with the Olerain next door, at 446.

BLAIR HOUSE   *200 East 58th Street*

A modern high rise with the name of the official U.S. government guest house in Washington, D.C., where high-ranking visitors are entertained.

BLEECKER COURT   *77 Bleecker Street*

The lobby and interiors are high tech, but the component parts and buildings, which were put together in 1981 to form Bleecker Court, are of much earlier vintage.

The name of the street and building was taken from the family whose farm occupied the area; the property was ceded to the city in 1809–1812.

BLENNERHASSETT, THE   *509 West 111th Street*

A redbrick and stone six-story building with elaborately treated windows and fire escape. Built in 1903 by George F. Pelham and Max Lieberkind.

The name is carved in stone over the porch doorway; it is spelled with a hyphen.

Harman Blennerhassett (1765–1831), an Irish-born associate of Aaron Burr, was involved in Burr's plan to form a separatist territory in the American West.

BLERVIE HALL   *565 West 144th Street*

A turn-of-the-century building of six stories and basement in sooty white brick.

BLITHEBURN   *272 West 123rd Street*
(southeast corner Frederick Douglass Boulevard)

A turn-of-the-century or older building; five stories of red brick, with fire escape.

BLOOMINGDALE   *852 Amsterdam Avenue*

A five-story turn-of-the-century tenement building.

The Bloomingdale Road was the old name for upper Broadway (also known as the Boulevard) which ran north to the village of Bloomingdale ("vale of flowers"), from West 23rd Street.

BLUE BELL   *1 Bennett Avenue*

A six-story building of the 1920s with appropriately blue trim.

BOLIVAR, THE   *230 Central Park West*
(southwest corner West 83rd Street)

A rather plain building with a handsome Art Deco doorway to which has, unfortunately, been added an ugly modern canopy. The building has also been given new windows.

Simón Bolívar (1783–1830) is known as the Liberator of South America and led the revolution against Spanish rule in the early years of the nineteenth century.

BOLTON   *501 West 176th Street*
2940-56 Amsterdam Avenue

A large six-story building with four open bays on the avenue. Occupies the blockfront between West 176th and West 177th streets. Bombed-out, but now being renovated by a government agency.

Bolton is a borough of Lancashire, England.

BONAVISTA   *362 Riverside Drive*
                              (southeast corner West 109th Street)

A ten-story building with bayed windows and an open court on Riverside Drive, circa 1900.

BONNY CASTLE   *601 West 191st Street*
                              (northwest corner St. Nicholas Avenue)

A six-story redbrick building with a decorated stone frieze across the ground-floor facade, circa 1900.

Sir Richard Bonnycastle (1791–1847) was a British officer in the War of 1812; he published important works on the topography of North America.

Twin to *Highland Court*.

BONSALL   *323 East 10th Street*

A five-story building on Tompkins Square North, circa 1890. The upper part of the building is brick painted white.

A virtual twin to the *St. Marie* next door.

BONTA-NARRAGANSETT   *210 West 94th Street*
                              (southeast corner Broadway)

A seven-story circa-1900 building.

BORCHARD   *220 West 98th Street*
                              (southeast corner Broadway)

A white-brick and limestone building of the post–World War I era; thirteen stories with bayed windows.

BORDEAUX, THE   *549 Riverside Drive*
                              (southeast corner Tiemann Place)

Six stories with basement and open court; built in 1905. L. A. Goldstone, architect.

The seaport of Bordeaux is in southwestern France.

BOWNETT, THE   *11 West 81st Street*

An unusually handsome 1908 Beaux Arts building of twelve stories, with iron and stone balconies and a mansard roof. The plot is only fifty feet wide. Designed by Ditmars and Brite, architects and builders, *The Bownett* had originally one ten-room apartment on each floor.

The original advertisement described the building as "overlooking Manhattan Square and Central Park in a neighborhood devoted to private residences of the cultured, refined, and wealthy."

The building is now known as *The Planetarium* from the Hayden Planetarium at The American Museum of Natural History across the street.

BRADFORD, THE   *210 West 70th Street*

A sixteen-story redbrick building of the 1920s.

BRADSHIRE   *709 West 176th Street*

Colonial-style stone apartment house with an English-sounding name (there's actually no county named Brad).

BRANDER   *418 Central Park West*
                                     (southwest corner 102nd Street)

A ten-story Renaissance-building. An open court in front has a fountain and columns; an arched entrance is to the right.

Named for the original builder, F. Bränder, who was active on the West Side in the 1890s.

BRANDON, THE   *201 East 78th Street*
                                     (northeast corner Third Avenue)

This eighteen-story 1930s orange-brick building has handsome stone trim of a vaguely oriental–Art Deco design. One of the few large buildings erected on Third Avenue while the el still ran by.

Brandon is the name of cities in Canada and the United States.

BREEN TOWERS   *241 Avenue of the Americas*

A light-brick 1950s high rise "owned and managed by the estate of Joseph Breen."

BREMER BUILDINGS   *201 East 82nd Street*

Bavarian-Victorian exuberance with an elaborate entrance on the side street and shops along Third Avenue. Even the fire escapes on this 1890 building are pleasant to behold.

BRENSONIA   *224–226 Eighth Avenue*
                                     (between West 21st and West 22nd streets)

Twin to the *Romanza*.

BRENTMORE   *88 Central Park West*
                                     (southwest corner West 69th Street)

A twelve-story building with open-court entrance, now modernized. Built of brick and limestone with iron balconies on the fourth and tenth floors. Circa 1900.

Brentmore. *This Central Park West building of circa 1900 has an open entrance court. The three units on each floor are served by two passenger elevators, necessitating long "private halls." The apartment on the West 69th Street side is a duplex.*

BRETTON HALL   *2350 Broadway*
(east side Broadway, between West 85th and West 86th streets)

A twelve-story building; circa 1900. Heavily ornamented, it has bayed windows. The cornice has been removed and the entrance modernized.

Now a hotel with suites of one to four rooms, "furnished or unfurnished."

Bretton Woods is an old resort in northern New Hampshire, noted as the birthplace of the International Monetary Fund in 1944.

BREVARD, THE   *245 East 54th Street*

This thirty-story apartment house was built in 1975 but was left unfinished until sold to Brevard Associates in 1981; the new owners have marketed the apartments with the slogan The Affordable Condominium.

Brevard is the name of a resort town in North Carolina, near Asheville.

BREVOORT, THE   *11 Fifth Avenue*
                                    (between East 8th and East 9th streets)

A late-1950s high-rise apartment house with the name written in freestanding flowing blue script letters above the cantilevered metal canopy. The name is that of the famous old Hotel
Brevoort that occupied this location from 1854 until its demolition to make way for the present apartment house.

Queen Emma of the Hawaiian Islands stayed at the Brevoort
in 1866, and in later years it was a favorite rendezvous of New
York's French colony as well as "Village" writers and artists.

The name Brevoort is that of an ancient New York family
whose landholdings in this part of Manhattan were extensive.

Diagonally across Fifth Avenue, at the northwest corner of
9th Street, was the celebrated house of Henry Brevoort, demolished for the *Fifth Avenue Hotel*.

BREVOORT EAST   *20 East 9th Street*

A massive addition to the *Brevoort* on Fifth Avenue. The architects were Boak & Road for this project of builder-owner Sam
Minskoff & Sons.

An inaugural brochure with floor plans (no separate dining
rooms) for this twenty-six-story building proclaimed the Brevoort East to be ". . . Proud Heir to an Illustrious Name."

BREWSTER   *21 West 86th Street*

A fifteen-story brick building of the 1920s.

Counties and towns in Texas and New York are called
Brewster.

BREWSTER, THE   *1400 Fifth Avenue*
                                    (northwest corner West 115th Street)

This five-story limestone Renaissance Revival building of
circa 1897, was first apartments, then the Fifth Avenue branch
of the State Bank, then apartments again. The Fifth Avenue
side is now occupied by the Vineyard Baptist Church, the basement by Mr. Soul's Funland.

BRIARTON   *322 West 84th Street*

A six-story redbrick building of the early twentieth century.

BRIDGE APARTMENTS
                                    West 178th and West 179th streets,
                                    Wadsworth and Audubon avenues

Brown & Guenther designed these four 32-story towers,
which were built in 1964. The individual names are The Wadsworth, The St. Nicholas, The Park, and The Audubon. The
buildings were erected over the approaches to the George Washington Bridge and have suffered from the automobile-produced
smog rising from the highway.

BRIERFIELD   *215 West 83rd Street*

See *Surrey*.

BRIGHTON   *215 Audubon Avenue*
(southeast corner West 176th Street)

A six-story white-brick building with basement, circa 1900.
[See also *Carlton/Regency/Pavilion*.]

BRISTOL   *300 East 56th Street*
(southeast corner Third Avenue)

The only clue to the name of this huge 1970s building is the
discreet monogram *B* on the glass entrance door.

The name evokes images of England: the great old port city
of Bristol is at the mouth of the Severn.

Britannia. *Detail of medieval-*
style stone decoration.

BRITANNIA   *527 Cathedral Parkway*

Medieval motifs enliven this large nine-story building. Ten
grotesque medieval figures serve as corbels for mock balconies.
The entrance is an open court.

BRIXFORD   *140 West 79th Street*

A twelve-story red brick building of the 1920s.

BROADDYKE   *4761–4779 Broadway*
(northwest corner Dyckman Street)

A rather large six-story 1920s building with an entrance to
the subway in its basement.

BROADMOOR, THE   *235 West 102nd Street*
                                   (northwest corner Broadway)

A 1920s sixteen-story building with new windows.
The Broadmoor is a famous resort hotel in Colorado Springs,
which opened in 1918.

BROADMOOR, THE   *315 West 23rd Street*

A thirteen-story building of the 1920s recently converted
into a cooperative.

BROADVIEW   *606 West 116th Street*

The architects were Schwartz & Gross for this 1907–1908
Paterno Brothers building. When it opened, there were four
apartments to the floor at annual rents of $700 to $1,600. A
glass entrance has been added.

BROADWAY, THE   *230 West 101st Street*
                                   (southwest corner Broadway)

An old seven-story building.

BROADWAY ARMS   *89–91 Fairview Avenue*
                                   (northeast corner Broadway)

A six-story tan-brick building of the 1920s, with an open
bay on Broadway.

BROCKHOLST, THE   *101 West 85th Street*
                                   (northwest corner Columbus Avenue)

Now somewhat down at the heels, this apartment house
was hailed in the *Architectural Record and Guide:* "A truly
noble building . . . [which] will, in the generations to come,
stand as a landmark of the latest type of hotel—that wherein
the families occupy their suites of apartments—their homes all
the year 'round, and are enabled to take their board in the
building. . . There is a great future for these 'apartment
hotels.' "

The Brockholst is a six-story building of circa 1890. The name
is chiseled on the building's stone facade. In the lobby stood a
"magnificent chimney mantel, such as one would expect in one
of the old English castles."

The original lobby decor was by Tiffany Studios, and on the
west side of the entry hall was the coat of arms of the Livingston
family (Brockholst was a favorite forename among members of
that family).

The apartment hotel had a restaurant catered by one Mr.
Costa (who was also in charge of the Mutual Life Insurance
Company dining room). The rent was $350 a year for one room
with bath; nine rooms and bath went for $1,500 a year.

One of the two builders was Mr. T. E. D. Power, who was

Brockholst

related to the Livingston family and who was hailed for having "embellished the West Side."

Anthony Brockholst was brought over to New York in 1674 by Governor Sir Edmund Andros and served the colonial government in various capacities until his arrest in 1690 during Leisler's Rebellion. Brockholst Livingston, a descendant, owned "Bellevue Place," his home on the East River, which is the site of what is today Bellevue Hospital.

BROMLEY, THE   *139 East 35th Street*

Amenities promised to early tenants of this circa-1940 structure included a photographic darkroom. The promotional brochure bore the developer's seal on its cover: a large *T* superimposed on a scene of two buildings, encircled by the motto You Will Be Happier in a Tischman Apartment.

The name is indicated only by a discreet *B* on the glass door. Bromley is the name of a Vermont ski area and a borough of Southeastern London.

BROOKDALE HALL   *50 East 34th Street*

Modern white and gray brick building.

BROOKFIELD   *450 Riverside Drive*

A 1910 building of ten stories. The eight-room apartments originally rented for $1,500 to $2,100 a year, and prospective tenants were assured by the brochure that all the hall attendants were "white boys."

BROOKS—VAN HORN   *117 West 17th Street*
                                         112 West 18th Street

In 1982 this 1920s building was converted to a thirty-five-unit loft condominium with "simplexes" and duplex penthouses. Prices ranged from $136,000 to $310,000.

BRYN MAWR   *333 East 66th Street*

A medium-sized apartment house of 1964, recently converted to cooperative ownership.

The name is most likely inspired by the famous women's college in Pennsylvania. The words are Welsh for "fair hollow."

BUCHANAN APARTMENTS   *160 East 48th Street*

Picture a handsome Georgian-style building with landscaped interior courtyard, two separate entrances, a location in the midst of towering corporate headquarters, midway between Turtle Bay and Grand Central Terminal. Picture all that with 294 apartments—many still rent-controlled or stabilized—and you realize why the *Buchanan* has an extraordinarily low turnover in tenants.

This fifteen-story apartment house with penthouse takes its name from the old Buchanan farm located on the site in the nineteenth century. Built in 1928, the *Buchanan* was an early victim of the depression and went bankrupt in the 1930s. It had the dubious distinction of being the largest apartment house in the city managed by a single trustee in bankruptcy. Neither financial problems nor its Third Avenue location near the rumbling el prevented it from remaining a chic—as well as convenient—place to live. In 1937 the *Buchanan* numbered among its tenants such society names as William O'D. Iselin, Eva Drexel Dahlgren, and Frederick C. Havemeyer.

A decade or so ago there were reports of severe maintenance problems, but in recent years things seem to have improved.

BUCHOVA APARTMENTS   *219 West 88th Street*
                                     (northeast corner Broadway)

A twelve-story 1920s building.

BUCKINGHAM HOTEL   *101 West 57th Street*
                                   (northwest corner Sixth Avenue)

Built as a residential hotel and still so today. In 1933 it advertised that it was home to many of New York's "finest families."

The *Buckingham* is one of a number of hotels that were built for residential occupancy. Some of these, including the Dorset at 30 West 54th and the Warwick at 65 West 54th, were residential in the 1930s but are mainly transient today.

BUTTERFIELD HOUSE   37 West 12th Street

A cooperative apartment house built circa 1962 and designed to blend into this block of town houses. It occupies the site of the home of General Daniel E. Butterfield (1831–1901), Union general and composer of the taps bugle call. A memorial to the composer-soldier has been erected near Grant's Tomb on Riverside Drive.

BUXLEY HOUSE   360 East 65th Street

A redbrick 1960s apartment house with an English-sounding name.

BYRON, THE   165 East 32nd Street

This prosaic apartment house of the 1960s presumably honors George Noel Gordon, Lord Byron (1788–1824), English poet, traveler, lover, and freedom fighter, although it may be just a family name (the builder-owner was Byron Associates).

The elaborate introductory brochure, with floor plans, stressed such features as free gas, central air-conditioning, and sound-deadening walls. A five-room apartment on the third floor went for $315 per month.

C. DE BELLIS   413 East 12th Street

A six-story tenement. The name on the pediment is probably the builder's.

CALEDONIA   28 West 26th Street

This seven-story white-brick building of circa 1900 has an unusually handsome Beaux Arts ground floor.

Caledonia is the ancient Latin name for Scotland.

This is one of the many buildings in New York in which O. Henry is said to have lived.

CALUMET   509 West 135th Street

A circa-1900 apartment house whose name is the word for the traditional American Indian peace pipe.

CAMARGUE, THE   301 East 83rd Street
                              (northeast corner Second Avenue)

A 1970s set-back tower with a landscaped entrance and lots of balconies. This was supposed to be a twenty-eight-story building, but it ended up with thirty-one stories, in violation of the law.

The Camargue is a marshy island in southern France, between the great and little Rhône rivers in Bordeaux.

CAMBRIA   *347–355 West 55th Street*

An eight-story building of the 1920s, with open-court entrance.

Cambria is the Latin name for Wales.

CAMBRIDGE   *60 West 68th Street*

An eleven-story 1920s redbrick building.

CAMBRIDGE, THE   *500 East 85th Street*
(southeast corner York Avenue)

A 1970s tower with nicely landscaped pool and entrance driveway.

CAMBRIDGE HOTEL   *141 Central Park North*

An old six-story building that has seen better days.

CAMBRIDGE HOUSE   *337 West 86th Street*

A 1920s redbrick building with sixteen stories and penthouses and with a later marble entrance.

CAMDEN RESIDENCE HALL   *206 West 95th Street*

Formerly called the Camden. Six stories and basement; built on the H-plan in 1906 by A. B. Knight. Now considerably run down.

CAMELOT   *301 West 45th Street*

A 1960s apartment house whose name is that of the legendary town of Britain's King Arthur. The word came into widespread use after the Lerner and Lowe musical *Camelot* opened on Broadway in December 1960, and the name was applied by starry-eyed journalists to the Washington, D.C., of John F. Kennedy's presidency.

CAMPANILE, THE   *450 East 52nd Street*

Although not as famous or large as its neighbor across the street, *River House,* this elegant stone tower predates *River House,* and it, too, originally had a dock where the private yachts of its tenants could be moored—a feature eliminated by the construction of the Franklin D. Roosevelt Drive in the late 1930s. *The Campanile* was built in 1926–30; Van Wart & Wein were the architects, and T. E. Rhoads & Co. the builders. It was virtually the only luxury building in what was then not much better than a slum area, and the contrast between the luxurious yachts at *The Campanile* and the slum children playing on the East 53rd Street dock provided the raw material for Sidney Kingsley's play *Dead End.*

Dead End opened in 1935 and ran for 686 performances.

Campanile. *The imposing Venetian-Gothic style entrance to the building faces the driveway of* River House *across East 52nd Street.*

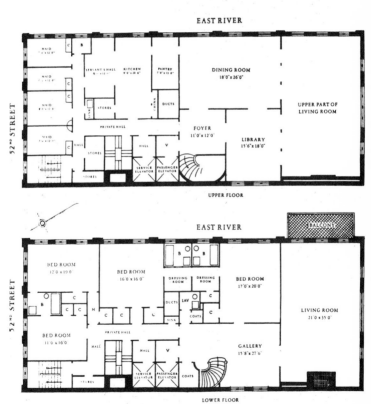

Campanile. *A "typical" fifteen-room duplex apartment in this small but elegant building.*

Campanile. *This penthouse-apartment has seven rooms and many terraces. Could this be the ultimate in New York dream apartments?*

Kingsley's inspiration for the play was a statement of Thomas Paine's: "the contrast of affluence and wretchedness is like dead and living bodies chained together." The setting reinforced the social-consciousness theme of this depression-era drama. The conflict between the "Dead End Kids" and the wealthy tenants of "East River Terrace Apartments" provided theatergoers of the time with a play that was given a stunning production and won the Theatre Club Award.

When the building opened, much was made of its name and location: "Reminiscent of Venice," the brochure read, "and its colorful Grand Canal—on the shore of the East River."

The name derives from the Italian word for a bell tower, and indeed with one apartment to a floor, the tall building does bear a faint resemblance to a bell tower, especially in the architect's original drawings of the building as viewed from the East River. In 1932 apartments in this cooperative were priced at $50,000 to $65,000.

Alexander Woollcott was a longtime resident; his third-floor apartment was the scene of his famous Sunday breakfasts. His friends made fun of the remoteness of the building: Franklin P. Adams suggested that the apartment take an Indian name, "Ocowoica," an Ojibway word meaning, according to Adams, "the little three-room apartment on the East River that it is difficult to find a taxi cab near"; but it was Dorothy Parker who gave it the name that stuck: "wit's end."

The roster of glamorous and wealthy residents over the years is truly outstanding: Noel Coward, John Barry Ryan, Arnold

Saint-Subber, Ralph Pulitzer, Greta Garbo, and Henry Luce and Clare Boothe Luce, among others.

CAMPOS PLAZA (NYC Housing Authority)
635 East 12th Street
(continues to East 14th Street)

This new complex of buildings, with almost five hundred apartments in all, has as its namesake Pedro Albizu Campos, a Puerto Rican nationalist.

CANNON POINT SOUTH   *45 Sutton Place South*
(between East 54th and East 55th streets)

This white brick building dating from 1958 has nineteen stories and a penthouse. The architect was P. Resnick.

Cannon Point extended into the East River off East 52nd Street until the Franklin D. Roosevelt Drive was built.

CAPERNACK   *188 St. Nicholas Avenue*
(southeast corner West 120th Street)

A seven-story dilapidated redbrick building; circa 1900.

CAPITOL HALL HOTEL   *166–168 West 87th Street*

A nine-story orange-brick building of the 1920s.

CAPRICE   *320 East 58th Street*

Redbrick 1960s apartment house with its name on the canopy.

CARLTON/REGENCY/PAVILION

Carlton House, London, was the residence of the Prince Regent of England (later George IV). Built as the home of Lord Carlton in 1708, it was redone in the latest style by Henry Holland circa 1790.

The last nine years of the reign of England's King George III (1811–1820) were marked by the monarch's illness and temporary insanity; and in that period the governing of the country was vested in his son as the Prince Regent.

Militarily and economically, politically and socially, the Regency period was marked by dramatic upheavals in Great Britain and the world.

However, in the popular mind, then as now, the carefree, dis-
solute life led by the prince and his set was most important, to-
gether with new developments in domestic architecture and deco-
ration. Ever since, "Carlton" and "Regency" have been
synonymous with a pleasure-centered, comfortable, and carefree
life style.

At Brighton, on the coast, a summer palace, known as the
Royal Pavilion, was built by the Prince Regent in a bizarre,
mock-Oriental style. The town became a fashionable resort, and
the architecture of the Pavilion and its imitations at Brighton
served as the inspiration for countless seaside resorts of the late
nineteenth century.

[See also entries for Regency *and* Pavilion.*]*

CARLTON ARMS HOTEL
160 East 25th Street
(southwest corner Third Avenue)

A five-story building; circa 1920s.

CARLTON HOUSE
680 Madison Avenue
(East 61st to East 62nd streets)

This fashionable apartment-hotel was built in 1952 in the
Georgian style. K. B. Norton was the architect. There are fifteen stories and a penthouse.

CARLTON HOUSE EAST
220 East 57th Street

A 1960s blue-brick building with no visible name.

CARLTON PARK
1065 Park Avenue

One of the few named residential buildings on Park Avenue—in this case a comparative newcomer—is this 1970s tower
in buff brick and travertine.

CARLTON REGENCY
137 East 36th Street

A huge tower in the 1970s style, with a canopied entrance
on Lexington Avenue, despite the posted address of record.
Lyra & Araye were the architects for this centrally air-conditioned building.

CARLTON TOWERS
200 East 64th Street
(southeast corner Third Avenue)

This 1960s building's Third Avenue side has a sunken plaza,
which was first occupied by a New York version of Paris's Le

Drugstore; after that it was a print gallery, and now it is the successful and popular Fiorello's Restaurant.

CARLYLE *77 West 85th Street*
(northeast corner Columbus Avenue)

A six-story building of circa 1915 with nice fire escapes.

CARLYLE, THE *35 East 76th Street*

Built in 1930–31 as an apartment hotel by the Calvin Morris Corporation (Bien & Prince, architects) on a site previously occupied by two old apartment buildings (the Lenox Hill and the Carrolton), the thirty-eight-floor, 426-foot-high *Carlyle*—with its sleek Art Deco lines and graceful tower (which doubles as a smokestack)—has dominated the skyline of the Upper East Side for over half a century. The building is filled with wealthy tenant-owners who live there (entrance on East 77th Street) and the more or less transient guests of the hotel who stay there (entrance on East 76th Street).

For more than a decade after it was built, *The Carlyle* was a bit out of place in a neighborhood of brownstones and shops and cheap restaurants; but in 1948 two things helped to put it in the limelight: (a) its owners built new premises for the Parke-Bernet Galleries (then located at 575 Madison Avenue), and the art galleries, good restaurants, boutiques, and carriage trade soon followed (and the Carlyle's view of Central Park was preserved); and (b) Harry S Truman, then president of the United States, began to stay at *The Carlyle* during his visits to New York, and his little walks in the area became front-page stories around the world. *The Carlyle*'s owners, City Investing Company, then sold the building to the Rockefeller Brothers, then leased it back and operated it. Later the building was bought by realtor Peter Sharp, who co-oped it in 1970.

During the 1960s President John F. Kennedy often stayed at *The Carlyle,* and among the apartment owners have been Henry Ford II and Colonel and Mrs. Edgar Garbisch (she was a daughter of Walter P. Chyrsler).

The 76th Street lobby is surely one of the most attractive public spaces in the city, and the Bemelmans Bar and the Café Carlyle are suitable embellishment for this luxurious establishment. Parke-Bernet has now fled to the far east (York Avenue and East 72nd Street), and the gallery with its sculpture of *Venus Bringing the Arts to Manhattan* was largely vacant in 1983.

The building was named for the Victorian writer Thomas Carlyle (1795–1881) because the builder's daughter admired his work.

CARNEGIE

*In 1901 Andrew Carnegie (1835–1919), the steel magnate,
built a splendid mansion for himself and his family on Fifth
Avenue at East 90th Street. At the time the area was not very
built up, and the entire neighborhood came to be called Carnegie
Hill.*

*A decade earlier Carnegie, who had emigrated to Pennsylva-
nia from Scotland as a boy and eventually controlled much of the
American steel industry, provided funds for the auditorium at the
intersection of West 57th Street and Seventh Avenue that still
bears his name and has been the focus of the neighborhood ever
since.*

CARNEGIE HALL STUDIOS   *160 West 57th Street
(southeast corner Seventh Avenue)*

Built in 1891, this is an early mixed-use building, for high
above the gold and white auditorium are studio apartments incorporated into the original structure to provide living and
working spaces for musicians and others. In recent years, the
eviction of rent-controlled tenants was marked by bitter name
calling. Interestingly, the old Metropolitan Opera House at
Broadway and West 39th Street incorporated apartments into
the structure when opened in 1883.

CARNEGIE HILL TOWER   *40 East 94th Street
(southeast corner Madison Avenue)*

This 1982 buff-brick condominium featured a picture of Andrew Carnegie in its logo, whereas the advertisement stressed
the location, the views, and the amenities.
Sample prices: three bedrooms from $371,000, studios from
$130,000.
On this site, before *Carnegie Hill Tower,* was Hollywood, a
turn-of-the-century apartment building.

CARNEGIE MEWS   *211 West 56th Street
(northeast corner Broadway)*

This thirty-two-story tower of the 1970s may well be among
the tallest of the city's "mews"—usually thought of as low-rise
stables along a courtyard or alley.
In 1983 police raided two "brothels" in the building. According to newspaper reports, the one on the fifth floor catered
to the "pay for pain" trade while that on the eighth floor offered
straight prostitution without torture. Both were said to be controlled by organized crime.

CARNEGIE TOWERS   *115 East 87th Street*

This thirty-eight-story, 198-unit rental apartment of 1973 has an elaborate stepped entrance on the 87th Street facade. Built into the first few stories is the Robert F. Kennedy Public School, with its own entrance on East 88th Street.

CAROL TOWER   *360 East 72nd Street*

A huge white-brick building with central tower, on the site of Upper Manhattan's first "model tenement," built in 1880 and demolished in the early 1960s to make way for the present apartment house.

The original building, designed by Vaux and Radford, was erected by an organization called the Improved Dwellings Association, which was one of several devoted to helping poor people live in reasonably healthy surroundings, an aim mandated by the laws of 1867 and 1879 regulating tenement houses.

CAROLINE, THE   *210 Sherman Avenue*
(southwest corner West 205th Street)

A 1970s fifteen-story redbrick building; one of the few new buildings in this neighborhood.

CAROLUS, THE   *29 Charles Street*

This six-story turn-of-the-century building has applied heraldic decoration, tastefully arranged.

The name is Latin for Charles.

CAROLYN COURT   *565 West 162nd Street*

This large turn-of-the-century building is next door to Lydia Court on West 162nd Street and backs up to *Rosbert Hall* on the corner of Broadway and West 163rd Street.

CARROLLTON   *601 West 168th Street*
(northwest corner Broadway)

A six-story redbrick building; circa 1900.

Charles Carroll, who signed his name "Charles Carroll of Carrollton" after his estate in Frederick County, Maryland, was, when he died in 1832, the last surviving signer of the Declaration of Independence.

CARTERET   *208 West 23rd Street*

A seventeen-story building of the 1920s carrying its name on a handsome stone entrance.

Captain Philip Carteret of the village of New Haarlem was prominent when British power was restored in New York in 1674.

CARVEL COURT
80 St. Nicholas Avenue
(northeast corner West 114th Street)

A nondescript seven-story circa-1900 building.

There is no Carvel ice cream store in the building, we assure you. The inspiration for the name may well have been *Richard Carvel*, a best-selling novel published in 1899 by the American author Winston Churchill.

CARVER HOUSES (NYC Housing Authority)
1475 Madison Avenue

This project of thirteen buildings and over twelve hundred apartments honors George Washington Carver (1864–1943), black agronomist and promoter of black entrepreneurship. He was on the faculty of Tuskegee Institute in Alabama.

CASCADE
10 Manhattan Avenue

A six-story building erected at the turn of the century.

CAST IRON BUILDING, THE
67 East 12th Street

Originally the James McCreery Dry Goods Store, this 1860s cast-iron behemoth was converted to apartments in the early 1970s.

The shops and elaborate columns of the ground floor are most attractive.

CASTLE COURT
540 West 122nd Street
(southeast corner Broadway)

A six-story building of red and black brick with limestone trim; with carved outset corner, columned porch, and central court; circa 1905. Built by Neville & Bagge. The exterior is in superb condition.

CASTLE VILLAGE
120–140–160–180–200 Cabrini Boulevard

George F. Pelham II was the architect for these five twelve-story buildings overlooking the Hudson between West 181st and West 186th streets. They were built in 1938 on the site of the large and elaborate "Paterno Castle" (as it came to be known), home of Charles V. Paterno, one of the major New York City real estate developers of the early twentieth century.

The buildings, which were described in the original brochure as "conceived and constructed by Dr. Charles V. Paterno," offered many attractions that were then new. "Tenants may lease space in the large fireproof ramp garage for the storage of automobiles within the Castle Village grounds. This is the first large, multi-car garage to be built in Manhattan in conjunction with an apartment project. Thus Castle Village for the first time offers Manhattan apartment dwellers a garage on the premises."

The first-floor apartments are about 200 feet above the level of the Hudson River; those on the top floor, about 300 feet.

CASTLETON, THE   *569 West 142nd Street*
                                 (northeast corner Broadway)

A six-story building of 1906; Neville & Bagge, architects.
A twin to the *Saguenay*.

CATHEDRAL

In the four hundredth anniversary year of the discovery of America there was a burst of building activity on Morningside Heights. On 27 December 1892 the cornerstone was laid for the Protestant Episcopal Cathedral of St. John the Divine on West 110th Street between Morningside Park and Amsterdam Avenue. West 110th Street was widened between Riverside Park and Seventh Avenue (now Adam Clayton Powell, Jr., Boulevard) and renamed Cathedral Parkway, a name to which New Yorkers have largely been indifferent, still calling the street by its number.

The first architects of the cathedral were Heins & La Farge. Although work had begun, their plans proved unsatisfactory, and in 1911 the architects were replaced by Cram & Ferguson who were in turn replaced by other architects. The cathedral had been designed to be the biggest Gothic-style church in the world, and it is no less than 601 feet long. Work continued until 1941, when it was stopped on account of World War II. It resumed in 1974, but the church is still far from finished.

Eighteen ninety-two was also the year that Columbia University decided to move its campus uptown close to the cathedral, forming, it was hoped, "the Acropolis of America."

At the same time numerous apartment buildings—most of them of modest scale—were built in the neighborhood around the university and the cathedral; this housing stock is still largely intact and includes a great number of the named buildings listed in this book.

Cathedral Court Apartments (Morningside Drive) *before occupancy.*

CATHEDRAL COURT   *44–47 Morningside Drive*

This turn-of-the-century building has a set-back entrance with an archway linking two sections of the building.

CATHEDRAL COURT   *541 West 113th Street*

A six-story turn-of-the-century building; a twin to *Robert Watt Hall.*

CATHEDRAL PARKWAY APARTMENTS
535 Cathedral Parkway

A plain fourteen-story structure built by Samuel Rosoff and Sons in 1925. The architect was Robert T. Lyons. The building has rather small apartments of three to six rooms. A typical lay-out was three rooms with foyer, bath, and "maid's toilet." Among the features of the building were "annunciators."

CATHEDRAL PARKWAY HOUSES
424 Cathedral Parkway
125 West 109th Street

Two towers built in 1975 by Davis, Brody & Assocs. and Roger Glasgow. There is a central plaza.

CATHEDRAL STUDIOS   *610 West 111th Street*

This six-story building with fire escape and elaborate windows was built in 1906.

CATHERINE   *466 West 149th Street*
                                (southeast corner Amsterdam Avenue)

A plain five-story redbrick building erected circa 1900.

CATHERWOOD COURT   *661 West 179th Street*
                                (northeast corner Broadway)

A five-story redbrick building of the basic Pelham design.

CAYUGA   *324 West 83rd Street*

A seven-story building with fire escape. The first two stories
are of limestone. A handsome stone balcony is over the door. A
fire escape connects the two wings of this apartment house, a
twin to the *Rexton* at 320.

The Cayuga Indians are a branch of the Iroquois and have
given their name to the largest of the Finger Lakes in upstate
New York.

CECILIA   *202 West 78th Street*

[See *Rose.*]

CEDARCLIFF   *48 St. Nicholas Place*

A six-story building of the 1920s.

CEDARLEIGH   *303 West 122nd Street*
                                (northwest corner St. Nicholas Avenue)

A large six-story white-brick building of circa 1915, occupying the irregularly shaped block bounded by West 122nd
Street, West 123rd Street, and St. Nicholas and Manhattan avenues. It overlooks the 28th Precinct House.

CENTENNIAL APARTMENTS
                                210–214 East 25th Street

This rather grandiose grouping of three similar buildings,
with separate entrances and red brick trimmed with stone,
dates from around the time of the U.S. Centennial celebration
in 1876.

The name is prominently displayed on the central cornice.

CENTRAL   *33–39 Macombs Place*

A six-story turn-of-the-century red and buff brick building.

CENTRAL CONDOMINIUM   *250 West 88th Street*

A former hotel that in the early 1980s underwent a "gut renovation" resulting in sixty-one apartments.

CENTRAL PARK STUDIOS   *15 West 67th Street*

A fourteen-story building, one of a row of artists' studio-living quarters on this street; built in the early twentieth century.

CENTRAL PARK TERRACE   *461 Central Park West*
(northwest corner West 106th Street)

A six-story 1920s building.

CENTRAL PARK VIEW   *414 Central Park West*
(northwest corner West 101st Street)

A sixteen-story building; circa 1900.

CENTURY   *95 West 119th Street*
(northeast corner Lenox Avenue)

A seven-story turn-of-the-century building with fire escapes and floral swags decorating the windows.

Century Apartments. *The ground plan for this twin-towered landmark on Central Park West. Most of the apartments are small but luxurious, featuring dropped living rooms, large foyers, and terraces.*

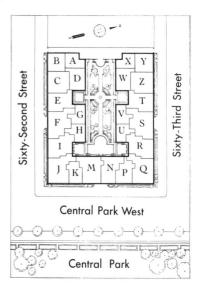

CENTURY APARTMENTS   *25 Central Park West*
(West 62nd to West 63rd streets)

Irwin S. Chanin was the architect of this huge Art Deco apartment building erected in 1931 on the blockfront between West 62nd and West 63rd streets, a site formerly occupied by the Century Theater. The thirty-one-story building contains more than four hundred suites, and it originally advertised "luxury in two rooms or seven."

The original brochure for the building stated: "The Century Apartments are an effort on the part of the Chanin Organization to create in the incomparable setting of Central Park West and Columbus Circle, small and moderate-size homes in which beauty, comfort, and pride of possession are added to the engineering and scientific achievements of those who have had a part in their plan and construction. With this humanitarian view, the impersonal calculations of the engineer and the cold research of the scientist have been invoked to mould these residences to every possible requirement of metropolitan modes of life."

The building has become a landmark of the area. Well-maintained, it is still rental.

CEZANNE, THE　　　　　　　　*61 Jane Street*

An undistinguished redbrick 1960s building, one of a number named after artists in that period, including the *Van Gogh* and the *Picasso*.

Paul Cézanne (1839–1906) was the French Post-Impressionist painter.

CHALFONTE　　　　　　　　*200 West 70th Street*
(southwest corner Amsterdam Avenue)

A fifteen-story building of the 1920s. Chalfont (without the final "e") is a village in England, where Milton lived and William Penn was buried; it is also a borough of Pennsylvania where, according to tradition, New York City's favorite Indian chief, Tammany, was buried.

CHALFONTE　　　　　　　　*51 East 97th Street*
(northeast corner Madison Avenue)

A six-story building with elaborate windows; circa 1900.

CHALFONTE　　　　　　　　*507 West 135th Street*

Part of a whole block of circa-1900 apartments.

CHALFONTE, MARLBOROUGH, CLINTON
502–512 Amsterdam Avenue

A series of six-story buildings along the west side of Amsterdam Avenue between West 84th and West 85th streets, dating from circa 1900. The three entrances, each of which has paired granite columns, have these names above the doors.

CHALK HOUSE　　　　　　　　*150 East 77th Street*

This white-brick 1960s apartment house originally bore this name in honor of its builder, the real estate tycoon O. Roy Chalk. The name is no longer in evidence.

CHALMONT　　　　　　　　*180 St. Nicholas Avenue*
(northeast corner West 119th Street)

A severe but rather elegant building with seven stories and a basement.

A twin to *Grampion Apartments.*

CHAMBOLD COURT   *66–72 Fort Washington Avenue*

Built circa 1900 in the late French Renaissance style with an open court at the entrance. The cornice, which must have been elaborately decorated, has been removed.

CHAMPLAIN ARMS   *165 Bennett Avenue*
(northeast corner West 189th Street)

A six-story tan-brick building of the 1920s.
The French explorer Samuel de Champlain (ca. 1567–1635) made his first voyage to Canada in 1603.

CHANTILLY   *1855 Adam Clayton Powell, Jr., Boulevard*
(northeast corner West 113rd Street)

An elaborate six-story redbrick building with limestone trim; built at the turn of the century.
Chantilly is a town in northern France, renowned for its horse racing and formerly for its lace manufacture. A famous French royal palace is situated there. The *Chantilly*'s neighbors have also been named after French royal palaces, including *Palais Royal, Versailles,* and *Fontainebleau.*

CHAPIN, THE   *530 East 84th Street*

A five-story brick apartment house with marble entrance, possibly a 1960s renovation of an older building.
Named for its proximity to the Chapin School at 100 East End Avenue.

CHAREL HOUSE   *40 East 80th Street*

"Conceived and built as a co-op" in the 1960s, this beige-brick apartment house was said to feature a marble vestibule and sills, attended elevators, solid wood doors, and solid masonry walls.
The name refers to the developer.

CHARLEMAGNE   *532 West 111th Street*

One of a row of three identical turn-of-the-century buildings. Like its neighbors, the *Romana* and *Amele Hall,* this white-brick apartment house has an arched entrance in the Gothic style.
When the building opened, the advertisements stressed that spaciousness was "the keynote of these . . . elevator apartments" of three to seven rooms which rented at $540 to $1,350 a year.
Charlemagne (742–814) was the first Holy Roman Emperor. The name seems to refer to the nearby Gothic Cathedral of St. John the Divine, as do several other medieval names in the vicinity.

CHARLES, THE   *229 West 111th Street*

Abandoned.

CHARLESTON COURT   *601 West 163rd Street*

When this turn-of-the-century building was built at the corner of Broadway, the Deaf & Dumb Asylum and the old Yankee Stadium were its neighbors here on Washington Heights.

CHARLOTTE COURT   *2 South Pinehurst Avenue*
(northwest corner West 176th Street)

A twin to *Emily Court*.

CHARLTON HOUSE   *2 Charlton Street*

A 1960s redbrick building.
Charlton Street was named in 1807 for Dr. John Charlton, a British surgeon who came to New York with the British forces during the American Revolution and stayed after the war to become one of the city's prominent physicians.

CHART HOUSE   *304 East 55th Street*

This brownstone apartment house is among the smallest of the named buildings.

CHATEAU D'ARMES   *46–52 Fort Washington Avenue*

One of a series of buildings in this neighborhood with entrance court and elaborately decorated doorways in the French Renaissance manner.
The name givers apparently intended to refer to an armory, although the French word is *salle d'armes*.

CHATEAU EAST   *222 East 75th Street*

This small white building with blue canopy (possibly a renovation of an older building) dates from the 1960s when "East" was a popular appendage to almost everything as a synonym for "chic."

CHATHAM GREEN   *185 Park Row*

A monolithic apartment complex of 1961. Park Row was originally Chatham Street, and the nearby court district was called Chatham Square in honor of William Pitt, first earl of Chatham (1708–1778), whose championing of the North American colonists in their opposition to British taxation policies won him favor in pre-Revolutionary New York.

CHATHAM TOWERS   *170 Park Row*

Kelly & Gruzen were the architects for this 1965 project that dominates the skyline of Chinatown and stands sentinel over its companion project, *Chatham Green*.

CHATILLION
214 Riverside Drive
(southeast corner West 94th Street)

Seven stories and basement of white brick and limestone; turn of the century.

The department of France and suburb of Paris spell this name without the second "i."

Chatsworth Apartments, *before the building of the Annex.*

CHATSWORTH
346 West 72nd Street
(southeast corner Riverside Drive)

The *Chatsworth* was built in 1904. John E. Schlarsmith, the architect, designed it in the most lavish Beaux Arts style with finely carved stonework and ironwork. The building's location— it overlooks the Hudson at the beginning of Riverside Drive and Riverside Park—has made its exuberant architecture familiar to countless motorists and joggers.

CHATSWORTH ANNEX
340 West 72nd Street

The annex was added in 1906 and offered apartments of five to fifteen rooms renting from $1,000 to $4,500 a year. "Views are panoramic, and cannot be duplicated in New York," stated the brochure. The parlors were of white mahogany, libraries of regular mahogany, and dining rooms of mission oak.

The *Chatsworth* and the *Chatsworth Annex* had their own electric generator and refrigerator plant, a conservatory, billiard parlor, cafe, barbership, valet, hairdresser, and tailor.

The name Chatsworth is taken from the enormous country house of the dukes of Devonshire which, with its elaborate gardens, superior architecture, and enormous art collections, has become synonymous with wealth, taste, and nobility.

CHAUTAUQUA, THE
270 West 88th Street
(southeast corner West End Avenue)

A twelve-story white-brick building of the 1920s.

Chautauqua, an upstate New York village, gave its name to a program of adult education in the arts, sciences, and humanities that was developed in the resort. Begun in 1874, the program continues today. Lectures were arranged on the Chautauqua circuit throughout the United States.

CHELSEA

Four or five New York neighborhood names seem to have a special attraction for the builders and architects who name apartment buildings: Sutton, Gramercy, Murray Hill, and Chelsea, among them. All are areas with rather ill-defined boundaries.

Chelsea in the eighteenth and early nineteenth centuries was a village that took its name from a house built by Jacob and Teunis Somerendyke sometime before 1750; the house stood on present-day West 23rd Street and about 200 feet west of Ninth Avenue. They sold it to Captain Thomas Clarke, a retired British army officer, but it burned down about 1777 and was replaced by Chelsea House, which occupied the site from about 1777 to 1852. It was in that house that Clement Clarke Moore wrote his celebrated poem A Visit from St. Nicholas *in December 1823.*

At the time the poem was written and even several decades later, Chelsea was the area lying between West 19th and West 24th streets, from Eighth Avenue to the Hudson. Like many popular neighborhoods in New York, it has steadily extended its boundaries. Now one of the centers of "gentrification" in New York, it is roughly West 14th Street to the low West 30s.

CHELSEA   *300 West 21st Street*

The name appears over the door of this six-story 1920s red-brick building with fire escapes. It has a rather handsome but dilapidated entrance.

CHELSEA COURT TOWER   *365 West 20th Street*
                                   (northeast corner Ninth Avenue)

A 1920s building of fifteen stories; white brick, with an open bay on Ninth Avenue. The entrance has been modernized. A 1934 brochure advertised "housekeeping apartments"; the building is in the process of becoming a cooperative.

CHELSEA EAST   *12 West 18th Street*

Finished condominium lofts in a 1983 conversion with J-51 tax abatements. Prices start at $100 per square foot.

CHELSEA HALL   *253 West 16th Street*

This six-story 1920s–1930s building has a handsome coat of arms carved in stone over the front door and again at the top of the building. The front door has remarkably fine grillwork, and the building has casement windows.

CHELSEA HOTEL   *222 West 23rd Street*

Although renowned throughout the world today as *the* hotel for resident and visiting bohemians—of every persuasion—the *Chelsea* actually started out in life as a very proper cooperative apartment house in 1884, when it was built as a "home club" by that foremost architect of the cooperative movement Philip G. Hubert.

Preceded by the *Rembrandt* (1882), the *Spanish Flats* (1883), and the St. Catherine (Madison Avenue and East 53rd Street, 1884), the *Chelsea* is the earliest Hubert building still extant in New York City.

It was planned that, of the *Chelsea*'s one hundred suites of three to twelve rooms, seventy were to be owned by shareholders in the home club, and thirty were to be rented out at $600 to $1,200 a year. The rents from these flats and the ground-floor stores—with projected revenues of $10,000 per year—were supposed to be enough to ease the burden of the shareholders and insure the financial stability of the *Chelsea*. Initially all the apartments were subscribed for (or rented), and the future looked secure. Alas, such was not to be the case. The economic roller coaster of the late nineteenth century proved too much of a burden, and in 1905 the cooperative was dissolved and the *Chelsea* reopened as a residential hotel.

Since then its reputation as the hostelry of bohemia, *par excellence,* has never paled. Artists such as John Sloan and Arthur B. Davies; writers such as O. Henry, Thomas Wolfe, Edgar Lee Masters, and Brendan Behan; musicians such as Virgil Thomson; plus assorted dress designers (Charles James), rock singers, and poets *manqués.* Because of Andy Warhol's memorable film *Chelsea Girls,* sixties vice came to be identified with the once staid cooperative in the public's mind.

Today, as the Chelsea neighborhood for which the hotel was named becomes increasingly "gentrified," the *Chelsea Hotel* has begun to take on an almost establishment air: its resident bohemians seem to frown on the wild goings-on of the past decades, and instead have assumed the manner of responsible arts-establishment types.

CHELSEA HOUSES (NYC Housing Authority)
430 West 26th Street

Built in 1963–1964, this project is named for the historic neighborhood where it is situated.

CHELSEA LANE APARTMENTS
16 West 16th Street

A 1950s–1960s buff-brick high rise of fourteen stories consisting of two buildings with an interior garden court. An additional entrance is 15 West 15th Street.

CHELSEA MANOR   *300 West 23rd Street*

The first brochure issued for this 1920s apartment house carried no name, but it was soon given one.

In the words of a later brochure, "The new Chelsea Manor house proudly lifts its nineteen stories and penthouse on 23rd Street at Eighth Avenue to dominate the Chelsea district with even greater distinction than that with which an earlier manor house ruled a different and far less interesting scene."

The small apartments offered—one to three rooms—were originally designed as "business women's apartments" and "business men's apartments."

CHELSEA MEWS   *148 West 23rd Street*

An early-twentieth-century building that has undergone conversion. It offers "loft-style apartments with huge living space . . . woodburning fireplaces."

CHELSEA PARK HOUSE   *321 West 29th Street*

A 1940s redbrick building of six stories with fire escapes; somewhat modernized.

CHELSEA TOWN HOUSE   *320 West 30th Street*

A seven-story redbrick building of the 1940s.

CHELSMORE APARTMENTS   *205 West 15th Street*

This six-story building is in three sections that are separated by courts. The building has fire escapes in the courts, casement windows, and one of the finest Art Deco entrances in the city.

CHEPSTOW
215–217 West 101st Street
(northeast corner Broadway)

A pre–World War I thirteen-story redbrick building with a beautiful entrance.

Chepstow is a town in England not far from Bristol.

Cherokee. *View of one of the open courtyards showing a staircase with its distinctive outward curve.*

CHEROKEE, THE
507–523 East 77th Street
508–524 East 78th Street
(at Cherokee Place)

Built in 1909–1912 as one of the architect Henry Atterbury Smith's model tenements for improving the living conditions of those with modest means, *The Cherokee* is still a handsome structure, with its open inner courtyards approached by vaulted and tiled passageways, and windows adorned with balconies. The staircases leading to the individual apartments (there are no interior halls or stairs) from the open courts are constructed in such a way that even large objects can be maneuvered up and down the relatively narrow space. Some tenants still call these staircase features "coffin corners," alluding to the days when wakes were held at homes and coffins were often seen being carried up and down the stairs.

The adjoining John Jay Park is on land donated by Mrs. William K. Vanderbilt, who was also involved in the movement to provide improved housing for the working classes. *The Cherokee*, which was formerly called the *East River Houses* or the *Shively Sanitary Tenements*, is one of the best examples inspired by that movement.

Green-glazed terra-cotta ornament and Spanish tile roofs are

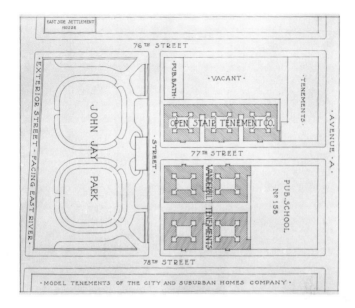

Cherokee, *ground plan. Here the buildings are called "Vanderbilt Tenements," after the philanthropist who provided the money to build them. The "Open Stair Tenement Co." flats have been replaced by the* Pavillion. *Avenue A is now York Avenue.*

nice additions to the sombre buff-brick surfaces. *The Cherokee* has aged very well.

The name Cherokee, applied to the apartments and the bordering street, derives from the old Cherokee Democratic Club on East 79th Street between First and York avenues. This was one of the local "wigwams" (each named after an Indian tribe in deference to the mythical patron of the organization St. Tammany, famous sachem of the Lenni-Lenape Indians) of the Tammany organization. In an area of mostly poor immigrants it obviously was a powerful influence.

The club's building has been turned into an apartment house, but the substation post office for Zip Code 10028 is still called Cherokee (First Avenue and East 80th Street).

[CHEROKEE DEMOCRATIC CLUB]
334 East 79th Street

The present bland building on the site of one of the landmarks of old Yorkville is a recent replacement for the eclectic splendor of the smoke-filled clubhouse.

CHESAPEAKE
155 Audubon Avenue
(southeast corner West 173rd Street)

Twin to *Shenandoah* at 145 Audubon Avenue.

CHESAPEAKE HOUSE, THE   *201 East 28th Street*

This huge tan-brick building of the 1960s–1970s is named after the famous bay in Maryland and Virginia, which is synonymous with seafood to New Yorkers.

CHESTER COURT   *96 West 119th Street*
                                (southeast corner Lenox Avenue)

An eight-story circa-1900 building. An elaborate door decorated with female masks is at the center of the apartment house's porch.

CHESTER HALL   *201 West 107th Street*
                              (northwest corner Amsterdam Avenue)

A six-story elevator building built in 1907; B. Levitan, architect; I. Judis, builder.

CHESTERFIELD   *260 Riverside Drive*
                                (northeast corner West 98th Street)

This ten-story circa-1900 building has an open-court entrance on the side street.

The fourth earl of Chesterfield's letters to his son, published in 1774, were much admired for their instruction in polite behavior.

CHESTERSHIRE   *570 West 183rd Street*

A six-story building with bowed windows. Its name is an ill-inspired attempt at Anglicization. The county of Chester in England is Cheshire.

CHEYNEY, THE   *344 West 23rd Street*

A ten-story white-brick building recently converted into a condominium. Advertisements call it "a bit of London in Manhattan" and claim that the building is "in keeping with the character of London's Cheyney Walk." The well-known London street is, however, spelled Cheyne. Forty-four simplex, duplex, and penthouse apartments are included.

CHILMARK HALL   *501 West 143rd Street*
                                (northwest corner Hamilton Place)

A six-story white-brick building decorated with coats of arms at the top.

Chilmark is a town on Martha's Vineyard.

Twin to the *Wellington Arms*.

CHISLEHURST, THE   *455 Fort Washington Avenue*
                          (between West 180th and West 181st streets)

A five-story redbrick building standing between *The Hazelhurst* and *The Pinehurst*.

Chislehurst is a village in Kent, England, famous in modern history as the refuge of Napoléon III of France and Empress Eugénie after the fall of the Second Empire in 1870.

CHURCHILL, THE *300 East 40th Street*

A gargantuan 1970s white-brick tower with landscaped plaza.

Most likely named for Sir Winston Churchill (1874–1965), British prime minister and honorary U.S. citizen.

CIRCLE, THE *114 Morningside Drive*

Built in a curving line at the point where Morningside Drive comes down the hill to meet Amsterdam Avenue.

CLAIBORNE HOUSE *444 East 84th Street*

A 1960s redbrick apartment house with balconies.

CLAIRE *350 West 118th Street*

Six stories and basement with porch entrance containing three granite columns. Built in 1906–1907 by Robert M. Silverman.

A twin of the *Rosedale.*

CLARA COURT *503 West 111th Street*

A six-story turn-of-the-century building with columned porch entrance and fire escape.

CLAREMONT

Claremont Avenue, which runs north seven blocks from West 120th Street, near Riverside Park, takes its name from an eighteenth-century manor house known as "Claremont," that stood nearby, just a short distance from Grant's Tomb.

The manor house was built by George Pollock, a wealthy Irish-American merchant whose nephew, St. Clair Pollock, known as "the amiable child," is buried nearby. Claremont, in Surrey, England, is said to have inspired the naming of the New York mansion. This house, much altered, stood until 1952, when it was torn down. In its last century it was the Claremont Inn, a favorite summer rendezvous of Manhattanites, providing dinner and dancing overlooking the Hudson.

CLAREMONT, THE   *229 East 12th Street*

A seven-story building of the 1890s.

CLAREMONT   *55 Tiemann Place*

A six-story white-brick and limestone building with an open-court entrance. The right cornice has been removed; the left is of Spanish tile.

CLAREMONT   *608–612 West 184th Street*

Twin to *Augher Villa*.

CLAREMONT COURT   *530 Riverside Drive*

Six stories and basement in red brick, with fire escapes; built on open-court plan by the architect G. Kiester in 1907.

CLAREMONT HALL   *601 West 112th Street*

A seven-story turn-of-the-century redbrick building with three bays.

CLARENCE   *312 West 93rd Street*

Built in 1904 by George F. Pelham, architect. The six-story redbrick building with fire escape is a twin to *The Riverview* next door.

Clarendon, *the West 86th Street entrance.*

CLARENDON

137 Riverside Drive
(southeast corner West 86th Street)

This handsome and well-preserved building with an elaborate metal canopy has twelve stories. Built in 1907 by the architect Charles E. Birge, it is best known as the New York home of William Randolph Hearst for many years.

Hearst originally stayed at the Hoffman House when he first arrived in New York in 1895; then he owned a town house at 123 Lexington Avenue. He moved to the *Clarendon* in 1907, leasing the thirty rooms on the top three floors. Following a dispute with the owner, Ronald McDonald, Hearst bought the entire building for $900,000. He lost it to the mortgage holders in 1938.

Clarendon was a name well-known in New York during the British colonial period. Edward Hyde, Viscount Cornbury (1661–1723), the son of the second earl of Clarendon, was first cousin to Queen Anne, and was sent over to govern New York and New Jersey in 1702. He was a sort of remittance man. He had an incorrigible habit of dressing in women's clothes and scandalized the population by promenading the ramparts of the Battery on summer evenings dressed in gown and pearls. He was sent home in 1708, not for this fault, but for the inefficiency and dishonesty of his administration. He became the

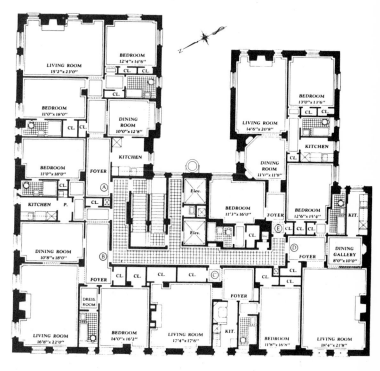

Clarendon. *Here the public hall is long, but the long, narrow "private halls" within individual units have given way to spacious foyers from which the other rooms flow.*

third and last earl of Clarendon. His Irish wife (born Kitty O'Brien) died in New York and was buried in Trinity Church in 1706.

CLARENDON   *605 West 112th Street*

A six-story turn-of-the-century building, now modernized.

CLARICE   *400 West 50th Street*

A well-kept nineteenth-century redbrick building.

CLARIDGE HOUSE   *201 East 87th Street*

A thirty-story tower on Third Avenue, with a drive and porte-cochere entrance on the east side of the building—between East 87th and East 88th streets—enhanced by a pleasant garden.

CLARIDGE'S   *101 West 55th Street*
(northwest corner Avenue of the Americas)

A recently renovated 1920s redbrick building with its long side along Avenue of the Americas.

The name is taken from the famous old hotel in Brook Street, London, which has been in operation for over a century.

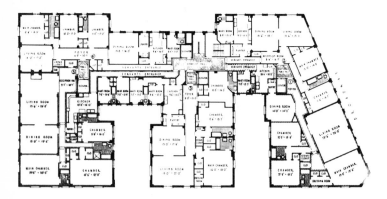

Clebourne. *Typical floor plan of this building on an irregularly shaped plot. There are five units on this floor. Note the "servants entrance" leading from the service hall and elevator to the individual apartments, a nice feature dating back to the time when help was cheap and plentiful and tradesmen always used the service elevators.*

CLEBOURNE
255 West 105th Street
924 West End Avenue
(northeast corner West 105th Street and West End Avenue)

Stone detailing on an otherwise routine 1920s building with a porte-cochere entrance in the side street.

CLEMENTINE
139 East 26th Street

A six-story walk-up of gray brick; circa 1900.

CLERMONT SOUTH
445 East 80th Street
(northwest corner York Avenue)

A nineteen-story white-brick apartment house; circa 1966. [See also *Robert Fulton* for discussion of name Clermont.]

CLERMONT TOWER
444 East 82nd Street

A gray-brick high rise of circa 1966; surrounded by a rather forbidding wrought-iron fence, which gives the place a somewhat institutional look.

CLIFDEN
265 Riverside Drive
(southeast corner West 99th Street)

An eleven-story tan brick and limestone building; circa 1900.

CLIFF DWELLERS' APARTMENTS
240 Riverside Drive
(northeast corner West 96th Street)

When this building was put up in 1914, the Mayan motifs embellishing the facade were extremely avant-garde. The architect Herman Lee Meader used southwestern animal life, naturalistically carved, in a frieze. Even a buffalo skull is to be found amid the ornamentation.

Early in this century people who lived and worked in tall buildings—an uncommon experience at the time—were popularly known as cliff dwellers. Henry Blake Fuller, the Chicago novelist, published a book in 1893 entitled *The Cliff Dwellers.* From the nature of the decor of this building it seems that the architect also had in mind the cliff dwellings of the American Indians in the Southwest.

CLIFFCREST
936–938 St. Nicholas Avenue
(southeast corner West 157th Street)

An old six-story building whose once elaborate entrance has been cemented over.

The name indicates its commanding position on "Sugar Hill"—the area of West Harlem that has traditionally been the home of the most prosperous black New Yorkers—near the apartment where Duke Ellington lived (now a National Historic site, marked with a plaque).

CLIFFHAVEN COURT   *217–225 Haven Avenue*
                            (northeast corner West 176th Street)

A twin to *Hudson Court*.

CLIFFORD   *160 West 119th Street*
                (southeast corner Adam Clayton Powell, Jr., Boulevard)

A five-story building with a rather unusual arched doorway with squat columns. Elaborate porch on the Adam Clayton Powell, Jr., Boulevard side.

The ground floor houses the New Look Restaurant. The No Littering, No Dogs sign seems to be largely ignored.

CLIFTON   *2010 Adam Clayton Powell, Jr., Boulevard*

A seven-story circa-1900 building of red brick and limestone, with a new cornice; nicely maintained.

CLINTON ARMS RESIDENTIAL HOTEL
                              244 West 99th Street
                              (southwest corner Broadway)

A seven-story redbrick building of the turn of the century. In its early days it was known as The Navarre.

CLINTON HOUSES (NYC Housing Authority)
                              1744 Lexington Avenue
                              (East 104th to East 110th streets)

A federally funded project of 749 apartments in Upper Manhattan. Named after De Witt Clinton (1769–1828), U.S. senator, mayor of New York City, governor of New York State, and "godfather" of the Erie Canal.

This project dates from 1965.

CLINTON TOWER   *790 Eleventh Avenue*

A high-rise apartment tower with an adjacent courtyard, playground, and low-rise building. Hoberman & Wasserman, architects; 1975.

CLOISTER, THE   *321 East 43rd Street*

This stone and brick Tudor-style building is part of the *Tudor City* group.

The name, meaning a covered walk or a monastic retreat, is not inappropriate given the late-medieval touches in this apartment house's architecture.

CLOISTER ARMS   *609–615 Fort Washington Avenue*

A six-story white-brick building; circa 1920.

The Cloisters, which houses the medieval collection of the Metropolitan Museum of Art, was not built until 1934–1938; however, the sculptor George G. Barnard had assembled portions of monastic cloisters on the site many years before.

CLUNY   *133 West 72nd Street*

This small apartment building of the 1920s once had a grand lobby entrance with an ornately carved facade in the medieval style appropriate for its name, which recalls both the French abbey and the Paris museum. Now, alas, all that is gone, and storefronts cover the ground floor.

COLISEUM PARK APARTMENTS
345 West 58th Street
350 West 60th Street

Sylvan & Robert Bien were the architects for this 1957 "Title I" slum clearance project.

Red-brick, no frills buildings with a large garden court between the north and south buildings, directly behind the New York Coliseum on Columbus Circle.

COLLECT POND HOUSE   *366 Broadway*

A handsome circa-1900 office building, which now has ten residential floors above two commercial floors. The clean lines of the building have been disfigured by a modern doorway.

Originally the Bernard Semel Building, it was renamed by Zuberry Associates, the developer, for a body of water that was nearby in colonial days.

COLLEGE PARK APARTMENTS
630 St. Nicholas Avenue

Six-story fire-escape building of the 1960s.

The college referred to is presumably the City College of New York (now City College, City University of New York).

COLLINSON   *225 West End Avenue*
(northwest corner West 70th Street)

A nondescript six-story building with an open-court entrance on the West End Avenue side; circa 1900.

COLONIAL, THE   *411 West 115th Street*

A simple building, less elegant than its neighbors on nearby Morningside Drive. In turn-of-the-century style, with the fire escapes on the outside.

A twin of *The Munroe* next door.

COLONIAL COURT   *600 West 142nd Street*
                                        (southwest corner Broadway)

The pediment has been removed from this six-story building.
The name is carved in stone with a crown at the top. The grand
entrance has three granite columns. Built in 1907 by Moore &
Landsiedel, architects.

COLONIAL HOUSE   *409 East 87th Street*

A small (five stories), well-maintained turn-of-the-century
apartment house resembling several of its neighbors in this
quiet Yorkville block; opposite St. Joseph's Church.

COLONIAL HOUSE   *611–617 West 112th Street*

This six-story building still bears its former name, the Ma-
ranamay. A handsome structure of red brick and limestone,
with big windows; it has lost its cornices.

COLONIAL PARKWAY   *409–417 Edgecombe Avenue*

A thirteen-story redbrick building of the 1920s, facing Colonial Park. During the 1920s the building was home to many
black intellectuals of the Harlem renaissance.

COLONNADE EAST   *220 East 60th Street*

Despite the name, no colonnades are in evidence.

COLONNADE 57, THE   *347 West 57th Street*

A forty-five-story condominium tower completed in 1982;
prices range from $130,000 for studios to $200,000 for two-
bedroom apartments.
   No colonnades here, either.

COLONY, THE   *31 East 1st Street*

A five-story tenement with its name inscribed in gold over
the door. Directly across the street breadlines form outside the
offices of the *Catholic Worker*.

COLONY, THE   *302 East 77th Street*

A name of elegant connotations for a somewhat down-at-the-
heels walk-up tenement situated between the Squid Row and
Lion's Rock restaurants.

COLONY HOUSE   *30 East 65th Street*

A white-brick 1960s apartment house. The awning prominently displays the name *The Colony,* suggesting some association with the famous restaurant that once graced the
neighborhood.

COLORADO   *76 West 82nd Street*

One of three contiguous matching buildings—the others being the *Nebraska* and the *Lyndhurst*—put up in 1891 by the Macdonald & Lozier Company. Each has five stories, a basement, and an arched entrance. The *Real Estate Record* described the buildings as having "attractive fronts of mottled brick and stone. . . . The Nebraska," it went on to say, "takes in half the block front on the avenue (Columbus) between 81st and 82nd and has a number of stores on the first floor." The buildings bear a strong resemblance to the *Endicott* across Columbus Avenue.

In 1892, the buildings were sold to Henry B. Slaven (1853–1904), famous at the time as the excavating contractor for Ferdinand de Lesseps during the French attempt to build a canal across the isthmus of Panama in 1880–89. The tenants complained that there was too much sun along the Columbus Avenue side, so Slaven installed awnings on the windows—apparently a noteworthy innovation at that time.

COLOSSEUM   *435 Riverside Drive*
                                    (southeast corner West 116th Street)

Built by Schwartz & Gross in 1910, this structure curves around the corner of West 116th Street and Riverside Drive.

A bronze plaque to the left of the entrance states that Harlan Fiske Stone (1872–1946), dean of the Columbia Law School and later chief justice of the U.S. Supreme Court, lived here between 1920 and 1925.

The similarity of this curving building to the Colosseum amphitheater in Rome gives the name.

COLUMBIA, THE   *275 West 96th Street*
                                    (northwest corner Broadway)

The plot on which this building stands has one of the most troubled and controversial histories of any in the recent history of the city. It was assembled in the 1960s and was to be the site of an Alexander's Department Store. Fierce opposition on the part of "community leaders" led to the cancellation of plans. A luxury apartment building was then proposed but also aroused opposition. The plot sat vacant until 1982 when the Zeckendorf interests finally constructed a 31-story condominium apartment building with 303 units.

COLUMBIA COURT   *431 Riverside Drive*
                                    (northeast corner West 115th Street)

Seven stories and basement; with modernized entrance. The name is from nearby Columbia University.

COLUMBUS   *550 West 157th Street*
                                    (southeast corner Broadway)

A nine-story white-brick building of the early twentieth century.

COLUMBUS HOUSE   *386 Columbus Avenue*

A narrow 1983 building, almost of the "sliver" type, containing sixteen stories with twenty-four condominiums, "apartments, duplexes, and studios."

COLUMNS   *32 West 40th Street*

An eleven-story redbrick and limestone building of the 1920s, with columns at the second- and third-floor windows and at the top. Formerly the *Engineers Club,* the building has in recent years been converted into a cooperative.

COMMANDER HOTEL   *240 West 73rd Street*

A tan-brick building of the 1920s, with the initials *CH* on the stone coats of arms flanking the entrance.

[COMMUNITY CHURCH AND
APARTMENTS]   *10 Park Avenue*

The congregation of the Community Church in the 1930s, at a cost of $3,500,000 erected this multipurpose building of twenty-nine floors, with stores and three-, four-, and five-room apartments, plus a church in the adjoining annex. A gourmet bakery now occupies the Gothic-style ground floor.

CONCORD HALL   *468 Riverside Drive*
(southeast corner West 119th Street)

George F. Pelham was the architect for this 1906 building of nine stories on the central-court plan. When it opened, it featured a "colonial style dining room" for tenants. Annual rents were from $1,400 to $2,000.

The name is taken from Concord, Massachusetts, site of the first battle of the American Revolution, where "once the embattled farmers stood, and fired the shot heard round the world."

CONCORDE APARTMENTS   *220 East 65th Street*

A striking T-shaped tower with a pleasant garden, pool, and cascading fountains at the entrance; circa 1980.

The French word for "harmony" or "agreement," the name has in recent times come to be synonymous with the Franco-British supersonic plane.

CONFUCIUS PLAZA   *19 Bowery*
2 Division Street

These apartments near the Manhattan Bridge were designed by the architects Horowitz & Chun in 1976. Named after China's philosopher-statesman-moralist-writer who lived from 551 to 479 B.C.—an appropriate choice given the large Chinese population in the neighborhood.

CONGRESSIONAL HOTEL   *483 West End Avenue*

A narrow twelve-story redbrick building of the 1920s; now rather run-down.

CONNAUGHT TOWER   *300 East 54th Street*

This 1980 high-rise tower was converted to a co-op in 1982. The vest-pocket park next door has a huge red abstract sculpture by Alexander Liberman as its focal point.

Connaught was one of the four ancient kingdoms of Ireland, but to many New Yorkers the name evokes visions of the fashionable Connaught Hotel in London's Mayfair district.

CONTEMPORA, THE   *111 Third Avenue*

This 1960s white-brick apartment house just below East 14th Street stands near the spot where Peter Stuyvesant's orchard was planted in the seventeenth century. The last surviving pear tree of that orchard grew here until 1867, when it was struck by two wagons and died—only two years before a descendant, Rutherfurd Stuyvesant, built New York's first apartment house, on East 18th Street, the *Stuyvesant*.

CONTINENTAL APARTMENTS
321 East 48th Street

This modern white-brick building adjoins the imposing Libyan Mission to the United Nations.

CONTINENTAL EAST   *353 East 83rd Street*
(northwest corner First Avenue)

Typical late-1960s set-back tower, with landscaped driveway entrance.

CONTINENTAL TOWERS   *301 East 79th Street*
(northeast corner Second Avenue)

Thirty-five-story tower with balconies. Bought by Invesco (the Gouletas family business; sister Evangeline Gouletas, wife of Hugh Carey, a former governor of New York) in 1981 to be turned into co-ops (Invesco also owned *Plaza Four Hundred,* at 400 East 56th Street). Nice pots of trees and flowers at the entrance.

CONVENT COURT   *452 West 149th Street*
(southwest corner Convent Avenue)

A building of six stories and basement with bayed windows that have been painted with pitch or black tar.

The numerous ecclesiastical names of the apartments in the vicinity of Convent Avenue—and the name of the street itself—were inspired by the Convent of the Sacred Heart and the sev-

eral schools administered by the nuns housed there in the nineteenth century. The convent grounds were located on a tract of
land in what was once the village of Manhattanville, bordered
by St. Nicholas Terrace, West 130th to West 135th streets,
and Convent Avenue.

Although the original building burned in 1888, the
schools—including Manhattanville College of the Sacred Heart—
remained here until 1952, when they were moved to the former
Ogden Reid estate at Purchase, New York.

The Convent Avenue site is now the South Campus of City
College, CUNY.

[See also the various names beginning *Saint.*]

CONVENT VIEW   *110 Convent Avenue*
(southwest corner West 133rd Street)

A five-story and basement building with a small interior
court, built circa 1900, when it looked onto the site of the Convent of the Sacred Heart. The view is now of the south campus
of the City College.

COOPER ARMS   *10 Cooper Street*

A six-story dark-brick building of the 1920s.

The American novelist James Fenimore Cooper actually lived
in New York City for only a short time of his life. He often
wrote about the city, however, and received an honorary degree
from Columbia in 1824.

COOPER GRAMERCY   *251 East 23rd Street*
(northwest corner Second Avenue)

This huge brown-brick tower has a school for the deaf on the
ground floor of its East 23rd Street side. Built on the site of an
old piano factory, the building honors both the not-too-distant
Gramercy Park and Peter Cooper (1791–1883), a longtime resident of the area.

CORDOVA COURT   *610 West 178th Street*

An old five-story building, neighbor and sister to Granada
Court at 604.

Córdoba, or Cordova, and Granada are cities and provinces
of Spain.

CORINNE   *521 West 135th Street*

One of a row of small apartment buildings along West 135th
Street, many of which have women's names.

CORINSECA   *209 West 97th Street*
(northwest corner Amsterdam Avenue)

The name—of unknown origin—is over the door of this
seven-stories-and-basement building of circa 1900.

CORNICHE   *301 East 87th Street*

Brown brick and buff brick with hexagonal corner balconies.
The French word for "cornice" or "rocky ledge," the name
brings to mind the winding mountain roads of the Riviera near
Monte Carlo.

CORNWALL, THE   *255 West 90th Street*
                                       (northwest corner Broadway)

A redbrick building with twelve stories and basement by
Neville & Bagge; 1909. The top three stories are elaborately ornamented. Carved masks decorate the doors of the imposing
entrance.
Like many buildings by this firm of architects, it has a British name: Cornwall is a county in southwestern England.

CORNWALLIS   *201 West 108th Street*
                               (northwest corner Amsterdam Avenue)

A six-story turn-of-the-century building.
Charles Lord Cornwallis was the British general defeated by
the Americans at the decisive Battle of Yorktown in October
1781. The following month he appeared in New York City and
from there sailed to England. He was later governor and commander in chief of the British forces in India and viceroy of
Ireland.

CORONET   *57 West 58th Street*

Built circa 1880–1890, this building is handsomely decorated with stone vases over most of the windows. A coronet dec-
orates the entrance which has been modernized. On the ground
floor are shops and the popular restaurant Thursdays.

CORSI HOUSE (NYC Housing Authority)
                                        306 East 117th Street

This East Harlem project built in 1973 is of relatively modest scale (only 171 units) and honors the memory of Edward
Corsi, executive director of LaGuardia Memorial House.

CORTLAND   *510 Cathedral Parkway*

A twelve-story brick and limestone building of the turn of
the century, with unusual tree-trunk stone decoration on the
third floor, and balconies on many windows.
The Van Cortlandt family was one of the most prominent
Dutch dynasties of New York.

COURT REBELLE   *416–422 West 122nd Street*

As described in the original brochure, this six-story building
of 1912–1913 featured large apartments of six, seven, and eight

rooms with a wall safe in the main chamber (i.e., master bedroom) of each apartment.

The name would appear to be a Frenchified tribute to the
American Revolution, since the brochure pointed out that the
building faced "Fort Horn [rock] where the famous battle of
Harlem Heights was once fought."

COURTNEY HOUSE   *55 West 14th Street*

This large 1960s building has twenty stories, penthouses,
and corner balconies; affords a direct view of the heavily Hispanic shopping district on West 14th Street.

COURT WASHINGTON   *245 Fort Washington Avenue*
(southwest corner West 170th Street)

A huge and solid six-story building of circa 1900 with entrance court and interior court (hence the name); a twin to the
slightly smaller apartment building called *The Fortress*.

COURTWOOD   *600 West 169th Street*
(southwest corner Broadway)

Twin to the *Carrollton*.

CRAGMOOR   *801 Riverside Drive*

A six-story tan-brick building of the 1920s.

CRAGSMOOR   *419 West 115th Street*

Sister to *The Munroe* and other buildings on the street.

CRESCENT COURT   *195 Claremont Avenue*
(southwest corner Tiemann Place)

Six stories and basement in white brick and limestone; by
Neville & Bagge, 1906.

CRESTON   *839 West End Avenue*
(southwest corner West 101st Street)

A large 1920s building with elaborate limestone base and
narrow open courts; entrance on West 101st Street.

CRILLON   *74 West 85th Street*

Twin to the *Sudeley*.

The name is derived from the Hôtel Crillon on the Place de
la Concorde in Paris; originally the palace of the Crillon family,
it is now a world-famous hotel.

Crillon. *The intricately carved stonework almost obscures the name over the door of this small apartment house.*

CRILLON COURT, THE   *779 Riverside Drive*

Six-story building with set-back entrance, fountain, and blue fire escapes.

CRITERION ARMS   *526 West 111th Street*

A handsome six-story turn-of-the-century building with open-court entrance. The decoration is unusual: stained-glass windows at the back of the court, and a row of stone carvings of medieval workmen, such as masons and builders in the front, a reference to the construction of the Cathedral of St. John the Divine, the entrance of which is only a few steps away.

CROMARTIE   *551 West 172nd Street*
(northwest corner Audubon Avenue)

A five-story salmon-colored brick building of circa 1900.
Cromarty is a county and town in northern Scotland that has given its name to several earls of the Mackenzie family.

CROMWELL APARTMENTS
601–605–607–609 West 137th Street
600 Riverside Drive

Six-story buildings in the English Renaissance style; built in 1907 by Bing & Bing, with Emery Roth as architect. Connected by an open court; central arched entrance and recessed fire escapes.

The six-story *Cromwell Annex* at 604–608 Riverside Drive was added about 1915.

Roth seems to have had a predilection for the name Cromwell, as he was the architect in 1927 of the *Hotel Oliver Cromwell* on West 72nd Street.

Oliver Cromwell (1599–1658), leader of the parliamentary forces in the English Civil War, was lord protector of England from 1653 until his death.

CROYDEN, THE   *12 East 86th Street*

Built in the 1920s as a hotel, this buff-brick building with handsome classical limestone trim has three sections. The earliest section has seven stories, and the later ones, built on the site of the car barns of the old Metropolitan Street Railway, have fifteen stories. The building extends to West 85th Street. Completely renovated into apartments in the 1970s and now known by its address.

Croyden is a town in the English county of Surrey, near London, formerly the site of the palace of the archbishop of Canterbury.

CRYSTAL COURT   *555 West 160th Street*
                                              (northeast corner Broadway)

A six-story circa-1900 building with crowned crockets at the top.

CUMBERLAND HOUSE   *30 East 62nd Street*

This modern redbrick apartment bears a plaque testifying that Theodore Roosevelt lived in a house on the site from 1895 to 1897.

Cumberland, a county in the northwest of England, is associated with the dukes and earls of Cumberland, whose London residence was "Cumberland House."

CURLEW   *250 West 78th Street*

A five-story nineteenth-century building.
The curlew is a shorebird.

DACORN   *452 Fort Washington Avenue*

A six-story circa-1900 building with a nicely decorated entrance and ornamental coats of arms on the facade.

DAG HAMMARSKJOLD TOWER
                                                240 East 47th Street

A striking condominium tower of 1982 honoring the memory of Dag Hammarskjöld (1905–1961), the Swedish diplomat who served as secretary-general of the United Nations from

1953 until his death. A bust of Hammarskjöld adorns the corner of the building.

DAKOTA, THE   *1 West 72nd Street*

The undoubted queen of New York's apartment buildings is *The Dakota.* Since the day ground was broken for it a century ago, it has consistently attracted public attention. Along with the Vatican, the White House, and Buckingham Palace, it is arguably the best-known residential address in the world.

Edward S. Clark of the Singer Sewing Machine Company put up the building in 1884 as one of the city's first luxury apartment houses. The architect was Henry J. Hardenbergh, who also designed the Plaza Hotel and many other buildings in New York. The town houses behind *The Dakota* on West 73rd Street are also his work.

Clark had great faith in the future of the West Side as a residential area, and he needed it when he put up *The Dakota,* because at the time the neighborhood was one of shanties among which goats happily grazed. The name is generally supposed to have been given the building because it was so far uptown it was "almost in Dakota Territory," but it must be remembered that gold was discovered in the Dakota Territory in the 1870s and it was the scene of a great land boom beginning in 1878. The name was then synonymous with riches. As the inventory shows, many buildings in New York were then named for western territories. The sculptured bust of an Indian chief adorns the facade.

The fountain court, the grand entrance on West 72nd Street, and the four corner elevators were striking innovations in their time and, along with the picturesque exterior decoration, which is medieval and Victorian at the same time, remain fascinating

Dakota. *The West 72nd Street entrance.*

today. The interiors, however, as many architectural critics have pointed out, show very little imagination, despite their size. When the building opened, it had its own restaurant looking out over Central Park, an amenity that, given the sparse settlement of the neighborhood, must have been a boon to the tenants. The first seven floors were for tenants, the eighth and ninth for their staffs; the tenth floor was a playroom for children. The sixty-five apartments had from four to twenty rooms.

In 1960 the building, which had been rental from the first, was threatened with demolition. A plan was worked out so that the tenants could buy their apartments, and a high rise, the *Mayfair Towers,* was put up on the *Dakota* parking lot.

The Dakota in recent years has attracted many tenants from the performing arts, including Leonard Bernstein, Ruth Ford and Zachary Scott, Lauren Bacall and Jason Robards, and John and Yoko Lennon. The building, already famous, received worldwide attention in 1980 when the former Beatle John Lennon was shot at the front entrance. For months admirers brought flowers to the spot.

The Dakota was the scene of the movie *Rosemary's Baby* (1968) and is probably the only apartment building in the world to have had books written about it, among them Stephen Birmingham's *Life at the Dakota.*

DALLAS COURT   *600 West 144th Street*
                                        (southwest corner Broadway)

A white-brick building of circa 1900.

George Mifflin Dallas (1792–1864), grandson of Benjamin Franklin, was vice president of the United States between 1845 and 1849 under James K. Polk.

DANDREW LANE   *425 West 24th Street*

A five-story redbrick building of the 1920s, directly across the street from *London Terrace.*

Twin to *Susany Lane.*

DANIEL   *98 Park Terrace East*

A redbrick building at West 217th Street. The park in the address is Isham Park.

DARTMOUTH   *509 Cathedral Parkway*

A twin to the *St. Albans.*

DAVID ARMS   *340 East 90th Street*

A valiant but unsuccessful effort to spruce up a small apartment house: ochre stucco above buff brick, with a brown canopy, and fire escapes disguised as balconies!

DE BOULOGNE   *526–528 West 112th Street*

A six-story turn-of-the-century building. Vaguely French Renaissance in feel. Twin to *The Huguenot* next door.

The Bois de Boulogne is a vast wooded park at the outskirts of Paris.

DE HOSTOS APARTMENTS (NYC Housing Authority)   *201 West 93rd Street*

The project dates from 1969 and contains 223 apartments.

It is named for Eugenio Maria de Hostos (1839–1903), Puerto Rican poet, essayist, educator, and political philosopher. He lived for a time in New York and was an early advocate of statehood for Puerto Rico.

DE KOVEN   *708–714 West 181st Street*

A six-story tan-brick building with green trim; 1920s.

Reginald De Koven, who was a New York music critic and composer, wrote the operetta *Robin Hood* in 1890, of which the hit song was "Oh Promise Me."

DELANO VILLAGE   *West 139th to West 142nd Street*
                       (Fifth Avenue to Lenox Avenue)

A 1957 complex of sixteen-story apartment houses.

The Delano family, to which Franklin Delano Roosevelt's mother belonged, has been prominent in New York since the eighteenth century.

DE LEON   *52 West 112th Street*

Seven stories of red brick, with fire escapes and open bay on the street; circa 1900.

Juan Ponce de León (1460–1521), Spanish explorer, discoverer of Florida, and, appropriately for one of New York City's major ethnic groups, governor of Puerto Rico (1509–1512).

He died while searching for the legendary "Fountain of Youth."

DE PEYSTER   *529 West 111th Street*

A six-story brick and stone building with handsome iron entrance and lamps flanking the doorway; circa 1900.

Named for the family that once owned the property. Described by Dixon Wecter, the historian of American society, as the "dull but canny De Peysters," they were major landowners in New York City.

DE SOTO   *215 West 91st Street*
                               (northeast corner Broadway)

A plain white-brick building of thirteen stories, built in the early 1920s.

Hernando de Soto (ca. 1500–1542) was the Spanish explorer who discovered the Mississippi River.

DE WITT   254 West 82nd Street

A heavily ornamented circa-1900 six-story building, with basement, bay windows, and handsome wrought-iron gates at the entrance.

Jan de Wit (or De Witt), a miller, put up one of the earliest windmills in New Amsterdam in 1622. Built in partnership with the Dutch West India Company, the windmill stood outside the boundaries of the city in present-day City Hall Park. The descendants of de Wit were long prominent in New York City history.

DEAUVILLE HOTEL   103 East 29th Street

Circa 1900; the front with columns and an ugly modern marquee.

Deauville is a stylish resort town on the channel coast of France.

DEERFIELD   676 Riverside Drive
(southeast corner West 145th Street)

Fine stone carvings of oak clusters with the initial *D* at the center decorate this eleven-story building, which is also embellished with stone balconies.

Deerfield is the name of several American towns, most notably the seventeenth-century town in Massachusetts, now a famous historic restoration.

DEL MONTE   102 West 75th Street
(southwest corner Columbus Avenue)

An old seven-story building with a heavily rusticated ground floor. The entrance has been poorly "modernized."

Del Monte, California, was a fashionable summer resort when this apartment house went up at the turn of the century.

DELAWARE, THE   520 West 122nd Street

Sister building to *The Grant* and *The Sarasota,* and possibly named for the Delaware Indians (also called the Lenni-Lenape) who inhabited the mid-Atlantic states, including what is now Manhattan. The white settlers gradually pushed them westward until they ended up settling with the Cherokees; some migrated to Ontario, Canada.

The English name for the tribe, as well as for the state and river—comes from Thomas West, Lord De La Warr, the first colonial governor of Virginia (1609–1618).

DELLA ROBBIA   740 West End Avenue
(northeast corner West 96th Street)

A thirteen-story dark brick building with an open bay on West 96th Street; 1920s.

Luca Della Robbia (ca. 1400–1482) was a notable Florentine sculptor of the Renaissance period.

DELMONICO'S

502 Park Avenue
(northwest corner East 59th Street)

Built in 1928 as the Delmonico Hotel by Benjamin Winter—to the designs of Goldner & Goldner, architects—this thirty-two-story building was named after a famous old New York restaurant, even though there was never any official connection.

One of the longtime tenants of the Delmonico Hotel was television host and *Daily News* columnist Ed Sullivan. In the 1970s the building was converted into a cooperative and renamed *Delmonico's.*

Among the prominent commercial tenants of the building are Regine's, the popular restaurant-discotheque, and Christie's, the London auctioneers, which opened a New York branch here in 1977.

The original Delmonico's Restaurant opened in 1837 on William Street in Lower Manhattan and over the years moved uptown—with the fashionable crowd—ultimately settling at its tenth site, 531 Fifth Avenue. The Swiss-born Lorenzo Delmonico (1813–1881) made New York famous as a center for fine restaurants and dining.

DEMARAN COURT

52–54 St. Nicholas Place

A five-story building of circa 1920.

DESHLER

124 West 114th Street
(southwest corner St. Nicholas Avenue)

A seven-story building. Twin to the *White Hall.*

DEVON RESIDENCE

306–308 West 94th Street

Twin buildings—dating from circa 1900—with slightly differing porches have been combined to form the *Devon Residence.* Formerly known as *Earls Court* and *Norfolk;* the name *Earls Court* still appears over the doorway of number 306.

Devon is an English county.

DEVONSHIRE HOUSE

28 East 10th Street

Despite its solidly aristocratic British name, this 1920s apartment building has a decidedly Hispano-Moresque look in its architecture.

The dukes of Devonshire, with their country seat at Chatsworth in Derbyshire, are among the wealthiest and grandest of the English noble families.

DEXTER HOUSE HOTEL

345 West 86th Street

A fifteen-story plain brown-brick building of the 1920s.

DIKEWOOD ARMS   *200 Dyckman Street*
                              (southwest corner Seaman Avenue)

A six-story 1920s building.

DOMEN EAST   *301 East 73rd Street*

Buff brick of the 1970s.
The name derives, perhaps, from the Greek and Latin root
for "house."

DONAC   *402 West 20th Street*

An odd little five-stories-and-basement building of 1897,
with an off-center recessed entrance to the right and bay windows. The architect was C. P. H. Gilbert.
The name is above the door and stands for *Don* Alonzo Cushman, the builder who developed Cushman Row, the group of
buildings at 404–418 West 20th Street, as well as many other
Chelsea blocks in the 1840s.

DORCHESTER   *110 East 57th Street*

The name of this 1970s white-brick apartment building is
visible on a tasteful brass plate beside the entrance.
On the ground floor is the Chantilly Restaurant.
Dorchester is a name long associated with the British nobility, with one of London's most famous hotels, and with Thomas
Hardy's Wessex novels; it stems from the principal town of the
county of Dorset, England.

DORCHESTER   *131 Riverside Drive*
                              (northeast corner West 85th Street)

The Riverside Drive entrance to this twelve-story turn-of-
the-century redbrick and limestone building has a handsome
stone balcony above the door. There is an open-court entrance
on West 85th Street.

DORCHESTER TOWERS   *155 West 68th Street*
                              (West 68th and West 69th streets,
                              Broadway and Amsterdam Avenue)

An enormous white-brick high rise built in 1965. Several
wings and setbacks; thirty-three stories at its tallest.

DORILTON APARTMENTS   *171 West 71st Street*
                              (northeast corner Broadway)

Few apartment houses in New York have received more
abuse from critics than this elaborate twelve-story Second Empire confection. When the building was put up in 1902—Janes
& Leo, architects—it was denounced by the *Architectural Record*
of the day as an "architectural aberration," and architectural
writers are still criticizing its statuary, mansard roof, and grandiose entrance. The building is well maintained, however, and

affords a striking contrast to the bland 1970s buildings that now surround it.

DORLEXA, THE   *318 West 100th Street*

An eight-story brick building of the turn of the century.

DORRENCE BROOKS, THE *337 St. Nicholas Avenue*
(northeast corner West 138th Street)

A six-story 1920s building of variegated brick, on Dorrence Brooks Square.

Dorrence Brooks, born in 1890, served as a private with the 369th Regiment, an all-black unit. He displayed great bravery in action during World War I, was brevetted when the officers of the unit were decimated, and was killed in action a few months before the armistice in 1918.

DORSET, THE   *150 West 79th Street*

Built in 1910 on the H-plan by Schwartz & Gross, architects. The eleven-story building with fine wrought-iron balconies on the corners was remodeled in 1937 by Boak & Paris, architects, and the originally large units were subdivided.

Dorset is a county in southern England.

DOUGLAS   *201 West 121st Street*
(northwest corner Adam Clayton Powell, Jr., Boulevard)

and

DESMOND   *2026 Adam Clayton Powell, Jr. Boulevard*

Two adjoining circa 1900 buildings.

Douglas *and* Desmond.

DOUGLAS   *357 West 115th Street*

This turn-of-the-century building has a very elaborate projecting cornice, six stories, and a basement. The name appears above the doorway.

A twin to *Helen Court* next door on Morningside Avenue.

DOUGLAS COURT   *546 West 147th Street*
                                        (southeast corner Broadway)

A six-story building of circa 1900.

DOUGLASS HOUSE (NYC Housing Authority)
                                        880 Columbus Avenue

This enormous complex with its "Douglass Addition" contains over two thousand apartments in five buildings between West 100th and West 104th streets.

Erected in 1958 (addition: 1965), the project honors Frederick Douglass (1817–1895), black orator, abolitionist, journalist, who was born into slavery in Maryland and rose to prominence as a social reformer and fighter for justice.

DOVER HOUSE   *205 East 77th Street*

A 1970s buff-brick apartment house.

Dover is a port in Kent, England, famous for its chalk cliffs; it is also the name of Delaware's capital.

[DOWNTOWN COMMUNITY SCHOOL]
                                        235 East 11th Street

A cooperative conversion of one of the four-storied buildings of the Third Street Music School Settlement complex.

DIPLOMAT, THE   *311 East 71st Street*

A white-brick 1960s apartment house.

DREW—HAMILTON HOUSES (NYC Housing
Authority)   *210 West 142nd Street*

This mid-1960s project of some twelve hundred apartments honors two disparate New Yorkers with connections to the local neighborhood: Monsignor Cornelius J. Drew (1895–1962), beloved pastor of St. Charles Borromeo Church on 142nd Street, and Alexander Hamilton (1755–1804), America's first secretary of the treasury, whose residence "The Grange," built in 1802, is a neighborhood landmark.

DRY DOCK   *355 East 4th Street*

A typical turn-of-the-century building of six stories, with the original name chiseled over the entrance.

The name derives from the building's proximity to Manhattan's first "dry dock" for the repair of ships. Instituted in 1825, the dock soon had several marine railways added to its works at the East River shore near East 10th Street and Avenue D.

The Dry Dock Savings Bank began as a repository for seamen's deposits from this same dry dock.

DRYDEN EAST *150 East 39th Street*

A post–World War II building with a later modernized entrance. A faded sign near the top would seem to indicate a prior career as a residential hotel.

John Dryden (1631–1700) was an English poet and dramatist.

DUANE PARK. *165 Duane Street*

A ten-story building of circa 1900 with pseudo-mansard roof; formerly industrial, but now converted to residential use.

The street and the little park are named for James Duane (1733–1797), first mayor of New York (1784–1789) after the British evacuation.

DUDLEY *100 West 87th Street*
(southwest corner Columbus Avenue)

A small five-story building with fire escape; built at the turn of the century and recently repainted.

Dudley is a British earldom.

DUNBAR APARTMENTS
2588 Adam Clayton Powell, Jr., Boulevard

By the late 1920s Harlem, which had begun to be *the* black district after the turn of the century, was overcrowded and contained some of the worst slums in the United States. John D. Rockefeller, Jr., who was active in slum clearance, purchased from the Astor family a five-acre tract of land at West 149th and West 150th streets in 1928 and commissioned the architect Andrew J. Thomas to build what has been referred to as "the first large cooperative for blacks," occupying the entire block bounded by West 149 and West 150th streets, and Adam Clayton Powell, Jr., Boulevard (then Seventh Avenue) and Frederick Douglass Boulevard (then Eighth Avenue). The six walk-up buildings contained over five hundred apartments, which were sold to carefully screened tenants. Numerous members of the black elite made their homes there, including Paul Robeson and Bill "Bojangles" Robinson.

The development, which has interior courtyards and playgrounds, was named for Paul Laurence Dunbar (1872–1906), an important black American poet. William Dean Howells, at the peak of his fame as a literary critic in the late nineteenth century, called Dunbar "the first man of African descent and American training to feel Negro life esthetically and express it lyrically." A portrait medallion of Dunbar is placed over the entrance of the apartments, along with an ox, an eagle, and other symbols.

In its early days the development held the Dunbar National Bank, then the only bank in Harlem owned by blacks. Like the cooperative, the bank was a victim of the depression and closed in the early 1930s. Buyers were unable to make their payments, and in 1936 Rockefeller declared a moratorium on payments, returned their equity to tenants who had moved in, and assumed the ownership of the *Dunbar Apartments* himself. The buildings were later sold several times and fell into increasing disrepair. In 1970, however, the development was declared a landmark, not only for its role in black history, but also for being "Manhattan's earliest large garden apartment complex."

In 1982 an $11.8 million renovation was instituted, and upon its completion, apartments were again offered as cooperatives. Signs on the building refer to this project as The New Dunbar.

DUNCRAGGAN   *867 West 181st Street*

A large, six-story 1920s building with a new entrance.

DUNDONALD FLATS   *71 West 83rd Street*

A five-stories-and-basement building of red brick built in 1885 by Jardine, Kent & Jardine, architects. It is built farther out on the sidewalk than the row of town houses on the street and the right side affords from its windows an unusual view up the street. It has been recently, and tactfully, restored; new windows have been put in, the brick has been cleaned, and antique-style lamps now flank the entrance.

Dundonald is a Scottish earldom held by the Cochran family.

DUNKLIN BUILDING   *112–114 Charlton Street*

Built circa 1910, this small apartment building is also the home of the American Renaissance Theater and the P. J. Charlton pub.

DUNSBRO   *120 East 31st Street*

Although the canopy reads "Lexington Residence Hotel," the original name over the door of what appears to be an apartment house of the 1870s is *Dunsbro*. There are a pillared portico, mansard roof, and bowed windows.

DUNWELL PLAZA   *1920 Amsterdam Avenue*

A 1960s redbrick high rise overlooking Trinity Cemetery.

DUPLEX 81   *215 East 81st Street*

A peculiar ten-story building, probably of the 1970s, with lots of iron balconies on a yellow stucco facade.

D Y C K   A R M S   *1825 Riverside Drive*
                                    (northwest corner Seaman Avenue)

A six-story white-brick building of the 1920s. The last address on Riverside Drive.

D Y C K M A N

William Dyckman built his farmhouse at present-day West 204th Street and Broadway in the Inwood section in 1783, replacing the family house that had been destroyed by the British in the Revolution. It remains today as the only eighteenth-century farmhouse in Manhattan; given to the city by the Dyckman descendants in 1915, it is open to the public. The style is typical Dutch colonial.

The Dyckmans were seventeenth-century arrivals in New Netherland, and members of the family held various civic offices. At one time they owned the largest farm on Manhattan—400 acres—in the vicinity of their house.

The Dyckman family has given its name to many apartment buildings in the neighborhood, as well as to a street. Surprising variants among the apartment building names are Dikewood *and* Broaddyke.

D Y C K M A N   A R M S   *35–41 Seaman Avenue*
                                    (northeast corner Cumming Street)

A 1920s five-story building of light-brown brick; ornamented and with a stepped entrance.

D Y C K M A N   H O U S E S (NYC Housing Authority)
                                             215 Nagle Avenue

Located on West 204th Street, this project takes its name from the nearby Dyckman House.

Almost three thousand people live in the 1951 federally funded complex.

D Y C K M A N   P L A Z A   *1–9 Seaman Avenue*
                                    (northeast corner Dyckman Street)

A seven-story tan-brick building of the 1920s.

D Y C K V I E W   *2–12 Seaman Avenue*
                                    (northwest corner Dyckman Street)

A five-story white-brick building of the 1920s; built on the open-court plan.

E. H. FRIEDRICHS   *140 Sullivan Street*

The name and date—"Established 1868"—are on the pediment of this small, formerly commercial building, which has been converted in recent times to residential apartments.

EARLS COURT   *306 West 94th Street*

See *Devon Residence.*
Earl's Court is a London neighborhood.

EAST HILL TOWER   *233 East 86th Street*

A 1982 high-rise condominium, with studios, one- and two-bedroom apartments, and duplex penthouses.

EAST MIDTOWN PLAZA
East 23rd to East 25th Streets,
First to Second Avenues

Davis, Brody & Assocs. were the architects for this unusual mass of high-rise and low-rise apartment units.

EAST RIVER

To begin with, it is not a river. From the geological point of view the East River is technically an estuary connecting the Harlem River (also really an estuary) at East 125th Street with the waters of New York Harbor at the southern tip of Manhattan.

Now bordered by a limited-access highway formally named Franklin D. Roosevelt Drive, but usually referred to as the East River Drive, the banks of the East River were once dotted with the country estates of New York's first families in the eighteenth and early nineteenth centuries.

The Stuyvesants, the Beekmans, the Dyckmans, the Rhinelanders, and the Rikers all had country seats looking out toward the verdant hills of Long Island.

Jones Wood, a large picnic grounds on the river's edge in the East 70s, was once proposed as the main park of the city; but rather than sacrifice waterfront property to such a frivolous use, it was decided to place the park in the boulder-strewn empty area in the middle of the island and call it Central Park.

EAST RIVER HOUSE   *505 East 79th Street*

Philip Birnbaum was the architect for this 1960s apartment building between York and East End avenues.

EAST RIVER HOUSES (NYC Housing Authority)
418 East 105th Street

1. A project, dating back to 1941, taking its name from its location. A pedestrian bridge over the river connects the complex with Ward's Island Park.

2. An International Ladies' Garment Workers Union project on the Lower East Side, formerly called Corlear's Hook Houses, and dating from 1956; now known as *East River Houses*.

EAST RIVER NORTH APARTMENTS
426–434 East 118th Street

A circa-1900 six-story building; recently renovated.

EAST RIVER TERRACE   *306 East 96th Street*

A rather plain 1950s cooperative in red brick (S. Rapaport was the architect).

The location—near the East 96th Street approach to the FDR Drive—determined the name.

EAST RIVER TOWER   *1725 York Avenue*

A thirty-story brown-brick tower with cantilevered balconies at several corners.

EAST VIEW   *40 Morningside Drive*
(northwest corner West 118th Street)

The entrance is at 401 West 118th Street. This seven-story redbrick and limestone building with unusual window treatment was built in 1907 by Neville & Bagge. The view is to the east over Harlem Valley.

EAST VIEW TOWER   *382 Third Avenue*

A 1970s "sliver" building.

EASTGATE HOUSE   *350 East 52nd Street*

Another of the many 1960s buildings with "East" in their titles.

EASTGATE TOWER   *222 East 39th Street*

A 1970s high-rise set-back tower, with a "plaza" dotted with wrought-iron garden ornaments and a gazebo. On the ground floor, beside the entrance, is the Marmalade Restaurant.

EASTMORE HOUSE   *240 East 76th Street*

Built circa 1960, this was one of the earliest of the apartment houses that together transformed Second Avenue from an ethnic neighborhood of brownstones and small tenements into a neighborhood of junior executives and airline stewardesses.

EASTON   *153 East 18th Street*

A circa-1890 six-story walk-up of red brick with limestone trim; well maintained.

Easton (east town) is a popular name in English-speaking countries.

EASTWINDS   *345 East 80th Street*
(northwest corner First Avenue)

A 1970s tower in brown and buff brick, with a somewhat intimidating entrance.

EDGEWATER, THE   *540 East 72nd Street*

Frank Sinatra once lived in this 1960s white-brick building overlooking the East River at the far east of end of 72nd Street.

EDGEWOOD   *31 Tiemann Place*
(northwest corner Broadway)

A white-brick building with six stories and basement; circa 1900.

EDITH   *410 Central Park West*
(southwest corner West 101st Street)

A sixteen-story building; circa 1900.

Edna Court. *Emery Roth's plan for this early-twentieth-century building is a decided improvement over the previous generation's long narrow hallways. The larger apartments have servants' rooms.*

EDNA COURT   *220 Audubon Avenue*
(northwest corner West 176th Street)

A six-story redbrick building; circa 1900.

EDWIN, THE   *561 West 147th Street*
(northeast corner Broadway)

A six-story redbrick building of circa 1900. The name is inscribed on an elaborate cartouche over the entrance.

EL CASCO COURT   *205 West 103rd Street*

Dirty brown brick, with a limestone base and an open-court entrance. Built by the Paterno organization in 1901.
Casco is the Spanish for "helmet."

EL GRECO   *204 West 14th Street*

This small six-story 1940s building has an Art Deco marquee.
Doménico Theotokópoulos (1541–1614), Cretan-born painter who emigrated to Italy and then Spain, where he was called El Greco (the Greek).

EL MORRO   *606 West 137th Street*

Built in 1906 by Schwartz & Gross, architects, this six-story building has severe decoration and marble columns at the entrance.
El Morro is the castle guarding the harbor at Havana, which was captured by the American forces during the Spanish-American War of 1898.

EL NIDO APARTMENTS   *121 St. Nicholas Avenue*
(northwest corner West 116th Street)

Built circa 1900, this apartment house is typical of the heavily ornate buildings designed by Neville & Bagge.
Appropriately enough for a "family type" apartment, *el nido* is Spanish for "nest."

ELBE, THE   *660–666 Riverside Drive*
(northeast corner West 143rd Street)

George F. Pelham was the architect of this six-stories-and-basement building of red brick and limestone. Built on the rear-court plan, it dates from circa 1900. The entrance is porched, and there is a recessed fire escape. The cornice is missing.
The Elbe is an important river in Czechoslovakia and East and West Germany. In 1945 it was established as the line of demarcation between the British and Russian forces in Germany.

ELDORADO   *300 Central Park West*
                                           West 90th to West 91st streets

This twin-towered building is the farthest north of the famous row of Art Deco apartment buildings on Central Park
West. Twenty-eight stories tall, it was built in 1931 by Mar-
gon & Holder. The builders were the Elkay Builders Corporation.

Duplexes on the seventeenth and eighteenth floors had eleven
rooms and five baths.

El Dorado means "the gilded man" in Spanish and refers to
the legendary South American Indian chief who at the time of
the Spanish Conquest had himself sprinkled with gold dust
which he then washed off in a sacred lake.

ELDORADO   *206 West 21st Street*

A small four-story redbrick building of the 1940s with fire
escape and casement windows; now advertised as offering "exclusive studio apartments."

ELEANOR COURT   *317 West 93rd Street*

A twin to *Albert Court*.

ELISE   *200 West 111th Street*
                          (southwest corner Adam Clayton Powell, Jr., Boulevard)

A circa-1900 six-stories-and-basement building of light
brick. The entrance is on West 111th Street.

ELITE   *364 Third Avenue*

An elaborate, though narrow, six-story tenement-type apartment house of circa 1890, with stores on the ground level. The
name is proudly displayed above the top story, beneath a broken
pediment.

The name, which means "select, or best, of a group," derives
from the Latin for "chosen."

ELIZABETH   *248 West 105th Street*
                                           (southwest corner Broadway)

A six-story orange brick and limestone building with fire escapes. Built circa 1905; S. B. Ogden and Co., architects. Entrance on West 105th Street.

ELIZABETH, THE   *35 East 38th Street*

This 1970s buff-brick apartment house's name may be inspired by one of England's queens.

ELIZABETH COURT   *421 West 118th Street*

A six-stories-and-basement building of circa 1905.
A twin to the *Winthrop* next door.

ELLEN APARTMENTS
202 West 82nd Street

A small, five-story white-brick building of the 1940s with two- and three-and-a-half-room apartments. The fire escape has been combined with balconies.

ELLERSLIE COURTS
600 West 140th Street
(northwest corner Broadway)

A six-story building of rather severe red brick; circa 1900.

ELLIOT
173 West 81st Street

A five-story turn-of-the-century building with ground floor in rusticated stone and an arched doorway. Twin to its neighbors the *Prague* and the *Martha*.

ELLIOTT
61 West 86th Street
(northeast corner Columbus Avenue)

A typical corner building of the turn of the century, with five stories and fire escape. Very narrow—only three windows wide—on West 86th; long side on Columbus.

ELLIOTT HOUSES (NYC Housing Authority)
420 West 26th Street

This Chelsea project of 1947 has over six hundred apartments in four buildings.

The name honors the memory of John Loring Elliott (1868–1942), pioneer social reformer and a founder of the Hudson Guild, the Chelsea Association, and the National Association for the Advancement of Colored People.

ELMHURST
503 West 140th Street

A turn-of-the-century redbrick building trimmed with limestone.

ELMORE
201 West 116th Street
(northwest corner St. Nicholas Avenue)

A circa-1900 seven-story building, with towerlet corners, in reasonably good shape.

ELSINORE
502 West 151st Street

A circa-1900 six-story building that has been modernized.

Elsinore is a seaport city in Denmark and the site of Kronberg Castle, famous as the setting of Shakespeare's *Hamlet*.

ELWOOD
204 Edgecombe Avenue

A circa-1900 white-brick building. The door has Renaissance details.

EMAHREL, THE   *317 West 99th Street*

A severe white-brick building with eight stories and basement, circa 1900. The pediment has been removed.

EMBASSY   *50 Park Terrace East*

Late-1930s Georgian Revival. The park referred to in the address is Isham Park in Inwood.

EMBASSY HOUSE   *301 East 47th Street*

This typical 1960s white-brick apartment house is just down the street from the United Nations, hence the name.

EMBASSY TOWER   *154 West 70th Street*
                                                     (southeast corner Broadway)

An old twelve-story building handsomely renovated. The fifth floor has stone balconies.

EMERY TOWERS   *400 East 77th Street*
                                                     (southeast corner First Avenue)

Emery Fabor was the architect of this white brick apartment of the 1960s.

EMILY COURT   *315 East 80th Street*

Pleasant orange-brick six-story apartment house of circa 1930s, with updated windows and a beautifully maintained court entrance with flower gardens.

EMILY COURT   *4 South Pinehurst Avenue*
                                                     (southwest corner West 177th Street)

A six-story building of the 1920s decorated with a row of stone urns at the top.
A twin to *Charlotte Court*. The reference was surely to the Brontë sisters.

EMPIRE HOUSE   *200 East 71st Street*

An early-1960s white-brick building, one of the earliest of the apartment houses that sprang up along Third Avenue after the el was torn down in the mid-1950s.

EMROSE COURT   *204–208 West 109th Street*

Two smallish six-story buildings of circa 1920. The name is on a vertical banderole flanked by the entrance doors.

EMSWORTH HALL   *435 Convent Avenue*
(southeast corner West 149th Street)

A six-story building of tan brick with granite and limestone decoration and turretlike details at the corners; built 1912–1913.

Emsworth is a town in southwest Pennsylvania.

ENCORE, THE   *301 West 53rd Street*

A 1970s high-rise building in the theater district.

Endicott *after renovation, the Columbus Avenue entrance.*

ENDICOTT, THE   *101 West 81st Street*
(northwest corner Columbus Avenue)

When it opened as a hotel in 1889, *The Endicott* was conveniently situated a block from the new American Museum of Natural History and across the street from a station of the elevated railway. Designed by the architect Edward L. Angell, the hotel had six stories and extended along Columbus Avenue (then Ninth Avenue) from West 81st to West 82nd streets in a neighborhood of mainly single-family houses. Its luxurious appointments well became the elegance of the new West Side.

No building better illustrates the vicissitudes of the West Side in this century. *The Endicott* slowly declined with the neighborhood, becoming by the 1950s a run-down residence catering to a drifting clientele. In the 1960s and 1970s things worsened and the hotel's name became a byword for urban decay. *The Endicott* was a perennial focus of protests by West Side civic groups, who characterized it as the haunt of criminal elements. In 1972 it was the scene of no fewer than four murders.

A few years later, however, West Side renewal began to catch up with *The Endicott,* and in 1979 rehabilitation began. The building was converted into cooperative apartments. Handsomely appointed shops, including Endicott Booksellers and DDL Food Show (the latter owned by the movie producer Dino de Laurentis) occupy the ground floor on the Columbus Avenue side.

ENDICOTT APARTMENTS   *53 West 72nd Street*
(northeast corner Columbus Avenue)

When it was built circa 1900, this seven-story building of no particular distinction was known as the Janet.

ENDYMION   *342 West 117th Street*

Rising moons carved in stone flank the name of this building. The reference is to the Endymion of Greek mythology, who was a young shepherd loved by Selene, the moon goddess.
Twin to the *Midlothian* at 353 West 117th Street.
Now abandoned.

[ENGINEERS CLUB]   *32 West 40th Street*

See *Columns*.

ENID   *104 West 96th Street*

A six-story redbrick building with fire escapes, dating from the turn of the century.

ENVOY, THE   *781 West End Avenue*

A fifteen-story building of the 1920s.

ENVOY APARTMENTS   *444 East 87th Street*

A small white-brick building with fire escapes and a marble entrance; circa 1960—possibly a redo of two old tenements.

ENVOY TOWERS   *300 East 46th Street*

Another suitably "diplomatic" name for a modern apartment house in the UN neighborhood.
In 1974 an explosion caused by leaking gas at a neighboring building in East 45th Street resulted in extensive damage, and the tenants were relocated until the repair work was completed.

ERCO COURT   *4996 Broadway*
(southeast corner West 212th Street)

A six-story redbrick building of the 1930s.

ERNESTINE   *531 West 145th Street*

A sister building to the *Beatrice* and the *Leondra*.

ESSEX HOUSE   *325 East 41st Street*

Another of the handsome brick-and-stone Tudor-style buildings in *Tudor City*. The name is carved in stone over the door
and derives from the county in southeastern England. A con-
traction of East Saxon, the word is associated with one of Queen
Elizabeth's favorites, Robert Devereux, the second earl of Essex.

ESSEX HOUSE   *160 Central Park South*

Essex House was built in 1930 on part of the site of the
Spanish Flats. Frank Grad was the architect. The building's facade has Art Deco details. The lobby area has been changed
through the years.

The first brochure advertising the building read in part: "Today, residentially and socially, Central Park South is town! Historically, it was the first meeting place between Father Knickerbocker and Mother Nature "—meaning the building faces on
Central Park.

Despite the glowing prose, the building, which was opened
during the depression, was very slow to fill up. It was in the
hands of the Reconstruction Finance Corporation between 1932
and 1946. In 1975 it became a condominium.

ESTELLE   *145 East 82nd Street*
                          (northeast corner Lexington Avenue)

A handsome structure with a nicely carved brownstone doorway; circa 1900. This is the only survivor of an original group
of four similar contiguous buildings. The others were called
Miriam, Hudson, and Plymouth.

ESTLING, THE   *223 Riverside Drive*

A seven-story tan brick and limestone building; circa 1900.

ETHELBERT COURT   *601 West 149th Street*
                            (northwest corner Broadway)

A plain six-story building of the turn of the century.

The name is that of several petty kings of Kent, the Saxons,
and Angles in sixth-to-eighth-century Britain.

ETON HALL   *29 Claremont Avenue*

A twelve-story apartment house built by the architect Gaetan
Ajello in 1910. Restoration work was under way in 1983.
Shares a facade with *Rugby Hall* next door.

Eton and Rugby are both British public schools. The names
of the buildings are highly suitable for this academic neighborhood, directly across the street from Barnard College.

EUCLID HALL   *2349 Broadway*

This heavily ornamented circa-1900 building occupies the entire blockfront between West 85th and West 86th streets along Broadway. The entrance is now on West 86th Street.

The seven-story redbrick building with two bays overlooking Broadway and an elaborate balustrade at the top is now in poor shape and contains small apartments for "transients and permanents."

Euclid was a fourth-century Greek who gave his name to a form of geometry.

EUFAULA   *51 Hamilton Place*

A large six-story building in two sections, by the architect George F. Pelham circa 1905. A twin to the *Talladega*.

Eufaula is a city near Montgomery, Alabama, on the Chattahoochee River.

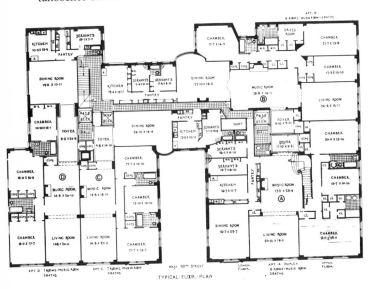

TYPICAL·FLOOR·PLAN

Evanston. *In the plan a music room, with fireplace, adjoins the living room in each of the four units on the floor. Note the comparative sizes of the tenants' tubs and those of the servants in their respective bathrooms. The servants have no sink.*

EVANSTON   *272 West 90th Street*
(southeast corner West End Avenue)

A twelve-story buff brick building, early twentieth century.

EVELYN, THE   *101 West 78th Street*
(northwest corner Columbus Avenue)

Red brick with elaborate terra-cotta ornamentation of cherubs, nymphs, dragons. Seven stories and basement with steps at entrance. One of the earliest and handsomest apartment buildings in the neighborhood; built by Emile Gruwé in 1886 across Columbus (then Ninth) Avenue from the then new American Museum of Natural History.

EVELYN ARMS   *203 West 98th Street*

A light brick six-story building of the 1920s.

EXCELSIOR, THE   *301 East 57th Street*

This towering apartment house of the 1960s—with its great height, huge lobby with an ornamental staircase illuminated by crystal chandeliers, and circular drive with porte-cochere—has its own "country club" on the fifth floor for tenant/owners, with swimming pool, sauna, cafe, gym, lounge, dining room, and sundeck.

Latin for "higher," *excelsior* is also the motto of New York State as well as the title of one of Longfellow's best-known poems: "A youth who bore, 'mid snow and ice,/A banner with the strange device,/Excelsior!"

EXCELSIOR HOTEL   *45 West 81st Street*

A plain, fifteen-story brick building of the 1920s.

[EXCELSIOR POWER COMPANY]   *33 Gold Street*

William C. Grinnell was the architect of this 1888 building in the Romanesque Revival style. A former generating plant for the Consolidated Edison Company, it had been vacant for some years. In the early 1980s, however, it and the adjacent vacant office building were converted into a 197-unit rental apartment building.

EXECUTIVE HOUSE   *225 East 46th Street*

A 1960s beige-brick apartment house.

FAIRFAX, THE   *201 East 69th Street*

This 1980 conversion of a 1930s office building has new fenestration and a new captioned canopy.

For many years the building was New York City headquarters of the Federal Bureau of Investigation and, as such, witnessed in the 1960s picketing by the Italian-American Anti-Defamation League. The group was protesting against the FBI's use of the word "Mafia."

When the FBI left the Upper East Side for its new home in the Federal Office Building on lower Broadway, one of this neighborhood's first big conversions to residential use took place.

Fairfax is a solidly aristocratic and eminently respectable English name, ideally suited to an apartment house. Thomas Fairfax (1693–1781) was the only resident English peer in America at the time of the Revolution.

FAIRFAX, THE   *1326 Madison Avenue*

A seven-story limestone and tan-brick structure with fire escapes.

FAIRFIELD   *97 Fort Washington Avenue*

The name of many towns and counties in the United States.

FAIRFIELD, THE   *423–431 West 121st Street*
                    (southeast corner Morningside Drive)

An early-twentieth-century structure with prominent stone balconies on most of the windows; under renovation.

FAIRHOLM   *503–507 West 121st Street*

Six stories, very plain, with a fire escape; built in 1905 by George F. Pelham.

FAIRMONT   *438 West 116th Street*
                    (southeast corner Amsterdam Avenue)

An old building whose name is a variation of the more usual "Fairmount"—both versions popular for centuries as names for parks or mansions in elevated situations, as, for example, Fairmount Park in Philadelphia.

FAIRMOUNT MANOR, THE   *401 East 86th Street*

White-brick; circa 1960.

FAIRVIEW COURT   *175 Claremont Avenue*

A rather large white brick and limestone building of six stories and basement, with open-court entrance; circa 1900.

FALKLAND, THE   *880 West 181st Street*
                    (southeast corner Riverside Drive)

A six-story white-brick building; circa 1900.
Falkland is a title of England's Cary family.

FANWOOD, THE   *112 East 17th Street*

This elaborate structure of the 1870s was one of the earliest apartment buildings in New York to be equipped with an elevator.
Fanwood was the name of President James Monroe's estate in Upper Manhattan, where he spent the last year of his life (1830–1831).

FARNHAM   *53 East 97th Street*

A six-story building with limestone base; circa 1900.
Farnham is the name of a town and castle in Surrey,
England.

FIFE ARMS   *251 West 87th Street*
                                      (northwest corner Broadway)

Seven stories and basement in white brick; fire escapes; turn-
of-the-century. The name is chiseled among floral decorations
above the columned entrance.
Fife is a county in Scotland.

[FIFTH AVENUE HOTEL]   *24 Fifth Avenue*

This apartment building was formerly the Fifth Avenue Hotel, famed for generations as a gathering place for Greenwich
Village literati. The present building, dating from the 1920s,
is on the site of the Henry Brevoort house, erected prior to
1840, and later owned by Charles de Rham and George F.
Baker before its demolition.

FINCH, THE   *61 East 77th Street*

This last remainder of Finch College, an expensive women's
school now defunct, is a recent conversion of some of the old
classroom buildings and a dormitory. The other college buildings, on East 78th Street, have been transformed into a private
preparatory school.

FIORA-VILLE   *616 West 116th Street*

Built by Schwartz & Gross in 1907, this ten-story building
was said to be "Parisian architecture."
It is a twin to the unnamed building next door at 620 West
116th Street.

FIRESIDE, THE   *226 East 95th Street*

"Discover the new 90s. . . . It's hot!" A new cooperative of
1983, with twenty-nine apartments.

FIRST HOUSES (NYC Housing Authority)
                                              130 East 3rd Street

Built as public housing during the depression, this was the
first project of the New York City Housing Authority. Named
a landmark in 1974 "to honor a great social experiment: the re-
sponsibility of society . . . to provide housing."
The opening ceremonies in 1935 were presided over by
Mayor Fiorello La Guardia, Governor Herbert Lehman, and
Mrs. Eleanor Roosevelt.

Unlike later high-rise projects, this development was more in the nature of a rehabilitation program for existing buildings and as such provided improved dwellings without destroying the neighborhood.

[FIRST REFORMED EPISCOPAL CHURCH AND APARTMENTS]   *315 East 50th Street*

This twelve-story redbrick apartment building with Gothic detailing incorporates the First Reformed Episcopal Church.

The Reformed Episcopal Church was organized in 1873 by dissidents from the Protestant Episcopal Church of the United States in a dispute over liturgical practices.

FITZROY PLACE   *442–446 West 23rd Street*

The nineteenth-century Italianate and Anglo-Italianate houses in this row across from *London Terrace* were single-family dwellings until around 1900, when they became rooming houses that catered to sailors from the Chelsea docks, which were berths for the Cunard and White Star lines along the North (Hudson) River. In the 1920s the buildings gradually became the property of Mrs. Louise Gard, a Swiss immigrant, who became noted as a landlady and friend of the sailors. She sold the houses in the 1970s, and they deteriorated badly.

Wells & Gay, the Chelsea real estate firm, began the restoration of the houses as cooperative apartments in the early 1980s. The name chosen for them is a historically valid one. Fitzroy Road ran near the line of present-day Eighth Avenue. It took its name from Charles Fitzroy (afterwards the first Baron Southampton) who married the daughter of Sir Peter Warren, one of the great property owners of eighteenth-century New York. Among his holdings were about 300 acres along the Hudson from present-day Christopher Street to about West 21st Street.

FLORENCE   *204 West 78th Street*

See *Rose.*

FLORENCE   *128 Second Avenue*

See *Alpine.*

FLORENCE MILLS APARTMENTS
                                         267 Edgecombe Avenue

This 1920s apartment house is named for the world-famous black musical comedy star who died in 1927.

FLORIDA   *1061 St. Nicholas Avenue*
                          (northwest corner West 163rd Street)

A six-story light brick and limestone building decorated with green terra-cotta; circa 1900.

FLORIDA COURT   *80 St. Nicholas Place*

A five-story buff building of the 1920s.

FOLIO HOUSE   *105 Fifth Avenue*

This, the old Barnes & Noble Bookstore Building, has been converted by Zuberry Associates to residential use.

Appropriately named, since "folio" refers to pages, numbers, and sizes of books.

FONTAINE, THE   *353 East 72nd Street*

The French word for "fountain" was bestowed on this slender, midblock tower, originally called The Eastsider, which was opened in 1982, having remained unfinished for a number of years.

FONTAINEBLEAU
1851 Adam Clayton Powell, Jr., Boulevard
(southeast corner West 113th Street)

Built circa 1900, the building has three bays and six stories of red brick.

Fontainebleau is a forest and town about thirty-five miles from Paris, most famous for its royal palace, which is now the summer residence of the presidents of France.

One of a series of buildings in this neighborhood taking their names from French royal palaces, including the *Palais Royal*, *Chantilly*, and *Versailles*.

FONTENOY   *492 Convent Avenue*

A five-story and basement building occupying the triangular site formed by the intersection of Convent Avenue and West 152nd Street.

At the Battle of Fontenoy on 11 May 1745 the French defeated the British and Dutch in a major encounter of the War of the Austrian Succession.

FOREST CHAMBERS   *601 West 113th Street*
(northwest corner Broadway)

A twelve-story early-twentieth-century building with open-court entrance and bayed windows.

FORESTERS HOME   *690 Columbus Avenue*

Dated 1886 on pediment. Four residential floors above Pozzo's Pastry Shop.

FORREST, THE   *251 West 81st Street*
                                                (northwest corner Broadway)

The name of this seven-story white-brick turn-of-the-century building is handsomely cut in stone amid decoration over the portico entrance.

FORT CHARLES COURT   *70 Marble Hill Avenue*

A five-story 1920s building with a large open-court entrance. For explanation of the name see *Fort Prince Charles Court.*

FORT PRINCE CHARLES COURT
                                                    108 West 227th Street

This six-story building with open-court entrance is on the highest point of Marble Hill.

The name is taken from a fort build nearby in 1776 by the American forces but captured by the British troops the following year and named for Prince Charles of Brunswick, brother-in-law of King George III of England.

FORT TRYON APARTMENTS
                                                    209 West 118th Street
                                      (northeast corner St. Nicholas Avenue)

A five-story building erected in 1907, with a central court and bay windows at the corners. The architect was John E. Schlarsmith. The modernized entrance is now painted gray.

Fort Tryon Park is at the north end of Manhattan Island and commemorates the site of a Revolutionary War outpost. Margaret Corbin, the first woman to serve in the Revolution, helped in the defense of Fort Tryon against the assault of the Hessian troops in November 1776.

William Tryon (1729–1788) was British colonial governor of New York from 1771 to 1778.

FORTRESS, THE   *235 Fort Washington Avenue*
                                       (northwest corner West 169th Street)

A twin to *Court Washington.*

FOSTER   *314 West 133rd Street*
                                      (southeast corner St. Nicholas Avenue)

A five-story building of the 1880s.

Stephen Collins Foster (1826–1864), the composer, spent much of his life in New York City where he wrote some of his most famous "Southern" melodies. He died in the charity ward of Bellevue Hospital.

FOWLER COURT   *400 Riverside Drive*
                                                   621 West 112th Street

A six-story red and white brick and limestone building with a gracious Parisian appearance, built in 1909, George F. Pelham, architect.

FRAMOR   *146 West 79th Street*

A smallish six-story redbrick building of the 1920s.

FRANCIS APARTMENTS, THE
                                        502–504 West 180th Street

An early-1920s five-story building.

FRANCONIA   *48 West 112th Street*
                              (southwest corner St. Nicholas Avenue)

Abandoned.
Franconia is a former dukedom of Germany that is now part
of Bavaria; but this building might also be named for the resort
village and mountain range in New Hampshire.

FRANKLIN   *204 West 94th Street*

A well-maintained six-story redbrick and limestone building
with a fine fire escape, circa 1900.

FRANKLIN ARMS   *961 St. Nicholas Avenue*

Six stories and basement with two open bays; circa 1900.

FRANKLIN PLAZA   *East 106th to East 108th streets,*
                              between First and Second avenues

A middle-income cooperative with 1,635 apartments in fourteen buildings; built in 1962.
[See also *Benjamin Franklin*.]

FRANT HOTEL RESIDENCE CLUB
                                        211 West 101st Street

A seven-story brick building of the 1920s.

FREMONT   *310 West 94th Street*

A seven-story building of circa 1900, with stone balconies.
The entrance is new and the fire escape has been added.
John Charles Frémont (1813–1890), the western explorer
and soldier, was nominated for the presidency in 1856; he spent
his last years in New York City.

FRIESLAND   *235 West 103rd Street*
                                  (northwest corner of Broadway)

An eight-story turn-of-the-century building of brick above
limestone; with fire escape and an iron fence around the front.
Friesland is a province in the Netherlands.

FRONTENAC   *122 West 112th Street*

A six-story redbrick building of circa 1900. A twin to the
St. Louis at number 118.

Louis, comte de Frontenac (1620–1698), was a governor of Canada; his administration was notable for exploration and development of the country.

FROST HOUSE   *1160 Third Avenue*

When this white-brick 1960s building opened, its ground-floor restaurant was a branch of Schrafft's. Now it is a Chinese restaurant.

G. WILKENS   *241 First Avenue*

The pediment of this otherwise unassuming four-story walk-up with storefront presumably bears the name of the man who built it in the late nineteenth century.

GAINSBORO   *2 Mount Morris Park South*
(southwest corner Fifth Avenue and West 120th Street)

A seven-story building of the turn of the century, with two bays, balconied windows, and original fence.

The reference is presumably to the English portraitist Thomas Gainsborough (1727–1788).

GAINSBOROUGH, THE   *222 Central Park South*

Built in 1907–1908 to the design of architect Charles W. Buckham, *The Gainsborough* is one of the most attractive and prominent survivors of the many "studio apartments" built around the turn of the century for artists and would-be artists.

There were originally fourteen duplex apartments (facing north over the park) and twenty-five simplex apartments (looking south), plus a ladies' reception room. The front apartments were cooperative, and the ones at the rear rented for $1,500 a year.

A portrait bust of Thomas Gainsborough adorns the facade of this grand old building, with huge windows and colorful tiled frieze.

Among the current residents are Candice Bergen and her husband, Louis Malle.

GALAXY   *51 West 81st Street*
(northeast corner Columbus Avenue)

A twelve-story turn-of-the-century building of red brick with stone trim; has a majestic columned entrance on West 81st Street. Formerly the Hotel Colonial, a new canopy carries the new name.

The name was obviously inspired by the stellar shows at the Hayden Planetarium across the street at the American Museum of Natural History.

Galaxy, *1905. The private residences along West 81st Street have long since been razed and replaced by apartment houses, including the* Bownett *(now the* Planetarium Apartments*) and the* Excelsior Hotel.

GALENA

101 West 89th Street
(northwest corner Columbus Avenue)

A five-story redbrick building with the name chiseled above the door. In 1983 it was standing derelict—isolated by the slum clearance for the West Side Urban Renewal. The surrounding plots were used as neighborhood flower gardens.

At the time this apartment house was built Galena, Illinois, was famous as the hometown of General Ulysses S. Grant.

GALLERIA

117 East 57th Street

David Kenneth Specter and Philip Birnbaum were the architects for this multiuse condominium tower erected in 1973–1974 by Arden Realty, which—owing in large measure to New York's fiscal crisis—went bankrupt in 1976 and became a problem, then a bonanza, for Morprop, the real estate subsidiary of Morgan Guaranty Trust.

The spectacular quadruplex penthouse was said to be designed with millionaire philanthropist Stewart Mott in mind, but he never bought it. After serving as the scene of a fundraising party for that perennial candidate Bella Abzug, the penthouse was sold to a California millionaire who prefers anonymity.

Although inspired by *Olympic Tower,* the *Galleria* has not captured the public imagination or become a notable address as *Olympic Tower* has done.

The name is taken from Milan's famous shopping arcade, the prototype for this building's public space.

GALLERY CONDOMINIUM   *32 East 76th Street*

This modernistic glass and brick apartment is tucked into an L-shaped site beside the former *Madison Avenue Hospital.* The name derives from this art-rich neighborhood.

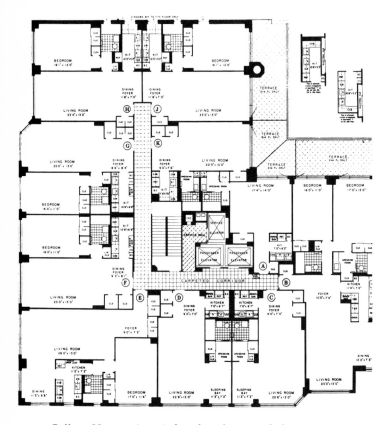

Gallery House. *A typical 1960s plan, in which maximum useable space was wrung from every square foot available. Note the combination entrance hall–dining area (here called "dining foyer"), the L-shaped living room, the windowless interior bathrooms and kitchens, and the efficient arrangement of service core and plumbing.*

GALLERY HOUSE   *77 West 55th Street*
                              (northwest corner Avenue of the Americas)

A 1960s high rise built by Horace Ginsbern & Associates.

GALSIE GARDEN   *19 Cumming Street*

A five-story dark brick building of the 1920s.

GANSEVOORT, THE   *95 Christopher Street*
                       (northwest corner Bleecker Street)

H. I. Feldman was the architect for this fifteen-story and penthouse building.

The Gansevoort family of Albany, New York, played leading roles in the American Revolution.

GARDEN GATE   *355 East 86th Street*
                   (northwest corner First Avenue)

A nineteenth-century building of four stories, remodeled in the 1920s; with an open bay on East 86th Street.

GARFIELD   *200 Claremont Avenue*
                (southeast corner Tiemann Place)

A turn-of-the-century building with six stories in red brick and limestone.

James A. Garfield was president of the United States in 1881.

GARNET HALL   *601 West 141st Street*
                   (northwest corner Broadway)

A circa-1900 six-story building elaborately decorated with urns, shells, and coats of arms in the School of Fontainebleau manner.

GARSON TOWERS   *500 East 87th Street*

A typical redbrick 1960s apartment building with a Gristede's grocery on the ground floor.

GATEWAY PLAZA   *397 South End Avenue*
                     (Liberty Street)

A gargantuan complex of apartments at Battery Park City, built on landfill near the World Trade Center. Isolated, but with sensational views. The Lefrak Organization was the developer. Rents started at $1,250 per month for a two-bedroom apartment in 1983.

GENDARME, LE   *135 Charles Street*

New York City's arms sculpted in high relief over a majestic balcony still adorn this 1895 building which, though now an apartment house, was formerly a precinct station house of the Police Department, a reminder of the days when Teddy Roosevelt was police commissioner and station houses were built to resemble palaces, not suburban bowling alleys.

During its last years as a precinct house, this building was the scene of an escape attempt by gays arrested during the fa-

Le Gendarme. *Once the Ninth Precinct police station, now an apartment house.*

mous "Stonewall Riots" in 1970. One man was killed after jumping out of a rear window.

Cut into the stonework is the Latin motto *Premium-virtutis-honos* (honor is the first of the virtues).

A *gendarme*—the word is French—is an armed officer of the state whose role is to maintain civil order. *Gendarmes,* in Paris, are to be distinguished from *policiers* (policemen), who are municipal officers.

GEORGE WASHINGTON COURT
4791–4797 Broadway
(northwest corner Cumming Street)

A large six-story building of the 1920s, with an open-court entrance.

Cumming Street, like Beak Street, was opened in 1925, when this area was being developed.

GEORGEAN COURT   *315 West 94th Street*

A building of seven stories, with two bays; circa 1900. The original columns flanking the entrance have been painted a bright gold. The name is a variant of Georgian.

Georgian Court at Lakewood, New Jersey, was the home of George Gould and was one of the most magnificent private residences in the United States in the nineteenth century. Another name derived from the Gould family is *Lyndhurst.*

GEORGETOWN PLAZA   *60 East 8th Street*

A soaring 1960s tower resting on huge pillars and surrounded by a somewhat disappointing open plaza; has rooftop pool.

GEORGIA   *564 West 160th Street*
(southeast corner Broadway)

Six-story apartment house, vintage 1900. Handsome entrance with fluted columns; floral decoration on windows.

GERALDINE   *61–63 West 106th Street*

Six stories; circa 1900.

GERARD, THE   *123 West 44th Street*

Now being redeveloped, and best-known for the Café Un Deux Trois, this thirteen-story brick building was built in 1893–1894 as an apartment hotel. It became a transient hotel known first as the Longwell and then as the Hotel 1-2-3.

It was named for the original proprietor, W. B. Gerard. The poet Ella Wheeler Wilcox ("Laugh and the world laughs with you") was at one time a resident.

The renovated building contains 123 one-to-three-bedroom apartments, with rents for one bedroom apartments beginning at about $900 per month.

GERKEN BUILDING   *90–92 West Broadway*

The front door of this thirteen-story Tribeca building has elaborate wrought-iron work spelling out the name in a lunette over the door. A pair of marble pillars flanks the entrance leading to an elaborate lobby.

Built circa 1895 as offices, presumably by or for a Mr. Gerken. The architects were Harding & Gooch. It was converted to residential use in the mid-1970s.

GERMANIA FLATS   *7–9 Second Avenue*

Twin abandoned five-story buildings of the late nineteenth century; the name is still visible on the pediment.

The Latin for Germany, the name may be related to the now-defunct Germania Bank, whose imposing headquarters building was located at the corner of Spring Street and the Bowery.

GERTRUDE, THE   *185–187 Audubon Avenue*
(northeast corner West 174th Street)

A severe five-stories-and-basement building; circa 1900.

GESSNER, THE   *87–91 Christopher Street*

A six-story building with fire escapes; with name and date—
1872—on front.

GIBRALTAR COURT   *40 Sherman Avenue*
(southwest corner Arden Street)

A five-story building of circa 1900, with a fancy balustrade
at the top.

GILFORD, THE   *140 East 46th Street*

A fine wrought-iron gate guards the entrance to this slightly
mysterious fifteen-story apartment building which was built in
1923 on the site of the old Gilford residence at Lexington Avenue and East 46th Street. Emery Roth was the architect of this
H-shaped, neo-Georgian brick structure. An early brochure
talked of "apartment comforts and hotel convenience at moderate cost."

Gilsey House *from a nineteenth-century print.*

GILSEY HOUSE   *25 West 29th Street*
(northeast corner Broadway)

Alderman Peter Gilsey lived, in the mid-nineteenth century,
on the northwest corner of Broadway and West 28th Street. He
was a large property owner in the area, as were his heirs. The
Gilsey office building occupied the west side of Broadway between West 28th and West 29th streets. In 1869–1871 the
Gilsey House Hotel was erected in the next block uptown. The
architect Stephen Decatur Hatch constructed it of cast-iron in
the Second Empire style. When it opened in April 1871, the

New York Times called it "one of the most imposing of our metropolitan palace hotels."

The *Real Estate Record* found "the most remarkable feature of
this building is its great height." (Nine stories, 125 feet.) "The
exterior of the building," the *Record* continued, "is an adaptation of the Palladian style of architecture; profusely adorned
with little detached double columns—Ionic on the first story
and composite on the others—interspersed with straight and
circular or segmental-headed windows, in pleasing variety and
rich in all the ornamentations peculiar to iron building. The effect is altogether grand and imposing and reflects high credit on
its author."

The neighborhood was then full of theaters. Across the street
from the hotel was Banvard's Museum (afterwards Daly's Theater). Apollo Hall (later the Fifth Avenue Theater) was nearby,
and in the Gilsey Building a billiard hall was turned into a
theater in 1874.

Gilsey House was one of the first hotels in the United States
to offer telephone service, and its name appears on the first
(1878) list of subscribers to the Bell Telephone Company of
New York.

Gilsey House was long popular with Southern visitors to New
York. Their wants were attended to by James H. Breslin, who
was referred to in the contemporary press as one of "the best
known and most popular of New York bonifaces." "Boniface,"
meaning a manager or tavern keeper, was then a popular word;
it derives from an eighteenth-century play by George Farquhar,
The Beaux' Stratagem, in which a landlord is named Will Boniface. Breslin's name survives today in the Breslin Hotel just
down the street at 1186 Broadway.

The hotel closed in December 1904, and the building was
converted into offices. In the 1970s it was once again converted,
this time into cooperative apartments—a project of Zuberry
Associates.

GLASS HOUSE FARM   *448 West 37th Street*

Eighteenth-century New Yorkers had to rely on imported
glass—which was very expensive—or the few American glass
products made in other colonies. In 1758 a glass manufactory
was established in New York on about thirty acres in the area
known as Newfoundland, on the North (Hudson) River between
present-day West 34th and West 40th streets. Nicholas Bayard
and Matthew Ernest took newspaper space "to inform the Pub-
lick, that the new erected Glass-House at Newfoundland,
within four miles of this City is now at work, and that any
Gentlemen may be supply'd with Bottles, Flasks, or any sort of
Glass agreeable to their Directions." They also advertised for
oak wood, which was used in stoking the furnace.

This promising project failed, and very shortly, because by
1763 the glass house was converted into a roadhouse, or tavern,
and the proprietor was offering the use of a stage coach to bring
patrons to Newfoundland from Lower Manhattan. The air there
was considered especially salubrious. The tavern did not last

PART II

long, either, and the glass house became a farm and remained as such up to the time of the Civil War, when the northward advance of the city gave commercial value to the land.

In 1982 a large office building on the site was converted into cooperative apartments under the historic name.

GLEN CAIRN
270 Riverside Drive
(northeast corner West 99th Street)

A twelve-stories-and-basement building of white brick.

Glen Cairn is an old title of the Scottish Cunningham family.

GLEN COURT
666 West 162nd Street

A large six-story building of buff brick; early twentieth century.

GLOUCESTER, THE
200 West 79th Street

Opened in 1975, a nineteen-story high rise with 272 apartments.

Gloucester is an English royal duchy, and the name is now widely spread over many parts of the world.

GOLDEN GATE
272 Manhattan Avenue
(northeast corner West 111th Street)

A seven-story turn-of-the-century building, now in disrepair.

The Golden Gate is the strait connecting the Pacific Ocean and San Francisco Bay.

GOMPERS HOUSES (NYC Housing Authority)
50 Pitt Street

This mid-1960s project on the Lower East Side is named after Samuel Gompers (1850–1924), the British-born American labor leader who rose from membership in the New York Cigar-makers' Union on the Lower East Side to become founder and first president of the American Federation of Labor.

GOODHUE HOUSE
20 East 35th Street
(southeast corner Madison Avenue)

A fourteen-story and penthouse building of the 1950s, de-signed by W. M. Dowling in a restrained classic style with traces of Art Moderne in the limestone trim.

GOTHAM TOWN HOUSE
153 East 57th Street

L. K. Levy and Philip Birnbaum designed this white-brick twenty-story and penthouse building of 1961.

GOTHIC HOUSE   *136 East 67th Street*

A white-brick 1950s building by Maxon-Feld, architects; with "spacious two- and three-bedroom apartments." Built on the site of the old Chapin Home for the Aged and Infirm, *Gothic House* was bought lock, stock, and barrel by the Soviet Union and now houses its mission to the United Nations.

GOUVERNEUR GARDENS
Franklin D. Roosevelt Drive
(at Jackson Street)

A six-building middle-income apartment complex on the Lower East Side near Jackson, Montgomery, and Henry streets. Frederic P. Wiedersum Associates were the architects for this 1963 venture.

Named for Abraham Gouverneur, French Huguenot merchant of seventeenth-century New York, who fled to Boston after the Leisler Rebellion was crushed. He was tried and sentenced to death *in absentia* for his efforts to overthrow the government.

GRACE APARTMENTS   *462 West 141st Street*

A new canopy and name on one of a row of handsome private houses of the turn of the century.

[GRACE INSTITUTE APARTMENTS]
250 East 65th Street

Built in 1961, an early example of the "mixed use" buildings that have come to be so much more common in the last decade. The first few floors, with an entrance at 1233 Second Avenue, house Grace Institute, a Roman Catholic school for women that specializes in practical and vocational subjects.

At 250 East 65th Street is the totally separate entrance to the high-rise apartment house.

The institute, which was formerly located on the West Side near Lincoln Center, owns the entire building.

GRACIE

Archibald Gracie emigrated from Scotland to New York at the close of the Revolutionary War and within a few years became one of the new nation's most prosperous shipowners.

At the beginning of the nineteenth century he built a mansion at Gracie Point (formerly known as Horn's Hook) overlooking the East River at East 88th Street. Here he entertained Washington Irving, Louis Philippe, and other notable visitors.

The Gracie family occupied the house until 1823. It was later bought by the city and was opened to the public as a museum. In 1942 it became the official residence of the mayor of New York.

Gracie Mansion, Gracie Square, and Carl Schurz Park form a charming and restful oasis at the far end of bustling East 86th Street.

GRACIE MANOR   *510 East 85th Street*

A 1956 apartment building of twelve stories.

GRACIE MANOR   *321 East 90th Street*

A recent rehabilitation of a five-story tenement; the name is in gold script on the door.

GRACIE MEWS   *401 East 80th Street*

A futuristic thirty-five-story tower of the 1970s; with "sculpture garden" public plaza, unusual vehicle driveway, and entrance with glass porte-cochere canopy.

GRACIE PLAZA   *1701 York Avenue*

A thirty-five-story luxury rental and cooperative building of 1972, with nicely landscaped entrance. Its early history was marred by owner-tenant strife.

Built on the former site of St. Joseph's Orphan Asylum, which was originally housed in one of the city's most striking country seats, the Kenyon/Prince mansion of 1799.

GRACIE SQUARE GARDENS   *525 East 89th Street*
                                  515 East 89th Street
                                  520 East 90th Street
                                  530 East 90th Street

A complex of pleasant six-story redbrick buildings grouped around a central garden court between East 89th and East 90th streets.

A few nice neo-Georgian details at doors and windows suggest the late 1930s as the probable date of construction.

Built on the former site of the House of the Good Shepherd, a Catholic asylum for girls. Next to it is a monumental landmark Art Moderne building, originally an asphalt plant built in 1944.

GRACIE TOWERS   *180 East End Avenue*

This buff-brick 1970s apartment building between East 88th and East 89th streets looks right down on Gracie Mansion across the street.

Graham. *Elaborately carved stone-work distinguishes the entrance of what was originally planned as the Upper East Side's first apartment-hotel.*

Graham, *detail of one of the entrance columns.*

GRAHAM, THE   *18 East 89th Street*
(southwest corner Madison Avenue)

Built in 1891 and heralded as the Upper East Side's first apartment hotel, this massive seven-stories-and-basement building, with its distinctively elaborate doorway, has long since lost its original name and luxurious amenities. Nevertheless, the handsome detailing and large—often still rent-controlled—apartments—plus a location near "Museum Mile," continue to make it a most desirable address.

The builder and architect was Thomas Graham, who also erected a row of town houses, now demolished, adjoining the taller, L-shaped apartment building on East 89th Street. In September of 1891 the *Real Estate Record and Guide* noted that Mr. Graham had overextended himself financially, and the building was in the hands of receivers. Only a few months before, an issue devoted to the development of the still largely unimproved East Side had featured *The Graham,* describing it as ideal for "young married couples and small families whose associations, whose friendships, and whose kith and kin are on the east side

of the Park, and who would not for one moment think of crossing over to the West Side to reside." The article went on to
explain that like so many of the new apartment hotels on the
West Side, *The Graham* would consist of suites of from two to
six (or more) rooms, each with a bath; there would be no kitchens in the smaller flats, for ". . . you do not do any cooking in
them . . . instead you take the elevator down to the first floor,
and, entering the spacious dining room, partake of your meals
without the trouble of having to do your own marketing or your
own cooking. . . . You need not keep any servants, for every
day your beds are arranged and your rooms dusted by bright and
neat chambermaids." *Sic transit gloria Grahamensis.*

GRAHAM COURT
*1923–1937 Adam Clayton Powell, Jr., Boulevard
(northwest corner West 116th Street)*

Built in 1901 by Clinton & Russell, architects, for the Astor
family; eight stories and basement with rather severe limestone
on the second floor. The top story is handsomely sculpted with
garlands of fruits and flowers. Occasional balconies break the facade. Built on the courtyard plan, the building has eight elevators and is considered the finest apartment building in Harlem. It was the prototype for *The Apthorp,* designed by the same
architect and built by the same family.

Graham Court's *inner courtyard.*

GRAMERCY

In 1831, when real estate developer Samuel Ruggles drained a swampy section north of the city and laid out sixty-six building lots centered around a park modeled after London prototypes, he called the area Gramercy, since that was how the locals had referred to it since the mid-seventeenth century. The Dutch settlers had called the neighborhood Kron Moerasje, *that is, "little crooked stream." This gradually became* Crommeshie *and was eventually Anglicized into "Gramercy."*

One of the first residents was Ruggles's son-in-law, the New York diarist George Templeton Strong, who lived at 74 East 21st Street from 1849 on. As Allan Nevins wrote in his edition of Strong's diary: "It was a pleasant district, for Union Square was only half a dozen blocks to the southwest, Madison Square even closer on the northwest, and Gramercy Park at the door; and it was destined to become a historic area, for within a narrow circle were the residences at various times of Washington Irving, Bayard Taylor, Chester A. Arthur, Samuel J. Tilden, the Cary sisters, Horace Greeley, and Peter Cooper and Abram S. Hewitt, and the birthplace of Theodore Roosevelt."

The Gramercy Park Historic District includes the old Friends' Meeting House (1859; now a synagogue); the Mrs. Stuyvesant Fish mansion at number 19, later owned by Benjamin Sonnenberg; and the Players Club, founded by actor Edwin Booth in 1888. A statue of Booth as Hamlet stands in the middle of the park itself, where admission is still restricted to key-holding residents of the immediate area.

GRAMERCY, THE   *34 Gramercy Park East*
(northeast corner Gramercy Park South, East 20th Street)

The *grande dame* of Manhattan's cooperative apartments, *The Gramercy* was built in 1883 as a cooperative and is still going strong—it even has its original Otis hydraulic elevator and distinctive stained-glass, marble, and Minton-tile lobby (no glass or aluminum travesties here, thank you)—and continues to reign over the city's only private park from its regal perch at the corner of East 20th Street and Gramercy Park East.

Although first conceived as a hotel, the building was sold to a group of businessmen who announced: "This elegant new apartment house [will be] conducted upon the 'cooperative' or

Gramercy. *The front en-
trance to New York's oldest
cooperative apartment house,
built in 1883 and still going
strong.*

'Home Club' plan. The Gramercy is located in one of the most
desirable, accessible, and fashionable quarters of the city." Plans
called for three flats on each of the nine floors, with nineteen of
them reserved for shareholders, and the remainder (including
"bachelor flats" on the top floor) to be rented out as sources of
revenue for the owners. Today most of the seven-to-eleven-room
suites have been cut up, the Louis Sherry's restaurant on the
eighth floor that provided a convenient dining room is long
gone, and the special horse-cab service for tenants has disap-
peared. However, *The Gramercy* still maintains a dignified old
New York ambience that its residents adore.

Over the years a number of people prominent in the arts and
letters have lived at *The Gramercy,* among them DuBose Hey-
ward (author of *Porgy,* later to become Gershwin's *Porgy and
Bess*), James Cagney, Mildred Dunnock, and Margaret Hamilton, a current resident.

GRAMERCY ARMS   *145 East 15th Street*

Buff brick of the 1960s. The name is indicated by a *G* on
the door.

This is an example of "Gramercy" being used in preference
to "Stuyvesant," even though the latter is, geographically, more
appropriate.

GRAMERCY ARMS   *102 East 22nd Street*

A delightful redbrick ten-story apartment house which man-
ages to express itself in two styles of the twenties: Tudor red
brick and Art Deco tiles. Casement windows.

GRAMERCY EAST   *301 East 22nd Street*

A huge white-brick 1960s apartment.

GRAMERCY GREEN   *150 East 18th Street*

This tan-brick 1960s apartment house is memorable only in that it covers the site of New York City's *first* apartment house, *The Stuyvesant*, at 142 East 18th Street.

GRAMERCY HOUSE   *8 Gramercy Park South*
(southeast corner Park Avenue)

A six-story brown-brick building of the 1930s.
Gramercy Park South is actually East 20th Street between Park and Third avenues.

GRAMERCY PARK APARTMENTS
151 East 19th Street

A modest six-story apartment house of circa 1910; at the end of a beautiful block of row houses.

GRAMERCY PARK HABITAT *205 East 22nd Street*

"A touch of the country in the heart of the city," according to an advertisement for this 1983 renovation-conversion of an old warehouse. Two-bedroom apartments start at $215,000 in this condominium.

GRAMERCY PARK TOWERS   *205 Third Avenue*

A 1960s white-brick building.

GRAMERCY PLAZA   *130 East 18th Street*

A 1960s white-brick building; across from the fabled Pete's Tavern, in O. Henry country.

GRAMERCY ROW   *134 East 22nd Street*

Probably a 1960s–1970s rehabilitation of some earlier tenements or row houses; redbrick balconies, et cetera.

GRAMERCY SPIRE   *142 East 16th Street*

Remarkable for the somewhat bizarre Chinese pagoda entrance to a 1960s building that's actually on Third Avenue.

"GRAMERCY—THIRD"   *151 East 20th Street*

This group of modest four-story brick buildings was put together in the nineteenth century to form the Homeopathic Hospital Medical College. The poet William Cullen Bryant, editor of the New York *Evening Post,* was president of its board.

In recent times the building has been divided into small residential apartments.

GRAMERCY TOWERS   *32 Gramercy Park South*

A 1960s redbrick building at the corner of Third Avenue.

GRAMERCY TOWERS   *4 Lexington Avenue*

This important example of Renaissance-style architecture began its life in 1915 when the Russell Sage Foundation commissioned Grosvenor Atterbury to build a *palazzo* for its headquarters. Plaques, escutcheons, sculptural bas-reliefs, and the chiseled motto For the Improvement of Social Living Conditions, all attest to the wealth of the organization and its high-minded attitudes. After the foundation left the building, it was used by other groups, including Catholic Charities.

In recent years the building has been converted to residential use, and the handsome exterior has been beautifully preserved and maintained.

Gramont, *photographed in 1925. The nine-story building to the left of the Gramont is the* Marion *at 2612 Broadway.*

GRAMONT   *215 West 98th Street*
                                        (northeast corner Broadway)

A large 1920s apartment building. Next door at 207 West 98th is the *Gramont Annex:* eight stories, with elaborate window decor and the name in Gothic letters over the entrance; also circa 1920s.

Gramont is the name of a noble French family outstanding for several centuries for its soldiers, statesmen, and memoirists.

GRAMPION APARTMENTS (NYC Housing Authority)
182 St. Nicholas Avenue

This federally funded rehabilitation project of thirty-six apartments takes its name from the Grampion Hotel, which had previously occupied the premises.

The Grampion Hills are a range of mountains separating the Highlands from the Lowlands in Scotland.

GRAND CENTRAL TOWERS
230 East 44th Street

A 1960s white and tan brick apartment house, a block from Grand Central Terminal.

GRAND VIEW
315 West 116th Street

Abandoned.

GRAND VIEW
390 Wadsworth Avenue

A six-story 1920s building with a roof of green Spanish tile.

GRANITE, THE
20–23 Morningside Avenue
(northeast corner West 116th Street)

The base of this handsome building is granite. There are balconies of limestone and bay windows. The pediment has been removed.

GRANT

Ulysses S. Grant (1822–1885) served as eighteenth president of the United States (1869–1877), after having served as commander of all Union soldiers during the Civil War.

After his term in office (which was marked by several scandals) he went on a round-the-world tour and wrote his memoirs.

He also moved to New York City. In 1884 Grant and his wife bought a town house on East 66th Street just off Fifth Avenue.

On 23 July 1885 Grant died, and the citizens of his adopted residence not only gave him a spectacular funeral, they immediately began to raise funds for a suitable monument.

Grant's Tomb, overlooking the Hudson at West 122nd Street in Riverside Park, was completed in 1897 and has been a familiar sight—and landmark—of the city ever since.

GRANT, THE   514 *West 122nd Street*

Built in 1905 by George F. Pelham on the long-hall plan, with six stories and basement; in buff brick and stone.
Only a few blocks from Grant's Tomb.
Twin to *The Sarasota* next door.

GRANT COURT   610 *West 113th Street*

A six-story building with a fire escape in the center and three granite columns at the entrance.

GRANT HOUSES (NYC Housing Authority)
                                                 1320 *Amsterdam Avenue*

This project, bounded by Broadway, Amsterdam Avenue, and West 124th and West 125th streets, contains almost two thousand apartments in nine buildings.

GRAUSTARK   135 *Lenox Avenue*

A six-story building of circa 1905. Abandoned.
Named after George Barr McCutcheon's novel of 1901 which, despite having a heroine named Miss Guggenslocker, was one of the great best-sellers of the time. Connoisseurs of bad writing have long treasured the book, which contains such gems as " 'You brute,' hissed the Countess."

GRAYSTONE   100 *West 74th Street*
                                       (*southwest corner Columbus Avenue*)

A narrow, smallish circa-1900 five-story building with its long side on the avenue. The name is still visible.

GREENHOUSE, THE   26 *West 27th Street*

A new name for a turn-of-the-century building of pinkish brick and limestone; seven stories with fire escapes.

GREENHOUSE EAST   328 *East 86th Street*

A sixteen-story sliver building; circa 1980.

GREENPARK, THE   7 *Park Avenue*
                                        (*northeast corner East 34th Street*)

This huge apartment house of the 1920s is a long way from London's Green Park, one of the most delightful of that city's many oases. However, the original brochure for the New York building put it this way: "He who lives on Park Avenue is fashionable, he who lives on Murray Hill is aristocratic; but he who lives at 7 Park Avenue is both. Here, where the Murrays, the Gileses, and the Hoffmans once did their farming, where the old families of New York still have their residence, 7 Park Avenue offers, two-, three- and four-room apartments designed for pleasant living."

GREENTREE AT MURRAY HILL, THE
240 East 31st Street

The 1982 developer's advertisement reads, "unique luxury condominiums with individuality." The base is the former parish house of the Protestant Episcopal Church of the Good Shepherd *(anno Domini MCMI),* and the plain matching brick superstructure rises to a height of eight stories.

GREENWICH

The Indian settlement of Sapokanikan became known to the English settlers of New York as Greenwich Village in the late seventeenth century, presumably because it was a convenient barge ride away from the center of town, just as Greenwich down the Thames from London was.

A favorite spot for country estates, a refuge from the diseases, plagues, and disorders of Lower Manhattan, Greenwich Village became part of New York in 1825 and later deteriorated into a slum (except for the mansions at Washington Square and lower Fifth Avenue) as the fashionable citizens of the growing metropolis left it behind and poor immigrants moved in.

When artists, writers, and musicians began living in "the Village" early in this century because of its low rents and European atmosphere, it gained a reputation as a refuge for bohemians that it still retains despite the rows of houses and blocks of apartments that house office workers and their families.

GREENWICH
446 Central Park West

A seven-story building; circa 1900.

GREENWICH COURT
117 West 13th Street

A six-story neo-Georgian building of the 1920s, with fire escapes, that blends in nicely with the older town houses on the block.

GREENWICH HOUSE   *247 West 12th Street*

A 1980s residential conversion of a six-story turn-of-the-century warehouse-loft with beautiful brickwork on the facade. The old loading bays have been turned into an entrance and large plate-glass windows.

GREENWICH TOWERS   *105 West 13th Street*

A late 1950s–early 1960s redbrick building with a modernistic entrance.

GREENWICH.V (*sic*)   *26–28 Horatio Street*

A late-nineteenth-century six-story walk-up tenement with a fire escape and a nicely wrought iron fence along the street.
The name is written over the door.

GREGORY HOUSE   *222 East 35th Street*

A six-story 1930s redbrick building near St. Gregory the Illuminator Armenian Orthodox Church on Second Avenue at East 34th Street.

GREGORY HOUSE   *440 East 79th Street*

A redbrick 1960s apartment house.

GREGORY TOWERS   *460 East 79th Street*

Sister building to *Gregory House,* from which it is separated by the Jacques Coeur restaurant.

GRENVILLE HALL   *5000 Broadway*
                              (northeast corner West 212th Street)

A six-story 1930s redbrick building.
The Grenvilles were one of the great eighteenth-century families of British statesmen.

GREYCOURT   *2139 Adam Clayton Powell, Jr., Boulevard*
                              (southeast corner West 127th Street)

Matches the *Oakhurst* and the *Parkhurst.*
Abandoned.

GREYLOCH DWELLINGS   *601 West 143rd Street*
                                      (northwest corner Broadway)

A circa-1900 six-story building with entrance on Broadway; decorated with stylized carved anthemion medallions.

GREYLOCK
*61 West 74th Street
(northeast corner Columbus Avenue)*

This pre–World War I seven-story fire-escape building is rusticated on the ground floor.

Greylock, in northwestern Massachusetts, is the highest mountain in the Berkshire Hills.

GREYSTONE APARTMENTS
*212 West 91st Street
(southeast corner Broadway)*

A thirteen-story brick building of the 1920s.

GREYTON COURT
*630 West 141st Street
(southeast corner Riverside Drive)*

An eleven-story brown-brick building of the 1920s–1930s.

GRIFFON, THE
77 Park Avenue

It's hard to say whether this nice old 1920s apartment house memorializes a breed of English hunting dogs, or a mythical beast with the head and wings of an eagle and the hindquarters of a lion, fabled to guard the gold of the Scythians.

In either case, it's a most unusual name for a Manhattan residence.

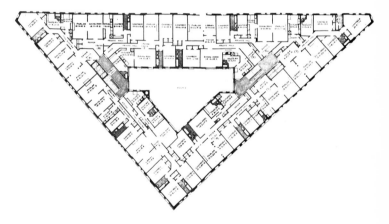

Grinnell. *An unusual floor plan for an unusual triangular plot. The central court and two elevator banks, coupled with long internal hallways, are typical of the era when it was built. Note that many of the dining rooms and maids' rooms are on the court. Architects, and, presumably, tenants, were not disturbed when the kitchen was not placed directly next to the dining room, as is customary today. In the "A" apartment on the Audubon Place–West 157th Street corner, the food has to cross a hall and a pantry on the way from the kitchen to the dining room, and in the "E" apartment it has to go down a long hall past two maids' rooms to get to the table.*

GRINNELL   *800 Riverside Drive*

A nine-stories and basement building with a granite base and a penthouse on one corner; 1920s. It fills an oddly shaped corner formed by the intersection of West 157th Street, Riverside Drive, and Audubon Place.

Probably named for George Bird Grinnell, an anthropologist and authority on American Indians, who was also an employee of the city of New York.

GROVE APARTMENTS   *49 Grove Street*

A 1920s apartment building. Each fire escape has the initial *G* worked in wrought iron.

GUARDSMAN, THE   *64 East 93rd Street*

A plain 1950s redbrick apartment house with seven stories and marble entrance; faces the famous public school built at enormous expense in 1969 to look like the redbrick armory that was demolished to make way for the school!

Only the west facade of the National Guard's Squadron A Armory still stands—a "folly" that serves to remind old-timers of the polo matches and colorful uniforms of the cavalry troops who once paraded here.

The building name recalls the equestrian tradition of the neighborhood.

GUILFORD, THE   *151 East 81st Street*

A circa-1900 bow-fronted apartment house of eight stories, with typical columned entrance and external fire escapes.

Towns in Maine and Connecticut are known by the name Guilford.

HABITAT   *154 East 29th Street*

Buff-brick apartment house.

The name was possibly inspired by the widely publicized dwelling built for the Montreal world's fair in 1967.

HADDON HALL   *324 East 41st Street*

One of the component buildings of *Tudor City.*

The namesake of Haddon Hall is the mansion belonging to the Dukes of Rutland in Derbyshire, England, a notable relic of the medieval period.

In the twentieth century the name achieved widespread familiarity when Charles Major published his best seller of 1902, *Dorothy Vernon of Haddon Hall,* a sequel to the earlier *When Knighthood Was in Flower.*

HADDON HALL   *596 Riverside Drive*
                                 (southeast corner West 137th Street)

The once grand entrance of this circa-1900 six-story building has been modernized and has a wheelchair ramp.

HADRIAN   *225 West 80th Street*
                                     (northeast corner Broadway)

A ten-story white-brick building of 1903 by John H. Duncan, the architect of Grant's Tomb, with a handsome classical porch appropriate for a building named for the Roman emperor Hadrian (A.D. 76–138), famous for his patronage of art and architecture.

HAGUE, THE   *547 Riverside Drive*

A handsome circa-1900 building with open-court entrance. The front walls are decorated with escutcheons adorned alternately with leaf and drapery swags.

Many buildings of the era, such as *The Hendrik Hudson,* have names that recall New York City's Dutch heritage which was emphasized at the time of the Hudson-Fulton celebrations of 1909. However, in this case the name probably refers to Charles Hague, a prominent builder of apartments on the Upper West Side.

HALCYON HALL   *404 West 150th Street*

The halcyon is a mythical bird that had the power to charm winds and waves into calmness. "Halcyon days" are days of peace and tranquillity.

HALIDON COURT   *3679–3681 Broadway*
                                 (southwest corner West 153rd Street)

This turn-of-the-century building looks out over Trinity Cemetery at the corner of Broadway. Handsome stone female masks decorate the doorway.

Halidon is the place in northern England where King Edward III of England defeated the Scots in 1333.

HAMILTON COURT   *164–168 Lenox Avenue*
                                 (northeast corner West 118th Street)

Abandoned and burned out.
[See also *Alexander Hamilton.*]

HAMILTON GRANGE   *310 Convent Avenue*
                                 (southwest corner West 143rd Street)

This six-story building, constructed circa 1912–1913, had an elevator and only large apartments. The brochure stated: "The plumbing is the acme of hygiene, the product of unstinted

expense . . . syphon jet flushometer toilets. . . . The artistically
designed [lobby] ceiling [is] in keeping with the rich onyx marble walls, palms, and Oriental rugs."

HAMILTON HALL   *420 Riverside Drive*
(northeast corner West 114th Street)

A twelve-story 1920s building of white brick. Although it
has lost its cornice and its original doorway lamps, the building
retains some vestiges of glamour.
There is an initial *H* over the door.

HAMLET COURT   *600 West 165th Street*
(southwest corner Broadway)

A six-story white building of circa 1900.

HAMPSHIRE   *46–50 West 9th Street*

A six-story building dated 1883. It has an attractive concierge's window to the left of the entrance, and elevators.
Although it is not a twin to the *Portsmouth* next door, its architecture is sympathetic, and the names indicate an obvious
link. Like the *Portsmouth,* it is extremely well maintained.
Hampshire is a county of England.

HAMPTON, THE   *80–82 Perry Street*

A six-story nineteenth-century building with its original
fence.
Hampton Court, on the Thames in England, is one of the
most famous royal palaces.

HAMPTON HOUSE   *28 East 70th Street*

A fifteen-story 1920s building with Spanish-tile roof, designed by Emery Roth. The buff brick and limestone is decorated with displayed eagles over the doors. La Goulue Restaurant is on the ground floor.

HANOVER HOUSE   *442 West 57th Street*

A twelve-story middle-of-the-block building of buff brick;
circa 1960. A distinctive feature is the many corner balconies
that have been enclosed by the tenants to make sun rooms.
The British dynasty of Hanover reigned over the colony of
New York from 1714 to the American Revolution and is commemorated in Hanover Square and Hanover Street.

HARBOR VIEW TERRACE (NYC Housing
Authority)   *525 West 55th Street*

This federal "turnkey" project of 337 apartments on the far
West Side was completed in 1977.
The name derives from its proximity to the last big passenger
terminal for ocean liners still in operation in New York City.

HARDING   *455 West 44th Street*

A nineteenth-century building of six stories; recently and neatly renovated.

HARDWICK HALL   *314 East 41st Street*

Part of the *Tudor City* complex. In 1928 rents ranged from $1,500 to $2,500 a year.

Named for one of England's most historic and popular stately homes, Hardwick Hall, today a National Trust property in Derbyshire, which was originally built by Bess of Hardwick and now belongs to the earls and dukes of Devonshire.

HARFAY   *324 East 85th Street*

A seven-story white-brick apartment house of the 1960s. Its made-up name is written in gold on the glass entrance door.

HARKNESS, THE   *61 West 62nd Street*
(northeast corner Columbus Avenue)

Twenty-seven floors with 293 apartments, built in 1980.

Incorporates the site of the short-lived Harkness Theater for Dance which faced Broadway and was named for its patron Rebekah Hale Harkness, married to a member of the Harkness Standard Oil family.

HARLEM RIVER HOUSES (NYC Housing Authority)   *221 West 151st Street*

The home of two projects: Harlem River Houses of 1937, with 577 units, and Harlem River Houses–II of 1965, a building with 116 apartments.

Both are named for the nearby Harlem River, which separates Manhattan and the Bronx.

The 1937 construction is "the first federally constructed, federally owned housing project in New York City." The chief architect was Archibald Manning Brown.

HAROLD   *437 Manhattan Avenue*
(northwest corner West 118th Street)

Elaborate carved entrance with putti over the door. A second entrance at 351 West 118th Street has been blocked up.

HAROLD COURT   *1456 St. Nicholas Avenue*
(southwest corner West 183rd Street)

A three-story building of variegated red and black brick in a tapestry effect; circa 1900.

HAROLDON COURT   *215 West 90th Street*
(northeast corner Broadway)

A thirteen-story redbrick and limestone building of the 1920s.

Harperly Hall. *The restaurant was decorated in the simple Arts and Crafts style becoming popular at the time the building was erected, with much use of bare wood. Note the wall seat with pillows at the rear. A touch* à la Japonaise *are the stenciled peacocks and plants on the walls above the wallpaper.*

HARPERLY HALL
41 Central Park West
(northwest corner West 64th Street)

This circa-1900 building was built as a luxury apartment house with apartments of two to nine rooms renting from $600 to $6,000 annually. H. W. Wilkerson was the architect. Unusual for the time, a woman, Mary Linton Bookwalter, was "Decorator-Architect" and "Chairman [*sic*] of the Building Committee." Among the features stressed by the management were a filtered water system, extra guest rooms, a trunk room for each apartment, and a cold storage room.

HARRIDGE HOUSE
225 East 57th Street

A modern apartment house of tan brick.

[HARRISON]
111 West 96th Street

A series of five-story turn-of-the-century buildings, formerly known as Harrison (111), Daniel Webster (113), Andrew Jackson (115), and Phil Sheridan (117). The buildings have been unified by a new brown plaster front with four entrances at the numbers indicated, but no name has been given to this cooperative apartment complex.

HARTCOURT   *258 West 97th Street*

A smallish seven-story redbrick building with bay windows, circa 1900.

HARTFORD, THE   *60 West 75th Street*
(southeast corner of Columbus Avenue)

This grand old six-story building with a rusticated ground floor has its name in gilt over the entrance-hall door.

HARTLEY HALL   *482–484 Central Park West*
(southwest corner West 109th Street)

A seven-story circa-1900 redbrick building with fine sculptured stone trim.

HARVARD COURT   *707 St. Nicholas Avenue*

A redbrick and limestone building of circa 1900.
Harvard, the oldest and most influential university in the United States, was founded at Cambridge, Massachusetts, in 1636.

HATFIELD HOUSE   *304 East 41st Street*

Another of the Tudor-style buildings of *Tudor City*.
Hatfield House, Hertfordshire, is one of the most famous stately homes of England, the seat of the marquess of Salisbury.

HAVEN CLIFF   *112 Haven Avenue*

Similar to *Woodcliff* and *Hudson Cliff*.

HAWKINS   *204 West 81st Street*

A five-story turn-of-the-century building of brick with a later fronting of stucco; fire escape.

HAWTHORNE, THE   *211 East 53rd Street*

A typical 1970s white-brick building.
Nathaniel Hawthorne (1804–1864) was the New England novelist.

HAWTHORNE GARDENS   *4861–4873 Broadway*
(southwest corner West 204th Street)

Statues of lions guard the entrance to this orange-brick building of the 1920s; six stories with a courtyard entrance; touches of Spanish decoration.

HAZEL COURT   *221 Sherman Avenue*
(southeast corner West 207th Street)

A six-story dark brick building; circa 1900.

HAZELHURST, THE   *453 Fort Washington Avenue*
(southwest corner West 181st Street)

A next-door neighbor to both the *Pinehurst* and the *Chislehurst* apartments—all dating from the early twentieth century.

HEATHCOTE HALL   *609 West 114th Street*

Built by Schwartz & Gross for the Carnegie Construction Company in 1911. This nine-story building originally had seven apartments to a floor, with rents starting from $45 per month. The entrance has carvings of laurel around it, but the doorway itself has been modernized.

Caleb Heathcote (1666–1721) was a merchant and government official in colonial New York City and served as mayor from 1711 to 1713.

HEDSON APARTMENTS   *247 Wadsworth Avenue*

An undistinguished building of the 1920s.

HELEN   *511 West 135th Street*

A turn-of-the-century apartment house.

HELEN COURT   *14 Morningside Avenue*
(northeast corner West 115th Street)

A large building of the turn of the century facing Morningside Park; now considerably dilapidated and with a large sign on the entrance reading Positively No Loitering or Eating on Steps.

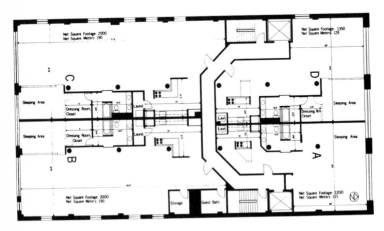

Hellmuth. *The floor plan of this building shows how a typical New York commercial loft building has been turned into four residential units. Unbroken space and large windows are accompanied by "island" kitchens, "sleeping areas" (not bedrooms), and a somewhat circuitous public corridor.*

HELLMUTH BUILDING   *154 West 18th Street*

Cooperative lofts in a conversion of an early-twentieth-century commercial structure. Named for original occupant, Hellmuth Printing Inks.

HEMISPHERE HOUSE   *60 West 57th Street*
(southeast corner Avenue of the Americas)

A high-rise white-brick building of the late 1960s.

The name presumably refers to the Western Hemisphere, likewise honored by the Avenue of the Americas, whose name was changed from Sixth Avenue in the 1930s.

HENDERSON HOUSE   *535 East 86th Street*

A 1961 cooperative in buff brick; built by I. Orlian & Sons. [See also *Henderson Place,* Part III.]

Hendrik Hudson Apartment House. *The navigator's name was actually Henry, and he was an Englishman, but his name was often given in its Dutch form since he made his famous voyage to New York for the Dutch East India Company.*

HENDRIK HUDSON, THE   *380 Riverside Drive*
(between Cathedral Parkway and West 111th Street)

When this enormous apartment building was put up in 1906 at Cathedral Parkway (West 110th Street) at Riverside Drive,

Hudson was very much on New Yorkers' minds because plans were already being made for the Hudson-Fulton celebrations of 1909. Many of the ornamental decorations on the building are now gone, but it is still a noble pile.

The architects for the L-shaped building of eight stories were Rouse & Sloan. The facade resembles that of Italian villas: the materials are limestone, brick, and terra-cotta, and the roof is of Spanish tile. When it opened, it featured a billiard room and a cafe in the basement, and the services of a barber and hairdresser were available. Annual rents ranged from $1,500 to $3,000.

A twelve-story addition or annex, now called the *College Residence Hotel* at 601 Cathedral Parkway (northwest corner Broadway), was built in 1908 by the same architects.

[See also *Hudson*.]

HENINGTON HALL   *214–216 East 2nd Street*

A six-story elevator building of circa 1900, still carrying its name and with the original columned porch at the entrance. The ground floor is now painted gold and adorned with graffiti.

HENNION   *521–523 West 180th Street*

Largely abandoned. A twin to the *Marion* at 517–519, which is well cared for.

HERBERT ARMS   *124 West 93rd Street*

A nine-story building of the 1920s; Robert T. Lyons, architect; Sam Rosoff & Sons, owner-builders. Because of the location near the low-rise Croton water pumping station, "tenants will always be assured of permanent light from three sides," according to the introductory promotional brochure.

The building and its twin, *Ralph Arms*, are in the neo-Georgian style much favored by architects in the 1920s.

HERBERT TOWERS   *327 West 30th Street*

A 1940s white-brick building with seven stories and fire escapes.

HEREFORD   *310 West 79th Street*

A twelve-story white-brick and limestone building of circa 1920.

The name is from a county in England.

HERLEON COURT   *214 Audubon Avenue*
                              (southwest corner West 176th Street)

A six-story circa-1900 building of red brick and limestone.

HERMAL COURT   *16–22 West 111th Street*

A small five-story building now provided with a new entrance and known as the "New West 111th Apartments."

HERMITAGE, THE   *330 East 43rd Street*

This handsome brick-and-stone building in the typically antiquarian style of *Tudor City* adjoins the Ford Foundation Building.

When originally opened in 1928, it was notable for "larger apartments," which rented for $750 to $2,600 a year.

The name refers to the quiet retreats of the European nobility—even if of palatial size—rather than to the place where a monk or hermit lives in solitude.

HERNANDEZ HOUSE (NYC Housing Authority)
189 Allen Street

This Lower East Side building of 1971 has 149 apartments. It is named for Rafael Hernandez, a local community leader.

HESPERION, THE   *600 West 180th Street*
(southwest corner St. Nicholas Avenue)

A five-story brick building, circa 1900.

Hesperia means "western," and *The Hesperion* is in the far west of Manhattan.

HESPERUS   *408 Manhattan Avenue*
(southeast corner West 118th Street)

This seven-story building with three bays overlooking Manhattan Avenue still carries its original name. Red brick with limestone trim; fire escape.

Twin to the *Parthenon.*

Hesperus is the Greek name for Venus, the evening star.

HEWLETT HOUSE   *60 East 12th Street*

A 1960s white-brick structure.

The owner, Ardor Realty, is located in the "Five Towns" area of Nassau County, so the name may refer to Hewlett, Long Island.

HIGH VIEW COURT   *175 Pinehurst Avenue*

A six-story open-court building of the 1920s.

HIGH VIEW MANOR   *10 Park Terrace East*

A six-story redbrick building of the 1920s–1930s.

HIGH VIEW TERRACE   *187 Pinehurst Avenue*

A six-story redbrick building of the 1920s.

HIGHGATE   *182 East 95th Street*

A 1982 rental in severely plain red brick, with "Rooftop Garden & Jogging Track." Entrance on Third Avenue.

The name recalls the section of London where Dick Whittington, Samuel Taylor Coleridge, and Andrew Marvell lived— and where Karl Marx was buried.

HIGHLAND   *519 West 152nd Street*

A columned entrance marks the front of this redbrick and limestone building of circa 1900.

A twin to the *Adriatic*.

HIGHLAND COURT   *600 West 192nd Street*
                          (southwest corner St. Nicholas Avenue)

Twin to the *Bonny Castle*.

HIGHMOUNT   *572 West 141st Street*

A redbrick structure built in 1905 on the center-court plan by Schwartz & Gross and B. N. Marcus, architects.

HILDA   *101 West 83rd Street*
                          (northwest corner Columbus Avenue)

A run-down old building of five stories with fire escapes and a rusticated ground floor. The shops in it are now closed.

HILDONA COURT   *341 West 45th Street*

An early-twentieth-century building of six stories, with an open-court entrance which has been modernized. Now a residential hotel.

HILL HOUSE   *137 East 26th Street*

An old (circa 1900) six-story apartment house.

The name, which appears on a red canopy projecting from the door, is probably a result of the fairly recent renovation. Herman Melville once lived just down the street.

HILLHURST   *160 East 91st Street*

An unusual nineteenth-century building with an undulating facade that includes a rusticated granite base. Eight stories with elevator. The original iron fence is in place.

HILLSIDE COURT   *35–25 Hillside Avenue*

A six-story white-brick building on the open-court plan.

HILLTOP, THE   *174 East 90th Street*

A new awning (and name, most likely) for a restored red-brick turn-of-the-century building. Bartholomew's cafe-pub is on the ground floor at Third Avenue.

The name is apt, as the street slopes away toward the East River just near this site.

HOERLE BUILDING   *306 West 21st Street*

A circa-1900 five-stories-and-basement building with fire escape.

HOHEN-AU   *249 East 77th Street*

This five-story tenement has an impressively captioned pediment inscribed "Hohen-Au 1886." Its twin to the east, at number 251, has had its name obliterated.

The building's name perhaps honors a German noble family (the countess of Hohenau was the morganatic wife of Prince Albert of Prussia) and is a reminder of the time when this part of Manhattan, known as Yorkville, was home to thousands of Germans, Czechs, and Eastern Europeans. The last influx was at the time of the Hungarian uprising of 1956–1957, but since then more and more of the old buildings, shops, and tearooms have given way to high-rise apartments and singles' bars.

HOHENZOLLERN   *495 West End Avenue*
(southwest corner West 84th Street)

An ornate nine-story turn-of-the-century building with granite columns at the entrance and iron balconies. The windows are lavishly decorated with stone. A moat surrounds the basement. Above the front door on West End are carved masks.

The Hohenzollerns were the ruling dynasty of Prussia and, after 1871, of the German Empire.

HOLLAND   *517 West 135th Street*

One of a row of turn-of-the-century small apartment buildings—each with porch entrance—along West 135th Street.

HOLLAND COURT   *315–317 West 98th Street*

The name is shown over the door of this eight-stories-and-basement building which has iron balconies on many windows.

[HOLLY CHAMBERS]   *33 Washington Square West*

Built in 1930 as the Knott Apartment Hotel by the architect C. F. Winckleman. In 1932 rates were "$70 per month up for apartments with bath, closets, refrigerators, etc."

Over the door in a cartouche are the entwined initials *HC*. The 1955 date on the side of the building refers to later improvements.

Now Hayden Hall, a dormitory for New York University.

HOLMES COURT   *31–39 Bennett Avenue*

A six-story building of the 1920s.

A twin to *Wendell Hall.* The reference is likely to Oliver Wendell Holmes (1809–1894), the Boston physician and writer.

[HORTON ICE CREAM FACTORY]
205 East 24th Street

This grand old redbrick factory, closed for many years, was converted to residential use in 1982. At one time Horton's ice cream was one of New York's favorites.

Hotel des Artistes. *View of one of the murals by Howard Chandler Christy in the Café des Artistes, originally the dining room of this apartment-hotel.*

HOTEL DES ARTISTES   *1 West 67th Street*

Perhaps the grandest of all the apartment buildings that aimed for a wealthy, artistic, bohemian group of tenants, "Des Artistes" (as it's known—hardly anyone uses "Hotel") was built in 1918 by developer Walter Russell (who'd built other "studios" on West 67th Street) to the wonderfully pseudo-Gothic designs of G. M. Pollard.

Originally the tenant-owners (it was always a cooperative) of these double-height apartments also enjoyed such amenities as squash courts, theaters, a ballroom (now leased to ABC television), and a restaurant, the Café des Artistes, which is still in operation and still adorned with the frolicking nymphs painted by Howard Chandler Christy, who was at one time a resident.

Writer Fannie Hurst occupied an especially baronial apartment from 1932 until her death in 1968. She recalled in her memoirs that when she and her husband moved in, the enormous apartment "swallowed our simple furniture at a gulp," as well it might, as it was a triplex with thirty-foot ceilings. Hurst promptly went on a buying spree in Europe and furnished the apartment in appropriate Gothic taste. She wrote later: "Guests find it an experience in contrast to come from the clatter and miscellany of New York streets into the conventional lobby of our apartment building, enter a conventional elevator operated by an attendant in conventional uniform and then into the Gothic quiet of architecture, furnishings and mood, removed by centuries from the scenes eighteen stories below." The Hurst apartment sold for under $140,000 in 1974, when New York co-op apartment prices had reached their nadir.

Another famous resident was Alexander Woollcott. When he moved into the *Hotel des Artistes,* he announced to his friends that he would like them to give him a china, linen, and silver shower. Franklin P. Adams (the famous newspaper columnist "F.P.A.") sent him a mustache cup, a handkerchief, and a dime.

Other notable residents have been Norman Rockwell, Isadora Duncan, Ellsworth Kelly, Noel Coward, and John V. Lindsay.

HOTEL 14 　　　　　　　　　　　*14 East 60th Street*

See *Bellaire Apartment Hotel.*

HOTEL MARGRAVE 　　　　　*112 West 72nd Street*
　　　　　　　　　　　　　　　　　109 West 71st Street

A handsome ten-story building of the World War I period distinguished by its beautiful iron and stone balconies. It is unusual in that it occupies a mid-block site with entrances on both side streets.

Margrave is a title of German nobility corresponding to the English marquess.

HOUSE OF LANCASTER 　　　*611 West 141st Street*
HOUSE OF YORK 　　　　　　*605 West 141st Street*

Twin buildings of six stories built circa 1900; now in poor shape and belying their royal names.

The House of York (the white rose was its badge) and the House of Lancaster (the red rose) were rival branches of the English royal family. Their contest for the crown of England, which lasted from 1455 to 1485, was known as the War of the Roses.

HOWARD, THE 　　　　　　*370 Fort Washington Avenue*

A 1920s six-story neo-Georgian apartment house whose name could be that of either the British noble family or the real estate developer's brother-in-law.

HUDSON

The Hudson River—also confusingly called the North River until midcentury—begins in the Adirondacks and joins the sea at New York City.

It was named for Henry Hudson, the seventeenth-century English navigator and explorer who entered New York Bay and proceeded up the river that was later to bear his name, thus giving the Dutch East India Company, which had financed his journey, their claim to colonies in North America.

In 1611 Hudson's crew mutinied while on another fruitless expedition in search of the Northwest Passage, and the explorer, his son, and a few others were set adrift in a small boat, never to be seen again.

On the occasion of the three hundredth anniversary of Hudson's voyage to New York and the centennial of steamboat navigation of the river he discovered, a grand celebration honoring the memories of Henry Hudson and Robert Fulton, the inventor of the steamboat, was held in New York City.

The Hudson-Fulton celebration of 1909 was a very important event in the history of the city. Exhibitions of art and antiques were held at the Metropolitan Museum of Art, and a great flotilla of ships in the style of Hudson's sailed past Manhattan Island as thousands lined the river's bank to see the spectacle.

HUDSON   *139 West 44th Street*

    See *Savoy.*

HUDSON   *3542 Broadway*
                              (northeast corner West 145th Street)

Six-story building with entrance on Broadway. Decoration is rich in geometric detail, and there is an elaborate copper cornice. The view of the Hudson River is an unusually nice one.

HUDSON, THE   *50 Horatio Street*

A six-story redbrick walk-up built circa 1890–1900 at the corner of Hudson Street. The name is over the new glass door in a space behind the main part of the building.

The building overlooks the all-asphalt Cpl. John A. Seravelli Playground.

HUDSON ARMS   *320 West 96th Street*

A six-story redbrick building of circa 1900; recently cleaned up but not improved—the handsome cartouche and lamp fixtures have been silvered.

HUDSON CLIFF   *120 Haven Avenue*

One of a trio with *Woodcliff* and *Haven Cliff.*

HUDSON COURT   *227–223 Haven Avenue*
(southeast corner West 177th Street)

A six-story white-brick building of the 1920s, with an elaborate doorway.

HUDSON HALL   *628 West 114th Street*

A six-story redbrick building with a recessed fire escape. Built about 1905 by the Paterno Construction Company; architects, Schwartz & Gross.

A twin to *Revere Hall* at 622.

HUDSON TOWERS   *301 West 72nd Street*
(northwest corner West End Avenue)

This twenty-three-story building, designed by the architect Arthur Weiser, has one of the strangest histories of any apartment building now standing in New York. It was originally designed as a combination hospital and hotel (you took your patient in and then spent the night in the hotel). It was partially constructed in 1924, at a time when West End Avenue was having a building boom. The idea, however, did not catch on, and financing ran out. The building sat, uncompleted and an eyesore for twenty-one years.

In 1940 it reverted to the city for tax arrears, and the city tried to sell it at auction and failed. In 1945 it was finally sold to developers who completed and rented it.

HUDSON TOWERS   *106–114 Pinehurst Avenue*

A six-story light brick building of the 1920s.

HUDSON VIEW   *520–540 West 145th Street*

The name on the several canopies unifies this group of spruced-up old apartment buildings on one of Harlem's main thoroughfares, which takes up almost the entire block between Amsterdam Avenue and Broadway and encloses at the ground-floor level Valerie's Boutique, the Moment of Truth Church, and the Afro-American Book Center.

HUDSON VIEW   *562 West 148th Street*
(southeast corner Broadway)

A six-story building with porch; circa 1905–1910.

HUDSON VIEW GARDENS   *116 Pinehurst Avenue*

The fourteen buildings on a six-acre plot of land between West 183rd Street and West 185th Street were built by George F. Pelham, Jr., architect, in 1924–1925. They were cooperative from the beginning with 356 apartments consisting of three to six rooms.

Many modern labor-saving devices were advertised by the buildings' brochure, including "motor-driven dish washers" (which sat in the kitchen sink), refrigerators, and a central telephone switchboard.

Heavily stressed to prospective tenants was the radio equipment, then very rare in apartments. "Four super-heterodyne Western Electric receiving sets will be installed in a room devoted to radio equipment," the brochure stated. "Each of the apartments will have four outlets, one connected with each receiving set, enabling residents to listen to a choice of all four programs at one time."

The kitchens were the object of much real estate hyperbole. Each had an incinerator. *"Facilis Descensus Averno!"* proclaimed the brochure. "Virgil's quotation, 'Easy is the road to hell,' did not apply to garbage until incinerators were invented."

Each apartment also had a refrigerator that made ice cubes, a process described in some detail, as it was a very new attraction.

HUGUENOT, THE   *530–532 West 112th Street*

A six-story turn-of-the-century building with recessed fire escape.

A Huguenot is a French Calvinist, many thousands of whom emigrated to England and America in the seventeenth century to escape persecution. There was a Huguenot settlement in New York City at a very early date.

HYPERION   *320 West 84th Street*

A six-story redbrick and limestone building of circa 1900; well renovated with new windows and entrance.

In Greek mythology Hyperion is one of the Titans, deities of enormous strength.

IDA   *54 St. Mark's Place*

A four-stories-and-basement house, probably dating from the 1870s; now painted red but with the name still proudly dominating the cornice.

IDLEWILD   *1854 Adam Clayton Powell, Jr., Boulevard*

Seven stories and basement with surrounding wrought-iron fence; circa 1900.

Idlewild is a remote area of Queens County near Jamaica Bay that gave its name to the airport now called John F. Kennedy.

ILLINOIS   *511 West 113th Street*

See *Louisiana*.

IMPERIAL, THE   *55–57 East 76th Street*

Built in 1882, this brownstone-fronted apartment house is
now dwarfed by its next-door neighbor, *The Carlyle*, but still
retains something of a *grande dame* air.

In 1883 it was listed as one of the first-class buildings with
vacant flats. *The Imperial* is a cooperative today.

IMPERIAL ARMS   *610 Riverside Drive*
(northeast corner West 138th Street)

Seven stories, circa 1900, elaborately decorated with lion
mask and coat of arms sculpted in stone above the door. The
north entrance has been bricked up.

Near to, but not a twin to, *The Royal Arms*.

Imperial Court.
*Photographed about
1928 (then the Las-
anno). The small
structure at the right
was the entrance to the
garage of the* New
Century *on West End
Avenue, the first auto-
mobile garage for ten-
ants in a New York
building.*

IMPERIAL COURT   *307 West 79th Street*

When this ten-story white-brick and limestone building was
build in 1906 to the designs of Schwartz & Gross, architects, it

was called Lasanno Court and contained apartments of from six to nine rooms renting from $1,200 to $2,500 a year. The owners offered to create even larger apartments by combining the six- and eight-room apartments.

Imperial Court *showing the garage entrance transformed into a synagogue.*

It is now a residential hotel offering one and one-and-a-half-room furnished apartments. The "commodious carriage entrance" has been bricked in to create a modern entrance entirely at variance with the design of the building.

IMPERIAL HOUSE   *150 East 69th Street*

This huge 1960 building, with its entrance drive and gardens, occupies the entire block from East 68th to East 69th streets, Third to Lexington avenues. Built just after *Manhattan House,* it was obviously inspired by its nearby elder sister.

INDEPENDENCE PLAZA
Washington Street at Harrison Street

A government-assisted project with various types of housing including restored townhouses of the late eighteenth century and high-rise towers. Built on the site of the old Washington Market and now adjoining Manhattan Community College.

INDIANA   *117 West 79th Street*

A circa-1900 building with seven stories and basement; original portico entrance with four stone columns and classical windows.

INGLEWOOD, THE   *718 West 178th Street*

Six-story turn-of-the-century apartment house with the same name as the California city where Los Angeles International Airport is located, which was incorporated in 1908.

The Scottish Gaelic word *ingle* meaning "fireplace" or "flame," has given rise to a number of domestic words, such as "inglenook."

INWOOD COURT   *130 Post Avenue*
                    (southwest corner West 207th Street)

A circa-1900 building; six stories of dark brick.

The Inwood area of Manhattan is more or less bounded by West 193rd Street, the Harlem River, and the Hudson, about two-fifths of it being parkland.

IOWA   *133–135 West 104th Street*

A circa-1900 seven-story building; once part of a row but now freestanding because of devastation on the block. Granite columns in front. Recently, and well, renovated.

IRENE HALL   *66 Post Avenue*

A twin to *Post Hall*.

IROQUOIS   *480 Convent Avenue*

The Iroquois were an American Indian confederacy that inhabited New York State; sometimes called the Six Nations.

IROQUOIS   *201 West 94th Street*
                    (northwest corner Amsterdam Avenue)

A five-stories-and-basement building (with original iron fence); circa 1900. The name is over the door.

IRVING

Streets, schools, and apartment houses have been named for that quintessential writer of Old New York, Washington Irving (1783–1859), whose comic history of his native town was published in 1809 under the pseudonym Dietrich Knickerbocker.

Although Irving made six long stays in Europe (once as U.S. ambassador to Spain) and spent more than half his adult life

*there, he never forgot New York, and few have written more af-
fectionately of the city. He wrote to a friend in 1824 about New
York: "there is a Charm about that little spot on earth, that
beautiful city and its environs, that has a perfect spell over my
imagination. The bay; the rivers and their wild and woody
shores; the haunts of my boyhood, both on land and water, ab-
solutely have a witchery over my mind."*

*His travel writing, his novels, his retelling of the legends and
tales of the Hudson River Valley, made him one of the earliest
American authors to be esteemed both at home and abroad.*

*"Sunnyside," his home on the Hudson, at Irvington in West-
chester County, has been preserved and is open to the public.*

IRVING   *118 East 17th Street*

This late-nineteenth-century brick and brownstone apartment house is just up the street from the so-called Irving House
where, in fact, the author never lived. Nearby is Washington
Irving High School.

IRVING ARMS   *222 Riverside Drive*
                              (northeast corner West 94th Street)

[See *Westsider Hotel*.]

IRVING COURT   *803 West 177th Street*

A 1920s redbrick neo-Federal apartment house of six stories.

IRVING HALL   *500 Cathedral Parkway*
                              (southwest corner Amsterdam Avenue)

A six-story turn-of-the-century building with fire escape and
open bay on Cathedral Parkway. Twin to *Miller Hall*.

ISABELLE   *213–215 West 111th Street*

A six-stories-and-basement building with porch.

ISHAM GARDENS   *222 and 229 Seaman Avenue*

On both sides of this block in West 214th Street. The buildings are tapestry brick with cupolas and armorial decoration.
The Isham family, who had a home in this part of Manhattan, donated the land for the nearby Isham Park in 1912.

ISHAM PARK PLAZA   *5009–5021 Broadway*

A large seven-story building with bits of terra-cotta decoration. The ground floor is shared by the Liffy *(sic)* Bar and the
Foxy Girl Boutique.

IVEY DELPH APARTMENTS, THE
19 Hamilton Terrace

A 1950s building in the Art Moderne style. The builder's name was Delph. Hamilton Terrace is a short street at the north end of St. Nicholas Park running between West 141st and West 144th streets.

[J. GOEBEL & CO.]
95 Bedford Street

The name and "est. 1865" is written at the top of this building which contains three floors of apartments above two garages.

JACKIE ROBINSON HOUSE (NYC Housing Authority)
2120 Lexington Avenue

This eight-story building at East 128th Street is named for Jack Roosevelt Robinson, the first black to play major league baseball. In 1947 he took part in the world series, playing for the Brooklyn Dodgers, and later said: "I experienced a completely new emotion when the National Anthem was played. . . . This time, I thought, it is being played for me, as much as for anyone else. This is organized Major League baseball, and I am standing here with all the others; and everything that takes place includes me."

JADAM, THE
420 Central Park West
(northwest corner West 102nd Street)

A six-story building of the 1930s–1940s.

JAMES LENOX HOUSE
49 East 73rd Street

An apartment building of the 1970s for senior citizens, sponsored by the Madison Avenue Presbyterian Church, which it adjoins, and built on the site of the former Presbyterian Home for Aged Women founded in 1866 by James Lenox and others. The building that was demolished to make way for *James Lenox House* dated to 1869.
[See also *Lenox*.]

JAMES WELDON JOHNSON HOUSES (NYC Housing Authority)
1844 Lexington Avenue

Built in 1948, this state-sponsored project in East Harlem honors the memory of James Weldon Johnson (1871–1938), a black American educator, poet, and diplomat who was a founder of the NAACP.

JEAN . . .
20 West 14th Street

This five-story building has an elaborate female statue posed over the door and a fancy entrance with two griffins couchant. Now in a state of disrepair the building may once have had a longer name, possibly "Jeanne d'Arc"?

JEANETTE COURT   *255 Audubon Avenue*
                              (southeast corner West 178th Street)

A six-story redbrick building; circa 1900.

JEFFERSON, THE   *324–28 West 51st Street*

A six-story, turn-of-the-century building on a presidential block (see *Washington* and *Lincoln*), that has seen better days.

JEFFERSON HOUSES (NYC Housing Authority)
                              300 East 115th Street

An eighteen-building complex, dating from 1959, and named for Thomas Jefferson (1743–1826), the third president of the United States, who lived in New York when he served as the nation's first secretary of state (1789–1790).

JEROME   *215 West 116th Street*

A typical turn-of-the-century seven-story redbrick building with columned porch.

Leonard Jerome built the racetrack called Jerome Park in the Bronx, which opened in 1866. He was also responsible for the boulevard running from Macomb's Dam to the racetrack, which still carries his name. He is probably more famous today, however, for being the grandfather of Sir Winston Churchill.

JEROME PALACE   *221 West 82nd Street*

Sam Minskoff was the builder of this 1920s brick building of fourteen stories and tower with a bay on Broadway. Extends along the east side of the avenue from West 82nd to West 83rd streets.

JESSICA   *625–627 West 138th Street*

A five-stories-and-basement building with four granite columns at the entrance; circa 1900.

JOAN D'ARC   *10–12 Pinehurst Avenue*

A six-story, circa-1900 apartment house.

The name is a fractured-French or Franglais rendering of the name of the Maid of Orleans (ca. 1412–1431), the warrior saint who enjoyed such popularity with New Yorkers that a statue, as well as a high school, commemorate her.

JOESAM COURT   *556 West 141st Street*

A very plain six-story 1920s apartment house.
Named for its builders, Joe and Sam?

JOHN ADAMS   *101 West 12th Street*

A 1970s luxury high rise occupying the whole blockfront along Avenue of the Americas between West 12th and West 13th streets.

When John Adams was vice president of the United States in 1789, he lived at "Richmond Hill," a house at Varick and Charlton streets that had been used by Washington as his headquarters and was later occupied by Aaron Burr. The site was not too far from this building.

JOHN HAYNES HOLMES TOWERS
1780 First Avenue

Built in 1969, and consisting of two buildings with 537 apartments, this project is named for the Reverend Dr. John Haynes Holmes (1879–1964), civic leader, rector of the Community Church, noted lecturer, and one of the founders of the NAACP and the American Civil Liberties Union.

JOHN MUIR, THE   *27 West 86th Street*

Built in 1926 by Sugarman & Berger, architects, with Sloan & Robertson as consulting architects, this fourteen-story building carries its name and a fleur-de-lis coat of arms over the front entrance. Handsome plaques adorned with masks run in a frieze between the second and third floors.

Named for the famous Scottish-born American naturalist John Muir (1838–1914), considered by many to be the godfather of today's environmentalist movement. He was instrumental in establishing Yosemite National Park. Muir Woods in California also honors him.

JOHN MURRAY HOUSE   *220 Madison Avenue*

This neo-Georgian apartment house of pre–World War II vintage stands on what was once the Murray family farm. The surrounding area is still called Murray Hill after the ancestral homestead where John Murray, brother of Robert Murray and champion of free public schools, died in 1808.

[See also *Murray Hill*.]

JOHNSON BUILDING   *107 West 25th Street*

A 1920s white-brick building of six stories, undergoing conversion into "living lofts" in 1983.

JOSEPHINE   *1785 Amsterdam Avenue*

A five-story redbrick turn-of-the-century beauty, now abandoned.

JULIETTE   *18 St. Nicholas Place*

Gothic arched windows and crenellations distinguish this five-story building of the 1920s.

JUMEL   *507–509 West 142nd Street*

These very elegant twin buildings have windows with sculptured stone surrounds.

JUMEL HALL   *429 West 162nd Street*
                                                 (at Edgecombe Avenue)

A 1920s six-story building named after the nearby Morris-Jumel Mansion, originally Roger Morris's summer home (1765) but later the property of Stephen Jumel (1754–1832), a Franco-American wine merchant, whose widow married Aaron Burr in 1833 but divorced him a year later and lived in the house until 1865. The surrounding land was sold off by her family until only the house remained.

KANAWHA   *203 West 111th Street*

Abandoned.
The Kanawha is a river in West Virginia.

KARG   *101 Delancey Street*

The name is written over the door of this six-story brick building which now has an Off-Track Betting parlor in its ground floor.

KATHERINE COURT   *110 Terrace View*

This four-story 1920s building is in Marble Hill near West 225th Street.

KATHMERE, THE   *601 West 135th Street*
                                                 (northwest corner Broadway)

Built in 1906, George F. Pelham, architect; six stories of variegated brick. The original cornice has been removed.

KATTERSKILL NORTH and KATTERSKILL SOUTH   *94 South Hamilton Place*
                                                 (northwest corner West 141st Street)

Twin seven-story buildings of circa 1900, now being renovated.
Katterskill Falls in Ulster County, New York, was a favorite subject for Thomas Cole and other painters of the Hudson River School.
Katterskill was Anglicized into Catskill in many place names of New York State.

KEITH ARMS   *340 West 87th Street*

A nine-story building of the 1920s.

KELMSCOTT   *316 West 79th Street*

This early-twentieth-century building of twelve stories has lion-mask decoration at the entrance and handsome balconies.

"Kelmscott" was the home of the English poet William Morris, one of the founders of the Arts and Crafts movement. The Kelmscott Press in Hammersmith, London, established by Morris, was important in the revival of fine printing in the late nineteenth century.

KENDAL COURT   *521 West 111th Street*

A six-story redbrick building with open-court entrance and granite columns at the entrance, built in 1903, Schwartz & Gross, architects. Well maintained.

KENILWORTH   *45 Pinehurst Avenue*
(northeast corner West 179th Street)

A six-story 1920s building.

Kenilworth, first published in 1821, is one of Sir Walter Scott's most celebrated novels. Set in the sixteenth century, it portrayed life in the court of Queen Elizabeth I.

KENILWORTH, THE   *151 Central Park West*
(northwest corner West 75th Street)

The Lenox Realty Company put up this building in 1908, employing as architects Townsend, Steinle & Haskell.

Although modestly advertised as "housekeeping apartments," the units were quite grand: each floor contained three apartments, one of nine rooms, two of ten rooms.

KENILWORTH, THE   *178 East 80th Street*
(southwest corner Third Avenue)

Twenty-five-story buff and brown brick tower of the 1970s. The orange balconies add a nice touch of color. The below-side-walk-level Kenilworth Plaza on the Third Avenue side never completely caught on with the public.

KENMAR   *101 West 77th Street*
(northwest corner Columbus Avenue)

One of the three five-story buildings of the same vintage, but its neighbors, Renfrew at 103 and Juannita at 105, have no visible sign of their original names.

On the ground floor of the *Kenmar* is the Museum Cafe, one of the earliest restaurants to be built when this stretch of Columbus Avenue was gentrified in the 1970s.

KENOSHA   *141 West 111th Street*

A six-story white brick and limestone building with porch, dating from circa 1900.

A city and county of Wisconsin, probably taken from the Indian.

KENSINGTON   *216 West 113th Street*

A six-story turn-of-the-century building.

One of several named for the Royal Borough of Metropolitan London, site of Kensington Palace, the official residence of Princess Margaret.

KENSINGTON COURT   *555–557 West 151st Street*
                                        (northwest corner Broadway)

Six stories in white brick; circa 1900.

KENSINGTON HOUSE   *200 West 20th Street*
                                    (southwest corner Seventh Avenue)

A fourteen-story white-brick building with casement windows and a frieze between the second and third floors. The handsome Art Deco entrance has bands of blue-and-gold mosaics.

KENT, THE   *216 West 102nd Street*
                                       (southeast corner Broadway)

A circa-1900 seven-story fire-escape building.

KENWAY   *462–466 Convent Avenue*
                                 (northwest corner West 150th Street)

This once handsome building, set on a triangular-shaped piece of land, is now abandoned.

KEYPORT   *642 West 172nd Street*

A five-story turn-of-the-century building.

KIMBERLY, THE   *222 East 80th Street*

White brick, 1960s; opposite the Hungarian Baptist Church.

KING, THE   *56 East 87th Street*

The architect George F. Pelham designed this 1904 apartment house for builder Joseph King—who named it after himself.

A six-story edifice with recessed fire escapes over the central doorway, *The King* is a well-maintained survivor in a neighborhood of mostly 1920s behemoths.

King Model Houses, *better known as "Strivers' Row," the 200 block of West 138th Street. In the distance, on the heights, is the City University of New York, rising above St. Nicholas Park.*

KING MODEL HOUSES

West 138th to West 139th streets between Adam Clayton Powell, Jr. and Frederick Douglass boulevards

David H. King, Jr., was responsible for this remarkable group of apartments and townhouses built in 1891. He employed three architects: James Brown Lord; Bruce Price and Clarence S. Luce; and McKim, Mead & White. The land on which it was built had been the country estate of Cadwallader D. Colden, who was mayor of New York from 1818 to 1820. "The land is dry, healthful and accessible," said a contemporary writer, "swept by the westerly breezes from the Hudson and within easy reach of the elevated."

The Model Houses received great attention from the press when they opened in April 1892. "It is the largest enterprise of its kind ever undertaken on Manhattan Island," said the *Real Estate Record.* "Nearly two hundred families will be supplied with separate homes. . . . The material chiefly used is buff brick from the Perth Amboy Terra Cotta Co., and the effect is bright and cheerful."

One of the most interesting features of the plan, almost unique in New York, was a street running parallel to West 138th and West 139th streets between the two rows of houses "as in Philadelphia, so as to give access to the rear of each house for grocery wagons and ash carts and thus permitting the 'business' part of housekeeping to be kept out of sight." It was emphasized that these cross streets were not "mere alleys, but broad enough for two wagons to pass." They were asphalted and closed by ornamental iron gates, and fountains and flower beds were placed at the intersections of the cross streets.

Model apartments furnished for inspection by prospective tenants are no new feature of New York life. The King Houses were opened to the public when they were finished. More than two thousand people came to view the model on a single Sunday in the spring of 1892.

In the decade after the King Model Houses were built, Harlem gradually became black. The houses were considered the most desirable residences in the district—along with *Graham Court*—and many prominent blacks, such as W. T. Handy, made their homes there. Because so many successful people lived there, the houses were nicknamed Striver's Row, a name that persists. After nearly a century the houses maintain their prestige in what remains the most desirable part of Harlem.

KINGS COLLEGE APARTMENTS
501 West 121st Street
(northwest corner Amsterdam Avenue)

Six stories and basement in brick and limestone; entrance-way, with eight polished granite columns. Built in 1906 by Neville & Bagge with typical center-court plan and a long lobby.

Kings College was the name of Columbia University between 1754 and 1784, referring to its founding by a grant from King George II of England.

KINGSLAND   *838–844 Riverside Drive*

A six-story tan-brick building; circa 1900.

KINGSLEY, THE   *400 East 70th Street*
(southeast corner First Avenue)

This 1983 tower—a self-styled "very special condominium residence"—was named shortly after Ben Kingsley, the British actor, won the Academy Award for his portrayal of the title role in *Gandhi*.

KINGSTON   *22–28 King Street*

Identical redbrick buildings of circa 1880, with elaborate stone trim corbels, cartouches, cabochons, masks.

KIPLING ARMS   *145 West 96th Street*

Gronenberg & Leuchtag were the architects of this fifteen-stories-and-penthouse white-brick building owned by Krumholz Bros., Inc. "Ready for occupancy September 1, 1927 . . . surpasses in many ways the best private houses."

Named for one of the most popularly successful writers of all time, Rudyard Kipling (1865–1936). The name still appears in gold lettering on the fanlight, but a neighborhood wag has transformed it into "Killing Arms."

KIPS BAY PLAZA   *East 30th to East 33rd streets, First to Second avenues*

Occupying a ten-acre site are the twin twenty-story build-ings of *Kips Bay Plaza*, built by William Zeckendorf's firm, Webb & Knapp as a Title I slum-clearance project in 1960–1965. The architect was I. M. Pei, and the architecture was—and still is "an invigorating departure from the type of apart-ments now found in Metropolitan New York," to quote the original promotional brochure. "Each room offers clean, balanced living space. To heighten the effect of spacious proportion, eight foot high doors and openings have been integrated in the design [of recessed, almost] floor-to-ceiling windows . . . free gas, music in the lobbies, elevators, and laundry rooms, views."

In the 1980s the owners of *Kips Bay Plaza* announced plans to make the building a cooperative, but legal difficulties derived from the original Title I charter caused delays.

William Zeckendorf of Webb & Knapp said, "the Bellevue site, which we renamed Kips Bay, was pure Webb & Knapp. Here we created something new in city housing—a sense of place and unity with buildings, gardens, and play areas—and have ever since been proud of what resulted."

The name refers to the nearby riverfront farm of Jacobus Hendrickson Kip. Born in New Amsterdam in 1631, Kip was the second son of Hendrick Kip, who came over from the Neth-erlands. The Kip house survived until circa 1850, when the northward march of the city made such large landholdings things of the past.

KIPS BOROUGH HOUSE   *303 East 37th Street*

A modest six-story building overlooking the entrance to the Queens-Midtown Tunnel; built between 1936 and 1940.

The name is from the original Dutch owner of the land.

KNICKERBOCKER VILLAGE
Catherine to Market streets, Monroe to Cherry streets

This Lower East Side housing project was completed in 1934 by Fred F. French (of *Tudor City* fame) with government assis-tance. It replaced a warren of slums known as the Lung Block because of their unhealthiness.

The name is taken from the fictional character invented by Washington Irving in his *History of New York, From the Begin-ning of the World to the End of the Dutch Dynasty . . . by Diedrich Knickerbocker*, first published in 1809.

Knickerbocker is an Anglicized version of the old Dutch name Knickerbacher and has come to stand for any New Yorker, especially one descended from the original Dutch set-tlers, and to symbolize *old* New York.

Among the more famous former tenants of *Knickerbocker Village* were Julius and Ethel Rosenberg and their sons.

KNOWLTON COURT   *558 West 158th Street*

Built by Neville & Bagge, architects, in 1907–1908. The six-story building with bay windows has an open court on Broadway. When it opened, the five-to-eight-room apartments rented for $480 to $1,200 a year.

L. SCHNEE BUILDING   *123 St. Marks Place*
(northwest corner Avenue A)

A buff-colored brick building dated 1907 on the pediment, with Renaissance stone details.

LA GUARDIA HOUSES (NYC Housing Authority)
250 Madison Street

This large complex of nine buildings on the Lower East Side is named for Fiorello H. La Guardia (1882–1947), one of the city's ablest and most popular mayors, who served from 1934 to 1945. He was responsible for initiating the City Housing Authority during his first term as mayor.

LA RESIDENCE   *1080 Madison Avenue*

When this eighteen-story sliver apartment house opened for inspection in 1980, it was called The Residence on Madison, and its location in the art-saturated neighborhood of the low Eighties was featured. The windows and inset balconies are attractive.

LA RIVIERA   *230 West 99th Street*
(southeast corner Broadway)

A seven-story building with columned entrance; circa 1900.

LA ROCHELLE   *57 West 75th Street*
(northeast corner Columbus Avenue)

Lamb & Rich were the architects of this 1896 apartment house. The columned facade on the Columbus Avenue side must always have been imposing, even when the Ninth Avenue el rattled by. Today it is cluttered with shops and open-air cafes.

La Rochelle, an important French seaport, has been synonymous with the history of the Huguenots since the sixteenth century, when it was their stronghold. New Rochelle, the Westchester County town, was founded by Huguenot settlers in 1688.

LAFAYETTE   *320 Manhattan Avenue*
(southeast corner West 114th Street)

A six-story turn-of-the-century building; very plain, built of brick; with a fire escape. Overlooking a square containing Bartholdi's statue of Lafayette and Washington, appropriately next door to the *Rochambeau*.

The Marquis de Lafayette visited New York several times during the American Revolution, in which he served on the American side, and received the freedom of the city in 1784. In 1824 he returned to a festive reception in New York.

LAFAYETTE APARTMENTS   *30 East 9th Street*

Built in the mid-1950s on the site of the old Hotel and Cafe Lafayette, a rendezvous for Greenwich Village intellectuals which was renowned for its cuisine. At one time the hotel was owned by Raymond Orteig, who offered $25,000 to the first man to fly nonstop from New York City to Paris. Charles Lindbergh won the prize in 1927.

H. I. Feldman was the architect for the present red-and-buff brick structures which, with twelve floors of apartments above the street-level commercial space, seemed mammoth when they were built, but have been dwarfed by more recent buildings.

LAMARTINE   *357–359 West 29th Street*

A series of seven-story town houses with bayed windows, united to form a cooperative apartment building.

Alphonse de Lamartine (1790–1869) was a French poet and orator who also served as France's minister of foreign affairs. This area is one of the old French neighborhoods of New York.

LANCASHIRE   *353–355 West 85th Street*

An eight-story building with a classical entrance adorned with coats of arms in stone; circa 1900 and well maintained.

Lancashire is a county in northwest England.

LANCASTER   *39–41 East 10th Street*

A renovated redbrick building of the 1890s.

Lancaster is a royal duchy of England.

LANCASTER APARTMENTS   *936 West End Avenue*

A seven-story building of circa 1900, with fire escapes; sits with the *Westbourne* on the triangle formed by West 106th Street, Broadway, and West End Avenue.

LANDMARK, THE   *300 East 59th Street*

A huge tower, built in 1982, at the entrance to the Queensboro Bridge: "Luxury living in a truly luxury building." However, despite the advertising slogan, the lobby and exterior are of the *brut* architecture often associated with government buildings.

LANDS END   *257 Clinton Street*

A large housing project under construction in 1983.

Clinton Street (known in the eighteenth century as Warren Street), once ended in a dock on the East River.

Langham Apartments. *The drawing room of J. B. Greenhut was furnished with a Salon painting, Louis XV/XVI Revival furniture, and an Aubusson carpet typical of stylish interior decoration at the time the building was completed, and now coming back into fashion.*

LANGHAM, THE   *135 Central Park West*
                              (West 73rd to West 74th streets)

This *château*-esque monument to luxurious living was built by architects Clinton & Russell in 1905 on the blockfront between West 73rd and West 74th streets.

The original layout had four apartments to a floor. Annual rents for these nine- and ten-room apartments began at $4,500. There were eight elevators, a mail delivery system, a refrigeration and ice plant, central vacuum, and a laundry *in the penthouse.* According to the promotional brochure "accommodations for men servants are found in the basement, if desired, as well as storage rooms." A rear carriage entrance completed the amenities.

The Langham has long been popular with celebrities. Some of the more famous tenants have been Basil Rathbone, Cyril Ritchard, and Lee Strasberg.

LANGHOLM   *200 West 112th Street*
             (southwest corner Adam Clayton Powell, Jr., Boulevard)

A five-story turn-of-the-century building with a beautifully decorated entrance.
Langholm is a Scottish place name.

LANSDOWN   *352 West 46th Street*

See *The Lyric*.

LAONIA   *400 West 153rd Street*

An old apartment house with a mystifying classical-sounding name.

LARCHMONT   *100 West 105th Street*
             (southwest corner Central Park West)

A seven-story building of red brick with ornate limestone decoration. Two entrances on Central Park West. Early twentieth century.
Larchmont is a town in Westchester County about twenty miles northeast of New York City on Long Island Sound.

LARCHMONT, THE
             2031 Adam Clayton Powell, Jr., Boulevard

Gray brick and limestone; circa 1910. Now abandoned.
A twin to *The Monmouth*.

LARRIMORE, THE   *444 East 75th Street*

Red brick, 1960s.

LATHROP   *46 West 83rd Street*

A white brick and limestone building of eight stories, with small balconies on some windows; circa 1920s.

LAURA COURT   *120 West 228th Street*

A twin to *Rose Court*.

LAUREATE HALL   *435 West 119th Street*
             (northeast corner Amsterdam Avenue)

A ten-story white-brick building whose name is appropriate for this scholarly neighborhood around Columbia University.

LAUREL—COURT   *552 West 141st Street*

Six-story building with wrought-iron fire escapes. The windows have severe but handsome stone decoration.

LAUSANNE, THE   *333 East 45th Street*

A bland 1970s building.
The name is that of the Swiss city on the shores of Lake Geneva.

LE TRIOMPHE   *245 East 58th Street*
                         (northwest corner Second Avenue)

At the Manhattan end of the Queensboro Bridge now stands New York's answer to Paris's Arc de Triomphe: a high-rise building of orange brick and tinted glass.

LEANDER   *801 St. Nicholas Avenue*

Plain redbrick structure with visible fire escapes.
Leander was a Greek mythological figure who was drowned while swimming the Hellespont to be with his beloved Hero, priestess of Aphrodite at Sestos.

L'ECOLE   *2 East 47th Street*

A 1977 apartment house on the site of the old Central Commercial School Annex.
L'école is French for "school."

LEEDS HOUSE   *307 East 11th Street*

A four-story cooperative conversion of an 1880s house.

LEFT BANK, THE   *99 Bank Street*
                         (between Greenwich and Hudson streets)

A tastefully done 1970s conversion of a late-nineteenth-century commercial building.
Bank Street takes its name from a branch of the Bank of New York which once stood in the area, and the apartment building's name puns on that.

**LEHMAN VILLAGE (NYC Housing
Authority)**   *1605 Madison Avenue*

This 1963 project was named for Herbert H. Lehman (1878–1963), the brilliant banker and politician who was governor of New York from 1932 to 1942, after which he distinguished himself as director of U.S. foreign relief and rehabilitation projects. Both he and his wife were noted for their philanthropic activities.

LENATHAN HALL, THE   *86 Fort Washington Avenue*

A six-stories-and-basement building of tan brick, with a dignified classical entrance, circa 1920.

LENMOR APARTMENTS   *58 East 1st Street*

Seven-story early-twentieth-century apartments with white-washed entrance.

LENOX

James Lenox (1800–1880) was the only son of a prodigiously successful Scottish-born merchant, Robert Lenox, who left his son an enormous fortune at his death in 1839.

The son devoted the greater part of his life and fortune to philanthropy and book collecting. On land that his father had bought in 1818, on Fifth Avenue between East 68th and East 71st streets, Lenox built his library and laid out the area with restrictive deeds around a pleasant square called Hamilton Place. The square is gone, but the area is still called Lenox Hill.

In the Lenox Library were the first Gutenberg Bible to come to the United States and many other rare books, as well as the first painting by J. M. W. Turner to be owned by an American. The library was eventually incorporated into the New York Public Library. The Frick Collection now stands on the site of the Lenox Library.

James Lenox was a great supporter of Presbyterian charities, including the Presbyterian Hospital, originally on Lenox land and now at Broadway and West 168th Street, and the Presbyterian Home for Aged Women, formerly on the site now occupied by the James Lenox House *at 49 East 73rd Street.*

Northern Sixth Avenue was renamed for James Lenox in 1887 in recognition of his generosity to the city of his birth.

LENOX   *101 West 118th Street*
                                (northwest corner Lenox Avenue)

A five-story orange-brick building of circa 1900; now partly abandoned.

LENOX COURT   *114 East 71st Street*

A seven-story circa 1900 redbrick building.

The name is chiseled above the door amid scrolling leafage, a reminder that this area was once part of James Lenox's extensive landholdings.

Lenox Avenue. This view looking north from West 113th Street, show-ing construction of the IRT subway in 1901. This thoroughfare was already amply supplied with apartment houses five or six stories in height, many of which are still standing and in use.

LENOX HALL   *83 West 115th Street*
(northeast corner Lenox Avenue)

   Six stories in red brick; built circa 1900 and now partially abandoned.

LENOX HOUSE   *301 East 78th Street*

   A 1970s buff-brick apartment house.

LENOX MANOR   *176 East 77th Street*

   Built on the site of the old Hebrew Benevolent & Orphan Asylum Society of the City of New York, this 1956 apartment house was designed by Sylvan & Bien, architects, and built by the Campagna Construction Company. The lobby was used for scenes in the Academy Award-winning film *Kramer vs. Kramer* (made in 1978). The building has recently become a cooperative.

LENOX TERRACE APARTMENTS
10 West 135th Street

   A large complex of luxury apartment houses built in 1957. S. J. Kessler & Sons were the architects for this pleasant group of redbrick towers occupying the stretch from Fifth to Lenox avenues, and West 132nd to West 135th streets.
   The little street leading from West 135th into *Lenox Terrace* is called Lenox Terrace Place.

LEONORA   *263 West 112th Street*

Abandoned.

LEONORI, THE   *26 East 63rd Street*

One of the few *old* named residences in the Madison–Park Avenue area still extant and still with its name prominently displayed. This grand old fortress—which has had its ups and downs since it was built at the turn of the century—now has in its ground floor Quo Vadis Restaurant (once the site of the Colony), Giorgio Armani, and Christatos & Koster, florists.

The name is a puzzle—a variant of Leonora? The Leonori has recently become a condominium.

LEONARD, THE   *245 East 30th Street*

The name is chiseled in stone over the entrance of this early-twentieth-century building.

Whether the namesake was Harry Ward Leonard (1861–1915), American inventor, or the building's original owner, is unknown.

LEONDRA   *533 West 145th Street*

A sister building to the *Beatrice* and the *Ernestine*.

LEROY   *133 West 113th Street*
(northwest corner St. Nicholas Avenue)

A seven-story circa-1900 building.

Jacob Le Roy was an eighteenth-century New York City politician and merchant. A street in Greenwich Village is named for him.

LESLIE COURT   *600 West 137th Street*
(southwest corner Broadway)

Built in 1907 by the firm of Bing & Bing, with Emery Roth as the architect, this six-story building has unusual strips of foliage ornamentation on its facade.

LESLIE HOUSE   *220 East 54th Street*

A 1960s redbrick apartment house with its name on a large brass plate, as well as on the canopy.

LESSTER, THE   *454 St. Nicholas Avenue*
(southeast corner West 133rd Street)

A 1880s five-story building with rusticated ground floor; semiabandoned. A twin to the *Raynor* next door south.

Could the name be a phonetic "Leicester"?

LEVEL CLUB CONDOMINIUM
253 West 73rd Street

Built in 1926 by Clinton & Russell, architects, as a meeting place for a Masonic organization. The name refers to the Freemasonic symbol, and the front of the building still carries a few Masonic references. Later a hotel, *The Riverside Plaza,* it was converted into condominium apartments in 1983.

LEXINGTON
144–146 East 22nd Street

A six-story walk-up apartment building located near the beginning of Lexington Avenue at Gramercy Park. This redbrick and limestone building of circa 1900 has a pillared porch.

LEXINGTON
167 East 72nd Street

A fifteen-story building recently made a cooperative; dating from the 1920s. In the ground floor is Le Bourgogne restaurant.

A new north-south avenue running from East 14th Street to East 30th Street was authorized by the New York State Legislature in 1832. Four years later it was named Lexington Avenue after the battle of the American Revolution. It was gradually extended northwards until 1870 when it reached the Harlem River. The section from East 14th Street to East 20th Street has always been called Irving Place after Washington Irving.

LEXINGTON HOUSE
141 East 56th Street

A twelve-story building of the 1950s.

LEXINGTON HOUSES (NYC Housing Authority)
1773 Third Avenue

This project of 1951 is centered on Lexington Avenue.

LEXINGTON TOWERS
160 East 88th Street
(corner Lexington Avenue)

White brick, 1960s, by Kary & Kavoitt, architects.

LIBERTY TOWER
55 Liberty Street

Designed by Henry Ives Cobb and built in 1909 at the northwest corner of Nassau Street, the tower may be described as "neo-Gothic chic." In 1978 the building was converted from offices into apartments.

LILLY, THE
119 Washington Place

A six-story early twentieth-century building.

LINCOLN

Abraham Lincoln (1809–1865), sixteenth president of the United States, was born in Kentucky and first rose to political fame in the Midwest; from 1847 to 1849 he served in Congress as representative from Illinois. After being defeated by Stephen Douglas for the U.S. Senate in 1858, Lincoln emerged as a contender for the Republican presidential candidacy in the elections of 1860.

The candidate delivered a speech at the Cooper Union in New York on 27 February 1860 that received wide attention and was instrumental in securing him the nomination at the Chicago convention. His speech in the Great Hall of the Union included the famous passage "Let us have faith that right makes might, and in that faith let us to the end dare to do our duty as we understand it," but it was on this occasion that the New York Times *dismissed him as "a lawyer that has some local reputation in Illinois."*

A year later Lincoln as president-elect and Mrs. Lincoln visited the city and were officially welcomed by the mayor. The Lincolns concluded a long day by hearing Verdi's new opera Un Ballo in Maschera *at the Academy of Music.*

After Lincoln's assassination his funeral cortege passed through New York on the way to Springfield, Illinois, where he was buried.

LINCOLN, THE   *306–310 West 51st Street*

Now more of a hotel, *The Lincoln* was built in 1907 (C. B. Meyers, architect).

The four- to six-room apartments rented initially for $600 to $900 annually.

Near the *Jefferson* and the *Washington*.

LINCOLN HOUSES (NYC Housing Authority)   *2142 Madison Avenue*

This 1948 Harlem housing project stretches from Park to Fifth avenues, from East 132nd Street to East 135th. There are 1,286 apartments in its 14 buildings.

LINCOLN PLAZA HOTEL   *140 West 69th Street*

See *Spencer Arms Hotel*.

LINCOLN PLAZA TOWERS   *44 West 62nd Street*
(corner Columbus Avenue)

An unusual thirty-story building, each floor with bay windows and dish-shaped balconies built of unfinished brick.

It stands next door to the Sofia Brothers, Inc., warehouse at 47 Columbus Avenue, one of the Art Deco landmarks of New York City. In 1983 plans to convert the Sofia building into apartments were announced.

LINCOLN SQUARE   *201 West 74th Street*
(northeast corner Broadway)

This 1920s fifteen-story redbrick building, recently renovated, is a "home for adults."

LINCOLN TOWERS   *West 66th to West 70th streets,*
Amsterdam Avenue to Freedom Place

Between Lincoln Center and the Old West Side rail terminus at the Hudson River, several housing projects were erected in the 1960s as part of the area's slum clearance program. The largest project was a Title I middle-class housing complex called *Lincoln Towers*. Containing some four thousand apartment units, *Lincoln Towers* was, recalled its developer William Zeckendorf in his autobiography, "the largest project we ever built. Our financial backer in this venture was Lazard Freres, and this . . . had regrettable results. Lazard Freres, aware of our exceeding our original budget at Kips Bay, was determined to keep costs down and profits at a maximum for this next development. . . . Lincoln Towers could have been one of the wonders of Manhattan, but this was not to be. When these towers are torn down, no one will mourn their passing."

Well, no one, that is, except the tenants who enjoy exceptionally comfortable, if not architecturally exciting, apartments at very nice rents.

The *Lincoln Towers* residents have an exceptionally strong and well-organized tenants' organization, headed for years by Shirley Quill, widow of the legendary Mike Quill, the outspoken head of the New York City transit workers' union. When the complex's management tried to install meters in the apartments and cease including the cost of electricity in the rents, ten thousand people showed up at a rally. Political support was forthcoming, and the meter proposal was withdrawn.

"I organized things . . . like a union," said Mrs. Quill to a *New York Times* reporter, "with each building like a department in a company, with its own building representative . . . and with floor captains."

LINCOLN-AMSTERDAM HOUSE
110 West End Avenue
(West 64 to West 65th streets)

Designed in 1976 by David Todd & Assocs., this reddish-orange brick building has extraordinary views across the nearby Hudson River.

LINDLEY HOUSE *123 East 37th Street*

A 1940s–1950s building.
The Lindley family was prominent in colonial New York.
See *Murray Hill*.

LIONEL HAMPTON HOUSES
West 130th to West 131st streets,
St. Nicholas Avenue to
Frederick Douglass Boulevard

A complex of low- and high-rise apartment buildings dating from circa 1974. Bond Ryder Associates were the architects.

Lionel Hampton (b. 1913) formed his own band in 1934, joined Benny Goodman in 1936, and is considered one of the most important contemporary jazz musicians.

He once lived at 337 West 138th Street.

"LITTLE ITALY APARTMENTS" *21 Spring Street*

An uninspired redbrick building, without any discernible architectural style, erected in 1982–1983 on a long-vacant plot of ground.

The building was sponsored by the community organization known as LIRA (for Little Italy Restoration Association).

LLOYD COURT
200 West 109th Street
(southwest corner Amsterdam Avenue)

An early six-story building.

LO RUTH TERRACE *216 East 28th Street*

An enigmatic name for this rehabilitated tenement sporting a new brick facade.

LOMBARDY *111 East 56th Street*

A neo-Veneto-Byzantine residential hotel of the 1920s.
Lombardy is a region in northern Italy whose capital is Milan.

LONDON HOUSE *420 East 80th Street*

A tan-brick structure opened in 1960 and named for the owners, the London family. Very 1950s marquee, almost a period piece.

LONDON TERRACE
23rd to 24th streets,
Ninth to Tenth avenues

Few residential buildings in New York sit on more historic land than this enormous complex of fourteen buildings containing over sixteen hundred apartments. The site once belonged to the family of Benjamin Moore, who was president of Columbia

London Terrace, *north side of West 23rd Street, looking west from Ninth Avenue in 1927 just prior to the demolition of the entire block to make way for the mammoth apartment house of the same name. This row of Greek Revival houses was built in 1845 by Clement C. Moore and named after a typical row of houses in London.*

(1801–1811), and one of the prominent New Yorkers of his day. In 1845 eighty row houses were constructed on the site by the architect Alexander J. Davis in imitation of the houses on terraces in London, hence the name.

When the houses were torn down in the 1920s, they were replaced by the present *London Terrace* built by Henry Mandel, who also built the *Parc Vendome* on West 57th Street. The cornerstone came from an old house of the Moore family and was laid in 1929 by a fifteen-year-old descendant of Benjamin Moore and his son Clement Clarke, author of *A Visit from St. Nicholas.*

When the building opened in 1930, it was one of the first to have staggered leases. Before that, most New York City apartment leases ran from October to October. At the opening three and a half rooms rented for $100 to $110, a studio for $70 to $75.

The building has an Olympic-sized swimming pool where the Billy Rose Aquacade, hit of the 1939 world's fair, was rehearsed. In the early days the doormen, dressed in London policemen's uniforms, were called out each morning by bugle and drilled in the courtyard before going on duty.

In 1932 the builder Mandel went bankrupt, and in 1934 *London Terrace* itself followed. In 1945 ten of the buildings were sold. Called *London Terrace Gardens,* these buildings contain about a thousand apartments and face on West 23rd and West 24th streets. The corner buildings, containing about seven hundred units, are called *London Terrace Towers.*

London Terrace. *This photograph circa 1930 shows a typical apartment's entrance hall and kitchen.*

LONGACRE HOUSE   *317 West 45th Street*

A residential hotel for women.

Longacre Square was the name of what is now Times Square until 1904. Longacre is also the name of a street in London's West End theater district.

LORAINE   *527 West 135th Street*

Turn-of-the-century.

LORRAINE, THE   *401 West 44th Street*

A nineteenth-century building of four stories, now painted red.

LOSSIE   *114 East 91st Street*

A five-story redbrick and brownstone apartment house of circa 1890; nicely restored, with original stoop.

LOTTA   *1961 Adam Clayton Powell, Jr., Boulevard*
                (northeast corner West 118th Street)

A five-story circa-1900 building with unusual bayed windows; now painted ochre. In the ground floor is the Three-Eyed Shrimp restaurant.

LOUIS PHILIPPE   *312–320 West 23rd Street*

The namesake of this four-story 1940s residence was king of France from 1830 until 1848.

Born in 1773, Louis Philippe sympathized with the revolutionaries but fled France during Napoléon's reign. He traveled to the United States and spent some time in New York City, from 1796 to 1800.

He was called the Citizen King because of his espousal of democratic ideals.

LOUISE   *100 West 85th Street*
                                    (southwest corner Columbus Avenue)

A circa-1900 very narrow redbrick building of five stories with turreted corners.

Gustave Charpentier's opera *Louise,* described as a paean to a city—Paris—was first performed in 1900. In 1908 Oscar Hammerstein presented *Louise* in New York City for the first time, with Mary Garden in the title role.

LOUISE   *250 West 112th Street*

Abandoned.

LOUISIANA   *507 West 113th Street*

An eight-story turn-of-the-century building of red brick, with a limestone base; some decor has been removed from the cornice.

Matches the *Illinois* at 511 and the *Michigan* at 517 West 113th Street. Around the corner were the Tennessee and the Arizona.

LOWELL, THE   *28 East 63rd Street*

This 1926 apartment house—residential hotel was designed by Herbert Lippman and Henry S. Churchill in the Art Deco style.

The tiled ground-floor facade has a mosaic over the door.

Long known as a chic address for rich out-of-towners keeping a small apartment in the city, who dined at the Passy restaurant downstairs.

LOYAL   *894 Riverside Drive*
                                    (southeast corner West 161st Street)

Stone Tudor roses and the gridiron commemorating the martyrdom of Saint Lawrence ornament the facade of this six-story tan-brick building of circa 1900; now dilapidated and partly boarded up.

LOYOLA   *477 Central Park West*
                              (southwest corner West 108th Street)

A five-story building; circa 1900.
Saint Ignatius Loyola (1491–1556) was founder of the Jesuit order.

LUCERNE   *505 West 143rd Street*

Six stories built on central-court plan by Neville & Bagge, architects; with pillared windows. Dates from 1906.
Lucerne is the name of a canton, city, and lake in Switzerland.

Lucerne Hotel. *The West 79th Street entrance has been modernized and a marquee added since this photograph was taken early in the century.*

LUCERNE HOTEL   *201 West 79th Street*
                              (northwest corner Amsterdam Avenue)

This brownstone and brick building is one of the Upper West Side's landmarks. Built in 1904—Harry B. Mulliken, architect—it is rich in grand details including, for example, a laughing mask over the service entrance on the Amsterdam Avenue side. The extraordinary columns flanking the entrance seem to derive from a Hollywood vision of an ancient temple. They are unfortunately now almost concealed by a later metal marquee, and the entire building is grimy and ill maintained. Nevertheless, the richness of its color and grandly conceived decoration make it a favorite stop for sightseers.

Lucerne Hotel. *This handsome roundel with carved mask was probably once a window over the service entrance on Amsterdam Avenue, now a vent clogged with debris.*

LUCETINE   *35 West 96th Street*

An eight-stories-and-basement building of white brick. Built in 1908 by Lawlor & Hasse, with apartments on the H-plan. Recently renovated, with a new canopy; well maintained.

LUCILLE   *122 West 114th Street*
(southeast corner St. Nicholas Avenue)

Abandoned and boarded up.

LUCILLE   *30–36 Sickles Street*

A six-story tan-brick building; circa 1920s.

LUCILLE   *525 West 135th Street*

Turn-of-the-century.

LUSITANIA COURT   *402–410 West 148th Street*

Built in 1907—Neville & Bagge, architects, E. M. Krulewitch, builder—*Lusitania Court* has six stories and basement. Krulewitch was also the builder of *The Sadivian Arms, Simna Hall,* and *Marimpol Court,* all of which still exist.

The open-court entrance has been modernized, but the elaborate original cornice is in place.

Lusitania was the Roman name for the region including Portugal and a portion of Spain. The enormous British passenger ship of the same name was sunk by German submarines in 1915 resulting in the loss of American lives, which was a major factor in the U.S. decision to enter World War I on the Allied side.

LUXOR, THE
600 West 115th Street
(southwest corner Broadway)

A twelve-stories-and-basement building of the 1920s. An elaborate metal canopy carries the initials *BD,* which also are chiseled on a cartouche above the door.

Luxor is the town on the Nile in upper Egypt, noted for its ancient ruins.

LYCEUM
35 Grove Street

Three tenements put together with a uniform pediment. The mustard-yellow brick is trimmed with brownstone and has delicate terra-cotta decoration. Dignified marble columns flank the front entrance, and the original fire escapes have been preserved. There is a handsome vestibule and a door with wrought-iron decoration.

A lyceum (from the Greek) is a building or hall where lectures are given. The word was extremely popular in the nineteenth century when attending lectures was a major amusement.

LYDEN GARDENS
215 East 64th Street

A redbrick building of the 1970s, across the street from the Manhattan Eye, Ear & Throat Hospital.

LYDEN HOUSE HOTEL
320 East 53rd Street

An apartment hotel in a handsome brick building of the 1930s.

LYDIA APARTMENTS
476 West 141st Street

New entrance to a five-story Broadway building on a block of beautiful private houses.

Lydia was an ancient kingdom of Asia Minor, closely allied to Greece and, later, Persia. Its last independent ruler was the fabulously wealth Croesus.

LYNDHURST
78 West 82nd Street

Lyndhurst is the name of the former Jay Gould estate on the Hudson, now the property of the National Trust for Historic Preservation.

[See *Colorado.*]

LYRIC, THE   *352 West 46th Street*

A large six-story building of circa 1904; George F. Pelham, architect. When new, four-to-seven-room apartments rented at $540 to $900 a year. The name is chiseled on the porch.

Originally known as the *Lansdown*.

M. MORAN WESTON COMMUNITY
APARTMENTS   *123 West 135th Street*

A series of small six-story brick buildings put together and renovated.

The sponsor of the project is St. Philip's Church (Protestant Episcopal), founded in 1810 and now standing on West 134th Street. The church purchased this row of buildings when the congregation moved uptown in 1910.

MACOMBS LANE   *29–31 Macombs Place*

A six-story turn-of-the-century building of red and buff brick.

Alexander Macomb, one of the American commanders during the War of 1812, lived at this site. His son operated a mill by damming the Harlem River at what is now Jerome Avenue and West 161st Street.

MCKENNA SQUARE HOME
                                       2103–2105 Amsterdam Avenue

Turn-of-the-century houses on the corner of West 166th Street, now being renovated.

MCKINLEY   *63 Perry Street*

A six-stories-and-basement building of the turn of the century with its name chiseled into the porch; each window with floral corbel; decorative fire escapes.

Named for William McKinley (1843–1901), twenty-fifth president of the United States (1897–1901); assassinated while attending the Pan-American Exposition at Buffalo, New York.

MCKINLEY   *111 East 7th Street*

Seven-story brick and limestone building of the late nineteenth century. Columns flank the windows on two floors.

[MADISON AVENUE HOSPITAL]
                                       30 East 76th Street

This redbrick 1920s building, formerly a private hospital, was converted to a cooperative apartment circa 1980—alas, without a name!

MADISON COURT   *1361 Madison Avenue*
                                 (northeast corner East 95th Street)

A well-maintained circa 1900 building of red brick above a
gray rusticated base; handsome pillared entrance.

Like so many buildings with "Court" in their names, this
one has a large central atrium-type court, surrounded on all four
sides by the building itself.

MADISON GREEN   *5 East 22nd Street*
                                 (southeast corner Broadway)

For eighty years the Flatiron Building dominated the skyline
of Madison Square South—until *Madison Green* was erected in
1982–1983, a tower of 425 balconied condominium apartments
topping the Flatiron and invading its "space."

The site was once occupied by the Bartholdi Hotel and the
ʼurtz Photographic Studios, where the American Art Associa-
on, forerunner of Sotheby Parke Bernet, had its galleries.

Madison Green takes its name from its commanding position
overlooking the trees of Madison Square which goes from East
23rd Street to East 26th Street and is bounded on the east by
the towers of insurance company headquarters built where the
original Madison Square Garden stood.

This was the site of one of the worst fires in New York's history: twelve firemen died fighting a blaze on the spot in 1966.

MADRID   *552 Riverside Drive*

A white-brick six-stories-and-basement building with fire escapes; circa 1900.

MAGNOLIA   *240 West 102nd Street*
                                 (southwest corner Broadway)

A circa-1900 six-story building with fire escapes and a classical entrance.

MAJESTIC   *63–65 Second Avenue*

A six-story elevator apartment building of the 1920s; the
ground floor was renovated with wood.

MAJESTIC
                2228–2230 Adam Clayton Powell, Jr., Boulevard

A six-story building in the manner of the architect George
F. Pelham.

MAJESTIC   *680–684 St. Nicholas Avenue*
                                 (southeast corner West 145th Street)

A seven-and-eight-story building, the number of floors varying with the hilly topography.

One entrance on St. Nicholas has been bricked up. There is
another at 356 West 145th Street.

Majestic. *When built circa 1900, this was the first building on the block. The photograph shows the building circa 1922.*

MAJESTIC APARTMENTS, THE
115 Central Park West (southwest corner West 72nd Street)

"The objective of the designers of the Majestic Apartments was to create a type of residence which would solve to the greatest possible degree the complexities—physical, psychological and social—of modern New York life."

So began the 1931 promotional brochure issued by the Chanin Organization for its newest venture, *The Majestic*—so named because it occupied the site of the old Hotel Majestic, built circa 1893 as a healthful uptown resort, a "house of good will" with a garden on the roof "overlooking fairyland," that is, Central Park.

By the late 1920s the idea of demolishing the by now out-of-date hotel took shape, and in 1929 the Chanins bought the property for $16 million and announced plans for a grand building with apartments of from eleven to twenty-four rooms.

The economic collapse brought about by the Crash of '29 caused these initial plans to be reconsidered, and in the summer of 1930 a new plan was unveiled—for a twin-towered apartment house with suites of three to fourteen rooms in the sleek Art Moderne style designed to take full advantage of the Central Park location. Work began on the redesigned building, with

Bruno Hauptman, later executed for the kidnapping and death of the Charles Lindbergh baby, among the many carpenters employed on the project. One of the legends of *The Majestic* is that part of the Lindbergh ransom money is hidden under the floorboards.

Cantilevered corner solaria, casement windows, and lots of terraces reinforced *The Majestic*'s promise: "thirty stories of sunshine."

But despite the location and the luxury, *The Majestic* was not a financial success. It went bankrupt in 1933, and vacancies were as common as notorious tenants (among them, Meyer Lansky and Lucky Luciano; Frank Costello was the target of an attempted assassination in the lobby of *The Majestic* in 1957).

In 1957 *The Majestic* became a cooperative and has since become a bastion of brokers, lawyers, bankers, and entrepreneurs with only the occasional entertainment figure (Milton Berle, Ted Lewis, Walter Winchell).

Today *The Majestic* remains one of New York's great apartment houses—still luxurious and aging gracefully more than half a century since its first tenants moved into what was then described as "a fine home distinguished by a name which already has symbolized luxurious living for more than a third of a century."

When letters are sent to residents with the address on the envelope merely saying "Majestic Apartments," they arrive.

M A K S E N   *472 West 147th Street*
                                (southeast corner Amsterdam Avenue)

A five-story salmon-brick building with limestone trim; circa 1900.

M A N C H E S T E R   *255 West 108th Street*
                                    (northeast corner Broadway)

A pre–World War I twelve-story white-brick building with an air shaft in the center; now being converted to a cooperative.

M A N C H E S T E R   *512 West 151st Street*

A seven-story building of brick and limestone; circa 1900. The cornice has been removed.

A twin to the *Marlborough*.

M A N C H E S T E R   H O U S E   *145 West 79th Street*

A building of the 1920s faced with irregular variegated stonework; has a fine coat of arms carved over the entrance.

M A N D E L   C O U R T   *920–926 Riverside Drive*
                                (northeast corner West 162nd Street)

A redbrick neo-Georgian building of the 1930s; six stories.

The Mandel interests were large builders in New York during the 1920s and 1930s, putting up *London Terrace* among other buildings.

MANHASSET, THE   301 West 108th Street
                                         300 West 109th Street

The Manhasset was built in 1904 on the west side of Broadway between West 108th and West 109th streets by Janes &
Leo, architects. Walter Reid and Co. were the builders. The
eleven-story building of salmon brick, gray brick, and limestone, with a two-story mansard roof, has no two stories the
same. At the time it was opened, annual rents were $1,800 to
$3,500.
   Manhasset Bay is an inlet of Long Island Sound as well as a
town on Long Island.

MANHATTAN

Hendrik Hudson is believed to have brought the name to Europe
from his voyage of 1609. It first occurs in writing on the Velasco
map of 1610 where it is written "Manahatin." Much ink has
been spilled over the origin of the name, but it seems clear that it
was taken from the Indian tribe that inhabited the island when
Hudson arrived. On the Velasco map they appear as the
Manahata.
   Throughout the seventeenth century there was confusion among
geographers and map makers as to the proper spelling of the name:
"Manhates," "Manhath," "Manatans," are just a few of the
variants. By the end of the century the name had pretty much
settled into the present form.
   Once contiguous with New York City, the island of Man-
hattan became the borough of Manhattan and the county of New
York within the consolidated city of 1898.

MANHATTAN   255 West 22nd Street

   A handsomely ornamented turn-of-the-century building. Six
stories, a basement with an iron fence before it, and a fire escape. The name is over a door flanked by columns.

MANHATTAN   244 East 86th Street

   An 1880s six-story redbrick building that still has its flag-
pole on the roof.

MANHATTAN COURT *16 Manhattan Avenue*
(southeast corner West 101st Street)

A turn-of-the-century building with center court; George F. Pelham, architect. Rents at the time it opened ranged from $500 to $1,000 annually.

MANHATTAN EAST *315 East 65th Street*

Another 1960s white-brick residence—this one with minimal landscaping.

MANHATTAN HOUSE *200 East 66th Street*

While the Third Avenue El still rattled along on its way to the Bronx, the farsighted New York Life Insurance Company tore down the old car barns in the block between East 65th and East 66th streets, and Third to Second avenues, and broke ground for *Manhattan House* (1950), a twenty-story luxury apartment building. By the time the el was torn down, *Manhattan House* stood—gleaming white and festooned with Bauhaus-type balconies—dominating the far East Side on the verge of its building boom.

Designed by Skidmore, Owings & Merrill, with Mayer & Whittlesey, the building attracted a solid group of tenants right from the start owing to its convenient location and good security.

The original rentals seem ludicrously reasonable now: a seven-room apartment went for $590 to $625 per month, gas and electricity included. The original brochure stressed the ownership and management by New York Life, as well as the solaria, gardens, lounges, and cross-ventilation (this was, after all, still in the pre-air-conditioning era). A mural by Attilio Salemne adorned the lobby, and the owner-developer bought the row of tenements on the north side of East 66th Street and renovated them, thus making the street a very pleasant one as well as insuring the views of *Manhattan House*'s tenants who are still, obviously, a very solid group: William H. Whyte, in his introduction to the recently reissued *WPA Guide to New York City* (1982), points out that *Manhattan House* has the greatest concentration of people listed in the Social Register of any building in the borough.

MANHATTAN PLAZA *400 West 43rd Street*
(between Eighth and Ninth avenues)

This 1970s federally subsidized project of seventeen hundred units has a tenant population that is primarily drawn from show business. Tennessee Williams, for example, had an apartment here.

The towers are far more attractive in design than most such large complexes. The tenants enjoy a health club, a racquet club, and other amenities.

MANHATTAN PLAZA   66–68 East 4th Street

A five-story building of circa 1900, with iron balconies and its original cornice.

MANHATTAN SQUARE STUDIOS
44 West 77th Street

Some of the Gothic detail has been removed from the facade of this cathedral-like building to reduce the hazard of falling stone, but enough remains to make it one of the most distinctive apartment buildings in the city.

Built in 1909—Harde & Short were the architects—as a cooperative; it was, as were so many buildings, later converted to rental; however, in 1970 it became a cooperative again.

When it opened, there were two apartments on each of its fourteen floors; the apartments had eleven or twelve rooms and three or four baths. The largest studio on the top floor measures twenty-five feet by forty-four, with an eighteen-foot ceiling!

The lower floor of the building was connected with the Hotel Manhattan Square next door west, and hotel service could be provided.

Manhattan Square is bounded by West 77th and West 81st streets, Central Park West, and Columbus Avenue. It was acquired by the city in the mid-nineteenth century and set aside for the American Museum of Natural History, the cornerstone of which was laid in 1874.

MANHATTAN TOWERS   2166 Broadway

[See The Opera.]

MANHATTANVILLE HOUSES (NYC
Housing Authority)   545 West 126th Street

This six-building project, built in 1961, derives its name from the early village of Manhattanville, which existed in this area from 1806 until it was swallowed up by the advance of New York City in the mid-nineteenth century.

Manhattan College (now in the Bronx) and Manhattanville College (now in Westchester) both were first located in the formerly sylvan Manhattanville area.

MANHILL APARTMENTS   222 West 83rd Street
(southeast corner Broadway)

A fourteen-story tan-brick building; 1920s.

MANITOU   143 West 111th Street

Abandoned.

The Indian word for the "Great Spirit"—akin to "God" or "Jehovah"; the name is given to hills, and other places where the Indians believed the Great Spirit dwelt (e.g., near Anthony's Nose on the Hudson River).

MANNADOS   *17 East 97th Street*

Built in 1905 by Schwartz & Gross, with a central court and porch entrance, this apartment house adjoins the Russian Orthodox Cathedral and has stores on the Madison Avenue ground-floor level.

Original rents were $1,000 to $1,500 annually.

"Mannados" was one of the several names for Manhattan Island in the seventeenth century.

MANOR   *400 East 63rd Street*

An old tenement with stores; renovated and painted and given a name, still faintly visible in silver paint over the new (1960s) entrance.

The name is Old French for "dwelling."

MANOR, THE   *333 East 43rd Street*

An appropriate name for one of the handsome Tudoresque components of *Tudor City*. This was the second unit completed, containing mostly small apartments for "young married couples who entertain a bit in their own charming homes . . . older people who take life easily . . . girls in groups of two or three who find they can create a desirable background for themselves on what is truly a minimum expenditure when they divide it up."

MANSFIELD   *567 West 149th Street*
                                                 (northeast corner Broadway)

This six-story building opened in 1907; J. Hauser was the architect. The apartments were described as "well arranged around a central court" and ran from five to seven rooms each at a cost of $600 to $1,000 yearly.

MANSION HOUSE   *525 East 82nd Street*

Plain white brick; 1960s.

Named for its proximity to Gracie Mansion, the New York equivalent of London's Mansion House, official residence of that city's Lord Mayor.

MANSIONETTES OF 1935, THE
                    210, 215, 220, 225, 230, 235 East 73rd Street

No, this isn't the name of a Broadway revue, it's the original name of a group of handsome redbrick apartment buildings on both sides of East 73rd Street between Third and Second avenues. When the fifth and last building of the group, number 235 East 73rd Street, was completed, the promotional brochure trumpeted: "Looking with confidence to the future, Bing & Bing, Inc., is proud to present a new residential building for those who have come to know that they need not sacrifice luxury in small apartments. We have created a unique and charming neighborhood on this pleasant street in the fashionable East Seventies. It has provided addresses of which its tenants may be proud. It has furnished homes in which they may enjoy every comfort. With the creation of this new building, more of these luxury homes—The Mansionettes of 1935—become available."

The message was loud and clear: people who in better days were used to living in mansions or large luxury apartments, but had to make do with more modest accommodations, thanks to the depression, were welcome to live in those "little mansions" on East 73rd Street.

And today the complex still provides a charming ambience for the block. The rents have gone up over the years, but today's tenants still value the "features which have made the Bing & Bing Mansionettes so popular: sunken living rooms, ornamental railings . . . supersize closets . . . radio outlets . . . built in hampers."

After almost half a century *The Mansionettes of 1935* are still playing to full houses!

MARBLE HILL
2 Marble Hill Avenue
(northeast corner West 225th Street)

A six-story white-brick building of the 1920s.

Marble Hill—an English approximation-translation of the Indian name for the area—formed part of Manhattan Island until 1895, when the course of the Harlem River was changed to allow navigation, thus putting Marble Hill physically in the Bronx. Politically it remains part of Manhattan.

MARBLE HILL HOUSES (NYC Housing Authority)
5220 Broadway

This 1952 project of almost seventeen hundred apartments is named for the neighborhood whose skyline it dominates.

MARBLE HILL VIEW
1 Marble Hill Avenue
(northwest corner West 225th Street)

A six-story building of the 1920s, with an open-court entrance.

MARBORO
171 West 79th Street

A plain fifteen-story building of the 1920s.

The name is one of the variants of the British ducal title Marlborough.

MARC ANTONY, THE
514 Cathedral Parkway

Built in 1911; Schwartz & Gross, architects; Paterno Construction Company, builders. A three-story brick building with stone base and open front court.

As with many of the Paterno buildings, the name commemorates a famous Italian: Mark Anthony (Marcus Antonius), circa 83–30 B.C., Roman orator, triumvir, and soldier.

Twin to the *Prince Humbert.*

MARGARET   *120 West 116th Street*

Abandoned.

MARIE   *61–69 East 86th Street*

A handsome and extremely well kept circa-1900 apartment building of seven stories, with a two-story limestone base and entranceway below five stories in tan brick; original bronze light at entrance.

MARIMPOL COURT   *521 West 122nd Street*

Built by Benster & Benster.
Twin to *Simna Hall* at 515, but it's lost its pediment.

MARION   *2612 Broadway*
(between West 98th and West 99th streets)

A nine-story building of circa 1900.

MARION   *221–223–225 West 105th Street*

Three seven-story turn-of-the-century buildings united by a joint pediment on which the name is emblazoned.

MARION   *100 St. Nicholas Avenue*
(northeast corner West 115th Street)

A seven-story brick building with fire escapes; distinguished by a series of strange ornaments on the roof that look like the prows of Viking ships.

MARION, THE   *517–519 West 180th Street*

This well-maintained building is a twin to the less well-kept *Hennion* next door.

[MARION FAHNSTOCK TRAINING SCHOOL]   *304 East 20th Street*

In its recent conversion to residential use this circa-1910 institutional building did not have the original name eradicated completely—it is still visible over the columned portico.

MARJORIE   *245 West 113th Street*

A twin to the *Teresa.*

MARK TWAIN
100 West 12th Street
(southwest corner Avenue of the Americas)

A six-story low-rise redbrick building of the late 1950s or the 1960s.

Mark Twain lived in New York at various periods in his life; his last residence was at 21 Fifth Avenue, the site of which is now marked by a plaque.

Marlborough. *A portrait of John Churchill first Duke of Marlborough (1650–1722) by Sir Godfrey Kneller.*

MARLBOROUGH
518 West 151st Street

A twin to the *Manchester.*

John Churchill, the great English general, was created duke of Marlborough in 1702, and his descendants have borne the title since. Their country house, Blenheim Palace, is one of the greatest private residences ever built. Marlborough House in Pall Mall was their London residence.

MARLBOROUGH HOUSE
245 East 40th Street

A huge balconied tower that has the distinction of being the headquarters of *New York* magazine (entrance on Second Avenue).

The lobby's crystal chandelier attempts to capture some of the splendor associated with the name Marlborough.

MARLO TOWERS
301 East 48th Street

The facade of this typical 1960s building is brightened by an abstract mural by William Bond. The inaugural brochure mentioned "the classic entrance with its distinctive cantilevered marquee" and, in the apartments themselves, "vanity alcoves for madame."

MARLTON HOTEL   *5 West 8th Street*

An eight-story apartment building of circa 1900, now a hotel.

MARSHALL   *117 West 15th Street*

A five-story brownstone with the name chiseled on the lintel; now being restored.

MARTHA   *169 West 81st Street*

Forms a group with its matching neighbors to the west—the *Prague* and the *Elliot*; each one a five-story turn-of-the-century building with rusticated ground floor and arched doorway.

MARTHA   *200 West 84th Street*
(southwest corner Amsterdam Avenue)

A six-story turn-of-the-century building of light brick and stone.

MARTIN LUTHER KING, JR., TOWERS
(NYC Housing Authority)   *90 Lenox Avenue*

This Harlem project of 1954 was later named to honor the memory of Dr. Martin Luther King, Jr., after his assassination in Memphis in 1968. Dr. King, born in 1929, achieved world-wide fame by his fearless leadership of the civil rights movement of the 1960s.

MARY LOUISE, THE   *19 East 65th Street*

Scott & Prescott were the architects for this small-scale, red-brick nine-story apartment house of the 1920s.

The name is over the door in Gothic script; next to Rita Ford Music Boxes in the ground floor commercial space.

MARYLAND   *201 West 105th Street*
(northwest corner Amsterdam Avenue)

A nondescript six-story turn-of-the-century building with fire escapes.

[MARYMOUNT MANHATTAN
APARTMENTS]   *220 East 72nd Street*

A huge mixed-use tower built in the 1970s on the original site of a row of brownstones owned by Marymount Manhattan College (on East 71st Street). The college occupies the first four floors, and the residential area is above—a neat solution in a handsome package.

MASARYK TOWERS   *81 Columbia Street*

A middle-income cooperative of the 1960s, originally priced at $3,000 for a two-bedroom apartment with balcony, with maintenance charges of $140 to $160 per month. The complex has its own library, school, and indoor pool.

Tomáš Masaryk (1850–1937) was the first president of Czechoslovakia, in office from 1918 to 1935. His wife was an American. Their son Jan (1886–1948) was a leader of the Czech government in exile during World War II.

MASCOT FLATS   *East 6th Street*
                                           (between Avenues C and D)

Abandoned, and with its street address number no longer visible, *Mascot Flats* is symbolic of what's happened to so many buildings in this Lower East Side area.

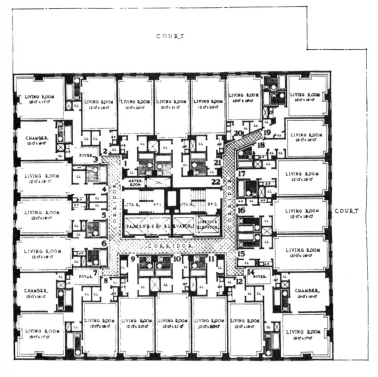

Master Apartment Hotel. *A typical floor plan for the late 1920s apartment-hotel showing twenty-two mostly one-room units off an H-shaped corridor. Note the small "pullman" kitchenettes, denoted here by the letters "S.P." (service pantry).*

MASTER APARTMENTS, THE   *310 Riverside Drive*
(northeast corner West 103rd Street)

Few apartment buildings in New York City have had a stranger origin than this stunning Art Deco masterpiece. Louis and Netti Horch, whose large fortune came from foreign exchange dealings, commissioned the twenty-nine-story building in 1929 from the architects Helmle, Corbett & Harrison and Sugarman & Berger. The Horches were under the influence of Nicholas Roerich, an emigré Russian artist who was an ardent Theosophist.

The building was to house the Master Institute, which was dedicated to Theosophical studies and to Roerich's own brand of spiritualism; the Roerich Museum, which held only paintings by Roerich; and the Corona Mundi Art Center. The unusual color scheme of the building's facade is directly related to the Roerich philosophy: it fades from purple brick at the bottom to blue and then to gray at the top to symbolize heavenly aspirations. The building's name refers to the Theosophical masters resident in Tibet, with whom Roerich, by his own account, was in constant communication.

In the early 1930s the building was the scene of great activity in the arts, but in 1935 the Horches parted ways with Roerich and transformed the lower floors of the building into the Riverside Museum. Roerich, whom the U.S. government suspected of being a Soviet agent, was convicted of tax fraud and fled to Russia, where he died in 1948.

In recent years the building has housed the Equity Library Theatre, which does revivals of plays and musicals.

MATILDA   *310 West 95th Street*

A circa-1900 seven-stories-and-basement building.

MAX MELTZER TOWER (NYC Housing Authority)   *94 East 1st Street*

This 1971 building is named for New York's Judge Max Meltzer.

MAYFAIR FIFTH   *96 Fifth Avenue*

A terra-cotta and white-brick 1960s building whose name conjures up visions of London's most fashionable residential area—located in the Borough of Westminster—so called because from ancient times until 1708 a popular fair was held there each May.

MAYFAIR 14th   *145 Park Avenue South*

A 1963 high-rise apartment house.

MAYFAIR HOUSE   *610 Park Avenue*
                                  (southwest corner East 65th Street)

A fifteen-story apartment hotel of 1925, J. E. R. Carpenter, architect.

This has long been a favorite of the carriage trade.

MAYFAIR MIDTOWN   *301 East 69th Street*
                                  (northeast corner Second Avenue)

A 1963 building of white brick with orange trim typical of apartment houses erected by the Mayfair group around Manhattan in the 1960s.

MAYFAIR SOUTH   *340 East 34th Street*

Built in 1961, this apartment house was designed by Leo Stillman and advertised rents of $68 per room (including gas and electricity) when it first opened.

Across the street at 333 East 34th Street is a sister building, Mayfair North.

MAYFAIR TOWERS   *15 West 72nd Street*

Built in 1963 and notable in its time as one of the first high-rise luxury buildings to be put up on the West Side in many years. *Mayfair Towers* was built on the former site of its next-door neighbor's—that is, *The Dakota's*—rose garden and generating plant that later was its parking lot.

MAYFAIR–207   *207 East 74th Street*

A 1960s white-brick building.

MAYFIELD   *15 East 10th Street*

A fine redbrick and limestone building in the collegiate Georgian style of the 1920s; six stories; now a cooperative.

MAYFLOWER   *245 East 87th Street*
                                  (northwest corner Second Avenue)

A 1960s–1970s apartment house with sunken entrance on Second Avenue. Converted to cooperative ownership in the 1980s, with two-bedroom apartments priced at $180,000.

MECKLENBURG, THE   *600 West 146th Street*
                                  (southwest corner Broadway)

A redbrick building with stone trim and windows coated with copper in contrasting green and red. Neville & Bagge were the architects in 1906.

Mecklenburg was the name of two grand duchies in the old

German Empire. The Mecklenburg Declaration, signed in Mecklenburg County, North Carolina, in 1775, was an early step in the American Revolution.

MEDFORD   *3900 Broadway*

A six-story white-brick building of the turn of the century, extending a full block along Broadway between West 163rd and West 164th streets.

Towns in Massachusetts, Oklahoma, Oregon, and Wisconsin are called Medford.

MEDINA, THE   *189 Claremont Avenue*

Built in 1906 on the central-court plan; F. S. Nute, architect, and J. O'Brien, builder. Six stories, with wrought-iron balconies on the second floor. Unusual geometric brickwork ornaments the top story and the keystone designs on the windows. Attractive arched entrance.

Medina, in Saudi Arabia, is one of the holy cities of Islam. Muhammad took refuge in Medina after his flight from Mecca in 622 and was buried in the mosque there.

Megantic's entrance is the doorway with a curved pediment: the glass-enclosed doorway is the "ladies' entrance" to James Cassidy's bar on the corner.

MEGANTIC   *201 East 30th Street*

This smallish building of six stories houses the Bank Cafe in its ground floor, but the rather elaborate entrance to the apartments is on East 30th Street. The name is above the door, but how this circa-1900 structure came to be named after a lake in Quebec remains a mystery.

MELBOURNE   *1295 Madison Avenue*

[See *Wales Hotel.*]

MELROSE   *480 Central Park West*
                                        (northwest corner West 108th Street)

A circa-1900 seven-story building with fire escape.
Melrose is a locality in Scotland containing what is generally considered the finest ruin in Scotland, an extremely ancient abbey.

MELVIN HALL   *56 Bennett Avenue*

A six-story building of the 1920s.

[MEMORIAL HOUSE]   *207 East 16th Street*

A 1983 conversion of a handsome stone structure built in 1887 as a gift to St. George's Protestant Episcopal Church (for use as a parish hall) from J. P. Morgan, a parishioner.

[MERCANTILE EXCHANGE BUILDING]
                                                      6 Harrison Street

This grand old building, dated 1884, was once the trading center for New York's butter and egg operations. Prices were based on output and other market conditions, and as many as seven million cases of eggs and three million tubs of butter changed hands each year, well into the 1930s.

In 1977 the disused Mercantile Exchange was purchased by Peter Gee and Paul Serra and renovated into fourteen residential units.

The building was subsequently sold to the Dia Art Foundation (a De Menil family foundation) and today houses artists and others involved in foundation-sponsored activities.

MERLEGH COURT   *274 Audubon Avenue*
                                        (southwest corner West 176th Street)

A six-story redbrick building; circa 1900.

METRO NORTH PLAZA   *310 East 102nd Street*

A 1976 urban renewal project adjoining the Vito Marcantonio School, these thirteen-story buildings are distinguished by the vertical pattern of the brickwork and the roughly textured surfaces of the lower stories, designed to discourage graffiti.

METROPOLITAN   *235–239 West 108th Street*

This six-story circa-1900 building has an open-court entrance.

MEYBERRY HOUSE   *220 East 63rd Street*

A white-brick, 1960s building designed by architect J. Riggio for a builder named *Meyer Ber*fond.

MEYERS' HOTEL   *116–119 South Street*

This handsome old brick Victorian edifice operated as a hotel and bar until a few years ago. Built in 1873 by John B. Snook at the southwest corner of South Street and Peck Slip and, 110 years later, converted into cooperative apartments.

MIAMI.   *519 West 121st Street*

Six stories and basement, with fire escapes; red brick with limestone trim; circa 1910.

Name with period is over the door. Opposite the Macy Manual Arts Building, one of the oldest buildings of Columbia University.

The name of several cities, counties, and rivers, which derives from the Indian tribe, now extinct, that originally inhabited what is now Indiana and Michigan.

MICHIGAN   *517 West 113th Street*

[See *Louisiana*.]

MIDDLETOWNE, THE   *148 East 48th Street*

Now the self-proclaimed—on its canopy—*Middletowne Hotel,* this structure dates from the 1920s.

MIDLOTHIAN   *353 West 117th Street*

This substantial six-stories-and-basement building has two bays on the street and visible fire escapes. Its name is written in stone scrollwork above the door.

A twin to the *Endymion* at 342 West 117th Street.

Midlothian is the county in Scotland of which Edinburgh is the seat. Sir Walter Scott's title *The Heart of Midlothian* refers to the Edinburgh jail.

MIDWAY HOTEL
216 West 100th Street
(southeast corner Broadway)

Formerly called the Allenhurst. A twelve-story building; the top two stories are decorated.

MILBURN COURT
65–71 Seaman Avenue
(northeast corner Academy Street)

A five-story redbrick building; 1920s.

MILDRED
217–219 West 111th Street

Abandoned.

MILL ROCK PLAZA
345 East 93rd Street

A 1970s thirty-story tower with an uninviting courtyard.

On 19 September 1700 one John Marsh requested permission "to build a mill on flowing Island near Hell Gate." This became known as Mill Rock, and during the War of 1812 it was used as a fortified gun emplacement to protect Manhattan from a possible British attack via Long Island Sound.

The site is now a park in the middle of the turbulent East River across from East 94th Street—visible, no doubt to the upper-floor residents of the *Mill Rock Plaza* apartments.

MILLER HALL
201 West 109th Street
(northwest corner Amsterdam Avenue)

A six-story building; a twin to *Irving Hall*. An entrance also at 998 Amsterdam Avenue.

MILTON
531 West 135th Street

John Milton (1608–1674), English poet and author of *Paradise Lost*.

MINERVA
357–363 West 118th Street

This fanciful Victorian building has seven stories and a double entrance.

Minerva was the Roman goddess of learning, called by the Greeks Athena.

MINERVA COURT
367 Wadsworth Avenue
(northeast corner West 191st Street)

A five-story building of the early 1920s.

MIRABEAU   *165 West 91st Street*
(northeast corner Amsterdam Avenue)

Large 1920s building of fifteen stories.

The Mirabeau family was prominent in France during the Revolution. One member, André, vicomte de Mirabeau, served in the American army from 1780 to 1785.

MIRAMAR   *452 Riverside Drive*

A nine-story white-brick building with armorial devices over the doorway and an open-court entrance; circa 1900.

MIRAMAR   *612 West 137th Street*

A twin to *El Morro.*

MODEL, THE   *48 Perry Street*

An "elegant, first-class building," according to a periodical of 1887; complete with marble, tiles.

[MODEL TENEMENTS]   *East 64th to East 65th streets,*
First to York avenues

Built on or near the site of the Colored Home, a nineteenth-century charitable organization founded in 1845. The present block of buildings was erected between 1900 and 1915 by the City and Suburban Homes Company, a group organized in 1896 to provide healthful and sanitary housing for working people. Their first project was on the West Side, and this East Side Model Tenement their second.

The buildings are now collectively known (at least internally) as "Stahl-York," after the present owner, Stahl–York Avenue Partners.

[MODEL TENEMENTS]   *East 78th to East 79th streets,*
York Avenue to FDR Drive

The contrast between this group of mostly quite plain buildings and the nearby *Cherokee* apartments is striking. Although a few of the individual buildings are blessed with open courts and a few interesting details of decoration, the general effect is rather bland.

When put up circa 1900 by the City and Suburban Homes Company, these were considered one of their finest accomplishments. At 520 East 79th Street is a plaque inscribed "To the memory of Henry Codman Potter, Bishop of New York, and in grateful recognition of his life of wisdom and courage and righteousness and service." The land on which these *Model Tenements* were erected was called the Protestant Episcopal School Tract on early maps, possibly explaining the involvement of Bishop Potter (1835–1908), noted social reformer and initiator of the plan to build the Cathedral of St. John the Divine on Morningside Heights.

MODERN   *40–42 West 127th Street*

A seven-story redbrick building; circa 1900.

MON BIJOU   *210–212 East 17th Street*

This late-nineteenth-century apartment house has Manhattan's most affectionate appellation chiseled over its pillared portico—*mon Bijou,* meaning "my jewel." Now *there* is pride of ownership!

MONMOUTH, THE   *2037 Adam Clayton Powell, Jr.,*
Boulevard

A twin to *The Larchmont.* Partly abandoned.

Monmouth is the name of counties in England and New Jersey.

MONT CENIS   *54 Morningside Drive*

A well-maintained six-story building with recessed fire escapes masked by masonry to give the effect of balconies. Schwartz & Gross were the architects.

This building matches *La Touraine.*

Mont Cenis (Monte Cenisio in Italian) is the historic pass over the Alps, traditionally the crossing point for Hannibal and his army. The Mont Cenis was the first tunnel through the Alps, opened in 1871. When this building was put up by the Paterno Construction Company, the Saint Gotthard, named after another Alpine pass, was down the street.

MONT CLEMENS   *8 Manhattan Avenue*
(southeast corner West 101st Street)

A circa-1900 six-story redbrick building now in poor condition. Built by Robert M. Silverman, a major developer of the neighborhood.

Mount Clemens, Michigan, is about twenty miles northeast of Detroit.

MONTANA   *35 Mount Morris Park West*
(southwest corner West 124th Street)

A six-stories-and-basement building of red brick with white trim; with doorway painted brown; circa 1900.

Montana was admitted to the Union as the forty-first state in 1889.

MONTANA, THE   *247 West 87th Street*
(northeast corner Broadway)

This twenty-seven-story twin-towered apartment building of 1984, designed by the Gruzen Partnership, is reminiscent in style of the splendid twin-towered buildings of the 1920s along Central Park West.

The name *Montana* carries on the Westside tradition of western states and territories in apartment nomenclature.

MONTALVO COURT   *723–727 St. Nicholas Avenue*
(northwest corner West 146th Street)

When this six-story building was put up in 1906—Lorenz Weikr, architect—it was described as being "French Renaissance in style." The subway stop is, literally, at the door.

García Ordoñez de Montalvo, Spanish writer of the late fifteenth century, is most remembered for his novel of chivalry *Amadís de Gaula,* in which, incidentally, the word "California" first appears.

MONTE CRISTO   *201 West 123rd Street*
(northeast corner Adam Clayton Powell, Jr., Boulevard)

A seven-story redbrick and limestone building; circa 1900.

Alexandre Dumas published his celebrated romance *The Count of Monte Cristo* in 1844. The hero took his name from the Italian island near Elba.

MONTE VISTA   *464 Riverside Drive*

Twin to the *Aquavista.*

The Orange and Paterson mountains of New Jersey can be seen from this part of Manhattan.

MONTEBELLO   *548 Riverside Drive*

Six stories and basement in red brick, with open-court entrance and bay windows; circa 1900.

A twin to *The Hague.*

Jean Lannes (1769–1809), a French officer under Napoléon, won a great victory at Montebello in Italy in 1800 and was created marshal of France and duc de Montebello in 1804.

Monterey. *Bartholdi's bronze sculpture of Lafayette and Washington is seen in the foreground.*

MONTEREY   *351 West 114th Street*
                                    (northeast corner Morningside Avenue)

An interesting and attractive building of the late nineteenth century; seven stories with a heavily rusticated base in the Richardsonian manner, surrounded by an iron fence and green hedges.

In the little square formed by the junction of West 114th Street and Manhattan and Morningside avenues stands Frédéric Bartholdi's statue of Washington and Lafayette which dates from circa 1900.

Monterey, which means "king's mountain" in Spanish, is the name of a city and bay in California, site of a Spanish settlement in the colonial era; the city was the capital of California until 1847.

MONTGOMERY   *230–242 East 86th Street*

An amalgam of seven four-story buildings of circa 1885; the central structure with cornice marked *Montgomery*. The ground floor houses Kleine Konditerei, Karl Ehmer, and Elk Candy ("the home of marzipan")—all relics of Yorkville's German heritage.

John Montgomery (or Montgomerie) was captain general and governor in chief of the Province of New York and New Jersey. He granted a charter to the city of New York.

MONTGOMERY   *302 West 114th Street*

A simple five-stories-and-basement building; a twin to the *Ruth*.

MONTPARNASSE   *25 West 13th Street*

A seven-story redbrick apartment house of the 1960s.

Montparnasse, which is the French equivalent of Parnassus, the mountain ridge in Greece celebrated as the haunt of the Muses, is the name of a neighborhood in Paris.

MONTREUX, THE   *342 East 67th Street*

This medium-sized 1960s apartment house is distinguished by an enormous mural of the castle of Chillon on Lake Geneva in the lobby . . . appropriate enough, for the castle is near Montreux in the Swiss canton of Vaud.

It was in this castle that François de Bonnivard, hero of Byron's *Prisoner of Chillon,* was held captive from 1530 to 1536.

MONTVALE   *89 St. Nicholas Place*

A 1905 building on the center-court plan. On opening, apartments rented for $300 to $1,300 a year.

MORAD BEEKMAN   *420 East 51st Street*

An unexceptional modern building near Beekman Place; owned by the Morad Organization.

MORAD DIPLOMAT, THE   *345 East 73rd Street*

Another of the Morad buildings of the 1960s.

MORLEIGH, THE   *74 West 68th Street*

A ten-story building of the 1920s.

MORNINGSIDE   *328 West 113th Street*
(southeast corner Manhattan Avenue)

Abandoned.

MORRIS HALL   *501 Cathedral Parkway*
(northeast corner Amsterdam Avenue)

A redbrick and limestone turn-of-the-century building of ten stories.

Lewis Morris (1726–1798) was a New York landowner, soldier, politician, jurist, and last lord of the manor of Morrisania in what is now the Bronx.

MORRIS PARK HOMES (NYC
Housing Authority)   *17 East 124th Street*

This late-1970s building for senior citizens was named for the nearby park, originally known as Mount Morris Square but renamed Marcus Garvey Memorial Park in 1973, in honor of the black leader.

MORRISON, THE   *360 East 57th Street*

Despite the address, the entrance to this 1980 apartment house is actually on First Avenue, where it is tucked in between a small bank building and an earlier (1960s) apartment house to maximize the use of the awkwardly shaped lot. Unfortunately for the tenants of the older building, *The Morrison* blocked out the windows in a line of apartments on its north side, causing great consternation and threatened lawsuits.

Morrison is an old English family name.

MORTON COURT   *974 St. Nicholas Avenue*

A six-story redbrick building of the 1920s.

MUMFORD   *535 West 111th Street*

A six-story turn-of-the-century building.

G. S. Mumford was a large landowner in this area.

MUNROE, THE   *415 West 115th Street*

A twin to *The Colonial*.

MURRAY HILL

*The East Thirties of Manhattan at the time of the American
Revolution were the property of the Lindleys and the Murrays,
prominent Quaker families with large mercantile interests in the
city. Robert Murray built a country house at the intersection of
present-day Park Avenue and East 37th Street. One of the most
enduring Manhattan stories took place at this house. On 15 September 1776 the British general Lord Howe landed with his
troops at Kip's Bay intending to pursue General Washington and
his forces which were withdrawing from the city. Although Robert Murray, like most of his family, was more or less a Loyalist,
his wife, Mary (née Lindley), entertained Howe to tea and cakes
(an alternate version is wine and cakes), intentionally or unin-
tentionally delaying the British until Washington and the Americans had made good their escape from the island. No flirtation
was likely, despite the tales that have sprung up since: Mrs.
Murray was a middle-aged Quaker lady, the mother of twelve
children. A play about this incident, entitled* Small War on
Murray Hill, *was produced on Broadway in 1957.*

[*See also* Lindley.]

MURRAY HILL   *136 East 36th Street*
                          (southeast corner Lexington Avenue)

A good-looking eleven-story redbrick building of the 1920s.

MURRAY HILL, THE   *115 East 34th Street*

A huge, new, gleaming apartment house of the 1980s.

MURRAY HILL EAST   *207 East 37th Street*

An apartment house of the 1960s–1970s.

MURRAY HILL EAST, THE   *149 East 39th Street*

This 1960s redbrick building lists itself as an "apartment
hotel."

MURRAY HILL HOUSE   *132 East 35th Street*

A redbrick 1960s apartment house.

MURRAY HILL MEWS   *160 East 38th Street*

Despite the last part of its name (which originally meant a place where a gentleman kept his falcons and/or horses), this is an imposing tower of twenty plus floors with a drive-through entrance and a small plaza which bears the legend: "Open to the public 9 A.M. to sunset."

MUSEUM APARTMENTS   *102 West 80th Street*

A turn-of-the-century building listed on older maps as the Anderson, with a recently modernized entrance and canopy. The pediment has been removed, and the fire escapes are linked to the stone balconies.

The name refers to the American Museum of Natural History, the rear of which is across Columbus Avenue.

MUSEUM TOWER   *15 West 53rd Street*

This high-rise luxury building was opened in 1983 as a source of income for the Museum of Modern Art, above which it rises. One of the selling slogans for the cooperative apartments was Have Picasso as Your Downstairs Neighbor.

NAGLE ARMS   *65–67 Nagle Avenue*
NAGLE COURT   *165 Nagle Avenue*

The name of these buildings and the street is taken from that of Jan Nagel, a seventeenth-century Dutch landowner in the area.

NASSAU   *238 Fort Washington Avenue*
(southeast corner West 170th Street)

A nondescript white-brick six-stories-and-basement building; circa 1900.

Maps of the 1620s refer to the Hudson River as "the Nassau" in honor of the Dutch military hero Prince Maurice of Nassau (1567–1625). The house of Nassau were the reigning Stadtholders of the Netherlands at the time the Dutch settled New York.

NATHAN HALE   *750 West 181st Street*
(southeast corner Fort Washington Avenue)

A large six-story white-brick building; circa 1900.

Nathan Hale was the Revolutionary War patriot, captured and sentenced to death by the British; his famous proclamation "I only regret that I have but one life to lose for my country" was a paraphrase of a statement by Cato, the Roman statesman.

NATHAN STRAUS HOUSES (NYC Housing Authority)
228 East 28th Street

This project was opened in 1965 and honors the name of the man who left the family business (R. H. Macy & Co.) to publish the humorous weekly *Puck* and who later became, in 1937, administrator of the U.S. Housing Authority.

[NATIONAL ARTS CLUB STUDIOS]
15 Gramercy Park South

This thirteen-story residential and work-space annex to the Gramercy Park home of the National Arts Club was erected in 1906 on East 19th Street, thus leaving intact the fine brownstone facade of the club on the park.

NAVARETTO
400 West 151st Street
(southwest corner St. Nicholas Avenue)

A five-stories-and-basement gray-brick building; circa 1900.
The small building may take its name from the triangular park it faces. A *navaretto* is a small boat.

NAVARRE, THE
226–228 East 14th Street

This faded but still elegant relic (circa 1880) of 14th Street's glorious era has bowed windows, stone pilasters, and a name barely visible over the portico under countless layers of paint.
Navarre, a former kingdom, is now a province of Spain; situated on the French border, this fabled region has been pivotal in history.

NEBRASKA
80 West 82nd Street
(southeast corner Columbus Avenue)

[See *Colorado*.]

NETHERLANDS
340 West 86th Street

Coats of arms and other decorations ornament this twelve-story building at the top and over the entrance. Built in 1909, Neville & Bagge, architects, the name recalls the original settlement of Manhattan by the Dutch.

NEVADA, THE
139 East 30th Street

A nice redbrick and stone apartment house, circa 1890, in a block of mostly low buildings and brownstones. The name—almost invisible—is in faded gilt paint over the door.
This is one of a number of buildings of the late nineteenth century named for the thirty-sixth state of the Union (admitted

in 1864). The word means, literally, "snow-covered" and is usually associated with mountains, as in Sierra Nevada.

NEVADA, THE   *78–80 Christopher Street*

Although the name is almost invisible on a heavily repainted plaque beside the front door, this late-nineteenth-century residence still stands demurely over an "all male entertainment center" in its basement.

NEW AMSTERDAM   *200 West 86th Street*

An eighteen-story building of brick and limestone with casement windows, dating from the 1920s.

New Amsterdam was the name of the early Dutch settlement on Manhattan Island, from 1623 or 1624 (the exact date is disputed) to the end of the Dutch period in 1664.

NEW CENTURY APARTMENTS
401 West End Avenue
(northwest corner West 79th Street)

The *New Century* was most appropriately built in 1900; William B. Frank was the architect and builder. This nine-stories-and-basement building of red brick has a distinctive rounded "towerlet" at the West 79th Street corner. The columned entrance is typical of the time.

The building has undergone various changes: the original cornice has been removed, and the large apartments were cut up in 1935. The small garage between this building and the *Imperial Court* became a synagogue in 1942 and is now Congregation Kehilath Jacob.

[See illustration page 186.]

NEW CHELSEA   *340 West 21st Street*

The name appears over the door of this six-story brick building.

[See also *Chelsea*.]

NEW MILBURN HOTEL   *242 West 76th Street*

A twelve-story 1920s brick apartment building made into a hotel; has an unattractive new canopy.

[NEWBURY]
250 East 87th Street
(southwest corner Second Avenue)

The name was dropped from this 1970s tower when the building went co-op. Nice entrance.

Newbury is a town in Essex County, Massachusetts.

NEWPORT

Although Newport, Rhode Island, was an important center of shipping and commerce during colonial times, it went into a period of decline during and after the American Revolution, only to be rediscovered—this time as a summer resort—by fashionable New Yorkers of the 1880s and 1890s.

The Wetmores, Goelets, Vanderbilts, Berwinds, and other society families, mostly from New York City, built "cottages"—more accurately described as palaces—in Newport.

This association with New York's millionaires, and Newport's connection with the America's Cup yacht races, has made the name of this town synonymous with old money and new excitement for a century.

NEWPORT   *2006 Third Avenue*
                                  (northwest corner East 110th Street)

Three brownstones, circa 1880s, put together to form a four-story apartment building with brownstone facade and trim. The name is still on the pediment, but a more recent inscription reads, *Libertad para prisioneros de guerra puertorriqueños.*

NEWPORT COURT   *111–117 West 104th Street*

Six stories with fire escape and center-court entrance. Built circa 1905 on a U-shaped plan; C. B. Meyers, architect. Its condition is semiderelict.

It formerly had a sister building at 148–152 West 104th Street called *Putnam Court.*

NEWPORT EAST   *370 East 76th Street*

A buff-brick late-1960s high-rise apartment building. The architect Philip Birnbaum designed it for the owner-builder Carol Management Corporation. A rooftop swimming pool was one of its attractions.

One of the early tenants here was Joe Namath, who lived at Newport East during his glorious days with the New York Jets.

NEW YORK TOWER   *330 East 39th Street*

This enormous balconied building of buff brick dates from the 1970s. The name is visible only on the doorman's cap.

NEW YORK TOWERS   *305 East 24th Street*

Buff brick with balconies; circa 1968.

NEW YORKER, THE   *1474 Third Avenue*

A J. I. Sopher & Co. sliver, recessed from the usual building line; buff brick above travertine.
Would Eustace Tilley have lived here?

NEW YORKER EAST, THE   *417 East 57th Street*

A late-1970s high rise on a smallish plot.

"NINE-G COOPERATIVE"   *19–35 West 93rd Street*

In 1967 nine town houses dating from the 1880s and 1890s were put together, given a uniform facade with three entrances—designed by Edelman & Salzmann—and divided into thirty-four apartments.

NINTH AVENUE FLAT   *744 Columbus Avenue*

Above the rather grand entrance of this five-story redbrick building of circa 1880 is inscribed "9th Ave Flat."

NONPAREIL   *87 St. Nicholas Place*

A six-story redbrick and yellow-stone building with granite columns in front, which has fallen on hard times.
The name, which derives from Middle French, means "peerless."
The building is a twin to the *Montvale* next door.

NORFOLK   *308 West 94th Street*

Norfolk is the name of an English county.
[See *Devon Residence.*]

NORLAND, THE   *668 Riverside Drive*
(southeast corner West 144th Street)

A six-story building of circa 1900, with an elaborate cornice supported by heavy corbels.
Norland Park was the family home of the Dashwoods in Jane Austen's *Sense and Sensibility*.

NORMA APARTMENTS   *112 West 15th Street*

Probably once a private house, this four-story building is only three windows wide; brownstone with later brick added to the first floor.

Norma is the name of a minor constellation and a celebrated opera by Vincenzo Bellini, first produced in 1831.

NORMAN   *43 West 93rd Street*

The name is chiseled in stone over the doorway of this handsome and well-maintained turn-of-the-century building. This ivy-covered eight-story structure has a grilled doorway.

NORMANDIE/NORMANDY

The French province of Normandy, so called because of settlement there by the "Northmen" (Vikings) in the ninth century, lies to the west of Paris.

In 1935 the French ocean liner Normandie, *on her maiden voyage to New York, set a new record for an Atlantic crossing: four days, three hours, and two minutes.*

The staterooms and salons of the Normandie *were magnificently decorated in the latest Art Moderne style by France's leading decorators, sculptors, and artists, and the ship caused a sensation in the United States. When France fell to the Germans in 1940, the* Normandie *was in New York harbor, where it was seized by the U.S. government as enemy property and confiscated. During the course of its conversion into a troopship, a fire broke out, and the* Normandie *was destroyed by flame and water.*

NORMANDIE   *100 West 119th Street*
                              (southwest corner Lenox Avenue)

A seven-story building with nice details; now almost totally abandoned.

NORMANDY, THE   *140 Riverside Drive*
                              (West 86th to West 87th streets)

Built in 1939 by the architect Emery Roth in the Art Deco style, this notable building has entrances on both West 86th

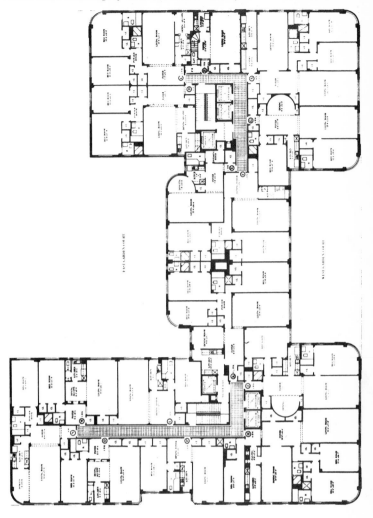

Normandy. *Semicircular dining alcoves and bedrooms with stream-lined and rounded corners feature in the floor plan of the Art Moderne Normandy. Two large "garden courts" and lots of large windows ensure extremely light apartments. Note that the "N" apartment has a "powder room," an early use of that expression in a New York apartment building.*

and West 87th streets with spectacular gold and blue mosaic-trimmed doorways. A glassed-in passage connects the side-street lobbies. Along the Riverside Drive facade is a handsomely maintained garden.

The name is spelled thus on the building itself, despite a number of reference books that give it the French ending *"-die."*

Normandy. *Detail of mosaic decoration at entrances.*

NORTHERN, THE   *100 Cabrini Boulevard*

Until 1938 Cabrini Boulevard was known as Northern Boulevard. The name was changed to honor the first American citizen to be canonized, Saint Frances Xavier Cabrini.

NORTHFIELD   *477 West 144th Street*
                                    (northeast corner Amsterdam Avenue)

An interesting five-story Italianate building with arched windows. On the ground floor is Dave's Unisex Barber Shop.

NORTHPORT   *74–78 West 103rd Street*

A circa-1900 five-story orange-brick survivor, oddly situated within a modern public housing development on Manhattan Avenue.

NORWOOD   *200 West 99th Street*
                                    (southwest corner Amsterdam Avenue)

A five-story nineteenth-century building now painted red.

NOTTINGHAM   *35 East 30th Street*

An extremely ornate glazed terra-cotta facade adorns the ground floor of this early 1920s redbrick apartment building. The frieze over the door is classical; the symbols of Freemasonry flank the frieze.

Nottinghamshire is the English county famous in the Robin Hood story.

OAKHURST   *2137 Adam Clayton Powell, Jr., Boulevard*
(southeast corner West 127th Street)

An early building (perhaps 1880s) of red brick with brownstone base; next door to, and matching, the *Greycourt* and the *Parkhurst*.
Abandoned.

ODHALL COURTS   *529–537 East 81st Street*

Five contiguous small apartments, circa 1885, with arched doorways enclosing sculpted terra-cotta panels of a female face, a bacchic head, a lion mask. In red brick and with the name in tarnished gold on the doors.

OENGLER   *718 Eleventh Avenue*
(near West 51st Street)

A five-story tenement with *Oengler—1898* engraved on pediment; now undergoing renovation.

OGONTZ, THE   *509–515 West 122nd Street*

Built in 1905 by Moore & Landsiedel, a typical six-story red-brick and limestone building with side-court (H-shaped) plan. The entrance is nice, but the pediment precarious.

Olcott. *Photographed about 1935. The empty lot in the right foreground originally was the site of the Da-kota's generator, and is now occupied by the* Mayfair Towers.

250 PART II

OLCOTT   *27 West 72nd Street*

Built in 1925 at a reputed cost of $4,500,000, the seventeen-story *Olcott* is one of several elegant apartment hotels on this stretch of West 72nd Street, just off Central Park West. Originally the residents could look out at *The Dakota* to the east, but that view was blocked in the 1960s by the construction of a huge white-brick apartment house.

The *Olcott*'s former dining room is now the Swiss Chalet Bar B. Q.

OLIVER CROMWELL   *12 West 72nd Street*

Built in 1927, at a cost of some $2,500,000, the *Oliver Cromwell* was designed by the architect Emery Roth (note the similarity to his *Ritz Tower*) and is today basically an apartment house, although it was originally an apartment hotel. The original dining room has become a public restaurant in recent years.

Its delightful balconies and terraces, adorned with urns, obelisks, and other ornaments, provide striking contrast to the sleekly Art Moderne *Majestic* next door.

The Oliver Cromwell is said to have been Emery Roth's personal favorite of all the apartment buildings he designed.

The exuberance of its vaguely Mediterranean Baroque architecture seems inappropriate for its dour namesake.

[See also *Cromwell*.]

OLYMPIA HOUSE   *279 East 44th Street*

A white-brick 1960s apartment house.

The name is from the religious center in the south of Greece where a sports festival in honor of Zeus was held every four years beginning in 776 B.C.

OLYMPIC TOWER   *641 Fifth Avenue*
(northeast corner East 51st Street)

Built in 1974 by Arlen Realty in partnership with Victory Development Corporation (i.e., Aristotle Onassis), *Olympic Tower* was designed by Skidmore, Owings & Merrill and rises 52 stories above Fifth Avenue, providing spectacular views of St. Patrick's Cathedral, Rockefeller Center, and Midtown Manhattan through its floor-to-ceiling window-walls.

An early brochure described *Olympic Tower* as "New York's first major multi-purpose condominium structure . . . a landmark ahead of its time, appealing to the New Yorker, the world citizen, and the world's business and diplomatic communities alike." Written in French, German, Spanish, and Japanese, the brochure went on to list the amenities offered: concierge, telex, gourmet shop, ticker tape, health club, restaurant, wine cellar, conference rooms, and design consultant—all aimed at prospective tenants who wished to live in luxury in Midtown and damn the expense. The building was the first to capitalize on the fact that New York had become a major international city, where wealthy people from all over the world wished to maintain a *pied-à-terre* (or more accurately, a *pied-à-ciel*) for their frequent sojourns in the city. As it was a condominium, propective tenant owners would not have to bear the onus of going before, and winning the approval of, a stuffy co-op board. All it took was money—and lots of it! The original purchase price of all the apartments totaled $47,000,000, with individual units going for $122,000 to $620,000. In the ensuing decade many apartments have been resold for many times their original cost.

Small fortunes have been spent decorating the rather nondescript apartment units. Stories about an Arab sheik installing his own *private* swimming pool in the huge apartment he'd bought went the round of the city's gossip trail for years.

Olympic Tower, whose name bespeaks its Greek connection (Olympic Airways was also owned by Onassis), was a success from the start and is still a residential address that doesn't need to be explained by exact street and number to a cabbie.

ONONDAGA   *747 Riverside Drive*
(southeast corner West 152nd Street)

Combined with the *Switzerland,* to which it is a twin, and, like it, trimmed in electric blue.

The Onondagas are a tribe of New York State Indians.

ONOWA   *650 West 172nd Street*

This five-story turn-of-the-century building still carries its name.

ONTIORA   *200 West 55th Street*
(southwest corner Seventh Avenue)

A five-story redbrick relic of the time when this was a quiet residential neighborhood of large apartment houses (*The Wyoming,* another survivor, is just across Seventh Avenue) and small ones of earlier vintage, such as this one, built circa 1885.

This now appears to be an annex of the Hotel Woodward at West 55th Street and Broadway.

The Ontiora Club is an exclusive private vacation community in the Catskills.

ONYX COURT   *193 Second Avenue*
(northwest corner East 12th Street)

A six-story elevator building of the 1890s with elaborate window details and a nicely maintained entrance with wrought-iron grate.

OPELIKA   *523 West 143rd Street*

A six-story building of the turn of the century. Opelika is a town in Alabama.

252   PART II

OPERA, THE
2166 Broadway
(northeast corner West 76th Street)

In 1930 the Manhattan Congregational Church forsook its old building and, in a move prophetic of the St. Peter's–Citicorp union of 1975, moved into a space within a neo-Gothic high-rise apartment hotel called *Manhattan Towers,* built at a cost of $2 million.

Over the years, as the congregation shrank and the residence gradually became a welfare hotel, *Manhattan Towers'* former glamour faded away.

In 1980 the building was converted to a cooperative apartment and rechristened *The Opera*; and the site of the former church was transformed into a theater—all symbolic of the rebirth of the Upper West Side.

A charming survivor from the earlier era is the handsome neo-Gothic doorway at 213 West 76th Street which still carries its original chiseled legend Entrance for Church and Towers.

ORCHID
170 West 78th Street
(southeast corner Amsterdam Avenue)

A pre–World War I five-story building with a stepped roof, bay windows, a rusticated ground floor, and a magnificent arched entrance.

OREGON AND MAINE
508 and 510 Ninth Avenue

Two six-story tenement buildings that have been joined to make a building taller and more pretentious than its neighbors. The facade is embellished with decorative details.

ORIENTA
302–304 West 79th Street

Built in 1904 by Schneider & Herter, builders and architects. Eight stories of Indiana limestone, "no terra cotta of any kind being employed," according to the original announcements. Apartments of five, six, and seven rooms rented from $660 to $925 per annum. There were four apartments to a floor, built on the H-plan.

A strange name for a building about as far west as you can get in Manhattan.

ORLANDO
311 West 94th Street

A tan brick and limestone building of six stories, with a handsome columned porch; circa 1900.

Orlando (or, in English, Roland) was the hero of Ludovico Ariosto's long poem *Orlando Furioso,* published in 1532.

ORLEANS
100 West 80th Street
(southwest corner Columbus Avenue)

A turn-of-the-century redbrick and limestone building of ten stories, with stone and iron balconies and a modernized entrance.

ORMISTON   *513 West 135th Street*

One of a row of named apartment houses.

ORMONDE   *101 West 86th Street*
(northwest corner Columbus Avenue)

A five-story turn-of-the-century building recently and neatly renovated and painted red with chocolate trim; matching building at the southwest corner of West 87th Street.

Ormonde is an Irish title of dukes and earls long held by the Butler family. Ormonde was also a famous racing horse which sold in 1892 for $150,000, then the "largest price ever paid for a single animal."

ORWELL HOUSE   *257 Central Park West*
(southwest corner West 86th Street)

Built in 1905–1906 by Mulliken & Moeller. At that time the purplish-brick building with limestone decoration had five-bedroom apartments with large reception halls, parlor, and library.

A twin to *Rossleigh Court,* it was known first as Central Park View, then later as Hotel Peter Stuyvesant. In recent years it became a cooperative apartment building under the name *Orwell House.*

OSBORNE, THE   *205 West 57th Street*

This large and handsome red-stone building has—remarkably for New York City—survived for nearly a century in one

Osborne. *The entrance lobby decorated by Louis Comfort Tiffany.*

of the busiest parts of the city. It was built in 1885 by Thomas
Osborne, a stone contractor, and was then considered far uptown for a residence. When Osborne went bankrupt, the building was finished by John Taylor. James E. Ware was the
architect.

The front of the building has eleven floors, the back sixteen.
The original elaborate porch has long since been removed, but
the lobby decoration by the Tiffany firm has remained. The
ground floor is now cut up into stores.

In 1962 the building became a cooperative.

OSCEOLA
490 Convent Avenue
(northwest corner West 152nd Street)

A triangular five-story building of circa 1900 standing at the
junction of Convent and St. Nicholas avenues.

The namesake (ca. 1800–1838) was the leader of the Seminole Indians in their war with the United States, 1835–1837.
There are several buildings with Indian names in this vicinity,
such as the *Amagansett*.

OSTEND
549 West 112th Street
(northeast corner Broadway)

A fortresslike but nondescript seven-story building of the
early twentieth century.

Ostend is a seaside town in Belgium.

OSTEND COURT
235–237–239 West 107th Street

A six-story double building of the early twentieth century.

OVERLOOK
812–820 West 181st Street
(southeast corner Pinehurst Avenue)

Marble columns decorate the entrance to this 1900s building.

OXFORD
205 West 88th Street

A fifteen-story building of the 1920s, with stock classical
decoration.

OXFORD EAST
333 East 49th Street

A 1970s building whose name conjures up both England's
ancient university and the smart Upper East Side.

OXFORD HALL   *454 Riverside Drive*

White-brick apartment house of the turn of the century. The other entry to the building, at 456 Riverside Drive, is called Cambridge.

[P.S. 8]   *29 King Street*

Now a condominium, this rather showy example of late-nineteenth-century civic architecture (the pediment bears the date 1886) was built as a public school. Converted to a residence circa 1981.

PACIFICA, THE   *327 East 34th Street*

A 1960s–1970s redo of an older building; the fire escapes are still visible.

The name is Latin for "peaceful" and is also the name of a town in San Mateo county, California.

PACKARD   *200 West 107th Street*
(southwest corner Amsterdam Avenue)

A circa-1900 five-story brick building. The ground floor is now occupied by a Hispanic funeral home.

Packard motorcars were first manufactured in 1900, and for the next half century they were among the most luxurious automobiles in the world.

PALACE   *809 West 177th Street*

A grandiose name for this Washington Heights building.

PALAIS ROYAL   *1864 Adam Clayton Powell, Jr.,*
Boulevard
(northwest corner West 113th Street)

This large, central-court apartment building of circa 1900 bears the name of a landmark building in Paris begun by Cardinal Richelieu in 1632. Entered from the Rue de Rivoli, the palace is notable for its central court garden in the eighteenth-century style.

PALAZZO GRECO   *115 Charles Street*

A nicely restored, gaily painted five-story building of circa 1890, now a "Greek palace."

PALISADE COURT   *601 West 139th Street*
(northwest corner Broadway)

A circa-1900 six-story building with bayed windows.

The Palisades of the Hudson are visible from the upper stories of this building.

Palermo. *Sealed up, hidden by scaffolding, and await-ing the wrecker's ball in 1984, this old apartment house reigned over East 57th Street long before the* Ritz Tower *or the* Gal-leria, *visible here in the background. See page 384.*

PALISADES ARMS   *91 Pinehurst Avenue*
                               (northeast corner West 181st Street)

A six-story building of the 1920s, with Renaissance details around the windows.

PANAMA   *569 West 150th Street*
                               (northeast corner Broadway)

Red brick, six stories.
The name gives us the approximate date of the building: the Panama Canal was begun by the United States in 1904 and opened in 1914.

PANMURE ARMS   *593 Riverside Drive*
                               (northeast corner West 136th Street)

Severe stone decoration with cartouches ornaments this six-story building with a central court; circa 1900.
Earl of Panmure was one of the titles of the Scottish family of Maule.

PARAGON   *113 West 115th Street*

A five-story building, semiabandoned. It formerly had a twin called *The Peerless* next door to the west.
A paragon is a model or pattern of excellence.

PARAMOUNT   *315 West 99th Street*

A white-brick building with eight stories and basement; circa 1900. The pediment has been removed, and the building recently cleaned and renovated. The name appears above the door.

PARC CAMERON   *41 West 86th Street*

A fifteen-story limestone and brick building of the 1920s, with an added hotel-style canopy.

PARC COLISEUM   *228 West 71st Street*

A new name on an old structure. The ground floor of this fourteen-story redbrick building has new picture windows.

PARC EAST TOWER   *240 East 27th Street*

Sleek high rise; circa 1975.

PARC—V   *785 Fifth Avenue*

This white-brick 1960s apartment house rising next to the venerable *Sherry-Netherland* was where La Banque Continentale opened for its brief days of glory during the go-go sixties. This was a bank that required a large minimum balance, was decorated with French eighteenth-century antiques, widely advertised its exclusivity, and failed. The name of the building is pronounced "Park Sank."

PARC VENDOME   *330–360 West 57th Street*

Henry Mandel, builder of *London Terrace,* was also the builder of *Parc Vendome,* which was put up on land that formerly belonged to Otto Kahn, financier and patron of the arts. Kahn is said to have offered the property at cost as a home for the Metropolitan Opera Company, but the offer was not taken up, and the property was sold to Mandel.

He constructed a building with several lobbies and towers on both West 56th and West 57th streets. The twenty-floor, 570-apartment building opened in 1931. Amenities included a gymnasium, pool, terraced gardens, solarium, and dining hall.

The property was sold in 1981 and refurbished for sale as a condominium. As the offer to prospective purchasers emphasized, "the Parc Vendome has been uncompromisingly restored to recapture the splendor of a bygone era." Private dining and banquet rooms could be reserved by owners; there was a private library and card room, a billiard room, a backgammon room, and a music room "complete with a grand piano." Prices for studios started at $94,000, for one-bedroom apartments at $165,000.

The name Vendome is taken from the Place Vendôme—the center of fashionable Paris—which in turn takes its name from the French eighteenth-century general Louis-Joseph, duc de Vendôme (1654–1712).

[PARK AND TILFORD BUILDING]
100 West 72nd Street
(southwest corner Columbus Avenue)

McKim, Mead & White were the architects of this six-story building of 1893, which was the home of Park & Tilford liq-

uors. Now handsomely converted to residential apartments, it
has been cleaned and fitted with new windows. Most of the
ground floor is occupied by a Natural Source food shop.

Frank Tilford lived in a townhouse on West 72nd Street between Broadway and West End Avenue in 1895.

PARK COURT   *403 West 115th Street*

Sister building to *La Touraine.*
The park referred to is nearby Morningside Park.

PARK EAST, THE   *235 East 86th Street*

"Surprisingly affordable luxury coops" are promised in this
twenty-story sliver of 1983.

PARK GALLERY TOWER   *125 East 55th Street*

A 1983 building of the sliver type, with one condominium
apartment on each of the thirty-six floors; advertised as "the
townhouse in the sky."

The name is from nearby Park Avenue.

PARK GRAMERCY, THE   *7 Lexington Avenue*

A 1960s buff-brick apartment house, just a few steps north
of Gramercy Park.

[See also *Gramercy.*]

PARK HILL   *135 Hamilton Place*

A large seven-story building occupying the triangle formed
by West 143rd Street, Hamilton Place, and Amsterdam Avenue. Dating from circa 1900, it has been renovated but lost its
ornamentation in the process.

PARK HOUSE, THE   *1245 Park Avenue*

Buff brick, 1960s–1970s, fifteen stories.

PARK LANE TOWER   *185 East 85th Street*

Built in the 1960s, this apartment building was designed by
F. H. Feldman and was one of the earliest of the set-back behemoths encouraged by a new zoning law that by the late 1960s
had become commonplace. The driveway entrance and surrounds are very nicely landscaped. There is a shopping plaza on
the East 86th Street side.

Park Lane, the street that runs along the east side of Hyde
Park in London, is noted for the Park Lane Hotel.

PARK LINCOLN   *321 Edgecombe Avenue*

An early 1920s building with a long canopy stretching to
the street.

PARK 900, THE

900 Park Avenue
(northwest corner East 79th Street)

One of the few buildings—perhaps the only one—on this stretch of upper Park Avenue to sport a name, even if it is only a rearrangement of the address.

The main entrance (on East 79th Street) used to be graced by a Henry Moore sculpture, but since the building's conversion into a cooperative, a work by the Mexican artist Francisco Zuñiga has taken its place.

Formerly occupying this site were the James Stillman Houses, a somewhat gloomy, vine-covered group which exuded an air of mystery and antiquity.

PARK REGIS

50 East 89th Street

Brown-brick and buff-concrete tower with balconies, circa 1980.

PARK ROYAL

23 West 73rd Street

Built in 1926, this sixteen-story edifice was designed by the ubiquitously popular George F. Pelham. As a hotel it featured a "gorgeous lobby . . . beautiful art fountain . . . terraces," making it an "ideal apartment home," according to a contemporary promotional piece.

PARK SUTTON

440 East 62nd Street
(southwest corner York Avenue)

Several blocks from either Sutton Place or the Park, but just around the corner from the Abigail Adams Smith Museum in the same block on East 61st Street.

[See *Sutton*.]

PARK TERRACE GARDENS

West 215th to West 217th streets,
and East and West Park Terrace

Five buildings of eight stories and penthouses, originally laid out in the form of three- and four-room "simplex" apartments and four- and five-room duplex penthouses. The gardens surrounding the buildings included 62,000 square feet.

The 1930s brochure advertising the Art Deco buildings points out their convenience to the "new Eighth Avenue subway."

Now converted to cooperative ownership.

PARK TOWERS

201 East 17th Street

A huge 1970s tower.

PARK TOWERS SOUTH

315 West 57th Street

A 1965 building; nineteen stories with 363 suites; in white brick.

PARK TOWERS SOUTH   *330 West 58th Street*

This late-1950s high rise is directly across from the New York Coliseum (1956). On the ground floor is a clutter of coffee shops and restaurants.

PARK VIEW   *317 West 116th Street*

Abandoned.

PARK WEST VILLAGE
West 97th Street to West 100th Street
Central Park West to Amsterdam Avenue

An enormous middle-class housing development completed in the late 1950s. The builder was Webb & Knapp, then one of the leading real estate developers in New York. The assembling of the plot, which was called the Manhattantown site, was the subject of much political scandal. William Zeckendorf, then head of Webb & Knapp, recalled in his autobiography: "A 1954 congressional investigation brought forth evidence that, though their projects were stalled, some sponsors of Title I projects and their business associates were doing rather well financially from their slum properties." At the invitation of Robert Moses, Webb & Knapp took over the project. "At Manhattantown," Zeckendorf commented, "which we renamed Park West Village . . . we wound up with a quite decent project." The seven buildings contain twenty-seven hundred apartments.

PARKER CRESCENT   *225 East 36th Street*

One of several "Parker" apartments, this one derives its name from the curved shape of the 1970s building.
In England curved rows of houses are usually called crescents, as in Bath Crescent.

PARKER 86   *444 East 86th Street*

One of the tallest in the Parker group: a thirty-five-story tower of the 1970s.

PARKER 40th   *305 East 40th Street*

A redbrick 1960s–1970s cooperative.

PARKER GRAMERCY   *7 West 14th Street*

This 1960s twelve-stories-and-penthouse redbrick building is many blocks from Gramercy Park. There is also an entrance at 10 West 15th Street.

PARKER 72nd   *520 East 72nd Street*

A fine river view.

PARKER TOWN HOUSE
3 Sheridan Square
(northwest corner Barrow Street)

A 1960s high-rise apartment house.

PARKHURST
2136 Adam Clayton Powell, Jr., Boulevard
(southeast corner West 127th Street)

Matches the *Oakhurst* and the *Greycourt*.
Abandoned.

PARKVIEW APARTMENTS
415 Central Park West
(northwest corner West 101st Street)

A 1920s redbrick and limestone-trimmed building with Georgian details including neo-Classical urns over the entrance.

PARKWAY
49 West 72nd Street

A sixteen-story 1920s brick building with Renaissance details.

PARTHENON, THE
400 Manhattan Avenue
(southeast corner West 117th Street)

A twin to the *Hesperus* to the north.
The Parthenon, which means "virgin's place" in Greek, is the temple dedicated to Athena on the Acropolis at Athens.

PATERNO
440 Riverside Drive
3 Claremont Avenue
(northeast corner West 116th Street)

A handsome building that curves around West 116th Street onto Riverside Drive, built by Schwartz & Gross about 1910. One of the few residential buildings in New York that curves its corner, the building is echoed across West 116th Street by the *Colosseum*.

The Paterno brothers were major builders in New York, especially on the West Side, in the first third of the twentieth century.

"PATTERSON APARTMENTS"
3 East 84th Street

Built in 1928 for Colonel Joseph Medill Patterson, the publisher of the *Daily News;* designed by Raymond Hood (who also did the News Building), it is distinguished by the exemplary Art Deco metalwork and grillwork enlivening the facade and the entrance.

PAUL JONES, THE
220 Wadsworth Avenue

A circa-1915 building with stone balconies, now becoming dilapidated.
John Paul Jones (1747–1792), American naval hero.

PAUL REVERE   *450 West 147th Street*
                                        (southwest corner Convent Avenue)

With its name written in gold script letters in the window light over the entrance, this turn-of-the-century brick and stone building stands beside the Macedonian Baptist Church.

Paul Revere (1735–1818), American silversmith and patriot.

Revere visited New York in 1774 and 1775 bearing letters from patriots in Boston.

PAULA   *15 West 108th Street*

A six-story building with typically elaborate windows and doors; turn of the century.

PAULA HOUSE   *341 West 30th Street*

A dilapidated nineteenth-century building; four stories of red brick.

PAULDING   *1349 Lexington Avenue*

A ten-story 1920s redbrick building with limestone base.

The Paulding family was prominent in old New York: James Kirke Paulding was a novelist who served as secretary of the navy, 1838–1841; and General William J. Paulding was elected mayor of New York in 1824 and reelected in 1826.

PAULINE   *16 Morningside Avenue*

Six stories and basement; circa 1900.

PAVILION, THE   *500 East 77th Street*

Designed by Philip Birnbaum and built in the early 1960s, this thirty-five-story white-brick tower was, when completed, the largest apartment structure in New York City.

One of its 852 units was the home of David and Julie Nixon Eisenhower in 1976.

The word "pavilion" originally meant a large, sumptuous tent (from the French word for butterfly, *papillon*) but now has come to mean any elaborate building or structurally independent component of a larger complex.

[See also *Carlton/Regency/Pavilion.*]

PAVONAZZA   *3671 Broadway*
                                      (southwest corner West 152nd Street)

A six-story, semiderelict apartment building of circa 1900; of imposing size, with an equally imposing Italianate name.

PAYSON

1803 Riverside Drive
(northwest corner Payson Avenue)

A white-brick building of the 1920s, with a modified Gothic entrance.

Payson Avenue is named for Dr. George S. Payson, who was minister of the Fort Washington Presbyterian Church, 1880–1920.

PAYSON HOUSE

7–15 Beak Street
(northwest corner Seaman Avenue)

A six-story white-brick building of the 1920s; now a cooperative.

Beak Street is a short street between Seaman and Payson avenues which was opened in 1925.

"PEGGY, JUNIOR, MANUEL, PUCHY . . ."

659 West 162nd Street

A six-story tan-brick building of the 1920s, with two bays. The entrance has been painted gray, and above it are listed nineteen given names—four of which we cite above—most likely the current juvenile tenants.

PEMBROKE

10 West 93rd Street

A six-story fire-escape building of white brick, built in the early 1900s.

Pembroke has often been a title among the English nobility, and there are many towns in the United States bearing this name, which derives from a county in Wales.

PENN STATION SOUTH

West 23rd to West 29th streets
Eighth to Ninth avenues

This 1962 slum clearance project of ten 21-story redbrick apartment towers was financed primarily by the International Ladies' Garment Workers Union and organized on a cooperative ownership basis for people of moderate incomes. The site was chosen, in part, because of its proximity to the garment trades district, and preference was given to members of the union as well as to people displaced by the new construction.

Penn Station South Cooperative has aged gracefully and is considered one of the best and most successful projects of its type. The winding landscaped roads and paths and the moderate rates (due in part to tax abatements) have helped to keep the turnover at 2 percent and the waiting time to get in at seven years.

In contrast to the experience at *Lincoln Towers*, tenants here embraced submetering of their electricity, rather than having it included as part of the maintenance charge. Savings were effected, but methods of generating power independently are now being explored.

The name, of course, derives from the project's geographical position ten blocks to the south of Penn Station whose name in turn reflects its origins as the grand terminus for the mighty Pennsylvania Railroad—now just a memory.

PEREGRINE, THE   303 East 49th Street
(northeast corner Second Avenue)

The building's developer promised "a most private and secure lifestyle" in a 1983 advertisement. "All the amenities you'd expect, plus greenhouses, jacuzzis, and more." The narrow site allows only one apartment per floor.

The name signifies a spirited falcon or a wanderer—a pilgrim.

PETER COOPER VILLAGE
East 20th to East 23rd streets,
First Avenue to the East River Drive

The companion housing development to *Stuyvesant Town,* with the same architects (Irwin Clavan and Gilmore D. Clarke) and developer (Metropolitan Life Insurance Company) and the same *rus in urbe* tranquillity.

The comfort, safety, and popularity of *Peter Cooper Village* may be gauged by the fact that there is an eleven-year waiting period to obtain an apartment there!

Peter Cooper (1791–1883) was a noted industrialist who built the first American locomotive (1830); promoted the laying of the Atlantic cable; founded Cooper Union for "the advancement of science and art" (1857–1859). His son-in-law, Abram S. Hewitt (1822–1903), served as mayor of New York City (1887–1888) after helping to demolish the Tweed ring.

PETER JAMES   201 East 25th Street

A redbrick 1960s apartment house.

PETER MINUIT   25 Claremont Avenue

This twelve-story white-brick building was erected in 1910. Gaetan Ajello, who was responsible for many residential buildings in this area, was the architect.

Peter Minuit (1580–1638) was the first director general of the Dutch colony of New Netherland and made the celebrated purchase of the island of Manhattan in 1626, paying the Indians in trinkets worth about sixty guilders.

PETER STUYVESANT   166 Second Avenue
(southeast corner East 11th Street)

A fifteen-story apartment building erected on land that was once Peter Stuyvesant's farm; across from the graveyard of St. Mark's-in-the-Bowery, where he is buried. A 1920s building with Gothic detailing designed by Emery Roth. This apartment house has also been called Warren Hall.

[See also *Stuyvesant Town*.]

PETER STUYVESANT   *252 Riverside Drive*
                                 (southeast corner West 98th Street)

Built in 1908; W. L. Rouse, architect. This ten-story building originally had three suites of nine or ten rooms on each floor, grouped around a central court.

PETER WARREN HOUSE   *51 West 10th Street*

Richard Morris Hunt's Tenth Street Studios occupied the site of this unremarkable apartment building from 1857 until 1956. The studios, which were not residences, were working quarters for scores of well-known painters, including Winslow Homer, Albert Bierstadt, and William Merritt Chase.

Named for Sir Peter Warren (1703–1752), the British vice admiral who resided in New York from 1730 to 1747 and acquired the land that is now Greenwich Village. After his return to London, he was knighted and served in Parliament.

PETERSFIELD, THE   *301 East 21st Street*

A huge redbrick and stone apartment house of sixteen stories; built in the Gothic taste circa 1930.

Named after Peter Stuyvesant's manor house, "Petersfield," which stood in this neighborhood until well into the nineteenth century.

PHAETON   *539 West 112th Street*

The brickwork around the windows gives this unusual building a proto–Art Deco feel. The very prominent fire escape extends across the front of the building above a modernized entrance.

In Greek mythology Phaeton nearly set the earth on fire while driving his sun chariot across the heavens and was slain by Zeus.

PHILLIEN   *411 West 114th Street*

A six-story redbrick turn-of-the-century building with the columned entrance so common in the area. Situated behind the Église de Notre Dame on the northwest corner of West 114th Street and Morningside Drive, a Roman Catholic church built in 1910.

PHIPPS HOUSES   *235, 239, 243, 247 West 63rd Street*
                      236, 240, 244, 248 West 64th Street

Built by the Phipps philanthropic interests between 1907 and 1911, these "model tenements" were prototypes for healthy

Phipps Houses. *West 63rd Street looking west in a photograph dated 15 January 1908*

housing for black laborers. Sold by the Phipps heirs in 1961, the buildings have since gone downhill.

The architects were Whitfield & King.

In 1982 plans for tearing down the buildings were made public, and the tenants reported housing-code violations.

PHIPPS PLAZA   *Second Avenue between East 26th and East 30th streets*

This middle-income project, built with Mitchell-Lama assistance, contains over sixteen hundred apartments and is part of the Bellevue South Urban Renewal Scheme. The mostly red-brick structures, nicely maintained and served by lots of stores and miniparks, go a long way toward avoiding the banal dreariness of most projects.

The name of this project is derived from its sponsor, Phipps Houses, Inc., a not-for-profit organization founded in 1905 by Henry Phipps (1839–1930), a longtime associate of Andrew Carnegie, and a well-known sportsman and philanthropist "dedicated to the creation of model housing at moderate cost."

The first Phipps Houses were built in 1906 on East 31st Street (torn down to make way for *Kips Bay Plaza*); the second were on West 63rd and West 64th streets (sold in 1961); later housing was put up at Sunnyside, Queens, and in the Bronx.

PHOENIX, THE   *160 East 65th Street*

Designed by Emery Roth & Sons and completed in 1969, this sheer tower with raised plaza is one of the more handsome apartment houses of recent years. A large abstract sculpture graces the entrance.

The name signifies not only a mythical bird but also anything deemed to be the best of its sort—a paragon of excellence and beauty.

PIANO FACTORY   *454 West 46th Street*
(southeast corner Tenth Avenue)

In the 1870s this was the home of the Wessel, Nickel and Gross firm of piano makers. The size of the building (actually an amalgamation of several buildings acquired as the firm grew) indicates the importance of this industry at a time when most middle-class American homes contained a piano.

In 1979 the factory was skillfully converted into apartments. The forty-nine apartments have a great variety of floor plans— simplexes, duplexes, undivided lofts, garden apartments, pent-houses—grouped around a central courtyard. The advertising slogan for the building was Old New York Revisited.

PICASSO, THE   *210 East 58th Street*

One of a number of 1960s apartment buildings named after well-known painters during the art appreciation boomlet of that go-go decade.

This gray-brick building with sunken entrance does have a large black-and-white Picasso print in the lobby.

Pablo Picasso (1881–1973), Spanish-born artist of the School of Paris.

PICKEN COURT   *706 Riverside Drive*
(southeast corner West 148th Street)

A ten-story tan brick and limestone building of the 1920s.

PIEDMONT   *316 West 97th Street*

A six-stories-and-basement redbrick apartment house dating from 1906. A. B. Knight, architect and builder, designed it on the H-plan.

The Piedmont is an upland region of Italy; in the United States the term is used to describe the area east of the Blue Ridge and Appalachian mountains from the Hudson River to central Alabama.

PIERMONT, THE   *201 West 21st Street*
(northwest corner Seventh Avenue)

A fourteen-story white-brick high rise of the 1950s.

Piermont is a town in Rockland County, New York, which was the eastern terminus of the Erie railroad in the mid to late nineteenth century. An enormous pier (where passengers once took the boat down to New York City) still juts into the Hudson here at the end of the Palisades.

PIERRE, THE   *Fifth Avenue and 61st Street*

A predominantly residential hotel of cooperative apartments, *The Pierre* was designed by Schultze & Weaver in 1928. Its green copper roof and graceful tower overlook Central Park and, in the early days of television, served as an antenna for local stations.

PIERREPONT, THE   *105 East 30th Street*

"A condominium for connoisseurs," read the advertisement for this 1984 semisliver building; in a block of mostly brownstone buildings, this twenty-story structure is conspicuous, to say the least.

PINEHURST, THE   *457 Fort Washington Avenue*
(northwest corner West 180th Street)

A six-story building of 1907; George F. Pelham, architect.
Pinehurst was the name of the estate of C. P. Bucking, a local landowner whose country seat gave its name to nearby Pinehurst Avenue as well.

PINEHURST TOWERS   *92–102 Pinehurst Avenue*
(northwest corner West 181st Street)

A six-story light brick building of the 1920s.

PLACID HALL   *736 Riverside Drive*
(southeast corner West 151st Street)

A six-story tan-brick building of circa 1900, with marble columns at the entrance and a marquee.
At the time this building was built, Lake Placid in the Adirondack Mountains of New York State was well on its way to becoming a noted resort; it was incorporated as a village in 1900.

PLANETARIUM, THE   *11 West 81st Street*

See *Bownett, The.*

PLANETARIUM APARTMENTS
430 Columbus Avenue

A red granite building of circa 1890 across the street from the American Museum of Natural History and Manhattan Square. The name was obviously added much later, since the Hayden Planetarium was not built until 1935.

PLAZA, THE
795 St. Nicholas Avenue
(southwest corner West 150th Street)

Seven stories and basement; circa 1900; in a semi-*palazzo* style.

PLAZA 50
155 East 50th Street

A 1970s white building.

"Plaza," whether stemming from the hotel or the old telephone exchange for the mid-Fifties (in the days before all-digit dialing) has long denoted chic and stature.

PLAZA FOUR HUNDRED
400 East 56th Street

This forty-story, 628-unit tower built in 1967 (architect, Philip Birnbaum) has an appropriately swank name, evoking no memories of Peter Doelger's Brewery which stood nearby until well into the present century.

PLAZA TOWERS
118 East 60th Street

This Miamiesque apartment building has the distinction of being the first to receive a building permit under the then (1962) new zoning regulations intended to limit density.

The original brochure (printed *before* the name was put up over the door, since it is not mentioned) called the new building "a residence of distinction for New Yorkers who care" and compared its entrance favorably to that of Versailles.

The fountain at the entrance of the thirty-three-story tower was designed by Raymond Loewy/William Smith, Inc.

PLYMOUTH
32–38 Fort Washington Avenue

The name is one plentifully scattered over the English-speaking landscape and has been given to bodies of water, cities, towns, counties, and the like. It derives from the city of Plymouth in Devonshire, England, which was incorporated in 1439.

PLYMOUTH
101 West 74th Street
(northeast corner Columbus Avenue)

This six-story turn-of-the-century fire-escape building has its length along the avenue.

PLYMOUTH
537–541 West 149th Street

A rather grandiose seven-stories-and-basement building of circa 1900, with elaborate stone decoration.

PLYMOUTH TOWER
340 East 93rd Street

A huge buff-brick building; circa 1980. The marquee has not only the name but two outline designs of a ship (the *Mayflower?*).

POCAHONTAS APARTMENT 620 *West 170th Street*

A 1920s building with six stories and an open court of orange brick, with fire escape.

Pocahontas (ca. 1595–1617) was the Indian princess said by the explorer Captain John Smith to have saved his life when he was attacked by her father's warriors. She later married the colonist John Rolfe and was received with honor in England.

POINCIANA, THE   434 *West 120th Street*
(southeast corner Amsterdam Avenue)

A ten-story early-twentieth-century building. The nice entrance with the name in gilt Gothic letters has lost its original marquee.

The poinciana is a tropical shrub or tree best known in the United States as the royal poinciana; it can reach a height of forty feet.

POLO   964 *St. Nicholas Avenue*

A five-story building of the 1920s; now abandoned.

Not far away is the former site of the Polo Grounds at West 155th Street.

POLO GROUNDS TOWERS (NYC Housing Authority)   2975 *Frederick Douglass Boulevard*

This 1968 project occupies the land once used by fashionable Harlemites of the 1880s for playing polo; in 1912 it became the site of an enormous stadium which could hold sixty thousand spectators. It was the home of the New York Giants baseball team until they moved to San Francisco in 1958. The Giants had been playing in the polo stadium since 1883.

POMONA   505 *Columbus Avenue*

A smallish five-story building with fire escape, on the west side of Columbus Avenue north of West 84th Street.

In Roman mythology Pomona was the goddess of fruits and fruit trees.

PONTCHARTRAIN, THE 312–316 *West 109th Street*

This eight-story building by George F. Pelham, architect, was put up in 1907 on the H-plan.

The name comes from the French nobleman who was chancellor of France in the early eighteenth century. He also gave his name to a lake, a hotel, and other places in New Orleans.

PONTIAC, THE
176, 178, 180, 182, 184 *West 82nd Street*
(southeast corner Amsterdam Avenue)

An old five-story building with five arched entrances, each with its own number, in two pairs with one single.

Pontiac was the Ottawa Indian chief (ca. 1720–1769) who led an attack on the British forces in Detroit in 1763.

PORTHOS, THE   *146–148 West 118th Street*

Built in the early twentieth century by Freedom & Feinberg, with architects Bernstein & Bernstein. A six-stories-and-basement building with limestone base and bay windows.

A twin to *The Athos* at 152–154 West 118th Street. Athos and Porthos were two of the three musketeers in Alexandre Dumas's celebrated novel.

Now abandoned.

PORTICO PLACE   *139–145 West 13th Street*

A conversion, circa 1981, of the handsome Greek Revival church built in 1846 on land owned by the Spanish-Portuguese Synagogue. Advertisements for the cooperative apartments called the building "the closest thing to Heaven."

The Reverend Samuel D. Burchard was minister of this church in the 1880s. On 2 October 1884, speaking for a deputation of clergymen calling upon James G. Blaine, whom he supported for the presidency, Burchard attacked the Democrats (who had nominated Grover Cleveland)—in Burchard's opinion, a "party whose antecedents have been Rum, Romanism, and Rebellion." Many observers believed this remark cost Blaine the presidency.

In 1954 the Village Presbyterian Church formed a partnership with the Brotherhood Synagogue, and the building was used for many years by both Jewish and Christian congregations.

Portsmouth

PORTSMOUTH   *38–40 and 42–44 West 9th Street*

A double building with two entrances, each with three columns and each carrying the name. A plaque indicates it was built in 1882. There are six stories; beautifully kept, with outside fire escapes.

POST HALL   *70 Post Avenue*

A 1920s redbrick building.

Post Avenue is named for the Post family, large landowners in the area in the eighteenth century who intermarried with the Nagel family for whom Nagle Avenue is named.

POWELL BUILDING   *105 Hudson Street*

A circa 1890–1900 Renaissance Revival building with a bizarre arrangement of decorative details. Formerly a bank, now converted to residential use.

POWELLTON   *221 West 97th Street*
                                   (northeast corner Broadway)

A seven-story pre–World War I building with fire escapes and open court on West 97th Street. The original iron fence surrounds the basement.

PRAGUE   *171 West 81st Street*

A twin to its neighbors: the *Elliot* on the west and the *Martha* on the east. Each is a five-story turn-of-the-century building with rusticated stone ground floor and an arched doorway.

Probably named for John Prague, a developer of West Side apartments at the turn of the century.

PRAGUE, THE   *77 West 87th Street*
                              (southeast corner Columbus Avenue)

A five-story building only three windows wide on West 87th Street. A Gothic-style entrance marks this turn-of-the-century building.

PRASADA   *50 Central Park West*
                              (southwest corner West 65th Street)

Charles W. Romeyn and Henry R. Wynne were the architects of this 1907 building, notable for its large size and for the banded limestone columns and elaborate carved decoration that distinguish its facade.

The twelve-story building was among the most elaborate in the most fashionable part of Central Park West when it opened, although never very highly praised by architectural writers, who have criticized its bulky feeling.

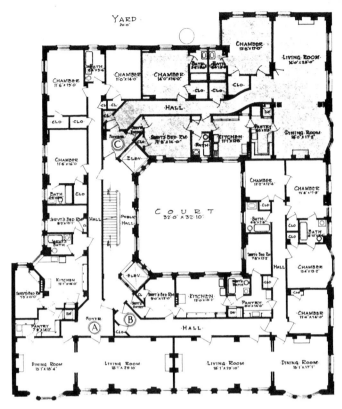

Prasada. *This distinctive building has an interior court and the inevitable long "private halls" within the apartments. Note the contortions in apartments "A" and "B" necessary to create corner dining rooms looking out over Central Park. To get from the living room in apartment "A" to the master bedroom it is necessary to pass the kitchen, maid's room, and delivery area.*

"Prasada" is the Sanskrit word for temple. Sanskrit studies were popular in the United States in the nineteenth century, among the Transcendentalists especially: Ralph Waldo Emerson, for example, was a student of the Sanskrit poem *Bhagavad Gita.*

PRASADA, THE   *26 West 9th Street*

Neo-Georgian redbrick apartment house of nine stories; erected in the 1920s.

PREMIER   *237 West 20th Street*

The name is over the door of this five-story redbrick building; built circa 1900 and now in rather poor condition.

PREMIER, LE   *112 West 56th Street*

A mixed-use condominium built by the Trump Organization
in 1982. Businesses occupy the first nine floors, including the
New York Health & Racquet Club; and the remaining floors are
residential, each floor with two two-bedroom suites.

PREMIER, THE   *333 East 69th Street*

Built in 1963. Mayer, Whittlesey & Glass, with William J.
Conklin, designer, were successful in fitting a fairly large building into a street of small houses.

PRESIDENT MONROE APARTMENTS
226 Lafayette Street
(southwest corner Prince Street)

A six-story white-brick building of circa 1900, with its original black cornice.
[See *Monroe.*]

PRESIDENTIAL TOWERS   *315 West 70th Street*

A 1960s luxury building of sixteen stories, with balconies on
the corners.

PRIMROSE   *551 West 174th Street*
(northwest corner Audubon Avenue)

A six-story building of red brick and limestone; circa 1900.

PRINCE HUMBERT   *520 Cathedral Parkway*

A twin to *The Marc Antony.*
Prince Humbert, heir to the Italian throne, was born in
1904 and reigned briefly as King Umberto II (from May to June
1946).

PRINCESS COURT   *3920 Broadway*
(northeast corner West 164th Street)

A six-story circa-1900 building with entrance on Broadway.
Stone balconies and bayed windows.

PRINTING HOUSE   *421 Hudson Street*

An eight-story circa-1910 structure converted in 1982 from
a printing trades building to cooperative apartments. Details at
the top include an open book surrounded by floral decorations.
In the conversion solar collectors were installed on the roof.

PRISCILLA   *61 West 10th Street*

Six stories; early 1920s. Contiguous to the *Standish.*
[See *Alden.*]

PROSPECT HILL APARTMENTS
333 East 41st Street

A redbrick six-story cooperative apartment building that is almost in the center of, but not part of, *Tudor City*.

Prospect Hill was the name given to the rise of land at the east end of 42nd Street which was cleared for the construction of *Tudor City*.

PROSPECT TOWER
45 Tudor City Place

The tallest building in the *Tudor City* group; no apartments face east toward the United Nations, since when it was built the site was a slaughterhouse. A stone plaque beside the entrance reads: *"Prospect Tower, designed & constructed by the Fred F. French Company. Anno Domini One Thousand Nine Hundred Twenty Seven."*

This was the first unit of *Tudor City* to be completed. The smallest apartments originally rented for $800 to $1,750 yearly.

[Pulitzer House]. *The main entrance to this palatial home of the famous publisher, now a cooperative apartment building.*

[PULITZER HOUSE]
11 East 73rd Street

A Venetian *palazzo* built for Joseph Pulitzer in 1903–1907 by McKim, Mead & White, and converted to apartments in 1934 by J. E. Casale. The facade, with its pillared grandeur, was used as the exterior of Crispin's Auction House in the 1982 movie *Still of the Night*.

PUTNAM   *602–604 West 162nd Street*

A six-story redbrick building of the early twentieth century, with columned porch.

General Israel Putnam commanded the American forces in New York in 1776, including those at Fort Washington, which stood near this building.

PYTHIAN ARMS   *135 West 70th Street*

Built windowless because of the secret rites of the Knights of Pythias, for whom the architect Thomas W. Lamb designed this neo-Egyptian fantasy in 1927.

After a dreary interlude as a branch of Manhattan Community College, the Pythian Temple was converted to residential use in 1982, a job that entailed, among other things, fenestrating the entire building. The architect of the conversion said, "It was like dealing with an enormous Rubik's Cube."

The lavish emblems of the Knights of Pythias were retained: winged lions are sculpted above the door. Across the front of the building are eight columns: four at the doorway are of colored stone.

Over the entrance is written, "If fraternal love held all men bound, how beautiful this world would be." Damon and Pythias were famous in antiquity as symbols of friendship. The Knights of Pythias is a fraternal organization.

The eighty-four condominium apartments in the conversion include one- and two-bedroom duplexes, maisonettes, and penthouses. The conversion received a 1981 American Institute of Architects residential design citation.

QUAKER RIDGE   *201 East 21st Street*

A 1970s white-brick apartment house.

In 1857 the Orchard Street Friends Meeting House moved to 144 East 20th Street.

QUEEN ANNE   *155 East 76th Street*

An early-1960s apartment house with a flashy lobby and buff-brick exterior.

The name is evocative of Old England. Britain's queen Anne reigned from 1702 to 1714 and had special connections with her colony of New York, granting, for example, land to Trinity Church.

QUEENSTON   *16 East 96th Street*
(southwest corner Madison Avenue)

This redbrick and stone building of circa 1900 has an entrance reminiscent of a Roman triumphal arch.

Across the street, on the northeast corner of East 96th Street and Madison Avenue, was George F. Pelham's *Arthur Hall* (1905), which had 819 rooms and "a ballroom for the special convenience of tenants." Now demolished.

Queenston, Ontario, near Niagara Falls, was the scene of a British victory over American forces in 1812.

QUIDNET, THE   *526 West 113th Street*

This eight-story building of variegated tan brick and limestone, with rather nice detailing, opened its doors on 15 April 1910. The architects were Mulliken & Moeller. It offered four large apartments, of between four and seven rooms, on each floor. The Champlin Realty Company offered leases of one to three years.

RAFFORD HALL   *601 West 144th Street*
(northwest corner Broadway)

A six-stories-and-basement building, built in 1907; George F. Pelham, architect. Although now run-down, the building has a fine view down Broadway.

RALEIGH   *121 West 72nd Street*

A tan brick and limestone building of fifteen stories; 1920s. Sir Walter Raleigh (1552–1618), English navigator, explorer, and writer.

RALEIGH   *71 West 92nd Street*

A seven-story building with fire escape, iron balconies, and an open bay.

RALPH ARMS   *134 West 93rd Street*

Twin to *Herbert Arms.*

RALPH J. RANGEL HOUSES (NYC Housing Authority)   *159–16 Harlem River Drive*

This 1951 project is named after a tenant, Ralph J. Rangel, whose brother has served as congressman from the district for many years.

RANCLEY   *2340–2346 Adam Clayton Powell, Jr., Boulevard*

A seven-story circa-1900 building with an imposing entrance.

RANDALL HOUSE   *63 East 9th Street*

A redbrick late-1950s apartment house with projecting marqueelike canopy surrounding the name in silhouette letters.

Thomas Randall, an eighteenth-century privateer, acquired the land surrounding Andrew Elliot's country home "Minto" and bequeathed it to his son, Robert Richard Randall. The estate consisted of most of the land between Washington Square and East 10th Street, from Fifth Avenue to the Bowery. When Robert Richard Randall, who never married, died in 1801, he left the estate to benefit retired seamen and stipulated that the land was never to be sold. Sailors' Snug Harbor—originally on Staten Island, now relocated to North Carolina—was the result of Randall's generosity.

RANDOLPH, THE   *135 East 50th Street*

A ten-story white brick and limestone building of the 1920s.

RANDOLPHO, THE   *272–274 Sherman Avenue*

A six-story light brick building of the 1920s.

RANSBY   *324 West 84th Street*

Circa 1900; a twelve-story redbrick building with a handsomely decorated entrance ornamented with a lion's mask.

RAPPAHANNOCK, THE   *23–25 West 119th Street*

A six-story brick building with limestone trim; a twin to *The Arlington*.
The Rappahannock is an important river of Virginia.

RAVENWOOD   *660 West 180th Street*
                                      (southwest corner Broadway)

A six-story building of limestone; circa 1900.

RAVENSWOOD   *118 East 91st Street*

A five-story apartment whose exterior has been covered in gray stucco, so there's no trace of its date—circa 1890—from the outside.
Edgar, Master of Ravenswood, was the lover of Lucy in Sir Walter Scott's *The Bride of Lammermoor*—better known to today's New Yorkers in Donizetti's operatic version.

RAYMOND   *257 West 111th Street*
                  (northeast corner Frederick Douglass Boulevard)

This once handsome redbrick building of seven stories has been abandoned.

RAYMORE COURT   *238 West 106th Street*

A large building of forbidding aspect, built circa 1900 around two courtyards, with fire escapes set into the back of the courts.

RAYNOR, THE   *450 St. Nicholas Avenue*

A twin to the *Lesster*, overlooking St. Nicholas Park.

RED HOUSE, THE *350 West 85th Street*

This six-story redbrick and stone building just off Riverside Drive is one of the most spectacular small apartment buildings in New York. The architects, Harde & Short, apparently meant to erect an Elizabethan manor house when they designed *The Red House* in 1904, but the ornamentation is Gothic and includes such unusual devices as a large dragon cartouche at the top of the building.

REGENCY EAST *301 East 64th Street*

Red brick; 1970s; one of the three *Regency* buildings in the area.
[See also *Carlton/Regency/Pavilion.*]

REGENCY NORTH *130 East 93rd Street*

A quiet 1930s building with a below-street-level entrance, above which is a discreet plaque reading, "Regency North" (although it's on the south side of the street).

REGENCY SOUTH *250 East 63rd Street*

A white-brick 1960s building.

REGENCY TOWERS *245 East 63rd Street*

This thirty-five-story 1960s apartment house was built by the Carlyle Construction Company, the builders of *Ambassador East, Gotham Towne House,* and *Olympia House.* Wechsler & Samesti were the architects.

REGENT *511 West 143rd Street*

A rather severe six-story building of the early twentieth century.

REGENT HOTEL *223 West 104th Street*
(northeast corner Broadway)

A seventeen-story red-brick building of the 1920s on a site occupied early in this century by the Hope Baptist Church. In 1983 the building was advertising apartments of one and two rooms. Formerly known as the Armstead.

REGENT HOUSE *25 West 54th Street*

A pleasant 1950s building next door to the "Rockefeller Apartments."

REILLY BUILDING *312 West 21st Street*

A nineteenth-century building of five stories and basement, with fire escape; now poorly kept.

RELDNAS HALL   *500 West 122nd Street*
                              (southwest corner Amsterdam Avenue)

A six-story buff-brick building with six granite columns at the entrance; circa 1905. The cornice has been removed.

REMBRANDT, THE   *31 Jane Street*

A 1960s redbrick apartment house.

Rembrandt Harmensz van Rijn (1609–1669) enjoyed a meteoric burst of renewed popular acclaim in the early 1960s when his *Aristotle Contemplating the Bust of Homer* was purchased by the Metropolitan Museum of Art.

RENAISSANCE   *72 West 88th Street*
                              (southeast corner Columbus Avenue)

A five-story fire-escape building of the turn of the century, with its long side on Columbus Avenue; now in poor condition and partly boarded up.

RENAISSANCE COURTS   *111 Ellwood Street*
                              (northeast corner Sherman Avenue)

Recent rehabilitation of a six-story redbrick building of the 1920s, with forty-eight units and a new name.

Ellwood Street, which runs only between Hillside and Sherman avenues, was laid out in 1891 and given its present name in 1911, but the origin of that name has escaped even the most diligent researchers.

RENE   *11 Manhattan Avenue*

Six stories built at the turn of the century.

RENOIR HOUSE   *225 East 63rd Street*

Named after Pierre-Auguste Renoir (1841–1919), the French Impressionist whose work enjoyed phenomenal popularity during the 1960s, when this building went up. Renoir's signature is reproduced on the building's canopy.

RENWICK, THE   *808 Broadway*

A 1982 conversion of a commercial building in the neo-Gothic taste; next to Grace Church, the masterpiece of James Renwick, Jr. (1818–1895), who was also the architect of St. Patrick's Cathedral and the old Corcoran Gallery (now the Renwick Gallery) in Washington, D.C.

The Renwick was built in 1888 by Renwick, Aspinwall & Russell.

RENWICK GARDENS APARTMENTS
332 East 29th Street

A redbrick building of the 1960s—nothing to do with James Renwick architecturally, at all.

REVERE, THE
400 East 54th Street

A high rise of 1972, built on the site of the old Fashion Institute of Technology.
[See also *Paul Revere.*]

REVERE HALL
622 West 114th Street

A six-story redbrick building of about 1905, with recessed fire escape.
A twin building to *Hudson Hall* at 628.

REXFORD
230 West 79th Street
(southeast corner Broadway)

A twelve-story building of the 1920s.
Twin to the *Sanford.*

REXMERE
328–330 West 85th Street

A circa-1900 white brick and limestone building of six stories, with tastefully modernized entrance.

REXMOORE
72–74 Vermilyea Street

A six-story building of the 1920s.

REXTON
320 West 83rd Street

A seven-story circa-1900 building with a recessed fire escape between the two bays facing the street. The windows are heavily ornamented, and the building has its original pediment.
A twin to the *Cayuga.*

RHINECLIFF COURT
788 Riverside Drive
(southeast corner West 156th Street)

A ten-story building with an open-court entrance; circa 1900.
Rhinecliff is a town on the Hudson River in Dutchess County that was popular as a summer residence for nineteenth-century New Yorkers.

RHINELAND, THE
244 Riverside Drive
(southeast corner West 97th Street)

Robert T. Lyons was the architect and builder of this six-story 1907 building of tan brick and limestone with an open-court entrance.

RHINELANDER, THE   *1327–1329 Lexington Avenue*

This huge 1920s Georgian-inspired apartment house runs from East 88th to East 89th streets. It has twin entrances and a three-story limestone base below eight more stories in brick. The water towers on the roof are hidden behind graceful urns and Palladian windows. They don't built them like this any-more—as evidenced by the 1960s banalities flanking *The Rhinelander*.

The name is taken from the Rhinelander family, one of New York's oldest. Originally in the sugar trade, they owned much of the land in the East Eighties and Nineties in the nineteenth century, and the Protestant Episcopal Church of the Holy Trinity at 316 East 88th Street is built on land donated by the Misses Rhinelander in 1895.

At one time many "old money" New York families had a RHinelander telephone exchange. BUtterfield came later—*Vide* John O'Hara.

RHINELANDER APARTMENTS   *12 Fifth Avenue*

A circa-1900 redbrick and limestone building with balconies; has a narrow town-house appearance. Three stories have been added to the original six.

RICACOURT, THE   *534 West 152nd Street*

An old center-court building whose name is Spanglish for "rich court."

RICHFIELD   *4 Manhattan Avenue*

A six-story building standing between West 100th and 101st streets, built at the turn of the century when this area was being developed.

RICHMOND   *147 West 79th Street*

A fifteen-story redbrick building of the 1920s, with exquisite terra-cotta details in the Renaissance manner.

RICHMOND HILL, THE   *27 Washington Square North (northeast corner MacDougal Street)*

This rather forbidding gray building of seven stories dates from circa 1900 and is at the end of a row of charming brick townhouses.

Richmond Hill was the name of a manor house built by Abraham Mortier in 1767 and occupied by George Washington during the American Revolution.

[See also *Greenwich Village*.]

Richmond Hill Apartment House. *Note how the builder of this early building failed to show any respect for the fine old townhouses in the rest of this historic block between MacDougal Street and Fifth Avenue.*

RIIS HOUSES (NYC Housing Authority)
454 East 10th Street

This large project dates from 1949 and is distinguished by an attractive open plaza constructed in 1966.

The namesake: Jacob August Riis (1849–1914), Danish-born journalist, writer, and social reformer. Riis was instrumental in helping to alleviate the desperate living conditions of the poor. Among his writings are *How the Other Half Lives* (1890); *The Children of the Poor* (1892); and *Children of the Tenements* (1903).

RIO GRANDE
RIO VISTA
15 Fort Washington Avenue
21 Fort Washington Avenue

Two early-twentieth-century buildings being rehabilitated in the early 1980s by the city of New York. On the side of the *Rio Vista* are the original painted advertisements for apartments.

RITZ TOWER
465 Park Avenue
(northeast corner East 57th Street)

Described in a 1931 promotional piece as "just a bit of Paris on Park Avenue," this elegant forty-two-story tower was designed by Emery Roth and Carrère & Hastings and built in 1925–1927; its construction was delayed by one of the worst building fires in New York's history.

The site is a small one for such a tall building. The gracefully decorated upper stories (with escutcheons, obelisks, terraces) compare favorably with the contemporary starkness of its next-door neighbor, *Galleria.*

The *Ritz Tower* started out as an apartment hotel and was owned for a time by William Randolph Hearst (who was forced to sell it in 1938 during the depression). It became a cooperative in 1955.

Among its roster of well-known tenants: Goodman Ace, Paulette Goddard, Irving Lazar.

On the ground floor are the Mitsukoshi Gallery (where Charles of the Ritz used to have headquarters) and the First Women's Bank (where Henri Soulé used to preside over Le Pavillon, the celebrated French restaurant).

RIVER ARTS   *159–00 Riverside Drive*

A seven-story redbrick building with white iron entrance; 1960s.

RIVER COURT   *427 East 52nd Street*

New, large, with a discreet—almost forbidding—entrance.

RIVER EAST PLAZA   *402 East 90th Street*

A 1970s redbrick condominium.

RIVER HOUSE   *435–447 East 52nd Street*

Bottomley, Wagner & White were the architects for this 1930s residential tower, surely one of the most luxurious and well situated ever built. Until the FDR Drive was completed in the early 1940s, a private dock allowed tenants and members of the River Club (in the same building) to moor their yachts right at their own dock.

Thirty stories high, with only seventy-three apartments that originally sold for $37,000 to $275,000, *River House* has been synonymous with wealth and power from the day it was built. Residents have included Angier Biddle Duke, Henry Kissinger, Cornelius Vanderbilt Whitney, Josh and Nedda Logan, and John Kenneth Galbraith. In recent years Gloria Vanderbilt was denied permission to buy an apartment in the building. She sued on the grounds that the board of the cooperative had rejected her because of her friendship with Bobby Short; the board said it had done so because she couldn't afford the apartment, priced then at $1.1 million.

A curving drive leads to an austerely beautiful black marble-floored lobby. Upstairs a "typical" apartment has twelve rooms, six baths, two fireplaces, and an extraordinary view of Long Island City.

River House. *Photographed about 1927, seen from the east and show-ing the yacht mooring at the water's edge that was a feature of this building until the Franklin D. Roosevelt Drive was put through in the 1940s.*

RIVER MANSION
337 Riverside Drive
(southeast corner West 106th Street)

Robert D. Kohn was the architect of this five-story building of red brick and limestone (built circa 1900), which has mini-versions of Italianate columns.

RIVER TERRACE
157–10 Riverside Drive

A 1960s redbrick building.

RIVER TOWER
420 East 54th Street

This thirty-eight-story residential tower was built in 1982; a Dubuffet sculpture graces the open plaza; the building goes through to East 53rd Street, where Youle's Shot Tower stood from 1821 to about 1920 (molten metal was poured through a

sieve at the top, fell into a well twenty-five feet below the
ground's surface, resulting in metal shot for guns).

Owned and developed by Harry Macklowe, *River Tower* was
aimed at the same affluent tenantry as *Olympic Towers* and *Gal-
leria*. There is a bilingual concierge, telex, and wine cellar. A
one-bedroom apartment rented for $1,880 per month in 1983.

RIVER VIEW   *3612–3618 Broadway*
(southwest corner West 149th Street)

Seven stories in red brick; turn-of-the-century. Buckman &
Fox, architects. The entrance is on Broadway.

RIVER VIEW TOWERS   *626 Riverside Drive*
(West 139th to West 140th streets)

A twenty-four-story "middle income" cooperative.

RIVERCLIFF   *628 West 151st Street*

Early-1920s building with set-back entrance.

The name derives from its position overlooking the Hudson
near Riverside Drive.

RIVERCREST, THE   *25 Fort Washington Avenue*
(southwest corner West 160th Street)

Built in 1906 by Schwartz & Gross and B. N. Marcus, architects; in red brick, with recessed fire escapes.

RIVERDALE   *67 Riverside Drive*
(southeast corner West 79th Street)

This unusually attractive building is heavily ornamented
with stone carvings; on each floor there are wrought-iron balconies with French windows supported by elaborate corbels decorated with floral swags. There is an open bay on Riverside
Drive and a portico entrance. This nine-stories-and-basement
building was put up in 1905 and at that time had two ten-room
apartments on each floor, with an annual rent of $2,000 to
$3,500.

RIVERFRONT   *555 East 78th Street*

Certainly an accurate name for the 1980 conversion of what
had been for many years a residence for women, the East End
Hotel. It faces directly on the FDR Drive and the East River.

RIVER'S BEND   *501 East 87th Street*

This handsome gray-brick apartment house of the 1960s was
built by Sheldon Solow. The architects were Paul & Jarmul, and
the early promotional literature stressed the rooftop health club
and breathtaking views.

The East River bends just above this address as it joins the
Harlem River.

RIVERSIDE MANSIONS

410 Riverside Drive
(northeast corner West 113th Street)

A grand building of the early twentieth century with gabled mansard roof and windows trimmed with limestone, thirteen stories and attics, the first three stories of rusticated granite. The porte-cochere is now enclosed and used as an entrance court. This well-maintained building has a marble entrance hall laid with Oriental rugs. Over the door is stained glass.

RIVERSIDE PLAZA

253 West 73rd Street

[See *Level Club Condominium.*]

RIVERSIDE STUDIOS

342 West 71st Street

Formerly the West View, this seven-story building has bayed windows. Circa 1900.

RIVERSIDE TOWERS

80 Riverside Drive
(northeast corner West 80th Street)

An undistinguished sixteen-story 1920s redbrick building.

RIVERVIEW

230–236 Seaman Avenue
(southwest corner West 215th Street)

A five-story white-brick building of the 1920s, with an open-court entrance. Built on the original site of the Seaman family farm, which occupied twenty-five acres between what is today West 214th and West 217th streets.

RIVERVIEW, THE

316 West 93rd Street

A six-story redbrick building of 1904; built by the architect George F. Pelham on the long-hall plan.
A twin to the *Clarence* next door.

RIVERVIEW APARTMENTS

602–616 West 135th Street

An early-twentieth-century five-story building with handsome fire escapes. The ornamental detail is now lost.

RIVIERA

790 Riverside Drive
(between West 156th and West 157th streets)

This huge apartment house of unusual shape was built in 1910 on a curved plot in Riverside Drive at West 156th Street.

The architects were Rouse & Goldstone, and the apartments—of five to ten rooms—were, as Andrew Alpern points out in *Apartments for the Affluent,* designed to attract middle-class tenants with upper-class pretensions. Libraries, butler's pantries, lavish lobbies, and ceremonial balconies were coupled with smallish rooms and long, awkwardly placed corridors and "private halls."

ROBERT FULTON

The American portrait painter, engineer, and inventor Robert Fulton (1765–1815) is still regarded as the inventor of the steamboat when, in fact, it is more accurate to say he was the first man to develop a commercially successful steamboat. His father-in-law, Robert Livingston of New York, held the monopoly on steamboat navigation on the Hudson River.

In 1807 Fulton launched the Clermont—*named for the Livingston estate in Columbia County, New York—which made the first successful trip to Albany by steam and launched a new era in the history of travel.*

Fulton lived at 1 State Street. When he died there in 1815, all business in the city was suspended, and guns were fired at the harbor forts while the funeral procession was wending its way to Trinity Church, where he was interred in the Livingston family vault.

In 1909 Fulton and the Clermont *were honored during the Hudson-Fulton celebration.*

ROBERT FULTON COURT   *559 West 156th Street*

A well-preserved turn-of-the-century building of brick and stone, with nice detailing.

ROBERT FULTON HOTEL   *228 West 71st Street*

[See *Parc Coliseum.*]

ROBERT FULTON HOUSES (NYC Housing Authority)   *421 West 17th Street*

This Chelsea project has almost one thousand apartments in eleven buildings and dates from 1965.

ROBERT WATT HALL   *549 West 113th Street*

Formerly called Claremont Court. A six-story white-brick building with fire escape; recently renovated and has new windows.

A twin to *Cathedral Court.*

ROCHAMBEAU   *312 Manhattan Avenue*
(northeast corner West 113th Street)

A twin to the *Lafayette.*

Jean-Baptiste-Donatien de Vimeur, marquis de Rochambeau

(1725–1807), French brigadier who served with General Washington during the American Revolution. He returned to France in 1783 and was made marshal of France in 1791.

ROCK FOREST   *255 Fort Washington Avenue*
                            (southwest corner West 171st Street)

A six-story building of circa 1900; in white brick and with an arched entrance.

ROCKCLYFFE, THE   *600 West 141st Street*
                            (southeast corner Broadway)

A plain six-story building with center court; built in 1905 by Schwartz & Gross and B. N. Marcus, architects.

"ROCKEFELLER APARTMENTS"
                            17 West 54th Street

From the time that this apartment building was erected in 1936, its architecture has been much admired. Harrison & Fouilhoux, the architects, employed four rows of cylindrical bay windows on the front which looks over the garden of the Museum of Modern Art.

Inside, the building contains rather small apartments, designed for single people or small families but incorporating the latest designs—radiators are concealed, for example. The building made such an impression that it was 100 percent rented before it was finished.

John D. Rockefeller, Jr., financed the building which is situated on land originally acquired for Rockefeller Center. The home of John D. Rockefeller, Sr., was around the corner at 4 West 55th Street.

ROCKFALL   *545 West 111th Street*
                            (northeast corner Broadway)

A turn-of-the-century building with two bays and open-court entrance. Stone balcony supports, but the balconies are gone.

ROCKLAND   *541–547 West 180th Street*

A six-story building with open-court entrance.

ROCKLEDGE HALL   *330 West 102nd Street*
                            (northeast corner Riverside Drive)

A twelve-story ornamented building of the 1920s, now housing a Buddhist church.

Rockledge is the name of towns in Florida and Pennsylvania.

RODIN STUDIOS
220 West 57th Street
(southwest corner Seventh Avenue)

Built on the site of an earlier apartment building, the Inverness, the *Rodin Studios,* named for the great French sculptor, Auguste Rodin (1840–1917), was the home of many notable writers and artists until converted to offices in the 1930s.

ROGER/MORRIS
474–476 West 158th Street

The *Roger* at 472 is next door to the *Morris* at 476. These twin buildings of the 1920s are collectively named for the wealthy New York Loyalist who built the imposing home in the Georgian-Federal style that still stands nearby in Roger Morris Park. Known today as the Jumel Mansion—after a later and more famous owner—the house was built as a summer residence in 1765 and was occupied by George Washington, who used it as his headquarters until he was forced to retreat in 1776 to New Jersey. Roger Morris fled to England with other Loyalists, never to return.

ROMA
234–236 East 50th Street

A turn-of-the-century building with fire escape and the name chiseled in stone over the portico—a name that recalls the Italophile period in New York's cultural life and real estate nomenclature.

ROMANA
528 West 111th Street

Along with the *Charlemagne* and *Amele Hall,* one of three identical eight-story white-brick buildings of the turn of the century.

ROMANZA
228–230 Eighth Avenue
(between West 21st and West 22nd streets)

A nineteenth-century white-brick building of six stories, in the middle of the block; its entrance is next to that of its twin, the *Brensonia*.

ROMEYN
56 West 111th Street
(southeast corner Lenox Avenue)

A seven-story brick building of circa 1900.
Romeyn is the name of a very old New York family, prominent in Dutch days, whose property is shown on the Castello plan of 1660, the oldest known map of the city.
Charles Romeyn was a well-known architect of the late nineteenth century whose buildings include the *Prasada*.

ROOKVILLE
247 Audubon Avenue
(northeast corner West 177th Street)

A six-story brick building; circa 1900.

ROOSEVELT, THE   *230–232 East 14th Street*

A virtual twin to its next-door neighbor *The Navarre* and probably named for Theodore Roosevelt, a local, as well as a national, hero.

ROSALIND   *111 West 106th Street*

A small early-twentieth-century building with fire escape.
Rosalind was the cross-dressing heroine of Shakespeare's *As You Like It.*

ROSBERT HALL   *560 West 163rd Street*
(southeast corner Broadway)

Redbrick, turn-of-the-century.

ROSCOE   *446 St. Nicholas Avenue*

Abandoned.

ROSE   *200 West 78th Street*
(southwest corner Amsterdam Avenue)

A smallish circa-1900 building with a rusticated ground floor and bay windows.
Identical buildings are the *Cecilia* at 202 and the *Florence* at 204.

ROSE   *20–22 West 109th Street*
(southeast corner Manhattan Avenue)

An old six-story building recently renovated; it now lacks its cornice.

ROSE COURT   *130 West 228th Street*

A six-story white-brick building of the 1920s, in Marble Hill.
A twin to *Laura Court.*

ROSE GARDEN APARTMENTS
235 West 70th Street

A white-brick seven-story building with open fire escapes and a modernized sunken entrance . . . but no sign of a rose garden.

ROSEDALE   *352 West 118th Street*

A twin to the *Claire.*

ROSEMERE   *145 West 127th Street*

A twin to the *Viola*.

ROSEWALL   *303–317 East 88th Street*

A six-story tan-brick building of the 1920s, with fire escapes.

ROSEWALL COURT   *5025–5035 Broadway*

An early-1920s building with seven stories, built around an open-court entrance reached by steps from the street.

ROSLYN, THE   *317 West 14th Street*

A five-story brownstone of the 1880s, with Art Deco entrance more or less matching that of *The Victor* next door.
Roslyn is a residential village on Long Island.

ROSSLEIGH COURT   *1 West 85th Street*
                                        (northwest corner Central Park West)

Built in 1905–1906 by Mulliken & Moeller as a twin to the Central Park View (now called *Orwell House*). This twelve-story building of purplish brick included apartments of four to eight rooms, renting for $1,700 to $3,100 annually. Among the allurements were "marble kitchens."

ROTHERWOOD   *717 West 177 Street*

An English-sounding name (there's a Rother River in Derbyshire) for this Washington Heights structure.

ROXANNE   *65 West 127th Street*

Abandoned.

ROXBURY TERRACE   *810 West 183rd Street*
                                        (southeast corner Pinehurst Avenue)

A large six-story building of the 1920s.
Roxbury is the name of towns in New York State and Massachusetts.

ROYAL ARMS, THE   *600 West 138th Street*
                                             (southwest corner Broadway)

Built circa 1906 by Thain & Thain, architects; six stories of red brick with fire escapes and unusual pillared walls.
Near to, but not a twin to, the *Imperial Arms*.

ROYAL YORK

425 East 63rd Street
420 East 64th Street

The first tenants of the *Royal York* could actually specify the colors of their kitchen appliances before moving in in 1955.

Greenberg & Ames were the architects of this 498-unit behemoth that was for a long time in the late 1950s and early 1960s a popular residence for young career people.

The *Royal York* has had its share of well-known tenants, among them Dr. Joyce Brothers and Eydie Gorme.

ROYALTON HOTEL   *47 West 43rd Street*

A twelve-story early-1900s·building that has its name chiseled above the door and also proclaimed by a neon sign. The handsome classical entrance is topped with a stone vase.

ROYALTY   *600 West 140th Street*

Six stories in white brick, turn-of-the-century, with bayed windows.

RUGBY HALL   *35 Claremont Avenue*

[See *Eton Hall*.]

RUPPERT TOWERS and YORKVILLE TOWERS   *East 90th to East 93rd streets, Second to Third avenues*

This enormous complex of redbrick towers was designed in 1974–1976 by Davis, Brody & Assocs. Handsome, if somewhat severe and monolithic, these were built with government assistance as Mitchell-Lama projects.

The site, in the part of Manhattan known as Yorkville, was formerly occupied by the Ruppert Brewery; once New York's favorite beer was brewed there. Colonel Jacob Ruppert, owner of the New York Yankees, built Yankee Stadium for his team. The beer is now a long-gone taste. Yorkville, because of its German population, once had more beer halls than any other part of Manhattan.

RUTGERS HOUSE (NYC Housing Authority)   *61 Pike Street*

Built in 1965, this five-building complex was named in honor of Henry Rutgers (1745–1830), an early New York entrepreneur and landlord whose farm was nearby. In addition to *Rutgers Houses,* a street and the state university of New Jersey were named after him.

RUTH   *306 West 114th Street*

A twin to the *Montgomery* at 302.

RUTH, THE   *449–453 West 123rd Street*
                    (between Morningside Drive and Amsterdam Avenue)

Charles Hensle was the owner of this building with two
wings. The first two stories are of Indiana limestone. The design
was said to be "Colonial, modernized." The reception hall,
however, was decorated and furnished "in pure Moorish style."
    The roof was provided with open-air clothes-drying frames,
and during the summer tenants could take the air in the roof
garden.

RUTHERFORD   *360 Riverside Drive*
                               (northeast corner West 108th Street)

A modest thirteen-story white-brick building; circa 1920.

RUTHMORE   *160 Sherman Avenue*

A six-story building of the 1920s.

RUXTON, THE   *50 West 72nd Street*

A sixteen-story 1920s building; facade of textured brick with
attractive Tudor-style decorations. The ground floor is now occupied by a Chinese restaurant.

SADIVIAN ARMS, THE   *695 St. Nicholas Avenue*
                               (southwest corner West 145th Street)

When built in 1906 by the architects Thain & Thain, *The
Sadivian Arms* had large apartments with servants' quarters. According to brochures, the dining rooms have "seven-foot quart-
ered oak, solid paneled wainscoting, and the floors in dining
room, parlor, library and music room [were] parquet birch."
The building had a roof garden "provided with palms, rugs, ta-
bles, and electric lights," and in winter a "winter-house [was]
made by roofing the garden with glass." Rents ran $600 to
$1,000 a year.
    All this grandeur is now departed, but the intriguing name
of the building is still emblazoned on a huge gilt coat of arms
over the arched doorway. On the ground floor are the Sugar Hill
Deli and the Solid Gold Variety Shop.

SAGUENAY   *538 West 143rd Street*
                                     (southeast corner Broadway)

A twin to *The Castleton.*
    The Saguenay is an important Canadian river noted for the
beauty of its scenery.

ST. AGNES   *41 Convent Avenue*

A very large seven-story building of circa 1900, with an
open-court entrance.

Saint Agnes was a Roman martyr, beheaded at the age of thirteen circa A.D. 304. Her feast is on 21 January.

ST. ALBANS   515 *Cathedral Parkway*

A plain ten-story white-brick and stone building of the turn of the century, with an open-court entrance.

St. Albans, England, has one of the finest medieval cathedrals in the British Isles, and the use of the name here is doubtless connected with the nearby Cathedral of St. John the Divine.

[ST. ANN'S SCHOOL]   80 *East 11th Street*

A handsome old redbrick school building with its name—and the date 1870—still emblazoned on the facade; now recycled as apartments. Next door is the Ritz nightclub.

ST. AUGUSTA   408–410 *West 130 Street*

A six-story buff-brick building; circa 1900.

ST. BENEDICT   601 *West 181st Street*
                    (*northwest corner St. Nicholas Avenue*)

A five-story tan brick and limestone building of circa 1900; the Chemical Bank has a branch on the ground floor.

Of the several Saints Benedict, the Italian monk who founded the Benedictine order at Monte Cassino circa A.D. 529 is perhaps the most famous.

ST. BRENDAN   598 *West 178th Street*
                    (*southeast corner St. Nicholas Avenue*)

A five-story redbrick and limestone building; circa 1900.

Saint Brendan was an Irish monk of the sixth century who in his legendary travels discovered a large island in the Atlantic, identified by some as North America.

ST. CABRINI TOWER   222 *East 19th Street*

A 1960s white apartment house, now used by staff of nearby Cabrini Medical Center.

Mother Cabrini, founder of the order of nuns who administer the hospital, was the first U.S. citizen to be canonized.

ST. CECILIA   49 *St. Nicholas Terrace*
                    (*southeast corner West 130th Street*)

A six-story white-brick building; circa 1900.

Saint Cecilia was a Roman virgin and patroness of music martyred circa 230. Feast day: 22 November.

ST. CHARLES   101 *West 72nd Street*

A six-story redbrick building of circa 1900; now repainted.

ST. CHARLES   *561 West 148th Street*

A typical turn-of-the-century building that's seen better days.

ST. DENIS   *200 Riverside Drive*
                              (northeast corner West 92nd Street)

Built about 1905, this redbrick building of nine stories and basement contained apartments of nine to ten rooms when it opened. The pediment has been removed. There is a columned entrance on West 92nd Street. The architect was George F. Pelham, and the builder J. Axelrod.

Saint Denis was called the Apostle to the Gauls and is the patron saint of France.

ST. ELIZABETH   *409 West 129th Street*

A six-story circa-1900 building.

Queens of Portgual and Hungary named Elizabeth are honored as saints.

ST. ELMO   *170 West 85th Street*
                              (southeast corner Amsterdam Avenue)

A five-story building of light brick built circa 1900; with its original pediment, recently cleaned, but with a poorly modernized corner ground floor.

St. Elmo was the title of a phenomenally popular sentimental novel by Augusta Jane Evans of Mobile, Alabama; published in 1867, the work sold over one million copies and gave its name to streets, hotels, and even towns.

Saint Elmo is the patron of sailors.

ST. EVONA   *3340 Broadway*
                              (northeast corner West 135th Street)

A six-stories-and-basement building of circa 1900; in white brick.

ST FRANCIS
     41 St. Nicholas Terrace (northwest corner West 129th Street)

A six-story white-brick building of turn of the century.

Saint Francis was born in Assisi in 1182, founded the Order of Lesser Brethren (Franciscans), and died in 1226. Feast day: 4 October.

ST. FRANCIS COURT   *583 Riverside Drive*
                              (northeast corner West 135th Street)

Six stories and basement; turreted on the corner; built in 1904 on the center-court plan. The architects were Neville & Bagge. Originally it had apartments of five to eight rooms, renting for $720 to $1,500 annually.

According to a 1983 exhibition in the bookshop of the Cathedral of St. John the Divine, Saint Francis is the patron saint of ecology.

ST. GABRIEL'S COURT   *202–204 East 35th Street*

Small 1920s brownstone building with a Spanish courtyard entrance.

Originally near St. Gabriel's Church, which was demolished during the construction of the Queens-Midtown Tunnel.

ST. GEORGE   *1125 Lexington Avenue*

A seven-story late-nineteenth-century brick and stone apartment house; fire escapes and stores at ground level indicate its less-than-patrician origins. The dignified entrance (new glass) has the name in stone above the door.

Saint George is the patron saint of England.

[ST. GEORGE HOTEL]   *49 East 11th Street*

This handsome brick apartment building with a decidedly up-to-date look is actually a 1970s conversion of a nineteenth-century hotel. The dark brick provides an interesting contrast to the gleaming white cast-iron building next door.

ST. GERMAIN   *33 Greenwich Avenue*

An early 1960s white and black apartment building.

St.-Germain on Paris's Left Bank is the site of much student activity; likewise, Greenwich Avenue cuts through the heart of New York's "Left Bank," Greenwich Village.

One of New York City's earliest apartment houses was called the St. Germain. It was located at the intersection of West 23rd Street and Broadway and was demolished to make way for the Flatiron Building in 1902.

ST. HELENA   *418–420 West 130th Street*

Six stories; in red brick; circa 1900.

Saint Helena was the mother of Constantine, the first Christian Roman emperor; her feast day is 18 August.

ST. JAMES COURT   *214 West 92nd Street*
(southeast corner Broadway)

A large seven-story building with two open courts on Broadway. The name appears over the entrance which is flanked by granite columns.

The popularity of the name St. James derives no doubt from its association with the royal palace in London, which was first used as a residence by Henry VIII. Although no longer occupied by the monarchs, it gives its name officially to the British court, foreign diplomats being "ambassadors to the Court of St. James's."

St. James's Tower. *Plan of a three-bed-room apartment in this 1982 high-rise luxury building. Note that two of the bathrooms have bidets and one has its own sauna. The dining room apparently has a structural column in one corner and the closet doors are of the bifold type. This apartment, on the nineteenth floor, was offered at $1,250,000.*

ST. JAMES PLACE   *543–545 West 146th Street*

A six-story redbrick building of circa 1900.

ST. JAMES'S TOWER   *415 East 54th Street*

This superluxury condominium tower has 106 apartments priced in 1982, when the building opened, at $330,000 to $7 million. Designed by Richard Roth of Emery Roth & Sons, *St. James's Tower* rises from a nicely landscaped plaza adorned with splashing fountains surrounding a glass-enclosed lobby-garden.

The building's developers were a British consortium headed by Michael Stevens. In London the firm's offices are located in the St. James's district, just off Piccadilly, hence providing inspiration for the properly Anglophile name.

The brochure for *St. James's Tower* is one of the most elaborate done for a New York apartment house, illustrated in color and boxed. The text was printed in English, French, and Spanish. Agents for the building had offices in London, Geneva, Houston, Nassau, and Kuwait. The motto for the building was "New York's New Place Between Beekman Place and Sutton Place."

St. James's Tower is on the site of the old Brevoort estate, where the New York family's palatial country seat, surrounded by gardens and fruit trees, stood until the 1860s, when the district became commercial.

ST. JOHN   *511 West 112th Street*

A six-story redbrick building with nice ironwork and a fire

St. James's Tower. *These floor plans for the south penthouse duplex apartment indicate such luxurious features as a library and game room, a dining room and breakfast room, a butler's room and a maid's room, and a separate service area near the service elevator, all typical of early luxury apartments but notably absent in recent years. Of course, the price reflects the luxury: the "common charge" (maintenance) was almost $5,000 a month.*

escape. The entrance treatment is similar to that of many London row houses. Turn-of-the-century.

The name is from the nearby Cathedral of St. John the Divine.

[See also *Cathedral*.]

ST. JOHN COURT
500 West 111th Street

This early-twentieth-century six-story building of salmon-colored brick, with an elaborate entrance, takes its name from the nearby cathedral.

[ST. JOSEPH'S HOME]
329 East 63rd Street

An apartment building made out of an old institutional structure. Interesting Victorian-Gothic architecture.

ST. LAWRENCE
413 West 128th Street

A five-stories-and-basement building; turn-of-the-century; still carrying its name above the door.

Lawrence Street, which no longer exists, ran diagonally between Convent Avenue and Broadway.

Saint Lawrence was a deacon of the early Roman church and martyr who was roasted on a gridiron.

ST. LOUIS
319 West 94th Street

A six-story building of circa 1900 retaining its original

name, but now advertised as a "residence hotel" offering "kitchen privileges."

Named for Louis IX, king of France (1226–1270), and crusader who was canonized in 1297.

ST. LOUIS   *118 West 112th Street*

A six-story redbrick building of circa 1900. A twin to the *Frontenac*.

ST. MARIE   *321 East 10th Street*

A five-story building of circa 1890 on Tompkins Square North. The upper part of the building is brick painted green.

A virtual twin to the *Bonsall* next door.

ST. MARKS   *115 East 9th Street*

The canopy of this white-brick 1960s apartment house shows no apostrophe in the name of the building, despite the fact that the next block is called St. Mark's Place.

ST. MARK'S FLATS   *122–126 St. Mark's Place*

St. Mark's Place is East 8th Street and takes its name from historic St.-Mark's-in-the-Bowery Church on Second Avenue and 10th Street.

This six-story building in the Renaissance Revival style, dating from circa 1880, is redbrick with stone trim. It is a twin to the *Tompkins Flats* across the street.

ST. MARY'S   *724 Eleventh Avenue*

This five-story tenement has "St. Mary's–1887" emblazoned on the cornice.

ST. MIHIEL   *165–171 Pinehurst Avenue*
                                      (northeast corner West 185th Street)

A six-story 1920s building.

One of the decisive battles of World War I occurred in September 1918 at Saint-Mihiel in northern France when American troops, in their first major offensive of the war, drove the Germans from a salient they had held since 1914.

ST. MONICA   *419 West 129th Street*

A six-story white-brick building; circa 1900.

Saint Monica was a Roman matron and mother of Saint Augustine; she died in Africa in 387. Feast day: 4 May.

ST. NICHOLAS

As Mrs. Schuyler Van Rensselaer pointed out in her History of New York in the Seventeenth Century: *"At New Amsterdam the celebration of Christmas and other old church festivals was not thought, as in . . . Massachusetts . . . a 'great dishonour' to God. Most characteristically Dutch were the St. Nicholas Day and New Year's Day observances."*

Saint Nicholas, better known today as Santa Claus, was a favorite patron saint in both old and new Amsterdam. The image served as the figurehead on the New Netherland, *the ship that brought the first Dutch colonists to Manhattan in 1624.*

Saint Nicholas was a bishop of Asia Minor who lived around A.D. *300; he was noted for his great charity and generosity.*

His feast day, December 6, is still observed annually by the New-York Historical Society, but thanks to the well-known poem

St. Nicholas Avenue, 1905. This view is looking south from West 117th Street, across Seventh Avenue (now called Adam Clayton Powell, Jr., Boulevard) toward West 116th Street. In the left foreground is Kilpatrick Square. Four newly built apartment houses are visible: from left to right they are Graham Court, *the* Wilhelmina, *the* Acadia, *and* El Nido.

by New York's own Clement Clarke Moore, A Visit from St. Nicholas, *he has become completely identified with the twenty-fourth day of December, not the sixth.*

ST. NICHOLAS   *10 St. Mark's Place*

A five-story house with its patron saint's name on the cornice. The building—circa 1870—provides a sober contrast to the flamboyant German Shooting Club next door at number 12.

ST. NICHOLAS   *52–56 St. Nicholas Avenue*

Six stories of buff brick; between West 113th and West 114th streets, with its original name visible; recently rehabilitated.

ST. NICHOLAS   *1589A St. Nicholas Avenue*

A six-story building of the early 1920s in the long unbroken block between West 141st and West 145th streets.

ST. NICHOLAS HOUSES (NYC Housing Authority)   *215 West 127th Street*

A mid-1950s project named for the nearby north-south avenue.

ST. REGIS   *3675–3677 Broadway*
(northwest corner West 152nd Street)

A buff-brick late-nineteenth-century building whose name (shared with the famous hotel as well as a lake in the Adirondacks) derives from an Indian tribe in what is now upstate New York and the province of Quebec. These Iroquois had been converted by French missionaries who named their settlement after Saint John Francis Regis (1597–1640), a nobleman-priest canonized in 1737.

ST. RITA, THE   *605 West 144th Street*

A sooty white five-stories-and-basement building, circa 1900, that has seen better days.
Saint Rita was a widow of Cascia, Italy, whose feast day is 22 May.

ST. TROPEZ   *340 East 64th Street*

Towering above the Maxwell's Plum restaurant, across East 64th Street, the entrance to this, New York City's first condominium, no longer bears the name it bore at its birth. However, the St. Tropez Cleaners on the First Avenue side gives vestigial testimony of the early 1960s' most publicized French resort.

St. Urban Apartments. *A watercolor rendering by Hughson Hawley dated 1905.*

ST. URBAN, THE
285 Central Park West
(southwest corner West 89th Street)

Built in 1904—Robert L. Lyons, architect—this massive building has a double entrance with a porte-cochere effect and little bowed windows on the facade. There is a single tower and an elaborate copper roof.

Could Saint Urban be the patron saint of apartment dwellers?

ST. VALIER, THE
90 Morningside Drive

The name of this seven-story turn-of-the-century building is more distinguished than its architecture. The name is probably taken from the seventeenth-century French-Canadian missionary bishop Jean Baptiste de La Croix Saint-Vallier.

ST. VERONICA
29 Convent Avenue

A six-story white-brick building; circa 1900.

Saint Veronica was the woman who offered Christ a cloth to wipe his face on the way to Calvary. The veil, imprinted with the image of Christ's face, is venerated at St. Peter's in Rome.

SALEM HOUSE, THE
520 East 81st Street

Redbrick, 1960s; sunken entrance.

Salem was a biblical kingdom and has been used as a poetical

name for Jerusalem—hence its popularity as a name in colonial
New England.

SALOME   *149 West 105th Street*

An abandoned building of 1900 with trompe-l'oeil shutters
and shades placed over the now boarded up windows. A Paterno
building.

Salome, Richard Strauss's opera based on Oscar Wilde's play
of 1894, had its American debut at the Metropolitan Opera
House in 1907; denounced as scandalous and sacrilegious by the
clergy of New York, it was withdrawn from the repertory.

SAMANA MANSION   *106 Fort Washington Avenue*

A six-story early-1920s nondescript apartment house.

Samaná is the name of a province of the Dominican Republic
and an island in the Bahamas.

SAN JOSE   *500 West End Avenue*
                                            (northeast corner West 84th Street)

A thirteen-story 1920s brick building.

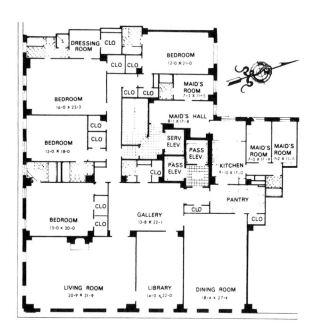

San Remo. *Plan of an eleven-room corner apartment in this luxury
building of the 1920s. Note the private elevator vestibule, the extremely
generous proportions of the rooms (the dining room is 18 × 27 feet), and
the servants' rooms at the back of the building on the court. By the time
the San Remo was built it had become chic to refer to the main entrance
foyer as the "gallery."*

SAN REMO   *145–146 Central Park West*
                                 (West 74th to West 75th Streets)

The twin towers of this huge apartment building are among the most distinctive silhouettes on the Central Park West skyline. H. R. H. Construction Company was the builder and Emery Roth the architect when the *San Remo* was put up in 1930 between West 74th and West 75th streets on the site formerly occupied by an apartment hotel of the same name.

The limestone base is heavily rusticated, and the two towers are crowned with templelike structures that rise to a height of thirty stories. The details are severely classical.

On 5 December 1980 the *San Remo,* which is a cooperative, celebrated its fiftieth jubilee. Its large apartments have long attracted notables, especially from the theater, and the celebration was attended by Tony Randall, Dustin Hoffman, and Diane Keaton, among other tenant-owners.

The town of San Remo on the Italian Riviera has long been a fashionable resort.

SANDGATE, THE   *311 East 75th Street*

This rather plain circa-1960 building has a black marble entrance and imposing canopy.

SANFORD   *229 West 78th Street*

Twin to the *Rexford.*

SANS SOUCI   *200 West 95th Street*
                                 (southwest corner Amsterdam Avenue)

This circa-1900 building of five stories and basement, in gray and white brick, is named for the palace of Frederick the Great at Potsdam. Without Care seems to be the motto of some of the present-day tenants.

SANS SOUCI   *131–133 West 124th Street*

Facing Marcus Garvey Memorial Park; seven stories with limestone on the first two and stone balconies.

SANTA MARIA   *520 West 114th Street*

An eight-story white-brick building of the early twentieth century, with nice marble entrance. One of a series of three buildings. The other two, *Tennessee* and *Arizona* at 508–514 West 114th Street, are now part of Columbia University's campus.

The *Santa Maria* was the flagship of Christopher Columbus on his 1492 voyage.

SANTA MONICA, THE   *345 West 70th Street*

Built in 1905 by A. B. Knight, architect and builder, *The Santa Monica* is two buildings with a center-court entrance. The six-storied building overlooks the railroad tracks and the West Side Highway from the end of West 70th Street but also has a fine view of the Hudson. The redbrick building with white-brick trim has been recently renovated with new windows.

Probably named for the city of Santa Monica, near Los Angeles, a popular resort at the time this building was erected.

SARASOTA, THE   *512 West 122nd Street*

Built in 1905, George F. Pelham, architect. A twin to *The Grant,* but in red brick.

A city and county of Florida, identified since the turn of the century with the winter headquarters of the Ringling Brothers circus.

SAVAGE   *323 West 83rd Street*

A very plain six-story building with fire escape.

SAVOY   *139 West 44th Street*

Still carries its original name of *Hudson* above the entrance, but a canopy reading *Savoy* has been added to the front of this four-story building.

Savoy was an Italian duchy, now mostly in France, that gave its name to the first (and only) reigning dynasty of Italy. "Savoy," when attached to swank hotels and apartments, as it is in many parts of the world, refers, however, to the former royal palace in London.

SAVOY   *452 West 149th Street*

A seven-story building with towerlets and green metallic decoration; circa 1900.

SAXON TOWERS   *201 East 83rd Street*

A 1960s redbrick nineteen-story apartment house by H. I. Feldman, architect. The original selling brochure proclaimed: "When they speak of residential living on the elegant East Side . . . they're sure to mention Saxon Towers."

SAXONIA, THE
601 West 136th Street (northwest corner Broadway)

Neville & Bagge were the architects of this 1907 six-story redbrick building.

SAXONY   *250 West 82nd Street*
                              (southwest corner Broadway)

A seven-story building of red brick; circa 1900; its grand old entrance now converted to a fast-food shop.

Saxony is a former kingdom of the old German Empire and now part of East Germany.

SCHERMERHORN, THE   *1100 Madison Avenue*

This ten-story apartment building of the 1930s takes up the entire west side of Madison Avenue between East 82nd and East 83rd streets. It is built on land originally owned by John P. Schermerhorn, a member of one of New York's old families.

SCHOMBURG PLAZA   *East 110th to East 111th streets,*
                    between Fifth and Madison avenues

Two octagonal thirty-five-story towers rise at the northeast corner of Central Park in pleasantly landscaped space. Gruzen & Partners, with Castro-Blanco, Piscioneri & Feder, were the architects for this 1975 project.

Arthur A. Schomburg (1874–1938) was a black historian. His collection of materials on black history was purchased by the Carnegie Corporation in 1926 and placed in the West 135th Street branch of the New York Public Library. Since 1979 the Schomburg Center for Research in Black Culture has been housed at 515 Lenox Avenue.

SCHUYLER ARMS   *305 West 98th Street*

The extremely elaborate entrance of this seven-stories-and-basement building is flanked by eight columns and leads to an attractive open-court entrance. Dates from circa 1900–1910. In 1981 it was handsomely renovated and became a cooperative.

Schuyler is an old New York family name. Philip John Schuyler (1733–1804) served as a major general in the Revolutionary War and was one of the first two U.S. senators from New York. His daughter married Alexander Hamilton.

Fort Schuyler in the Bronx, home of the New York State Merchant Marine Academy, was named for him.

SCHWAB HOUSE   *11 Riverside Drive*
                    (West 73rd to West 74th streets)

A redbrick high rise built in 1948 on the former site of the seventy-five-room mansion built in 1906 for Charles M. Schwab (1862–1939), president of U.S. Steel.

The Charles M. Schwab house, photographed about 1920. This view north along the west side of West End Avenue shows the rear view of the elaborate mansion at 11 Riverside Drive, torn down in the 1950s, and replaced by an apartment house called Schwab House. *The fourteen-story structure at West 74th Street is the Hotel Esplanade.*

SEAMAN TOWERS   *100–110 Seaman Avenue*

A seven-story 1920s building.

SEAPORT PARK CONDOMINUM
117 Beekman Street

A conversion of Beekman Hospital into twenty-six residential apartments.

The logo of the building includes the small lighthouse tower that formerly stood on the roof of the Seamen's Church Institute on South Street. It was placed there in 1913 by public subscription as a memorial to those who died on the S.S. *Titanic* the year before. When the Seaman's Church Institute was torn down, the lighthouse was placed on Water Street.

SEAPORT SOUTH   *130 Water Street*

Converted into condominium apartments during the early 1980s, with studios priced from $66,560. "Ideal for the corporate executive," the advertisements declared.

Semiramis Apartments. *The play,* The Heir to the Hoorah, *advertised on the billboard at the right, opened on 10 April 1905 at the Hudson Theater.*

SEMINOLE   *2020 Broadway*
                                   (northeast corner West 69th Street)

A recently renovated building of seven stories, circa 1900, with two unusually well carved seated stone lions above the entrance.

The Seminole are a tribe of Florida and Oklahoma Indians.

SEMIRAMIS   *137 Central Park North*

Built in 1901, this handsome residence has fallen upon bad times and in 1983 was a vacant shell awaiting redevelopment (it's owned by the city of New York). Its chance for a rebirth may be better than average, however, since the apartment house's namesake was a beautiful Assyrian princess who became the wife of Ninus, builder of Nineveh. After her husband's death she governed Assyria, built the city of Babylon; conquered Egypt, Ethiopia, and Libya; and waged war against India. All of these accomplishments are mixtures of myth and fact, transmitted by Greek historians. Her life served as the basis for operas by Gluck and Rossini.

SENATE EAST, THE   *335 East 51st Street*

A nondescript white-brick building of the 1960s.

SENATE STUDIOS   *206–208 West 92nd Street*

An eight-story building of the late nineteenth century, with balconies.

SENECA, THE   *213–217 East 84th Street*

This redbrick and brownstone antique has its name and date (1883) emblazoned on the cornice. Undergoing renovation in 1983; there are several little shops and boutiques in the basement.

Impossible to say whether the name refers to the tribe of Indians called Senecas who lived in New York State, or to the Roman Stoic philosopher Lucius Annaeus Seneca, who lived from circa 4 B.C. to A.D. 65.

SENIOR ARMS   *535 West 113th Street*

The proximity of Columbia College presumably gave this building its name. The eight stories have big windows and quasi balconies. An engaging decoration of coats of arms is found at the top of the building and over the entrance.

[SETON HALL]   *144 East 40th Street*

An old six-story building of one-room furnished apartments, originally decorated with "Swedish furnishings." Now the *Seton Hotel*.

St. Elizabeth Seton (1774–1821), a New Yorker, founded the Sisters of Charity.

SEVENTY-FIRST STREET STUDIOS
31 West 71st Street

This thirteen-story building of circa 1920 has a ground floor with later random stone decoration.

SEVERN ARMS   *170 West 73rd Street*
(southeast corner Amsterdam Avenue)

A twelve-story 1905 building by Mulliken & Moeller, architects, across from Verdi Square. The brick and limestone building has an open court on Broadway. A metal walkway at the roof level connects it to the *Van Dyke* on West 72nd Street. Many of the windows have handsome stone and iron balconies.

The Severn, celebrated by A. E. Housman in *A Shropshire Lad,* is, after the Thames, the longest river in England.

SEWARD APARTMENTS   *175–179 East 93rd Street*

Three of the original seven four-story apartment buildings of 1882 survive, in varying states of restoration or of neglect.

Named after William H. Seward (1801–1872) who was governor of New York and then secretary of state in Abraham Lincoln's cabinet. In 1869 he arranged for the purchase of Alaska from the Russians, a move his opponents called "Seward's Folly."

SEWARD PARK EXTENSION (NYC Housing Authority)

65 Norfolk Street

A federally funded project in Lower Manhattan.

SHAKESPEARE
151 West 123rd Street

A six-story building with columned entrance; circa 1900. Around the corner is the *Avon*.

SHANDON
463 West 43rd Street
(northeast corner Tenth Avenue)

This nineteenth-century building still carries its original name above the doorway; has five stories and basement.

SHARON
2 Manhattan Avenue
(northeast corner West 101st Street)

One of a series of six-story redbrick buildings with fire escapes along lower Manhattan Avenue, all put up circa 1906 by the builder Robert M. Silverman, characterized as "blunt and outspoken . . . a typical good fellow" in a real estate book of the era.

SHEFFIELD, THE
322 West 57th Street

A mixed-use high-rise building of the 1970s, with the first five floors used as offices. A drive runs to the west of the building between West 56th and West 57th streets.

SHELBURNE
219 Audubon Avenue
(northeast corner West 176th Street)

A six-story redbrick and limestone-trimmed building; circa 1900.

The second earl of Shelburne (1737–1805) was an English statesman who opposed the Stamp Acts and other policies of his government toward the American colonies. The Shelburne Hotel on St. Stephens Green in Dublin is one of that city's landmarks.

SHELBURNE HALL
110 Morningside Drive
(northwest corner West 121st Street)

A four-story circa-1900 building with three interior courts.

SHENANDOAH   *2338–2348 Frederick Douglass Boulevard*
(northeast corner West 135th Street)

This handsome old building opened in 1889. The *Record and Guide* of 5 January of that year commented favorably on the building. There are five stories and three entrances, and the building actually consists of nine brownstones put together.

Today, although the building still carries its name at the top, two of the three original entrances have been bricked up.

The *Record and Guide* commented: "The idea of naming the flat after an important river is not a new one. Builder McManus had previously named a block front of buildings which he erected on the west side of Eighth Avenue between West 119th and 120th after the historic Potomac."

SHENANDOAH, THE   *10 Sheridan Square*

This 1920s building of fourteen stories has stores on the ground floor. When it opened, it was advertised as "one of the imposing new modern apartment buildings rapidly changing certain sections of the Village."

SHENANDOAH   *145 Audubon Avenue*
(northeast corner West 172nd Street)

A large six-story redbrick building of circa 1900.

SHEPHARD HOUSE   *277 West 10th Street*
(northeast corner Washington Street)

The heavily rusticated granite base of this imposing building suggests its origin as a storage facility, the Shephard Warehouse, built circa 1894 in a fortress-like style echoing that of the *Archives Building* nearby.

Converted into apartments with new fenestration in 1978 by Bernard Rothzeid & Partners.

SHERBROOK   *264–266 Lexington Avenue*

An eleven-story building with terra-cotta medallion decoration and ivy growing over the front; circa 1920s.

SHERIDAN ARMS   *15 Sheridan Square*

This six-story 1930s building is of standard and nondescript design except for a few decorative swags and an incredible projecting canopy over the front door which looks as though it were taken from a motion picture palace.

The building looks out on Sheridan Square, a small triangle mainly known as a traffic hazard. Confusingly enough, the statue of General Philip Sheridan actually stands in the Christopher Street Park, just north of Sheridan Square.

SHERMAN HALL   *9–21 Sherman Avenue*
(southwest corner Sickles Street)

A 1920s redbrick building of six stories.

SHERMAN HALL   *165–175 Sherman Avenue*

A six-story light brick building of the 1920s, recently renovated.

SHERMAN SQUARE STUDIOS
160 West 73rd Street

Built in mock-Gothic style in 1929 by the firm of Tillion & Tillion. The studios were soundproofed for the use of professional musicians. The redbrick building has medieval-style windows on the first two floors and casements on the higher floors. Above the doorway is a charming stone figure of a medieval musician and the name in medieval lettering.

Sherman Square was named for General William Tecumseh Sherman (1820–1891), the Union general in the Civil War, famous for his march to the sea through Confederate territory in 1864. He retired from the army in 1883 and lived in New York City on West 71st Street.

SHERRY HOUSE, THE   *125 East 87th Street*

"An excellent address for gracious living," proclaimed the brochure for this 1960s brick building of 15 stories and penthouse, with 119 apartment units. Schuman & Lichtenstein were the architects.

SHERRY-NETHERLAND   *781 Fifth Avenue*
(northeast corner East 59th Street)

Completed in 1927, to the designs of Schultze & Weaver, and the firm of Ely Jacques Kahn, this forty-story apartment hotel, with its Gothic green-gabled roof, provides a fanciful contrast to the sleek 1960s banality of the General Motors Building across 59th Street to the south. A promotional piece of the 1930s proclaimed that the Sherry-Netherland was "more than a place to live—a new way of living [offering] ideal home life, either permanent or temporary." In the 1970s it became a co-op.

This high-rise château is built on the site of the old Hotel New Netherland which, when built in 1890, was the tallest hotel in the world. Two sculptured panels from the old Vanderbilt mansion on Fifth Avenue and East 50th Street were incorporated into the lobby decor.

The name is derived from linking that of Mr. Louis Sherry (1856–1926), renowned caterer and restaurateur, whose firm managed the hotel when it first opened, and the Netherland, which was the original hotel on the site.

SHIPS CHANDLERY CONDOMINIUM
245 Water Street

In 1983 the former home of Baker, Carver, and Morrell, "marine supplies," was converted into eleven condominium apartments.

When this late-eighteenth-century building was still directly on the waterfront, it was developed by Peter Schermerhorn for his own ship chandlery business. South Street, built on landfill, caused this structure to become less important, and it served in a number of ways until the whole area was developed in the 1970s as South Street Seaport.

SHIRBAR ARMS   *701 West 176th Street*

and

SHIRBAR TERRACE   *536 Fort Washington Avenue*

A six-story redbrick building of circa 1920, the front decorated with armorial beasts carved in stone.

SHORE VIEW   *448 Riverside Drive*

A twelve-story tan-brick building; circa 1900.

The "shore" is that of the Hudson, which the building faces.

SHOREHAM   *60 St. Nicholas Avenue*
(northeast corner West 113th Street)

Redbrick; seven stories; with decorated windows and fire escapes.

SICKLES GARDEN   *38–48 Sickles Street*

A redbrick five-story building of the 1920s, with a large central court.

Sickles Street was named for a family that settled in New York in 1693 and became large landowners in the area.

SILVER TOWERS   *100–110 Bleecker Street*

I. M. Pei & Partners built three concrete towers around an outdoor sculpture by Pablo Picasso in 1966. The buildings occupy the site of Bleecker to West Houston streets, between Mercer Street and LaGuardia Place.

Silver Towers, the two units on Bleecker Street, are owned by New York University; the third building is a cooperative.

Originally called University Village.

SIMNA HALL   *515 West 122nd Street*

A six-story building of circa 1905 by Benster & Benster with recessed fire escapes and rather elaborate brick and limestone details.

Twin to *Marimpol Court* at number 521.

SIXTY-SEVENTH STREET STUDIOS
27 West 67th Street

A fourteen-story building; the first ten stories of variegated brick, the top four of white brick. Built in 1903 as a cooperative building. The American painter Henry Ward Ranger was instrumental in organizing this venture. Among the early tenants were Robert Vonnoh and his sculptor wife Betsy Potter-Vonnoh.

The name appears above the entrance, which in summer months is attractively ivy-covered.

SMITH HOUSES (NYC Housing Authority)
21 St. James Place

Built in 1953, this Lower East Side project is in the neighborhood where Alfred E. ("Al") Smith (1873–1944) was born and grew up. Smith was active in New York City Democratic politics and served as governor of the state from 1919 until 1928, when he ran unsuccessfully for president.

St. James Place was formerly Old Bowery and was renamed to commemorate Smith's parish church.

SMITHSONIAN   *148 East 30th Street*

A five-story elevator apartment, possibly the rehabilitation of an older building. Very plain facade; circa 1960.

The Smithsonian Institution in Washington, named after its English benefactor James Smithson, was established in 1846.

SMITHSONIAN   *60 West 129th Street*
(southeast corner Lenox Avenue)

A seven-story building carrying its original name, with an elaborate stone porch; circa 1900.

SOHO GRAND, THE   *80 Varick Street*

This ten-story fortresslike building with vaguely Gothic details, standing between Watts and Grand streets, has been converted into "luxury loft" rental apartments. It is probably the most convenient building in the city for access to the Holland Tunnel.

[SOKOL HALL]   *525 East 72nd Street*

What started out as a Czech social club later became Coleman's and then the Phillips Auction Gallery. There are several apartments on upper floors.

SOMERSET   *385 Edgecombe Avenue*

A six-story circa 1900 building ornamented at the top.

The name of a county in the southwest of England (as well as counties in New Jersey, Maine, Maryland, and Pennsylvania), glamorized by association with the dukes of Somerset and their London residence, Somerset House (now a government building).

SOMERSET, THE   *1365 York Avenue*

A huge tower of the late 1970s, with a circular drive; the name is not visible, except on doormen's caps; the sister building to *The Stratford* at 1385 York (only the lobby decor differs).

SONOMA, THE   *191 Claremont Avenue*

Erected in 1906; F. S. Nute, architect, and J. O'Brian, builder; on the central-court plan.

Twin to *The Medina*.

Sonoma is the name of a county and town in California.

SOPHOMORE   *21 Claremont Avenue*

A ten-story white-brick building with balconies on many windows; circa 1900.

The name is appropriate for a building across the street from Barnard College.

SOROFEEN   *505 West 141st Street*

A six-story building with columned entrance; built circa 1906 and now in disrepair. The architects were Glasser & Ebert.

SOUND VIEW COURT   *260 Convent Avenue*

Presumably when this turn-of-the-century building opened, Long Island Sound could be seen.

Sound View *under construction about 1910. The Late English Gothic style buildings are those of City College, between West 138th and West 140th streets, built 1903–07. Like Morningside Heights, the Washington Heights area was extensively developed around the turn of the century.*

SOUTH PARK APARTMENTS   *435 West 57th Street*

A seventeen-story white-brick building of the 1960s.

SOUTH PENNINGTON AND NORTH PENNINGTON
801 West End Avenue
(northwest corner West 99th Street)

Two huge twin buildings extending along the west side of West End Avenue between West 99th and West 100th streets. The decoration of these twelve-stories-and-basement buildings is remarkable: a row of huge seashells is arranged at intervals along the top of each building.

The buildings were new in 1910, when they were described as "beyond doubt the most notable recent addition to the apartments of the metropolis." Rentals ranged between $1,200 and $1,800 annually.

SOUTHBRIDGE TOWERS   *90 Beekman Street*

Gruzen & Partners designed this Mitchell-Lama middle-income cooperative containing two- and three-bedroom apartments. Opened in 1971, the project houses thirty-five hundred residents.

The project lies just south of the Brooklyn Bridge and is bounded by Gold, Frankfort, Water, and Fulton streets.

SOUTHFIELD, THE   *145 East 35th Street*

A seven-story white brick and limestone building of roughly the 1920s.

Southgate. *Note the well-preserved Art Deco details and grillwork.*

SOUTHGATE   *433 East 51st Street*
                                      400, 414, 424, 434 East 52nd Street

This block-long 1930 brick fortress, designed by Emery Roth in the Art Deco style, has long been a landmark on this block of two famous towers, *River House* and *The Campanile*. A promotional brochure for *Southgate* when it first opened mentioned yearly rents of $700 for two rooms with bath and $2,100 for "studios of five rooms and bath" and stressed that Miss Scurry's Restaurant was on the premises for the convenience of the tenants.

SOVEREIGN, THE   *425 East 58th Street*

Sigmund Sommer, well-known owner of racehorses (his Sham ran second to Secretariat in the Kentucky Derby and Preakness Stakes), was the builder of this forty-eight-story tower of 365 apartments overlooking the Queensboro Bridge, between First Avenue and Sutton Place.

The architects were Emery Roth & Sons. There was a long lapse between *The Sovereign*'s construction and the time it finally opened in 1974, followed by many highly publicized fights between landlord and tenants about alleged gas leaks, burglaries, poor security, windows blowing out, et cetera.

In 1978–1979 *The Sovereign* went co-op—not without yet another round of charges, countercharges, and press releases.

The site was occupied in the early part of the century by the New York Orthopedic Hospital, whose buildings later housed the Mary Manning Walsh Home for the Aged, prior to its removal to York Avenue and East 72nd Street.

SOVEREIGN APARTMENTS   *411 East 83rd Street*

A small six-story apartment house with a very plain facade; possibly a conversion of an earlier building.

SOVEREIGN COURT   *535–537 West 151st Street*

An early-twentieth-century six-stories-and-basement redbrick building with fire escape.

SPENCER ARMS HOTEL   *140 West 69th Street (southeast corner Broadway)*

A handsome twelve-story building of 1906 with bay windows and wrought-iron balconies on some floors and limestone ornamentation.

In 1983 the building was renovated by Brandon Roth, architect, the old servant quarters on the roof being turned into duplex apartments, and the building renamed *Lincoln Plaza Hotel*.

SPRUCE RIDGE HOUSE   *245–251 East 25th Street*

A 1964 tan-brick building whose name is barely visible on a peeling wood sign. Certainly one of the most unassuming lobbies in all of Manhattan.

STADIUM VIEW   *445 Riverside Drive*

A twelve-story building of tan brick, with stone balconies handsomely adorned with ivy during the summer. At the time when this apartment house was constructed, circa 1900, plans to build an enormous stadium and marina on the Hudson River had been announced.

STAFFORD, THE   *622 Greenwich Street*

A modernized warehouse or commercial building with balconies added. Five stories, with an elaborate grille entrance.

STANDISH   *59 West 10th Street*

Contiguous to the *Priscilla*. Ionic colonnettes flanking each door; interesting; slightly bayed windows.
[See also *The Alden.*]

STANFORD   *502–504 West 113th Street*

Twin to the *Arlington* at 506–508 West 113th Street. George F. Pelham was architect of both buildings, circa 1905.

STANLEY COURT   *945 West End Avenue*
(northwest corner West 106th Street)

Built in 1906 by Charles E. Birge, architect. There were then two apartments of ten rooms and three baths to each floor at annual rents of $2,500. A Hollywoodesque entrance has been added.

STANLEY ISAACS HOUSES (NYC Housing Authority)   *403 East 93rd Street*

Three buildings and 636 apartments in this 1965 project named for Stanley M. Isaacs (1882–1962), New York City councilman, Manhattan borough president, and promoter of the 1964 New York World's Fair at Flushing Meadows.

STANWOOD   *321 West 55th Street*

A typical nine-story 1920s building of vaguely English appearance.

STELLA   *477 Amsterdam Avenue*
(southeast corner West 83rd Street)

A smallish building of five stories in pinkish brick; circa 1900. The porch entrance on West 83rd is without a street number and poorly maintained.

STELLA   *306 West 112th Street*

This rather elaborate seven-story redbrick building is now abandoned.

STEPHEN FOSTER HOUSES
West 112th to West 115th streets
Lenox Avenue to Fifth Avenue

One of the largest of the Harlem housing projects, consisting of ten buildings, each with thirteen or fourteen stories.
[See also *Foster.*]

STERLING   *76 West 86th Street*
                              (southeast corner Columbus Avenue)

Built at the turn of the century by Mulliken & Moeller, architects, this six-story building has an open court on West 86th
Street. When it opened, the apartments had seven to ten rooms
and rented for $1,000 to $2,300 annually.

STERLING   *203 West 113th Street*

Seven stories of red brick; a porch with three columns; fire
escape.

STERLING COURT   *326 Audubon Avenue*
                              (northeast corner West 181st Street)

A six-story buff-brick building; circa 1900.

STEWART HOUSE   *70 East 10th Street*

Stewart House occupies a historic site between Broadway and
Fourth Avenue across from Grace Church. Alexander T. Stewart's department store, "the cast-iron wonder," opened there in
1862 and was long considered one of the architectural and commercial landmarks of the city. In 1896 the store became Wa-
namaker's and finally closed in 1952. Four years later the building was destroyed by fire.
The present apartment building, of white brick, dates from
1960.
Alexander Turney Stewart (1803–1876), the Irish-born department store magnate, lived in a Fifth Avenue mansion at
34th Street; it was one of the wonders of New York in the second half of the nineteenth century. Stewart developed Garden
City, Long Island, as a planned community; but he is perhaps
equally famous as the man whose corpse was stolen from its
graveyard in St.-Mark's-in-the-Bowery and, only after ransoms
and negotiations, was finally interred at the Cathedral of the In-
carnation in Garden City.

STEWART HOUSE   *10 Mitchell Place*

This thirteen-story redbrick apartment building of 1928 is
just next to *Beekman Tower*. The architects were Turner &
Bowden.
The name refers to the owner of a house that formerly stood
here.

STIMSON HOUSE   *120 East 36th Street*

A 1960s redbrick building with marble entrance.
Henry Lewis Stimson (1867–1950), the distinguished American statesman, was born in New York City. He served as secretary of war from 1940 to 1945.

STOCKBRIDGE   *603–605 West 138th Street*

Schwartz & Gross were the architects of this 1908 building of six stories and basement.

A twin to the *Wiltshire*.

Stockbridge is a town in the Berkshire Hills of Massachusetts, originally founded as a model village for the Housatonic Indians. This tribe eventually moved to Wisconsin.

Edward Bellamy's novel about Shay's Rebellion, *The Duke of Stockbridge,* was a best-seller in 1900.

STRAND VIEW   *309 West 99th Street*

An eight-story building, circa 1900, of white brick and limestone, with iron balconies and a grille doorway.

Located near the strand, or shoreline, of the Hudson River.

STRATFORD, THE   *1385 York Avenue*

A high-rise apartment house of the 1970s; sister building to the *Somerset* next door; the name is not exactly prominent (one has to ask!). Lobby decor highlighted by a pair of large and stunning Italian still-life paintings.

Stratford-on-Avon in Warwickshire is celebrated as Shakespeare's birthplace. He and his wife were buried in the parish church there.

[See also *Avon* and *Shakespeare.*]

STRATFORD, THE   *26 East 81st Street*

An old (circa 1900) brick and stone building of eight stories, with decorative cornice and arched windows.

STRATFORD   *101 West 115th Street*
                               (northwest corner Lenox Avenue)

A six-story circa-1900 building with a beautiful porch.

STRATFORD   *369–373 West 116th Street*

Seven stories with fancy limestone decoration. Two stories with anthemion frieze below salmon-colored brick. The cornice has been lost.

STRATFORD ARMS   *117 West 70th Street*

A ten-story 1920s building distinguished by a fine stone carving of a crown with Prince of Wales ostrich feathers above the modernized entrance. Now houses several services for the blind.

STRATFORD-AVON   *210 Riverside Drive*
                               (northeast corner West 93rd Street)

A good-looking brown-brick building of twelve stories, with limestone trim; circa 1900.

STRATFORD AVON HALL *1270 St. Nicholas Avenue*
590 West 174th Street
(southeast corner)

Six-story white-brick building; circa 1900.

STRATFORD HOUSE *11–13 East 32nd Street*

A new and nondescript marquee adorns this twelve-story apartment building of circa 1900; in red brick and limestone and with bay windows.

STRATHMORE *404 Riverside Drive*
(southeast corner West 113th Street)

A Parisian-style marquee distinguishes this twelve-story building of circa 1900; in red brick and limestone. The original lamps flank the entrance.

STRATTON *342 West 85th Street*

A six-story turn-of-the-century building next door to *The Red House* and recently and beautifully restored; offering "mellow old-world ambience. . . . A new setting for life with style," according to advertisements.

Stratton is the name of a village in Cornwall, England, and a mountain and ski resort in Vermont.

STRIVER'S ROW *West 138th to West 139th streets,*
between Adam Clayton Powell, Jr.,
and Frederick Douglass boulevards

[See also *King Model Houses.*]

STUART ARMS *226 West 97th Street*

A rather narrow 1920s building: eight stories of brown brick and limestone.

The Stuart (or Stewart) family reigned in Scotland from 1371 to 1688 and in England from 1603 to 1688.

STUART STUDIO APARTMENTS
307 West 93rd Street

A late-nineteenth-century building of six stories, with a rusticated ground floor, arched entrance, and bayed windows. Formerly known as the Cliffside.

STUDIO HOUSE *239 East 77th Street*

A handsome renovation of a small town house or tenement, with new brick facade and large windows.

STUYVESANT TOWN

STUYVESANT TOWN

East 14th to East 20th streets
First Avenue to East River Drive

"A residential Community, owned and operated by Metropolitan Life Insurance Company. No provisions for air conditioning; no dogs permitted."

Thus ran the 1947 brochure for this peaceful oasis of undistinguished redbrick buildings in a parklike setting of shaded walks and pleasant playgrounds. The architects were Irwin Clavan and Gilmore D. Clarke.

Built on the site of the old Gas House District, *Stuyvesant Town* houses almost nine thousand families—in comfort and safety and at reasonable rents.

Peter (or Petrus) Stuyvesant arrived in New Amsterdam on May 11, 1647 to begin his service as Director-General of the colony of New Netherland. An able administrator, he was never popular with the colonists, mainly because he was against any form of representative government. Despite his efforts, the people of New Amsterdam won independent municipal government in 1653. Eleven years later, Stuyvesant was obliged to surrender his colony to the English. The following year he went to the Netherlands to defend his official conduct, but returned to New York where he lived on his farm, around present-day Third Avenue and East 14th Street until his death in 1672.

[See also *Peter Stuyvesant* and *Whitehall*.]

SUDELEY

76–78 West 85th Street
(southeast corner Columbus Avenue)

A smallish five-story building, circa 1900, standing with its twin the *Crillon* on a street of fine town houses surviving from the same era. Both buildings have elaborate entrances with carved-stone decoration and are very well maintained.

Sudeley Castle is one of the historic houses of England, the burial place of Catherine Parr, a wife of Henry VIII. In the nineteenth century it was owned by the Dent family. Mrs. Dent, who wrote a book about the castle, was born a Brocklehurst, and diagonally across West 85th Street is *The Brockholst*.

SULGRAVE, THE

571 West 139th Street
(northeast corner Broadway)

George F. Pelham was the architect of this 1905 building of six stories, with limestone band decor and a central court.

Sulgrave in Northamptonshire, England, is most famous as the home of the ancestors of George Washington.

A residential hotel called the *Sulgrave* formerly stood at East 67th Street and Park Avenue.

SUMMERFELD

521 West 112th Street

A 1920s plain white-brick building of eight stories.

"SUMMERSBY, THE"   *342–344 West 56th Street*

An 1898 building of seven stories and basement, with fourteen apartments and the name in quotes.

SUMMIT   *1428 Lexington Avenue*
(northwest corner East 93rd Street)

A six-story building; circa 1900; now somewhat dilapidated. The entrance at 156 East 93rd Street has been bricked up.

SUN VIEW   *188–196 Audubon Avenue*

A five-story apartment house facing east and living up to its name—at least in the morning.

SUNSET   *175 West 85th Street*
(northeast corner Amsterdam Avenue)

An old five-story building with its name in ornate type on the third floor. Now boarded up.

SURREY   *122 East 82nd Street*

A nine-story white-brick building; roughly 1920s.

SURREY, THE   *20 East 76th Street*

A quiet residential hotel, named for one of England's "home counties" (close to London) but with a popular French restaurant (Les Pléiades) in the ground floor. Ethel Merman had an apartment here.

SURREY, THE   *215 West 83rd Street*

A fourteen-story brick building of the 1920s, with penthouses.

SUSANY LANE   *429 West 24th Street*

A five-story brown-brick building, recently renovated.
A twin to the *Dandrew Lane*.

SUSSEX   *114–116 West 79th Street*

A fourteen-story building of the 1920s, with a new entrance. Sussex is an ancient name for the part of England lying along the English Channel.

SUSSEX, THE   *55 East 65th Street*

A fine old–circa 1890–apartment house of seven stories, completely renovated: the lower stories now painted chocolate brown and fire escapes modernized.

Just across the street from *the* fashionable restaurant of the 1980s, Le Cirque.

SUTTON

The buildings and streets called Sutton are tributes to the real estate acumen of Effingham Sutton, member of a New York shipping family, who, with James Stokes, bought the land at the east end of 57th Street about 1875.

Several brownstones were built, but rapid industrialization nearby caused the area to lose its appeal for the rich and well-established until the 1920s when a group of New York society ladies settled there, renovating brownstones or building new houses on Sutton Place, where the land sloped down to the East River.

The ladies were headed by Mrs. W. K. Vanderbilt and included Anne Morgan (daughter of J.P.), Miss Elizabeth Marbury and Elsie de Wolfe, and members of the Olin, Lorillard, Griswold, and Olcott families. They made the area fashionable, and it has remained so until the present, when huge apartment buildings crowd around the few remaining private houses overlooking the East River.

SUTTON EAST	*433 East 56th Street*
SUTTON GARDENS	*420 East 55th Street*
SUTTON HOUSE	*415 East 52nd Street*
SUTTON MANOR	*430 East 56th Street*
SUTTON MANOR EAST	*440 East 56th Street*
SUTTON MEWS	*412 East 55th Street*

Large 1955–1975 buildings, some of which were put up by the Doelger family, who owned much property in this, the area of their brewery on East 55th Street.

SUTTON TERRACE   *1161 York Avenue*
                                        450 East 63rd Street

A huge redbrick 1950s building with balconies overlooking Rockefeller University and the Equal Opportunity Building.

SUTTON VIEW   *347 East 53rd Street*

Vaguely visible on glass over the door, partly obscured by a canopy, the name is just barely accurate.

SWISS HOUSE   *262 West 23rd Street*

This small 1920s apartment house has its name spelled out in an elaborate wrought-iron pattern over the front doorway— apparently commemorating the Swiss lady who in the 1920s owned the houses now called *Fitzroy Place*.

SWITZERLAND   *740 Riverside Drive*
                               (northeast corner West 151st Street)

A large six-story building with modernized entrance. Now trimmed in electric blue.

SYLVIA   *59 West 76th Street*
                              (northeast corner Columbus Avenue)

The name of this turn-of-the-century building is in a beautiful cut-stone floral frame on the West 76th Street side. The ground floor is rusticated and contains Dobson's Restaurant.

"Who is Silvia? what is she . . . ?" asked Shakespeare in *The Two Gentlemen of Verona*.

SYLVIA   *501 West 133rd Street*

Six stories; turn-of-the-century; corrugated metal of recent vintage has replaced original cornice.

SYLVIA   *560 West 144th Street*

An open-court building of six stories and basement; with a fine porch. Matching it at the other end of the block is the Rosalind. In between are four buildings, numbers 520-550, called the Arthur, Henry, Lucille, and Ethelyn. The entire complex is known as Charlemagne Courts.

TAFT HOUSES (NYC Housing Authority)
                                        1740 Madison Avenue

This 1965 project in Spanish Harlem has, as its namesake, Robert A. Taft (1889–1953), the Ohio Senator, sometime presidential candidate, and co-author of the Taft-Hartley Law (regulating labor-management relations) who was known as "Mr. Republican." He was a strong advocate of better public housing.

TAINO TOWERS
East 122nd to East 123rd streets
Second to Third avenues

Silverman & Cika were the architects for this 1972–1979 complex of four gleaming white thirty-four-story towers—surely one of the most costly and luxurious public housing projects ever built.

From its inception, *Taino Towers* was meant to be better than the typical subsidized housing project. Local residents and community leaders worked with the architects in planning the buildings and amenities. But with enormous cost overruns, overly optimistic projections of rental income from the ground-floor offices and commercial spaces, and the energy crisis—making floor-to-ceiling glass walls a liability—things got out of hand. *Taino Towers* is still unfinished; the commercial space remains empty, and the tenants who do live there face an uncertain future in what has become the Versailles of public housing.

The name is taken from a tribe of ancient, now extinct Caribbean aborigines to honor the predominantly Caribbean-Hispanic population of the neighborhood. Murals by Rafael Rivera-García, depicting the culture of the Taino Indians, adorn one of the several public spaces (pool, gymnasium, meeting room).

TALLADEGA
61 Hamilton Terrace

A twin to the *Eufaula*.

The name is that of a city and county in Alabama, not far from Birmingham, where General Andrew Jackson defeated the Creek Indians in 1813.

TANYA TOWERS
620 East 13th Street

Built in 1974, this 137-unit apartment tower is a Mitchell-Lama project incorporating many amenities especially designed for the deaf tenants.

Named for Tanya Nash, for thirty-five years director of the New York Society for the Deaf, whose headquarters are at 344 East 14th Street.

TATHAM HOUSE, THE
138 East 38th Street

A recent conversion of a 1920s building, just across from the Cuban Mission to the UN.

TEMPLE COURTS
223 Second Avenue
(southwest corner East 14th Street)

A six-story apartment building of the 1920s, with its name on the porch entrance; next door to the Labor Temple.

TEMPLE HALL
100 West 121st Street
(southwest corner Lenox Avenue)

An interesting seven-story redbrick building put up in 1907; John Hauser, architect. There are bay windows with stained-glass panels at the top. Gothic details ornament the entrance and the cornice.

The name is taken from Temple Israel, which was also built in 1907 at 201 Lenox Avenue, at the northwest corner of West 120th Street. Noted for its lavish marble interior, the structure now houses the Mount Olivet Baptist Church.

TENTERDEN   *263–265 West 25th Street*

A nineteenth-century building of five stories and basement, with fire escape. Renovated some time ago and painted gray.

Tenterden is a town in Kent, England, giving its name to noblemen of the Abbott family.

TERESA   *243 West 113th Street*

A six-story redbrick building of circa 1900.

A twin to the *Marjorie*.

TERRACE, THE   *405 West 118th Street*

This six-story building of tan brick and limestone was built by Neville & Bagge in 1907 on the long-hall plan. There is a columned entrance with fire escape.

TERRACE COURT, THE   *202–208 Riverside Drive*
(southeast corner West 93rd Street)

A 1906 brochure for this building (dating from 1904) describes apartments with nine and ten rooms and two or three baths: "The bath rooms, which are walled with enamelled tile and floored with vitrified tile, are fitted up with the finest of plumbing; have Morris bath tubs with showers, oval porcelain basins and syphon jet closets with Kemey system of flushing, doing away with unsightly wooden cisterns."

The brochure stressed that the building offered "telephone connection affording both local and long distance communications . . . installed in each apartment." Rents were $1,300 to $2,600 annually.

TERRACE GARDEN   *189–199 Sherman Avenue*
(northeast corner West 204th Street)

The aptly named six-story 1920s building does indeed have a terraced garden entrance, planted and with a fountain in the center.

TERRY LANE   *433 West 24th Street*

A six-story early-twentieth-century building of brown and red brick, newly renovated and somewhat harmonizing with *London Terrace* across the street.

THALMAN, H.   *129 Charles Street*

A stable converted into a small apartment building.

THAYER COURT   *140–144 Nagle Avenue*
(southwest corner Thayer Street)

A five-story redbrick building of the 1920s.
Thayer Street was once known as Union Place and was renamed in 1911 to honor Francis Thayer, a local civic leader.

THELMA   *529 West 143rd Street*

A plain six-story brick building of the turn of the century.
Marie Corelli's sensational best-seller *Thelma* was published
in 1888.

THEODORE, THE   *217 East 86th Street*

A small 1920s apartment whose most prominent features are
the Tijuana Mexican Restaurant on the ground floor and the
name, which might well honor Theodore ("Teddy") Roosevelt,
who died in 1919.

THERESIA   *48 Carmine Street*

A narrow five-story building with this unusual name on the
pediment.

THOMAS-EDDY   *85 Eighth Avenue*

An austere five-story building; neat but uninspiring.

TOMPKINS FLATS   *115–119 St. Mark's Place*

The *Tompkins Flats* are identical to the *St. Mark's Flats* across
the street and have their name in raised tin lettering over the
entry. Remodeling has drastically changed the ground floor.
Tompkins Square, so named in 1833 in honor of Governor
Daniel D. Tompkins, is a sixteen-acre plot that had formerly
been known as Clinton Square and before that as Stuyvesant's
Meadows.
St. Mark's Place, the wide stretch of East 8th Street between
Third Avenue and Tompkins Square, held at that time "a range
of elegant buildings."

TOMPKINS SQUARE APARTMENTS
131–135 Avenue B

Five-and-six-story redbrick elevator buildings of the 1920s.
The entrance gates between are at present adorned with barbed
wire, a commentary on the neighborhood.

TOURAINE, LA   *50 Morningside Drive*

A six-story Schwartz & Gross building of 1906, matching the *Mont Cenis* next door, also developed by the Paterno Company.

Morningside Park, which the building faces, was opened in 1887. The many French names in the neighborhood are related to the presence of the Roman Catholic Église de Notre Dame, the first part of which was built in 1910.

Touraine is a province in France.

TOWER EAST   *190 East 72nd Street*

Built in 1961 by Emery Roth & Sons, *Tower East* was among the first of the sheer tower apartments. Shops, restaurants, and a movie theater occupy the ground floor on Third Avenue, and the main entrance is enlivened by its next-door neighbor, the Greek-temple-like bijou building of the Provident Loan Society (originally the 19th Ward Bank, 1908).

Devotees of grand movie theaters still mourn the loss of Loew's 72nd Street Theater, a mammoth house in the "Hindu" style, built in 1932 and featuring an "atmospheric" sky ceiling and enormous gilded columns, demolished for *Tower East*.

TOWER 53   *159 West 53rd Street*

A 1970s high rise.

TOWER WEST   *65 West 96th Street*
(northeast corner Columbus Avenue)

A twenty-seven-story 1970s high rise, part of the West Side Urban Renewal program. One of the Mitchell-Lama projects, the building was described in a newspaper headline of 1981 as "Tower West: Where Owners and the Tenants Wage a War."

TOWERS, THE   *720 Greenwich Street*

A warehouse converted into a seven-story apartment building with large ground-floor windows covered by metal grilles. Above the ground-floor doors are three herms.

TOWERS, THE   *250 West 85th Street*
(southwest corner Broadway)

A fourteen-story tan-brick building of the 1920s.

TOWN HOUSE   *330 West 45th Street*

A 1960s redbrick building of twelve stories.

TOWN HOUSE WEST   *5 West 91st Street*

A small six-story redbrick building of the 1970s, with neat gray-painted balconies.

TOWNE HOUSE, THE   *108 East 38th Street*

A 1925–1930 dark brick building with casement windows; the entrance has been redone, but the Art Deco–style doors appear to be original. Bowden & Russell were the architects for this period piece. The promotional brochure (complete with floor plans)—a spendid green and silver Art Deco period piece in its own right—offers this description:

"Simplex apartments . . . afford an intriguing and varied view from every room. Private terraces, of course, for a restful interval . . . fireplaces to give a cheerful note on crisp winter evenings. . . . A duplex apartment strikes a modern note. . . . The extra guest lavatory is located unobtrusively back of the gracefully curved stair in the main hall."

The Towne House is considered a very fine example of Art Deco architecture.

TOWNSEND HOUSE   *176 East 71st Street*

A white-brick building of the 1960s.

TOWNSLEY   *245 East 35th Street*

An apartment house of blue and white brick of the 1960s, with a name that *sounds* rather British.

TRACY TOWERS   *245 East 24th Street*

A redbrick cooperative apartment house of the 1960s.

TRAFALGAR   *233 West 99th Street*
(northeast corner Broadway)

A sixteen-story 1920s orange-brick building with casement windows.

Cape Trafalgar on the Atlantic coast of Spain was the scene of one of the greatest British sea victories, on 21 October 1805, when the Napoleonic forces were decisively defeated.

TRAFALGAR ARMS   *129 West 89th Street*

A six-story redbrick building of the 1930s.

TRAFALGAR COURT   *161 East 90th Street*

A redbrick 1930s–1940s building whose unusual lack of decorative detail results from having been Trafalgar Hospital until its conversion into apartments circa 1980.

TRAFALGAR HOUSE, THE   *120 East 90th Street*

A 1983 condominium conversion.

TRAUD HALL   *374 Wadsworth Avenue*

Red Spanish tile ornaments this six-story building of the 1920s, which has iron balconies and marble columns at the front entrance.

TRENT, THE   *124 East 91st Street*

A six-story circa 1900 redbrick building with handsome limestone entrance and trim, and original wrought-iron and glass doors.

Trent is the name of a river in Staffordshire, England.

TREVYLLIAN, THE   *140 East 17th Street*

A six-story elevator building of circa 1890, in red brick and limestone; the 1950s gray-marble lobby and entrance are unfortunate additions.

TRIANGLE, THE   *West 120th Street, St. Nicholas Avenue, and Frederick Douglass Boulevard*

A four-story building occupying nearly all the plot formed by the junction of three streets. Now abandoned.

TRINITY COURT   *518 West 111th Street*

A six-story building with open-court entrance; of brick and limestone, with a decorated brick pediment and fire escape. Dating from the turn of the century, the building, like several others in the neighborhood of the Cathedral of St. John the Divine, bears a religious name.

TRINITY HOUSE APARTMENTS   *100 West 92nd Street (southwest corner Columbus Avenue)*

Built in 1969 by Brown, Guenther, Battaglia, Seckler, this modern high-rise apartment house incorporates an extension of the Trinity School next door. Trinity's buildings are nineteenth-century, but the school itself was founded in Lower Manhattan in 1709 by Trinity Church.

TRINITY STUDIO   *550 West 153rd Street*

Huge copper-clad windows and the name *Trinity Studio* chiseled into a stone banderole over the entrance distinguish this early-1920s building which looks north over the open expanse of Trinity Cemetery, providing good light for the artist-tenants.

Trinity Cemetery, opened in 1843, is owned by Trinity Church in Lower Manhattan. Clement Clarke Moore, author of *A Visit from St. Nicholas,* was buried here.

[TROW'S DIRECTORY]   *201–213 East 12th Street*

A 1980s conversion of an old redbrick factory and adjoining commercial structure, both nineteenth-century buildings, the one on the corner of Third Avenue has Hudson's, the outdoors discount store, at street level.

Trump Plaza

TRUMP PLAZA   *163 East 61st Street*
                                (southwest corner Third Avenue)

A futuristic apartment tower with lots of glass and curves and balconies in a style that might be called Deco-Revival; very 1983; very close to Bloomingdale's.

Named for its developer, Donald Trump.

TRUMP TOWER   *1 East 56th Street*
                                    725 Fifth Avenue

"Imagine a tall bronze tower of glass. Imagine life within such a tower. Elegant. Sophisticated. Strictly *beau monde*. . . . You approach the residential entrance—an entrance totally inaccessible to the public—and your staff awaits your arrival. Your concierge gives you your messages. And you pass through the lobby. Quickly, quietly, the elevator takes you to your floor and your elevator man sees you home. You turn the key and wait a moment . . . to take in the view [of] New York at dusk.

Trump Tower

The sky is pink and gray. Thousands of tiny lights are making their way through Central Park. Bridges are becoming jeweled necklaces. Your diamond in the sky. It seems a fantasy. And you are home. Maid service, valet, stenographers, interpreters, multilingual secretaries, telex . . . hairdressers, masseurs, limousines, helicopters, conference rooms—all at your service. . . . If you can think of any amenity, any extravagance or nicety of life, any service we haven't mentioned, then it probably hasn't been invented yet."

So runs the glowing prose of the Trump Tower prospectus. Named for its developer, Donald Trump, *wunderkind* of the New York real estate kingdom, whose crowning achievement (so far) is this multiuse building that bears his name. Contains 263 condominium apartments, ranging in price from half a million dollars to ten million.

The retail and office space beneath the residential floors was designed to be equally glamorous, with tenants such as Asprey, Loewe, Charles Jourdan, and Cartier having shops in what was once space occupied by the old Bonwit Teller department store, enhanced by Tiffany & Co.'s air rights.

The site of Trump Tower was, of course, a residential area a century ago, when Vanderbilts, Whitneys, and Huntingtons all had ostentatious palaces near the intersection of Fifth Avenue and 57th Street. Now that tradition of ostentatious living has returned—with a bang—in *Trump Tower,* "the world's most talked-about address."

Trump Tower. *Plan of apartment "J." Note that the second bedroom is also suggested as a library or dining room. The walk-through kitchen has a small dining room at one end called "the breakfast room." Other features of this contemporary luxury building are a bidet in the master bedroom and the complete absence of any servants' rooms or service entrance, something unheard-of in earlier eras.*

TRYON GARDENS   *720–760 Fort Washington Avenue (at West 190th Street)*

The name is taken, as are many others in the vicinity, from Fort Tryon, a British military installation in northern Manhattan which, in turn, was named for William Tryon, the British governor of New York from 1771 to 1778.

TRYON TOWERS   *200 Pinehurst Avenue*

Built of two-color bricks with decorations and a green glass brick entrance, this circa-1930s building has casement windows with wrought-iron grilles.

TUDOR CITY   *East 40th to East 43rd streets, First to Second avenues*

In 1925 Fred F. French, a self-made man who believed in the efficacy of salesmanship (he thought Jesus Christ was "the best salesman of all time"), began secretly buying up the land on Prospect Hill, at the east end of 42nd Street, for a grandiose "White Collar City," where people could live well within walking distance of their jobs in Midtown.

By 1928 twelve buildings, all with British names and together containing a total of three thousand apartments and six

Tudor City. *View of*
The Manor *at 333
East 43rd Street, one
of several appropriately
named buildings in
this 1920s complex. In
the left foreground is
the park that residents
have managed to keep
for themselves rather
than redevelopment.*

hundred hotel rooms, constituted *Tudor City*—named after the family that ruled England from the fifteenth to the seventeenth centuries.

An early promotional brochure lauded this "city within a city, a garden spot in the center of New York" and asked weary straphangers, "What would you do with an extra two hours a day?" Amenities included restaurants, a grocery store, private school, medical staff, maid service, radio reception advisory service, private police force, garage, package room, book shop, taxi-calling system, and an eighteen-hole indoor golf course and an outdoor "Tom Thumb" course.

Owners of the slaughterhouses at the edge of the East River refused to sell, so the axis of *Tudor City* is toward the west and no apartment windows look east on what is now the site of the United Nations.

Tudor City was "designed, financed, constructed, and managed by the Fred F. French Companies," but the ingenious system of issuing shares and bonds to raise capital fell apart soon after the Wall Street crash of 1929, and Tudor City went into bankruptcy.

Much of the complex is owned by Harry Helmsley, who has been engaged in a sparring match with the tenants and the city over plans to build a high rise on land that has been a "private" park for *Tudor City* residents for more than fifty years.

The constituent buildings of *Tudor City* are all outstanding examples of neo-Tudor style, with fine brickwork—and stone-work—enhanced by mullions, escutcheons, turrets, crenella-tions, arcades. The pediments of the central buildings are crowned with stone fretwork copied directly from Hardwick Hall, the sixteenth-century country house of Elizabeth, the dowager countess of Shrewsbury, better known as Bess of Hard-wick, who was second in wealth and influence only to Elizabeth I, better known as Good Queen Bess.

The individual buildings are described in more detail under their own listings. See *Prospect Tower*, The *Manor, Tudor Tower,* the *Hermitage, Woodstock Tower, Haddon Hall, Hardwick Hall, Hatfield House, Windsor Tower,* and *Essex House.*

TUDOR HALL   *183 Pinehurst Avenue*

A six-story half-stucco building of the 1920s.

The Tudor dynasty reigned in England from 1485 to 1603, giving their name to a type of architecture shown, on a modest scale, in this building.

TUDOR TOWER   *25 Tudor City Place*

A twin to *Prospect Tower* in *Tudor City,* but originally with slightly lower rents of $800 to $1,700 annually, based on slightly smaller room sizes that, an early promotional brochure declares, "no one but an expert ever notices. . . . Life in Tudor City," it continues, "appeals especially to the younger set."

TURIN, THE   *333 Central Park West*
(northwest corner West 93rd Street)

A twelve-story white-brick building, the first two stories of limestone. Built about 1900, the building has two courts open to West 93rd Street. Albert J. Bodker was the architect.

Orginally, there were six apartments to a floor, each having six to nine rooms with two or three baths.

According to the original brochure, "Following the histories of London and Paris, it has always been proved that apartments on sunny corners fronting on large parkways have been the most desired and greatly sought after."

Turin is the Anglicized name of Torino, the northern Italian industrial city.

TURIN HOUSE APARTMENTS
609 Columbus Avenue
(West 89th to West 90th streets)

Built of pinkish concrete blocks in 1972, this nineteen-story high rise was designed by Holden, Yang, Raemsch & Corser. The odd-looking barred boxes attached to the sides of the build-ing are fire exits.

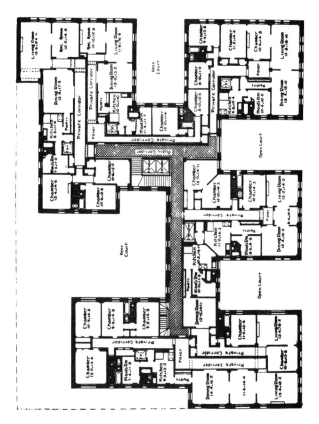

Turin. *An early floor plan with long public and private corridors and four open courts. Two of the apartments facing Central Park West have reception rooms as well as living rooms.*

TURNER HOUSE   *56 West 71st Street*

A large brownstone made into a small apartment building.

TURRETS, THE   *125 Riverside Drive*
                    (northeast corner West 84th Street)

This fortresslike building dates from the turn of the century. Nine stories tall, it is of white brick and limestone, with a magnificent stonework front decorated with nymphs. There are entrances on West 84th and Riverside Drive.

TURTLE BAY HOUSE   *249 East 48th Street*

A 1970s apartment building near Turtle Bay. The small inlet, called Turtle Bay because of its shape, was filled in many years ago.

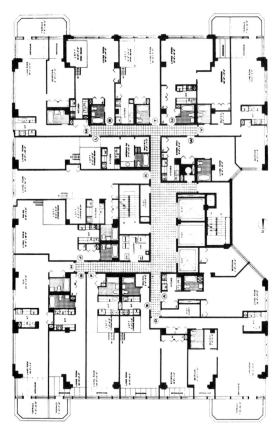

Turtle Bay Towers. *A typical floor of this 1970s conversion of what had formerly been an industrial building. Note the "loft" sleeping areas above the living rooms, made possible by the higher than usual ceilings. An unusual feature is "the greenhouse" in a number of apartments.*

TURTLE BAY TOWERS   *310 East 46th Street*

This highly successful redo of a 1929 commercial loft building was facilitated by its unusual set-back arrangement of the upper floors, which allowed lots of glassed-in terraces and solaria.

The old commercial building was severely damaged by an explosion in 1974 (the same blast that damaged *Envoy Towers*). When Paul Goldberger of the *Times* wrote up *Turtle Bay Towers,* he called the building "new luxury housing {that} can compete seriously with the buildings of a generation or two ago." The apartments with glassed-in terraces were called "Greenhouse Living Lofts" in the promotional literature.

TUXEDO   *65 West 70th Street*
(northeast corner Columbus Avenue)

This early-twentieth-century six-story medium-sized building carries its name in an armorial escutcheon on the West 70th Street side. The building is in red brick, with a rusticated ground floor.

The Cantina Mexican restaurant occupies the ground floor.

Tuxedo Park is a still-fashionable settlement at Tuxedo in Orange County, New York, where from 1886 on many New York City families built country houses. The "informality" of the place necessitated a break from the white-tie-and-tails costume men wore to dinner parties. Smoking jackets with black tie were substituted and soon became *de rigueur* elsewhere. Those who don't wear them a lot still call dinner jackets "tuxedos."

TUXEDO COURT   *30–34 East 128th Street*
(southwest corner Madison Avenue)

A six-story building of 1904; Neville & Bagge, architects. The name is above the door.

"TWIN PEAKS"   *102 Bedford Street*

Originally built in 1830, this small building was renovated in 1925 by Clifford Reed Daily, who half-timbered it to give the neighborhood more character.

Ulysses Court Apartments, *about 1911.*

ULYSSES COURT   *528 Riverside Drive*

Six stories and basement, with open-court entrance. The unusual entrance projects into the court and conceals the recessed fire escape. The name is in a handsome banderole.

The building is a few blocks from the tomb of President Ulysses S. Grant and dates from the same era (1897).

UNADILLA   *126–128 West 11th Street*
                                       (between Sixth and Seventh avenues)

A six-story building with fire escape and double marble pillars in front. The fire escape is placed over the portico in a way that is unusual and unobtrusive. There are unusually well defined lion's-head cartouches over the windows.

The name is written both in stone on the portico and in mosaics under the portico.

Unadilla is the name of a town in upstate New York.

The apartment building originally adjoined Rhinelander Gardens, a row of townhouses built by the Rhinelander family in the 1860s. They were demolished and replaced by Public School 41 in 1955.

UNIVERSITY HOUSE   *21 East 10th Street*
                                       (northeast corner University Place)

Begun in 1923 and opened in 1925, this handsome neo-Renaissance structure of mostly small suites (one or two bedrooms) was originally known as the Wordsworth and was one of the several large apartment buildings that began to change the Greenwich Village skyline in the 1920s. The architects were Sugarman & Berger. Initial rents were $1,200 to $3,200 annually; the highest rent—$3,600—was received for a penthouse studio of four rooms.

The name comes from its proximity to New York University, which dominates the neighborhood.

U.S. SENATE, THE   *235 Second Avenue*

Named for the upper house of the federal legislature, where William Maxwell Evarts of New York served from 1885 to 1889.

A twin to *The W. M. Evarts,* at 231 Second Avenue.

VALENCIA COURT   *317 West 95th Street*

A seven-story brick and limestone building of circa 1900.

Valencia is a Spanish province bordering on the Mediterranean.

VALENCIENNES, LA   *404 West 116th Street*

Matches its neighbor *La Touraine* on Morningside Drive.

Valenciennes is a small city in northern France captured by the German army in World War I and almost totally destroyed.

VALENTINE COURT
*228 Audubon Avenue
(southwest corner West 177th Street)*

A six-story building; circa 1900.

VAN BUREN
27 East 13th Street

A typical 1960s redbrick building named after one of the least notable U.S. presidents, Martin Van Buren (1782–1862), who served briefly as governor of New York State in 1829.

VAN CORTLANDT, THE
*1240 Park Avenue
(northwest corner East 96th Street)*

A nicely preserved relic of the 1905 era of apartment building, right at the point of Park Avenue where the tracks emerge from underground. Six stories in brick and limestone; the entrance porch has four polished granite columns. George F. Pelham was the architect; suites of seven, eight, and nine rooms rented for $1,000 to $1,400 annually in 1908.

The Van Cortlandt name is one of the oldest in New York, dating back to the 1630s. The Van Cortlandt Mansion and Park in the Bronx are vestiges of the enormous landholdings of this family.

VAN DYCK
*175 West 72nd Street
(northeast corner Amsterdam Avenue)*

A thirteen-story twin to the *Severn Arms,* built in 1905 by Mulliken & Moeller.

Sir Anthony Van Dyck (1599–1641), the Flemish artist, was court painter to King Charles I of England.

VAN GOGH, THE
*14 Horatio Street
(corner Eighth Avenue)*

A 1960s redbrick building—nothing worth cutting off your ear for. One of several in the neighborhood named after famous artists.

Vincent van Gogh (1853–1890), one of the greatest Post-Impressionist painters.

VAN HORNE
300 West End Avenue

A circa-1900 thirteen-story building with a handsome, nicely detailed rusticated base. Stone swags and corbels over the windows. The entrance portico is flanked by four columns.

The Van Hornes were early settlers of New Amsterdam. In 1743 Cornelius Van Horne went on record as regretting the decline of the Dutch tongue among New Yorkers.

VAN PRADT
524 West 112th Street

A six-story turn-of-the-century building.

VAN RENSSELAER   *15 East 11th Street*

This handsome redbrick and stone building has *Van Rensse-laer* chiseled over the door, while its adjoining pendant building has simply *V.R.* over its arched entrance. Both circa 1880 and both, after a checkered past, converted to cooperative apartments circa 1982 by Rockrose.

The name is a venerable one in New York's history: the first patroon, Kiliaen Van Rensselaer, never came to America, but later family members became enormous landholders in the Hudson Valley. Stephen Van Rensselaer (1764–1839) was a lieutenant governor of New York.

VAN VOORST   *123 Waverly Place*

This nine-story building in the 1920s Georgian style has a graceful marble entrance marred by a later aluminum canopy.

The Van Voorst family were among the earliest settlers of Manhattan and at one time were in possession of bowery (farm) number 8 of the Dutch West India Company.

VANCOUVER, THE   *314 West 94th Street*

George F. Pelham was the architect of this six-story building with a side court built in 1905. In 1984 it was converted into a condominium.

George Vancouver (1757–1798) was an English explorer who gave his name to Vancouver Island in British Columbia.

[VANDERBILT]   *4 Park Avenue*

This imposing structure, occupying the entire block between East 33rd and East 34th streets, was built in 1912 as the Vanderbilt Hotel, to the designs of Warren & Wetmore (who were also responsible for Grand Central Terminal).

The name recalls the family so closely associated with the New York Central Railroad.

In 1967 the building was converted to mixed office-apartment use and abandoned its old name in the process.

VARONA   *630 West 172nd Street*

A five-story turn-of-the-century building.

VAUX HALL   *780 Riverside Drive*
                                   (northeast corner West 155th Street)

A ten-story tan-brick building of the 1920s, with an open-court entrance.

Vauxhall was a famous pleasure garden in London, laid out in 1661 and described by English writers from Samuel Pepys to W. M. Thackeray.

VENDOME   *48 West 73rd Street*
(southeast corner Columbus Avenue)

A circa-1900 seven-story fire-escape building with a new name. Formerly known as the *Westport*.

The Place Vendôme is one of the principal squares of Paris, and in apartment-house nomenclature, the name is symbolic of luxury: the Ritz Hotel in located in the Place Vendôme.

VENICE   *515 West 135th Street*

One of a block-long row of circa-1900 apartment houses, each with its own name—in this case that of the Italian city known as the Queen of the Adriatic.

VENICE   *350 West 71st Street*

This circa-1900 seven-story building at the far west end of 71st Street has bayed windows overlooking the railroad tracks and the Hudson. The entrance has been modernized.

VENICE   *117–119 West 116th Street*

Abandoned.

VERMEER   *77 Seventh Avenue*

This 1960s apartment house is one of several in Greenwich Village named after famous painters—in this instance Jan Vermeer of Delft (1632–1667).

VERONA   *32 East 64th Street*

A magnificent neo-Renaissance *palazzo,* built in 1908 and still largely unchanged, except for the addition of stores along the Madison Avenue front when that street became commercial in the 1920s. The main entrance, with carved grotesque masks and twin bronze lamps, is especially striking.

The name is that of the Italian city, famous as the home of Romeo and Juliet.

VERSAILLES   *1845 Adam Clayton Powell, Jr., Boulevard*
(northeast corner West 112th Street)

A six-story, redbrick building of circa 1900.

Like the *Palais Royal, Chantilly,* and *Fontainebleau* in the same neighborhood, it takes its name from a French royal palace.

"VERSAILLES"   *250 West 91st Street*
(southwest corner Broadway)

A six-story turn-of-the-century building, now quite unpalatial in appearance. A twin building next door at 252 has a modernized entrance and has had its pediment removed, but apparently it has never been named. The name over the door includes the quotation marks.

VESTRY PLACE   *181–185 Hudson Street*
                                          (corner Vestry Street)

An eight-story loft condominium conversion of a building dating from circa 1910.

Vestry Street takes its name from the vestry of Trinity Church which ceded the land for the street to the city in 1802.

VICTOR, THE   *315 West 14th Street*

Five-story stuccoed brick building with a glass brick and metalwork entrance in the Art Deco style.

VICTOR HUGO   *200 West 114th Street*
              (southwest corner Adam Clayton Powell, Jr., Boulevard)

This turn-of-the-century seven-stories-and-basement building has a grand entrance with porch on Adam Clayton Powell, Jr., Boulevard but has fallen on evil times. A handwritten sign in the window reads "The Blood of Jesus Covers This House."

The celebrated French writer for whom the building is named lived from 1802 to 1885.

VICTORIA   *57 Second Avenue*

One of the few buildings with this name that actually looks Victorian: the resemblance to Victoria Station, London, is noticeable. Nine stories with elevator, in red brick with limestone trim; circa 1900.

VICTORIA, THE   *7 East 14th Street*

This huge white-brick apartment house of the 1960s—hardly Victorian in feeling—probably honors England's queen, who ruled from 1837 until 1901. An Australian state, a bridge in Canada, a waterfall in Africa, and a tower of the houses of Parliament in London were named for her as well.

VICTORIA   *250 Riverside Drive*
                                  (northeast corner West 97th Street)

A nine-stories-and-basement building of the turn of the century, covering half a block. There is a later canopy on West 97th Street.

VICTORIA   *175 East 62nd Street*

This 1960s white-brick building's name is invisible—but a few *V* monograms have been worked into the decor.

VICTORIA COURT *930 St. Nicholas Avenue*

This three-sectioned six-story apartment house of white brick was built toward the end of the reign of its namesake queen.

VICTORIA HALL *614–616 West 113th Street*

A seven-story redbrick building of the early twentieth century, with balconies.

Villa Norma. *Typical floor plan of this vintage Riverside Drive dwelling. Note that in this—and in several other plans—the bedrooms have been upgraded to "chambers."*

VILLA NORMA *835 Riverside Drive*

A large apartment house of the early twentieth century with three towers.

VILLAGE APARTMENTS *54 Barrow Street*

This circa-1900 Greenwich Village tenement was Hispanicized in the 1920s as a number of Village buildings were. The Spanish Revival touches include tiles around the doorway and on the roof. Take a look at 52 Barrow to see what the doorway was like before Spanish conquest.

[See also *Greenwich*.]

VILLAGE APARTMENTS, THE *45 Carmine Street*

A 1940s or thereabouts update of two five-story tenements.

VILLAGE LANDMARK, THE *259 West 10th Street*

An eight-story early-twentieth-century building of red brick. The original ground floor was a warehouse; a new upper story has been added.

VILLAGE TOWERS *15 Charles Street (at McCarthy Square)*

An eighteen-story centrally air-conditioned building of the mid-1960s, whose name is no longer visible but was featured in the original promotional brochure.

VILLAGE VIEW HOUSES *East 4th to East 6th streets First Avenue to Avenue A*

Five high-rise apartment buildings of the 1950s. Apartments with western windows do offer a view of Greenwich Village in the distance.

VILLAHERMOSA *1600 Madison Avenue (northwest corner East 107th Street)*

A turn-of-the-century building with a later name. Six stories of red brick and limestone; a new cornice and a new ground floor. Not architecturally restored, but clean and well kept.

Villahermosa ("beautiful town") is the name of towns in Spain and Mexico.

VILLARD HOUSES *457 Madison Avenue*

When the trustees of St. Patrick's Cathedral sold the land on Madison Avenue between East 50th and East 51st streets, across from the apse of the church, in 1881, the deed specified that the plot was to be used only for private dwellings, or "French Flats."

The magnificent U-shaped complex designed by McKim, Mead & White for Henry Villard, completed in 1883, turned out to be unique: several private houses masked as one, thus qualifying for inclusion in this list of multiple dwellings.

After years as private dwellings, the *Villard Houses* became the jointly owned headquarters of Random House Publishers and the Archdiocese of New York. In 1981 after protracted litigation they were incorporated into the new Helmsley Palace Hotel and their splendid interiors, noble facade, and courtyard continue to charm New Yorkers and visitors alike.

VIOLA *141–143 West 127th Street*

A white-brick six-stories-and-basement building with highly ornamental details; circa 1905.

VIOLA   *100 West 76th Street*
                                  (southwest corner Columbus Avenue)

This six-story turn-of-the-century building is now painted green. Stained-glass panels are inserted at the top of some upper-floor windows.

VIOLA   *257 West 112th Street*

Abandoned.

VIRGINIA   *226–230 East 12th Street*

An eleven-story redbrick building of the 1920s.

VIRGINIA, THE   *208–214 East 84th Street*

Four uniform brick and brownstone five-story buildings with smartly updated doorways, circa 1890.

VISCAYA CONDOMINIA   *110 East 71st Street*

This 1982 real estate adventure consists of an old town house with a slender high-rise tower built above it. The Townhouse Viscaya consists of five three-bedroom residences, the Tower Viscaya of sixteen two-bedroom *pieds-à-terre,* each one an entire floor. In 1982 the Town house apartments were priced at $700,000 to $1,235,000 and the Tower apartments at $582,000 to $675,000.

This type of construction, known as sliver building, was the target of restrictions passed in 1982, when the city acted to prevent further construction of this type.

The name is likely intended to share pleasurable association with Vizcaya (Biscay, in English), a province of Spain and a romantic palace in Miami, now a museum.

VIVIA   *393 Edgecome Avenue*

A six-story white-brick building; circa 1900.

VLADECK HOUSES (NYC Housing Authority)
                                         356 Madison Street

This huge federally funded project of twenty-two buildings on the Lower East Side dates from 1940 and is named for Baruch Charney Vladeck (1886–1938) who came to New York from Russia in 1908. He was associated with the *Jewish Daily Forward* and served on the City Council and as a member of the New York City Housing Authority, as well as being an editor, poet, and socialist.

VOLNEY, THE   *23 East 74th Street*

A former residential hotel, now converted to cooperative apartments, this fine old 1920s building, with an all-marble lobby, boasts a pleasant eating establishment called Adam's Rib.

Among the noted tenants in the past was Dorothy Parker, who lived there from 1953 to her death in 1967. She claimed to have moved there originally because she counted forty-three dogs in the building for her dog to be friendly with. She was fascinated by life in *The Volney,* which she said was full of well-to-do aging women with pasts. She wrote a play entitled *Ladies of the Corridor,* in which, her biographer notes, "the characters closely resemble then living inhabitants of the Volney."

The Comte de Volney (1757–1820), a noted French author and scholar, traveled in the United States as well as in Syria and Egypt.

VOLUNTEER   *100 West 78th Street*
(southwest corner Columbus Avenue)

A circa-1880 five-story building with modernized fire escape and badly redone facade.

VON COLON   *311 West 97th Street*

Seven stories and basement, a handsome porch with four granite columns, and name above entrance; circa 1900.

VONDALE   *18 Morningside Avenue*
(southeast corner West 116th Street)

A six-story turn-of-the-century building; which, when last seen, had a small garden growing corn and lettuce on the Morningside Avenue side.

VONDEL, THE   *171 East 83rd Street*
(northwest corner Third Avenue)

A six-story stone and brick apartment house of circa 1900, almost covered with fire escapes; columned entrance porch carved with name.

VON-HOFFMAN   *29 West 26th Street*

A nineteenth-century building of seven stories, with columns on floors three to five. Carries its name on top—probably that of the original builder.

W. M. EVARTS, THE   *231 Second Avenue*

Named for William Maxwell Evarts (1818–1901), a lawyer and statesman, who was attorney general under President Andrew Johnson, secretary of state under Rutherford B. Hayes, an anti-Tweed ring reformer, and senator from New York, 1885–1889.

This late-nineteenth-century building adjoins another, matching apartment house named *U.S. Senate.*

WACHUSETT   *170 West 75th Street*

A nineteenth-century building of five stories built of vari-colored brick. On the ground floor is the Boot Hill Bar.

Wachusett is an isolated mountain in Worcester County, Massachusetts.

WADSWORTH ARMS   *130 Wadsworth Avenue*
                                    (southwest corner West 180th Street)

A twin to *Wadsworth Court.*

James Samuel Wadsworth (1807–1864) was a Union general who was killed at the Battle of Chancellorsville. In 1862, while serving in the military, he was the Republican candidate for governor of New York.

WADSWORTH COURT   *129 Wadsworth Avenue*
                                    (southeast corner West 180th Street)

A six-story redbrick building of the 1900s period, with tow-erlets on the corners.

WADSWORTH GARDENS   *651 West 188th Street*
                                    (between Wadsworth Avenue and Wadsworth Terrace)

A group of small apartment buildings unified by their archi-tecture in the neo-Georgian style.

WADSWORTH MANOR   *45–49 Wadsworth Avenue*

A bland six-story 1920s building.

WAGNER HOUSE   *1450 Second Avenue*

A 1960s five-story building; possibly a conversion.

Near the Robert F. Wagner, Sr., Junior High School be-tween East 75th and East 76th streets.

WAGNER HOUSES (NYC Housing Authority)
                                    2396 First Avenue

This large project of over two thousand apartments in twenty-two separate buildings dates from 1958 and honors Sen-ator Robert F. Wagner, Sr. (1877–1953), father of the former New York City mayor Robert F. Wagner, Jr. The German-born senator from New York (1927–1949), who also served as lieu-tenant governor and state supreme court justice, is also the namesake of a junior high school on East 76th Street in Manhattan.

WALD HOUSES (NYC Housing Authority)

54 Avenue D

A 1949 project on the Lower East Side honoring Lillian D. Wald (1867–1940), founder of the Henry Street Settlement and New York's Visiting Nurse Service. A bronze bust of this tireless champion of public health and improved housing is enshrined in the Hall of Fame for Great Americans at University Heights in the Bronx.

WALDORF-ASTORIA TOWERS

100 East 50th Street
(southeast corner Park Avenue)

Cole Porter, Herbert Hoover, Douglas MacArthur, the Duke and Duchess of Windsor, Jacqueline Cochran, and Adlai Stevenson are just a few of the rich and famous who have occupied apartments in the towers of the Waldorf, whose own entrance and private elevators are completely separated from the enormous hotel which opened in 1931.

With forty-seven stories, the Waldorf-Astoria was called "the tallest and most beautiful hotel in all the world," and there are many who would still agree. The architects were Schultze & Weaver who even included such amenities as a private railroad siding under the hotel for those guests with their own private cars. The lobbies, public rooms, and much of the exterior gilt ornament have been recently refurbished in keeping with the *Waldorf*'s architecture of optimism: opulent Art Deco of the depression era.

The name is that of the old Waldorf-Astoria Hotel, at Fifth Avenue and 34th Street, demolished to make way for the Empire State Building. That hotel was so named because it was on the site of the old Astor mansions, Waldorf being the town in Germany where John Jacob Astor was born.

WALES HOTEL   *1295 Madison Avenue*

This turn-of-the-century nine-story building has been spruced up in recent years. It has lost its original cornice.

Originally it was an apartment house called the *Melbourne*.

WALLACE   *568 West 149th Street*
(southeast corner Broadway)

Built in 1907; George F. Pelham, architect; six stories on center-court plan. Named for its builder, Robert Wallace, a prominent developer.

WALTER ARMS   *216 West 101st Street*
(southeast corner Broadway)

A fifteen-story apartment building of 1924–1925.

Walter Arms. *The residence of Rev. J. Peters at 2648 Broadway, photographed in 1901. The house was demolished shortly after this photograph was taken and replaced by stores, which were replaced by the* Walter Arms *in 1924–25.*

Walter Arms. *This 1925 photograph shows the newly built but not yet fully occupied apartment house at Broadway and West 101st Street. The sign affixed to the corner of the building proclaims such amenities as "needle shower compartments, extra maid's lavatory, spacious cedar linen and guest closets, and spacious foyers."*

WALTON   *104 West 70th Street*
                                      (southwest corner Columbus Avenue)

A pre–World War I eleven-story building with bay windows on the fifth floor. The elaborate doorway has heavy stone decoration; above it is an iron balcony. The lobby has been modernized, and the building is well maintained.

Walton. *Photographed circa 1916, when it was the Hotel Walton. Note the Tenth Avenue Elevated tracks in the foreground and the taxi rank, with sign, at the corner of West 70th Street.*

WALTON HALL APARTMENTS
                                              325 East 72nd Street

This neo-Georgian apartment house was built in 1927 by Cox, Holden & Associates, architects. Its roof garden and "garden room" were highly praised at the time.

A virtual twin to *Walton Hall*—without a name—is at 333 East 57th Street.

William Walton's house on Pearl Street, which he built in 1752, was one of the landmarks of New York City during the nineteenth century. At different periods a private house, a boarding house, and a tenement, the building was not finally demolished until 1881.

WANAQUE   *349 West 47th Street*

An old building that has become a run-down rooming house.

What connection it has with a town in the Ramapo Mountains of New Jersey is anyone's guess.

WARREN HOUSE   *155 East 34th Street*

A white-brick 1960s–1970s apartment house.

WARWICK   *188 West 10th Street*
                                    (corner West 4th Street)

This plain old redbrick five-story building, with sparse applied decoration, dates from circa 1870. For decades the ground
floor was occupied by Joe's Italian Restaurant at 230 West
4th—Since 1933, as a sign over the door proclaimed. However,
just a few years ago the restaurant was closed, and the place now
has a melancholy, deserted air.

The name is that of a county, town, earldom, and castle in
England.

WARWICK   *92 St. Nicholas Avenue*

A redbrick seven-story building of circa 1900.

WARWICK ARMS   *101 West 80th Street*
                                    (northwest corner Columbus Avenue)

The name is handsomely chiseled over the door. This ten-
story building has classical decoration, including swags, executed in stone over the doors.

WASHINGTON

*Reverence for the Father of His Country reached an all-time high
in the years during which the centennial of his inauguration as
president was celebrated.*

*Washington took the oath of office on the balcony of the old
Federal Hall at 28 Wall Street on 30 April 1789, using a
bible hastily borrowed from the Masonic lodge. He lived in New
York City until August 1790, when the nation's capital was
removed to Philadelphia.*

*Exactly one hundred years later, Mayor Grant proclaimed the
centennial, and the board of estimate appropriated $15,000 for
fireworks and decorations. Stanford White designed a huge plaster triumphal arch which was built in the square that had borne
Washington's name since 1823. This arch, which was rebuilt in
marble in 1892, and several turn-of-the-century apartment*

buildings named for Washington are the principal relics of this gala civic observance.

WASHINGTON, THE   *115 Hamilton Place*

A typical turn-of-the-century apartment house, of generous size (it goes through to Amsterdam Avenue).

WASHINGTON, THE   *318–322 West 51st Street*

A twin to the *Jefferson* and a neighbor to the *Lincoln*.

WASHINGTON APARTMENTS
*2034–2040 Adam Clayton Powell, Jr., Boulevard
(southwest corner West 122nd Street)*

Opened in 1885. An eight-story building with a columned entrance on Adam Clayton Powell, Jr., Boulevard. Now considerably dilapidated, but once an elegant apartment house.

WASHINGTON ARMS   *328 West 11th Street*

A 1970s conversion of two old tenement-type buildings: an elevator studio apartment complex with handsome facade.

WASHINGTON COURT   *561 West 143rd Street*

A white-brick building of circa 1900; now shabby.

WASHINGTON COURT   *575 West 159th Street*

A coat of arms over the door distinguishes this old apartment house in the heart of Washington Heights, so named for Fort Washington, a Revolutionary stronghold.

WASHINGTON HEIGHTS, THE
*481 West 159th Street
(northeast corner Broadway)*

A six-story redbrick building on the center-court plan; built by Neville & Bagge, architects, in 1906.

WASHINGTON HOUSES, (NYC Housing Authority)   *1733 Third Avenue*

A late-1950s federal housing project.

WASHINGTON IRVING   *542 West 112th Street
(southeast corner Broadway)*

A ten-story central-court building by Neville & Bagge, architects; 1908.
[See also *Irving*.]

WASHINGTON IRVING
601 West 151st Street
(northwest corner Broadway)

A six-story redbrick building extensively ornamented with limestone. The entrance has been done over.

WASHINGTON IRVING HOUSE
145 East 16th Street

A 1960s white-brick apartment house, next to Washington Irving High School.

WASHINGTON SQUARE, THE
82–86 Washington Place

H. Hosenberger was the architect of this solid six-story building with limestone base and ornate cornice enhancing the tan brickwork.

WASHINGTON SQUARE VILLAGE
Bleecker Street at West Broadway

1956–58, architect S.J. Kessler; a New York University–sponsored complex of multi-colored high-rise buildings.

WASHINGTON VIEW
39½ West 4th Street

A five-story building of the 1880s, of brick trimmed with brownstone. The name is on the pediment, and the number is on the stoop.

The apartments indeed have a view of Washington Square.

WATERSIDE
East 25th to East 30th streets, at Franklin D. Roosevelt Drive

Unusually contoured towers perched at the edge of the East River, reached only by a bridge over the FDR Drive, provide comfortable apartments and sensational views for some sixteen hundred families.

The complex was designed by Davis, Brody & Assocs. in 1974.

WAUMBEK
300 West 107th Street
(southwest corner Broadway)

A circa-1900 seven-story redbrick building probably named after Waumbek Mountain in New Hampshire.

WAYNE
309 West 86th Street

A twelve-story brick and limestone building of circa 1910.

WAYWEST
380 West 12th Street

The building was originally the Hubert Warehouse. It was converted into a cooperative apartment building in 1979–1980.

358   PART II

WEATHERING HEIGHTS   *292 Lafayette Street*

These self-proclaimed "coop luxury lofts" are the "site of
Weathering Wall sculpture by Terry Fugate-Wilcox." The
rather bleak entrance hall is called an "elegant Deco lobby" in
the flyer found at the door.

WEBER   *1377 and 1379 Lexington Avenue*

The name *Weber* is in huge raised letters on the rooftop dor-
mer of this charming turn-of-the-century building. Five stories
with fine Renaissance-style decoration around the windows. A
relic of old, German Yorkville.

WEBSTER, THE   *171 East 81st Street*

The elaborate stone entrance to this circa-1900 building has
a little "concierge" window and seating area beside the doorway. The "modernized" storefront on Third Avenue detracts
from what is basically a nice—if somewhat begrimed—old
apartment house.

Daniel Webster (1782–1852), American statesman and orator; secretary of state, senator, and presidential candidate.

WEDGEWOOD HOUSE   *60 Fifth Avenue*

Possibly named to honor Josiah Wedgwood (1730–1795),
the British potter whose name is almost synonymous with one
of his factory's most famous products, a blue and white jasper-
ware that is still popular.

The 1960s building is of white brick and does have a blue
canopy, although the potter's name is misspelled.

WELLESLEY, THE   *200 East 72nd Street*

A dark-red brick tower built circa 1978 on a site that had
been cleared many years before.

The name evokes visions of a college campus in Massachusetts.

WELLESLEY, THE   *169 West 78th Street*

A very small old five-story building, with name and canopy
added later.

WELLINGTON, THE   *1290 Madison Avenue*
                          (southwest corner West 92nd Street)

A six-story brick and stone building with minimal decoration (pediment removed), circa 1900.

Arthur Wellesley, first duke of Wellington (1769–1852),
was the British military hero who defeated Napoléon at
Waterloo.

WELLINGTON ARMS   *500 West 144th Street*

Sits at the intersection formed by Hamilton Place and Amsterdam Avenue at West 144th Street.
Twin to *Chilmark Hall*.

WELLSMORE   *222 West 77th Street*

[See *Benjamin Franklin*.]

WELLSTON, THE   *161 West 75th Street*

A plain dark building of fifteen stories built in 1925; Rosario Candela, architect. Nice grillwork entrance. Above the door are the initials *AP* for the Paterno Construction Company.

WELLSWOOD   *122 East 91st Street*

Similar to the *Lossie* in date and style—one of three on this pleasant block of town houses and small apartments.

WENDELL HALL   *41–49 Bennett Avenue*

A twin to *Holmes Court*.

WESLEY TOWER   *210 West 89th Street*

A twelve-story white-brick building of the 1960s, with balconies at the corners.
John Wesley (1703–1791) was the founder of Methodism and a prolific hymn writer.
The building is only three blocks from the Church of St. Paul and St. Andrew on West 86th Street, one of the best-known Methodist churches in the city.

WEST COAST APARTMENTS, THE
95 Horatio Street

In the early 1980s a complex of warehouses and industrial buildings in the large area bounded by Horatio, Gansevoort, West, and Washington streets was converted into one of the biggest new rental apartment houses. The largest of the converted buildings was formerly the Manhattan Fruit and Meat Market. The loading dock areas have been fitted with glass, and the beautiful old copper decorative metalwork has been preserved. On the ground level are six stores. Many of the apartments are duplexes or triplexes.

WEST END HALL   *840 West End Avenue*
(northeast corner West 101st Street)

Built by George F. Pelham, architect, about the turn of the century, this big six-story building has a central court and a rather elaborate portico entrance with columns and colonnettes.

WEST END PLAZA   *378 West End Avenue*

A twelve-story building of the World War I period with classical decoration including a sculptured flame over the entrance.

WEST POINT   *336 West 95th Street*

A seven-story building with a grand arched entrance decorated with a handsome lion's mask; circa 1900. In recent years some effort has been made to spruce up the building: the lion's tongue, for example, has been painted a vivid red!

WEST POINT   *575 Riverside Drive*
(southeast corner West 135th Street)

A rather nondescript circa-1900 six-story building, steam cleaned in 1983.

The other academy is commemorated in its twin, the *Annapolis*.

Like several other apartment houses in the neighborhood, the building may have been given its name because of the proximity to Grant's Tomb, Grant being West Point class of 1843.

WEST RIVER HOUSE   *424 West End Avenue*
(southeast corner West 81st Street)

A 1983, twenty-two-story rental building of white and gray brick, with apartments containing one to three bedrooms.

WEST SIDE STUDIOS   *215 West 94th Street*
(northeast corner Broadway)

A poorly maintained twelve-story brick building of the post–World War I period.

WEST VILLAGE HOUSES   *Washington Street,*
between Bank Street and West 10th Street,
Christopher and Morton streets

Sponsored in 1973–1974 by the West Village Committee, Greenwich Village Community Housing Corporation (their logo carried the slogan Not a Sparrow Shall Be Displaced), this group of forty-two separate buildings of one-to-four bedroom apartments was put up at the height of the antideveloper, anti-high-rise feelings among Villagers, the most vocal being urbanologist Jane Jacobs, who has since moved to Canada.

In a classic case of "sweet lemons," the original brochure boasted, "These are walk-up apartments—an anachronism, perhaps to those New Yorkers who do not know the dangers of unattended elevators."

The five-story buildings were organized on a cooperative basis, the original investment being about $700 a room, with monthly maintenance charges of $104 per room. Heating and cooking were "all electric." The rather drab brick exteriors, the rise in electricity charges, and the lack of elevators and frills made *West Village Houses* less than an overnight success. But to-day, though not very visually stimulating, they appear to be fully occupied and are beginning to blend in with the miscellaneous array of old and new buildings forming the far West Village.

Westbeth. *The landscaped courtyard entrance.*

WESTBETH   *155 Bank Street*
                                 (between Washington and West streets)

Taking its name from two of the four Village Streets that mark its boundaries—West Street and Bethune Street—Westbeth Artists' Housing is a prime example of the idealistic optimism of the late 1960s, before double-digit inflation and expensive fuel put a damper on such projects.

In 1967 the J. M. Kaplan Fund purchased from the American Telephone & Telegraph Company the old Bell Telephone Laboratories Building—for $11.4 million. After alteration by Richard Meier & Assocs. in 1969, it opened in 1970 with a federal mortgage bearing 3 percent interest. It was thus the country's first subsidized housing for artists. The Kaplan Fund and the National Foundation on the Arts backed up the mortgage.

The realities of the 1970s, however, made rent increases, rent strikes, arguments, press releases, and frictional factions as much a part of *Westbeth* as the creative process.

In 1983 plans for co-oping *Westbeth,* paying off the HUD mortgage (now in arrears), and increasing the extremely low rents ($438 per month for a three-bedroom apartment!) were all put forth as solutions to *Westbeth*'s problems.

WESTBORNE COURT
*556 West 140th Street
(southeast corner Broadway)*

Owing to the lie of the land in this hilly part of Manhattan, this building of circa 1900 has six stories and basement on West 140th Street and seven stories on Broadway.

WESTBOURNE
519 West 143rd Street

A rather severe six-story building of the early twentieth century.

"Bourn" and "bourne" are archaic English words for "boundary" or "terminal."

WESTBOURNE
930 West End Avenue

A seven-story building with fire escape; circa 1900.

WESTERLY, THE
300 West 55th Street

A typically banal 1960s building; the architects were Herbert Fleischer Associates.

WESTLAND
723 West 177th Street

Boldly chiseled in stone over the door, the name of this fine old building of the early twentieth century sounds contrived but is not inappropriate now, considering the nearby bridge heading west to New Jersey.

WESTMINSTER
68 East 86th Street

A twelve-story brown-brick building of the 1920s. The heavy decoration at the top makes it look like some of the West Side buildings of the era.

Westminster is one of the boroughs of London, containing Westminster Abbey, the Houses of Parliament, and many other notable government buildings.

WESTMORE, THE
333 West 57th Street

An eight-story building with bowed windows; circa 1950s.

WESTMORE, THE
340 West 58th Street

An interesting series of bay windows marks this rather small 1950s building in the late Art Deco style.

WESTOVER APARTMENTS
253 West 72nd Street

A twenty-five-story building by Schwartz & Gross, architects, 1928.

W E S T P O R T   *48 West 73rd Street*

[See *Vendome.*]

W E S T P O R T   *636 West 172nd Street*

A five-story circa-1900 building.

W E S T S I D E R   H O T E L   *222 Riverside Drive*
                                    (northeast corner West 94th Street)

A seven-story white-brick building by Henry C. Pelton, architect, 1908. Formerly known as the *Irving Arms:* the old name can still be seen on the Riverside Drive entrance.

W E S T W I N D ,   T H E   *175 West 93rd Street*
                                 (northeast corner Amsterdam Avenue)

A large sixteen-story orange-brick building of the 1920s. Probably a recent name on the canopy. Two open courts on West 93rd Street.

W E S T W I N G   *108 West 111th Street*

Abandoned.

W H I T B Y   *325 West 45th Street*

Built in 1934 as a residential hotel, this now rather neglected building is named for the seaside resort town of Whitby in Yorkshire, England.

W H I T E   H A L L
                  1871–1873 Adam Clayton Powell, Jr., Boulevard
                                (southeast corner West 114th Street)

Seven stories and basement.
Twin to the *Deshler.*
Whitehall is a famous street in London, lined with government offices and on the site of a royal palace that burned in 1697. Peter Stuyvesant's residence, his "Great House," as it was called, stood at the corner of present-day Whitehall and State streets. The English governor Thomas Dongan made his headquarters there after 1686 and began to call the building and the street Whitehall, presumably after the royal palace in London. Whitehall was destroyed by fire in 1715.

W H I T E   H O U S E (NYC Housing Authority)
                                           2029 Second Avenue

The Reverend Gaylord White (1864–1931), a Presbyterian minister who also was founder and first president of the United Neighborhood Houses, is the namesake for this 1964 twenty-story building at East 104th Street.

WHITE HOUSE, THE   *262 Central Park West*
                                     (northwest corner West 86th Street)

A rather severe fourteen-story 1920s building of white brick with limestone base. The lobby is grand.

Built on the site of two buildings that were called the Mohonk and the Minnewaska.

WHITE HOUSE   *601 West 172nd Street*
                                     (northwest corner St. Nicholas Avenue)

A circa-1900 white-stone building of six stories, with a palatial arched entrance.

WHITESTONE, THE   *45 Tiemann Place*

The older address, 609 West 127th Street, is chiseled in stone above the door. West 127th Street became Tiemann Place, so named for Mayor Daniel F. Tiemann (1805–1899), who had a home on the north side of West 127th between Broadway and the Hudson. This early 1920s building has six stories and a basement and is of red brick with unusual green and yellow terra-cotta details, including lions' masks and Greek key frets.

WHITNEY AT MURRAY HILL, THE
                                     311 East 38th Street

A thirty-story 115-unit luxury condominium that featured pictures of A. T. Stewart's famous nineteenth-century mansion on Fifth Avenue and 34th Street in its advertisements, although that house was fully ten blocks away from the site.

[WHITNEY HOUSE]   *12 West 10th Street*

Now renovated into apartments, this early-nineteenth-century house was once the home of Isabel L. Whitney, a mural painter. She died in 1962.

WHITNEY HOUSE   *200 East 90th Street*

Modern versions of bay windows add a nice touch to this otherwise stark tower.

WILBRAHAM, THE   *1 West 30th Street*
                                     (northwest corner Fifth Avenue)

The Wilbraham was built as bachelor apartments in 1890, designed by the architects Jardine, Kent & Jardine. Each bachelor flat had two rooms and a bath. There was a dining room on the eighth floor of the nine-story building with a mansard roof.

"It may be said," according to the *Real Estate Record,* "that all the bachelor requires to do in such a house is to eat, drink, sleep, and be merry, and the servants and managers will take care of the rest."

Wilbraham. *Main entrance with its name beautifully displayed above the door. Note the zephyr carving on the right and the original lighting fixture.*

The building was modernized in 1935, offering at the time one- and two-room apartments. It then became commercial, with a number of firms selling textiles and other goods from India as tenants. A handsome banderole still carries the original name on the 30th Street entrance, however, even though it has recently been reconverted to residential apartments as the Tiffany.

WILLA VIEW APARTMENTS
1809–1811 Amsterdam Avenue

A late-nineteenth-century four-story walk-up building.

WILLIAM
243 West 98th Street (northwest corner Broadway)

A seven-story white-brick building of circa 1900, with fire escapes and stone and iron balconies.

WILLIAM HENRY
600 West 136th Street (southwest corner Broadway)

A six-story building; circa 1900.
Prince William Henry of England (later King William IV) was the first member of the British royal family to visit New York. Arriving in September 1781, while the city was still in the hands of the British forces, he received a respectful but enthusiastic welcome and was put up in a house on Wall Street for several days.

WILMINGTON   *230 West 97th Street*
                                          (southeast corner Broadway)

A large seven-story building of the early twentieth century.

WILSHIRE, THE   *301 East 75th Street*
                                      (northeast corner Second Avenue)

White brick with marble; the original 1965 brochure for this
now anonymous building boasted of a "lavishly appointed lobby
recapturing the atmosphere of the stately East Side."
Rents were listed then as $400 to $600 per month.

WILSHIRE HOUSE   *134 West 58th Street*

A 1920s building in a modified Gothic style.

WILSON HOUSES (NYC Housing Authority)
                                                   2040 First Avenue

A three-building project of 1961, named for Woodrow Wilson (1856–1924), twenty-eighth president of the United States.

WILTON   *601 West 164th Street*
                                       (northwest corner Broadway)

A six-story white-brick building with two bays on Broadway;
turn-of-the-century.
Wilton House in Wiltshire is one of the great homes of England, especially famous for its "double-cube" room.

WILTSHIRE   *602–604 West 139th Street*

Built circa 1908 by Schwartz & Gross, architects; six stories
of red brick, with fire escapes.
A twin to the *Stockbridge* on West 138th Street.
Wiltshire is one of the English counties.

WIMBLEDON, THE   *200 East 82nd Street*
                                       (southeast corner Third Avenue)

A 1970s high rise with driveway entrance enhanced by a
brass-shield-shaped nameplate and a little park with benches
and shade trees—but no tennis court!

WINDERMERE HOTEL   *666 West End Avenue*
                                      (northeast corner West 92nd Street)

A huge 1920s building with a tower at the top of its nineteen stories.
Lake Windermere in the Lake District of northern England
is the largest lake in England.

WINDSOR *400 East 71st Street*

Named, of course, after the British royal family and their suburban castle, this late-1970s apartment building occupies a site that had been vacant for such a long time, it became an unofficial playground and minilake (in the excavation hole) for the neighborhood.

WINDSOR ARMS *61 West 9th Street*

This nine-story building dates from 1926 and is in a vaguely Georgian style.

At the time of World War I the British royal family changed its name from Wettin, family name of Albert of Saxe-Coburg-Gotha, consort of Queen Victoria, to Windsor.

WINDSOR COURT *1469 Lexington Avenue*
(southeast corner East 95th Street)

Built circa 1890–1900; columns flank the main entrance. Seven stories, plus another "half-story" on East 95th Street where land slopes down to the east. Now painted gray and in good condition.

WINDSOR TOWER *5 Tudor City Place*

Part of the original *Tudor City,* this twenty-two-story apartment hotel had annual rents of $650 to $7,000 in 1928.

WINGATE, THE *201 East 37th Street*

Buff brick, 1960s.

WINGATE HOTEL *3440 Broadway*
(northeast corner West 140th Street)

Built in 1905; Schwartz & Gross and B. N. Marcus, architects. Seven stories, a center court, and recessed fire escapes; in red brick.

WINSLOW COURT *87 Hamilton Place*
(southeast corner West 141st Street)

Seven stories, circa 1900; with bands of wave scroll motifs on the second story.

WINTHROP *423 West 118th Street*
(northeast corner Amsterdam Avenue)

Six stories with a nice basement; circa 1905.
Twin to the *Elizabeth Court* next door.

WISE TOWERS (NYC Housing Authority)
124 West 91st Street

These two nineteen-story buildings date from 1965 and are part of that decade's Upper West Side clearance project.

Named for Rabbi Stephen S. Wise (1874–1949), founder of New York's Free Synagogue, activist in Jewish and Zionist affairs, and founder and president of the Jewish Institute of Religion.

WOLLASTON
231 West 96th Street
(northeast corner Broadway)

A seven-story building with fire escape, its long side on Broadway; circa 1900.

John Wollaston was an eighteenth-century American portrait painter who worked extensively in New York City, painting about three hundred portraits between 1749 and 1752.

WOODBURY, THE
19 East 95th Street

A twin to its next-door neighbor on Madison Avenue, the *Almscourt*.

WOODCLIFF
106 Haven Avenue

One of three identical five-story 1920s white-brick buildings standing on one of the highest points above the Hudson. The other two are the *Hudson Cliff* and the *Haven Cliff*.

WOODMERE
561 West 141st Street
(northeast corner Broadway)

An eight-story building of white brick, with open bay on Broadway; circa 1900.

WOODSTOCK HOTEL
127 West 43rd Street

The *Woodstock* takes its name from the town in Vermont. When the thirteen-story, three-hundred-room hotel opened in 1920, *Tavern Topics* noted: "There is a genuine significance in the name of the Hotel Woodstock. While maintaining service of the most up-to-date metropolitan caravansary, the management preserves the traditions of the Vermont folk who were instrumental in establishing the house and who today still form a large percentage of its clientele." One of the points of the interior decoration much stressed at the time was the embellishment of the public rooms with framed Japanese prints.

The hotel underwent a gradual decline as the Times Square area grew seedy after World War II, becoming a mixture of permanent residents and, eventually, welfare tenants. In 1978 a nonprofit group called Project Find began to turn the hotel into a residence for the elderly, to the relief of the small remaining group of permanent residents. In 1982 the *Woodstock* was being renovated as an apartment building.

WOODSTOCK TOWER   *320 East 42nd Street*

A *Tudor City* building. Described as an "elegant" building in 1928, when annual rents ranged from $800 to $3,000.

The name derives from a town in Oxfordshire, England, near Blenheim Palace, associated with Fair Rosamund, mistress of King Henry II. Elizabeth I, when heiress to the crown, was imprisoned at Woodstock by her half sister, Queen Mary.

WOODWARD HALL   *50 East 96th Street*
(southeast corner Madison Avenue)

This six-story tan-brick and limestone apartment house was designed by George F. Pelham in 1904. It has a central court and pillared entrance.

When it first opened, suites of five, six, and seven rooms rented for $720 to $840 annually.

John Woodward was a citizen of New York during the Revolutionary era, who took part in a raid on the offices of the King's Printer, James Rivington.

WOOLSEY, THE   *141 East 44th Street*

Typical 1920s building with central court entrance. No trace of the name on the door anymore. The building is dwarfed by its new neighbor, a gigantic office building with the name (and address?) "Two Grand Central Towers."

The name could refer to Joris Woolsey, a seventeenth-century New Yorker involved in the administration of an estate in the Turtle Bay Farm area.

Wyoming. *Photographed in June 1915, showing the now radically altered street-level facade along Seventh Avenue. The view is looking north toward West 55th Street and in the left distance may be seen the* Osborne *at West 57th Street.*

WYOMING, THE

166 West 55th Street
(southeast corner Seventh Avenue)

This mammoth twelve-story apartment building of 1906 is a real survivor. As the area has grown more and more commercial, most of the grand residential buildings that once graced this neighborhood have given way to new office towers and hotels.

Rouse & Sloan were the architects, and the annual rents at opening for the seven-to-thirteen-room suites ranged from $2,400 to $5,000.

The Wyoming Territory, organized in 1868, was admitted to the Union as a state in 1890.

YORK, THE

488 Seventh Avenue

Formerly the York Hotel, this elaborate building was converted to mixed commercial and residential use by Martin Swarzman & Partners in 1982. Floors one through six offered office suites; floors seven to twelve contained studio and one-bedroom rental apartments.

The name probably derives from the English prince who was responsible for New Amsterdam's final name: James, duke of York, later King James II.

YORK, THE

435 East 79th Street

A redbrick 1960s apartment house whose name comes from its location on York Avenue, a street named in 1928 in honor of Sergeant Alvin C. York, who was awarded the Congressional Medal of Honor and almost fifty other decorations for his bravery in World War I.

Prior to the renaming York Avenue had been Avenue A.

YORK HOUSE

401 East 58th Street

An amalgamation of brownstones and walk-ups, with its own private alley and gate; a bit of Greenwich Village near Sutton Place.

YORK MANOR

346 East 89th Street

A modern redo of one of the many small tenements on this block.

YORK RIVER HOUSE

1175 York Avenue

A huge modern building, one of several that transformed the area from one of gas tanks and tenements into a smart residential neighborhood.

YORK ROW

511–513 East 86th Street

A group of brownstones renovated in the 1920s and clad in a new facade with Federal-style doorways. The group was then christened *York Row* because during the Revolutionary War a battery of artillery from the county of Yorkshire in England had been stationed on a nearby knoll overlooking the East River.

YORKGATE
25 East End Avenue
(northeast corner East 80th Street)

A well-preserved 1920s building of fifteen stories; nice stone masks over the entrance.

YORKSHIRE
562 West 113th Street

An eight-story white-brick building of the early twentieth century, with modernized doorway.

Yorkshire is a county in the north of England.

YORKSHIRE HOUSE
401 East 81st Street

Tan brick, balconies—very 1960s.

YORKSHIRE TOWERS
305–315 East 86th Street
(northeast corner Second Avenue)

A 1960s white-brick pile designed by Slingerland & Booss and advertised as "New York's largest apartment building . . . the twenty-one story city-within-a-city [of] 695 apartments." The brochure promised "an ideal blend of Manhattan convenience, East Side distinction, suburban grace and country space." A health club is maintained for the residents.

On the site, in the nineteenth century, stood the Shepherd's Fold, an Episcopal home.

YORKVILLE TOWERS
East 90th to East 93rd streets
Second to Third avenues

See *Ruppert Towers*.

ZENOBIA, THE
217 Central Park North

The architect of this six-story redbrick building with odd crenellations on the roof was H. Anderson. Built in 1906, it featured large apartments.

Zenobia was queen of Palmyra, an ancient city of Syria, who fought against the Romans in the third century A.D. Also, *Zenobia* is the title of a best-selling novel published in 1837 by the American writer William Ware.

III

*Nooks and Crannies:
Named Residential
Enclaves*

F OLLOWING are the principal places in Manhattan that can be, and are, referred to by their inhabitants by name, rather than just a street address, but that are not, strictly speaking, multiple-unit dwellings under one roof.

AMSTER YARD   *211 East 49th Street*

This attractive little courtyard with its surrounding low-rise buildings was originally a starting point for the Boston stagecoach in the early nineteenth century. James Amster bought the whole complex in 1946 and renovated it for himself and his design firm; the other tenants were connected with design and the arts (Billy Baldwin, the decorator, lived here). Amster had been an assistant to Elsie de Wolfe in her interior decorating business.

In 1983 a thirty-one-story office tower called Crystal Pavilion rose nearby on Third Avenue, and the air rights to *Amster Yard* were sold to Cohen Brothers, the developers, thus ensuring the future of this peaceful enclave and the greater-than-allowable square footage of the Crystal Pavilion.

COLONNADE ROW   *428–434 Lafayette Street*

Only four of the original nine houses remain at what once was New York City's most elegant address. The architecture of this row between East 4th Street and Astor Place has been traditionally attributed to Alexander Jackson Davis. This magnificent relic of the city's vogue for attached row houses, made to look like one long Greek temple through the use of uniform colonnades, was originally called *LaGrange Terrace,* after Lafayette's estate in France, since it was built on Lafayette Place (now Lafayette Street).

GROVE COURT   *Between 10 and 12 Grove Street*

One of New York's peaceful oases of tiny houses built around a garden between Bedford and Hudson streets. The houses date from the 1850s but were "gentrified" in the 1920s when the name was changed from Mixed Ale Alley to *Grove Court.*

HENDERSON PLACE   *North side East 86th Street,*
between York and East End avenues

A charming block of small redbrick townhouses originally built by John C. Henderson for people of "moderate means" in 1882. Lamb & Rich were the architects.

Among the residents in recent years were Alfred Lunt and Lynn Fontanne of theater fame.

LAGRANGE TERRACE   *428–434 Lafayette Street*

[See *Colonnade Row.*]

MacDOUGAL-SULLIVAN GARDENS
Bounded by MacDougal,
Sullivan, West Houston,
and Bleecker streets

In the early 1920s this group of run-down row houses were acquired by the Hearth & Home Corporation and turned into a charming middle-class compound surrounding a central shared garden for residents only.

Carl Van Doren was one of the original inhabitants.

MILLIGAN PLACE   *Avenue of the Americas,*
between West 10th and West 11th streets

and

PATCHIN PLACE   *West 10th Street, between Avenue of the*
Americas and Greenwich Avenue

The small nineteenth-century houses in these adjoining culs-de-sac were originally built as workers' homes, but in the 1920s several well-known writers took up residence here, giving the place a reputation for bohemian intellectualism.

Among those residents were e.e. cummings and Djuna Barnes.

Milligan and Patchin were the names of the original owner and surveyor of this area in the late eighteenth century.

POMANDER WALK   *261–267 West 94th Street*
260–266 West 95th Street

Pomander Walk is a double row of twenty-seven small Olde

Pomander Walk

English–style houses, with its own central walk in the block between Broadway and West End Avenue. A London street of the same name lies in the suburb of Chiswick. In 1910 it gave its name to a play by the Anglo-American writer Louis N. Parker that was a hit in both London and New York.

Ten years later Thomas J. Healy, a New York restaurant owner, who was a great first-nighter, was so impressed by the play that he had King & Campbell design and build these little houses, their architecture inspired by the stage set. The first tenants moved in during 1922.

Upon seeing the re-creation, the playwright said: "You might have thought the houses were meant to be inhabited by very small dukes so stately were they in their tiny way."

Originally *Pomander Walk* was intended for tenants in the theatrical profession (it was an ancestor, therefore, of the 1970s *Manhattan Plaza*) and was occupied at times by famous actors and actresses including Madeleine Carroll and Louis Wolheim.

At the north end of the *Walk* there used to be a London suburb watchman's box with a private "bobby" sitting in it.

RENWICK TRIANGLE *114–128 East 10th Street*
23–25 Stuyvesant Street

The divergence from Manhattan's grid pattern due to the preexistence of a lane on Peter Stuyvesant's property was the happy accident that brought about Renwick Triangle between Second and Third avenues.

A group of Italianate houses—some now divided into apartments—was built by Mathius Banta in 1861. James Renwick, Jr., is thought to have been the architect. Restrictive deeds have kept the houses and the neighborhood from being redeveloped into oblivion.

SNIFFEN COURT   *150–158 East 36th Street*

A quiet enclave of old carriage houses and stables converted into residences during the 1920s. A Mr. John Sniffen was the builder of the original structures.

The sculptor Malvina Hoffman had her studio here.

TURTLE BAY GARDENS   *226–246 East 49th Street*
227–247 East 48th Street

In 1920 Mrs. Walton Martin assembled this group of twenty brownstones and had them remodeled in a modified Mediterranean style by Clarence Dean. A central garden was created, complete with fountain and paintings.

Among the tenants, past and present: Katharine Hepburn, Amin Khan, Tyrone Power, and Stephen Sondheim.

The name is taken from the original name for the inlet which has long since been filled in, and on which this complex now stands.

WASHINGTON MEWS *Fifth Avenue to University Place, south of 8th Street*

Nestled beneath the towering mass of the apartment building at 1 Fifth Avenue is the entrance to a row of what were once stables but which are now studios and residences of artists, sculptors, and distinguished members of the faculty of New York University.

The cobblestone paving, the old-fashioned lamps, and the deserted, quiet ambience are a welcome contrast to the honky-tonk of 8th Street.

On the other side of Fifth Avenue, extending to MacDougal Street, is MacDougal Alley, a cul-de-sac of studios.

IV

Names Writ in Water:
Demolished Buildings

ALBANY, THE   *1625 Broadway*

Built in 1876—John Babcock, architect—this typical old-fashioned apartment building with awkward layouts, which stood between West 51st and West 52nd streets, has long since been demolished.

Probably named for London's choicest and best-known multiple-unit residential building, Albany, built in 1785 as a private residence and converted into "chambers" for well-connected bachelors in 1803 by architect Henry Holland.

Albany still stands–in Piccadilly, next door to the Royal Academy of Arts in Burlington House–and its present tenants remain proud of its roster of illustrious past tenants, including Lord Byron, Lord Macaulay, Sir Harold Nicolson, and Edward Heath.

ARTHUR HALL   *45 East 96th Street*
                              (northeast corner Madison Avenue)

George F. Pelham was the architect of this 1905 building which boasted of parlors and libraries paneled in Louis XVI style and a private ballroom "for the special convenience of the tenants." Annual rents for a nine-room flat started at $1,600 when *Arthur Hall* first opened.

BACHELOR APARTMENTS
                                   225–229 West 69th Street

Schwartz & Gross were the architects for this specially designed accommodation of circa 1906.

FOUR SEASONS, THE   *145 West 41st Street*

Built prior to 1883, but listed in that year among the "first class apartments" with vacant flats.

GRENOBLE   *201 West 56th Street*
(southwest corner Seventh Avenue)

An apartment hotel of the late nineteenth century that once stood near the still extant *Osborne;* a Grenoble Market at the street level of *The Osborne* is a vestigial reminder. Demolished in 1930.

GROSVENOR, THE   *1 East 10th Street*
(northeast corner Fifth Avenue)

In 1874 *Scribner's Monthly* described *The Grosvenor* as "a type unique . . . since it secures the economy of multiple tenancy and cooperative living, with the atmosphere of home. . . . It is, in fact, a nest of elegant homes. . . . A success from the first. It opened with all its rooms leased for terms of years, while scores of desirable tenants eagerly enrolled themselves as candidates for the first vacancies that may occur."

Grosvenor is the family name of the dukes of Westminster, who own much property in Central London, for example, Grosvenor Square.

HANOVER   *2 East 15th Street*
(southeast corner Fifth Avenue)

Built in 1891; McKim, Mead & White, architects. A long-hall, awkwardly laid out apartment building.

HECKSCHER APARTMENTS   *277 Park Avenue*

Built in 1924 between East 47th and East 48th streets—McKim, Mead & White, architects—this enormous fortress was for many years one of Manhattan's best addresses. Residents included the Kennedy family.

Named for its builder, August Heckscher, Geman-born (1845) coal tycoon and real estate developer (the Crown Building at 57th and Fifth Avenue was originally the Heckscher Building and the first home of the Museum of Modern Art). His family is still prominent in New York's civic and cultural life.

HOFFMAN ARMS, THE   *640 Madison Avenue*
(northwest corner East 59th Street)

Now occupied by an office building, this corner was once the site of New York's oldest and most luxurious apartment hotel, *The Hoffman Arms.*

Samuel Verplanck Hoffman was born in 1802 in Clermont, New York, and came to the big city to make his fortune. He did—and before 1860 he had bought the land where he would later put up his apartment building, at a time when upper Fifth

and Madison avenues still were country lanes 'way out in the
sticks.

In the late 1870s Hoffman built a ten-story redbrick apartment house at 59th and Madison, which he called *The Hoffman
Arms,* both to immortalize himself and to share some of the
glamour associated with the Hoffman House Hotel on Madison
Square, one of Manhattan's favorite *rendezvous. The Hoffman Arms*
was a success from the day it opened and attracted a chic clientele, including artists, society figures, and the legendary financier Hetty Green (1834–1916), "The Witch of Wall Street,"
who *officially* lived in Hoboken to avoid New York taxes.

When Hoffman died in 1880, he left *The Hoffman Arms* to
his son Eugene Augustus and the land to another son Charles
Frederick. The latter sold out to his brother who entered the
ministry and became known as the richest clergyman in the
United States. When the Reverend Hoffman died in 1903, his
estate was valued at $6 million and included a copy of the Gu-
tenberg Bible bequeathed to the General Theological Seminary,
where he had once served as dean.

The Hoffman Arms was demolished in the early 1930s, sig-
naling the end of an era in apartment living.

HOLBEIN STUDIOS *Seventh Avenue and West 56th Street*

One of several studio apartment buildings in this area south
of Carnegie Hall.

Named for Hans Holbein (1497–1543), the German painter
renowned for his portraits of Henry VIII and his courtiers.

HOUSE OF MANSIONS
Fifth Avenue and East 41st Street

Across from the Croton Reservoir, now the site of the New
York Public Library, this was one of New York's first attempts
(1858–1859) to carry on the London tradition of elegant row
houses, in this case masked as one grand dwelling. Designed by
the noted architect and artist Alexander Jackson Davis, the
houses were described as "eleven independent dwellings, differing in size, accommodation and price, all combined as in one
palace." As another observed noted, "the architectural appearance" of the range of residences "much resembles an arsenal."

This real estate venture did not find favor among New Yorkers, and soon the Rutgers Female Institute occupied the northern part of the row. Most of the houses had been demolished by
1900 as Fifth Avenue had grown more and more commercial
below 59th Street.

LINCOLN ARCADE *1931 Broadway*

A complex of studios and studio apartments at West 65th
Street overlooking Lincoln Square, now demolished with the
march of progress brought about by the advent of Lincoln
Center.

This early version of artists' housing had originally been an office building but was converted during the transformation of this section of the Upper West Side to a center for painters. Milton and Sally Avery—newly wed—lived at *Lincoln Arcade* in 1926.

PALERMO, THE   *125 East 57th Street*

Named for the ancient Sicilian city, this apartment house was the last word in elegance when it was built in 1882, and a year later was mentioned as being one of the first-class apartment houses with vacancies. A ten-room apartment rented for $2,500 annually. Architects were Jardine, Kent & Jardine.

As late as the 1970s a few tenants were still enjoying their rent-controlled flats with marble fireplaces. In 1984 the block was in the process of being redeveloped. See page 256.

PLAZA HOME CLUB APARTMENTS
Fifth Avenue and West 59th Street

A never-completed cooperative apartment house on the site of the present Plaza Hotel.

The name is taken from the Grand Army Plaza at this intersection, with its Augustus Saint-Gaudens's statue of General Sherman and Victory.

RAYMOND, THE   *42–46 East 28th Street*

Now a parking lot, this site was occupied in the early part of this century by what the promotional brochure called "the most complete small suite apartment house in the City, with all modern improvements, such as cold storage (no ice), letter chute. . . . Electric cars pass the door . . . a most desirable residence only a short distance from Broadway."

REMBRANDT, THE   *152 West 57th Street*

This was supposedly the first of many cooperative apartment houses designed and organized by Philip Hubert and his Hubert Home Club organization.

Built in 1881, this building was immediately to the left of Carnegie Hall, predating it by almost ten years.

SONOMA, THE   *1730–1734 Broadway*
(northeast corner West 55th Street)

From circa 1900 an apartment house by this name occupied the site where Mutual of New York maintains its headquarters now.

The name is that of a county in California near San Francisco.

[SPANISH FLATS]   *150–180 Central Park South*
                                   145–175 West 58th Street

Built in 1882, the *Spanish Flats* comprised eight apartment buildings "each named for a city in Spain": Madrid, Cordova, Barcelona, Salamanca, Valencia, Tolosa, and Lisbon *(sic)*. The builder was José de Navarro, Spanish consul in New York and husband of the American actress Mary Anderson. The architect was the French-born Philip Hubert. The style was described as modern Gothic.

The buildings were planned to house seventy-six families and were among the most elaborate and expensive ever built in the city. In 1890 they were considered one of the six most costly structures in the city excluding federal and municipal buildings, the other five being St. Patrick's Cathedral, the Equitable Building, the Mills Building, the Plaza Hotel, and *The Dakota*.

An unusual feature of the buildings was their internal passageway, "almost a street in extent," which ran east and west from Seventh Avenue to the private street at the eastern end of the building. Supplies were delivered by means of this street.

The first advertisements for the building described them as having "air-cushion elevators with the assurance that if an elevator should drop from any floor, the occupants would fall soft."

The *Spanish Flats* were torn down in 1926, and the site is now occupied by the New York Athletic Club, built in 1929.

STEVENS HOUSE   *West 27th Street,*
                                   Fifth Avenue to Broadway

Built in 1870–1874, this was Richard Morris Hunt's second essay at apartment house architecture. It was named for its builder, Paran Stevens, and was dubbed "the first million dollar apartment."

After Mrs. Stevens followed society uptown to Marble Row on 42nd Street, *Stevens House* failed and later became the Victoria Hotel.

STUYVESANT, THE   *142 East 18th Street*

New York City's first apartment house, built in 1869, and pulled down in 1957, to be replaced by a routine apartment building named *Gramercy Green*.

Originally dubbed "Stuyvesant's Folly" because people were skeptical that French flats would ever be accepted in New York, the building proved to be a social and financial success. It *never* had a vacancy! There were no elevators, and its rather gloomy stairwells were used in the 1948 film *Kiss of Death* starring Richard Widmark as the villain who pushes an old lady in a wheelchair down the steps. Steam heat and electricity were installed later to augment the original stoves and gas.

Among the tenants were Mrs. George Armstrong Custer (widow of the unfortunate general), Calvert Vaux (co-designer of Central Park), Bayard Taylor (the novelist and world traveler), and the grand duke Alexis of Russia.

[See Introduction.]

Stuyvesant, *photographed in June, 1925. Built in 1869, the Stuyvesant was demolished in the 1950s to make way for the Gra*mercy Green *Apartments.*

TIFFANY HOUSE   27 East 72nd Street

Long since replaced by a stately 1930s apartment house, the imposing residence of Charles Lewis Tiffany at the northwest corner of Madison Avenue and East 72nd Street was actually three separate suites of duplex apartments within a unifying structure built in 1884 by McKim, Mead & White.

It was luxuriously decorated by Louis Comfort Tiffany, son of the man who commissioned but never lived in this "house of many mansions." The Tiffany family resided there almost until its demolition in 1936.

YOSEMITE, THE   550 Park Avenue

Now occupied by a typically classical Park Avenue cooperative apartment, "550" was once the site of an exceptionally grand residence called *The Yosemite,* built by McKim, Mead & White in 1891—undoubtedly named for Yosemite National Park, which was established with great fanfare in 1890.

The Yosemite was demolished in the 1920s.

V

Walking Tours

TOUR ONE: WEST SIDE SPLENDOR

The Upper West Side of Manhattan—defined as the area west of Central Park to the Hudson River and north of West 59th Street to the end of Manhattan Island—was late in being developed into residential neighborhoods.

Slowly at first in the 1880s, and then around the turn of the century in a spree of building, developers erected town houses, blocks of flats, and elegant apartment houses where only a few years earlier there had been nothing but farms, shanties, and country houses. An effort was made to call the area the West End after London's fashionable section, but the name never caught on. Broadway, laid out long before as the Bloomingdale Road, has always been the main artery of the West Side.

Because the area was not already densely covered with tenements, as were Downtown and the East Side, architects and builders vied with one another in erecting splendid rows of private houses, often with matching apartment buildings and stores at the avenue ends of each block.

Well in into the 1920s and 1930s, apartments for the middle class, erected on the main thoroughfares, such as West End Avenue and Riverside Drive, were remarkably large and comfortable. Along Central Park a dozen of New York's most interesting apartment houses rose, creating one of America's most distinctive skylines.

START OF TOUR: IND subway station at Central Park West and West 72nd Street

1 West 72nd Street is *The Dakota,* perhaps the most famous apartment house in the world. Across 72nd is:

115 Central Park West, the Art Moderne *Majestic.*

12 West 72nd Street is the *Oliver Cromwell* and 15 *Mayfair Towers* on the site that originally contained *The Dakota*'s generating plant. These two buildings facing each other across 72nd Street provide striking contrast between the architecture of the 1920s and the 1960s.

Two typical 1920s apartment hotels are the *Olcott* at 27 and *The Bancroft* at 40.

Crossing Columbus Avenue, on the southwest corner at 100 is the *Park and Tilford Building,* formerly commercial. Next door at 110 is the elegant *Hotel Margrave,* which extends through to West 71st Street.

At Amsterdam Avenue and 72nd on the northeast corner is the *Van Dyck;* behind it is a twin building, the *Severn Arms,* at 170 West 73rd Street. Together they occupy the entire east blockfront along Amsterdam Avenue between West 72nd and West 73rd, facing Verdi Square.

Around the corner at 160 West 73rd is the *Sherman Square Studios* with its medieval decoration.

The famous *Ansonia* stands between 73rd and 74th on the west side of Broadway. Its 73rd Street entrance is now bricked up. At 253 West 73rd Street is the *Level Club Condominium,* formerly the Riverside Plaza Hotel.

Returning to Broadway, at 2141–2157 is the *Astor Apartments,* recently renovated, and across Broadway is *The Opera,* formerly Manhattan Towers, built on the original site of the Manhattan Congregational Church. The arched Gothic doorway to the right of the main entrance leads to the Promenade Theater.

Eastward across West 78th Street is a series of typical small, usually five-storied apartment buildings of the late nineteenth century, such as *Florence* at 204, *Cecilia* at 202, and *Orchid* at 170. The striking brownish-red *Evelyn* is at the northwest corner of West 78th and Columbus Avenue.

Directly across Columbus Avenue is Manhattan Square, laid out as a park but now almost entirely occupied by the buildings of the American Museum of Natural History.

The long 77th Street block between Columbus Avenue and Central Park West contains Parc 77 at 50 and the *Manhattan Square Studios* at 44. The other buildings, although nameless, make an impressive group facing the museum.

South on Central Park West from 77th are the circa-1900 *Kenilworth* at 151, sharing the blockfront with the Universalist Church between 75th and 76th streets. Between 74th and 75th is the *San Remo* at 145–146, a noted 1929 eclectic building whose distinctive towers are a landmark of the West Side. Then comes the circa-1900 *Langham*.

Down West 73rd from Central Park West may be seen still standing some of the town houses built by Edward Clark of *The Dakota* when this area was first being settled.

END OF TOUR: back to IND subway entrance at Central Park West and West 72nd Street.

TOUR TWO: THE SOLID WEST SIDE

The vast majority of West Side apartments were designed for families with children. The original room counts in the larger buildings are staggering by today's standards—nine-, ten-, twelve-room apartments were the usual. As early as the 1930s many of the large suites were subdivided to suit changing ways of life. The gradual vanishing of servants, smaller families, and widespread financial problems during the depression were mainly responsible.

The flight of the middle class to the suburbs after World War II dealt a blow to the Upper West Side that brought about serious deterioration in many neighborhoods. Recovery in the form of renovation and rebuilding began in the late 1960s and has continued into the 1980s. Despite urban renewal, the building of Lincoln Center, and the expansion of institutions, a tremendous number of

apartment houses nearly a century old remain as solid
housing on the West Side.

This tour emphasizes the substantial apartments built
for family living from the 1890s to the late 1960s.
START OF TOUR: IND subway station at Central Park
West and West 86th Street.

257 Central Park West on the downtown corner of
West 86th Street, now called *Orwell House,* was formerly
the Stuyvesant and Central Park View. Across 86th at 27
is *The John Muir.* West on 86th Street, the vast *Belnord*
stands at 225, facing the *New Amsterdam* at 200.

The interesting *Euclid Hall* and *Bretton Hall* with their
similar flamboyant decoration face each other on the
downtown side of 86th and Broadway.

At 340 is the *Netherlands* with its handsome decoration
recalling the Dutch heritage of New York. Next door is
the *Clarendon* on the southeast corner of 86th and Riverside Drive (137), associated with William Randolph
Hearst, and *The Normandy* at 140 Riverside Drive, its entrance richly ornamented with mosaic in the Art Deco
manner.

The elegant *Dorchester* is at 131 Riverside Drive. South
on Riverside Drive, looking left on West 85th Street gives
a view of one of the best-maintained blocks on the West
Side, where *The Red House* (350) and *Lancashire*
(353) sit in Elizabethan splendor.

The Turrets at 125 is on the northeast corner of a street
officially designated on the signboards as Edgar Allan Poe,
but still known to locals as West 84th Street. Poe lived
during the summer of 1844 in a farmhouse nearby while
finishing *The Raven.*

At 79th and Riverside Drive is the *Riverdale.* On 79th
is *Imperial Court* at 307; the synagogue next to it was formerly the garage of the *New Century* at 401 West End
Avenue. Across 79th are the *Orienta* at 302–304 and the
Kelmscott at 316.

One of the most important buildings in the historical
development of West Side apartment living is *The Apthorp,* occupying the entire block bounded by West 78th
and West 79th, West End Avenue, and Broadway.

At 79th on the northwest and southwest corners of

Amsterdam Avenue are the *Lucerne* at 201, notable for its extravagant decoration, and *The Gloucester,* a 1960s building at 200.

The neighborhood on Amsterdam from 79th to 81st streets consists entirely of buildings erected at the turn of this century. In the 1980s a number of them have been restored and the street levels "modernized" in varying degrees of tastefulness.

The block on 81st between Amsterdam and Columbus contains a series of late-nineteenth-century buildings, which in most cases were the first to be built on their sites. They include the *Amsterdam, Prague,* and *Martha* at 175, 171, and 169.

At 81st and Columbus is *The Endicott,* one of the notable restorations of the early 1980s. The block facing Manhattan Square between Columbus and Central Park West is a reflection of the 77th Street block south of the museum, with handsome buildings including the *Galaxy* (51), *The Bownett* (11), and, on the corner of 81st and Central Park West, the enormous 1929 *Beresford,* which occupies the site of an older hotel of that name.

END OF TOUR: IND subway station at Central Park West and West 81st Street.

TOUR THREE: HARLEM OLD AND NEW

The history of Harlem begins in 1658, when it was established as a village outpost of the Dutch colony on the lower tip of Manhattan. It remained semirural and isolated, a place where the well-to-do had summer homes, until the last quarter of the nineteenth century. In 1879 the elevated railroad reached Harlem, and the area became much more urban. Many private brownstone houses, hundreds of which are still standing, were built at this time.

In 1901 the IRT Lenox Avenue subway opened, and Harlem became attractive to developers. Hundreds of apartment buildings were erected, especially along the wide and handsome avenues—Lenox, Seventh (now Adam Clayton Powell, Jr., Boulevard), and Eighth (now Frederick Douglass Boulevard)—in one of the classic real estate booms of New York history. Like all such booms, it collapsed—before World War I. The area had had a white population, but faced with thousands of empty apartments, real estate interests began renting to blacks who had been living in the West Thirties. By the 1920s Central Harlem was largely black. Two decades later East Harlem, which had been largely Italian and Irish, gradually became Hispanic.

The boundaries of Harlem have traditionally been vague. Today, it is considered by most New Yorkers to extend from Central Park North (West 110th Street) to West 155th Street, with some exceptions, such as Morningside Heights, and that is the area included in this tour.

The distances become great and the streets steep in Upper Manhattan, and it is recommended that this tour be made by automobile.

Harlem has a large stock of housing from the turn of this century but also contains numerous large-scale public housing projects built since World War II.

START OF TOUR: The Cathedral of St. John the Divine at Amsterdam Avenue and Cathedral Parkway.

South of the Cathedral on Cathedral Parkway are the *Cathedral Parkway Houses,* a 1975 housing project of advanced architectural design.

One Hundred Tenth Street from river to river has a more confusing array of names than any other thoroughfare in Manhattan: from the Hudson to Frederick Douglass Boulevard (Eighth Avenue) it is known as Cathedral Parkway, from Frederick Douglass Boulevard to Fifth Avenue it is Central Park North, and from Fifth Avenue to the East River it is East 110th Street.

A block east of the Cathedral is Morningside Avenue running along Morningside Park, landscaped by Frederick Law Olmsted to preserve the naturally rugged terrain below Morningside Heights. A left turn off Cathedral Parkway onto Manhattan Avenue leads to Morningside Avenue. At the junction of Morningside Avenue and West

115th Street is a small square in which stands the statue of Washington and Lafayette by Frédéric Bartholdi. Facing the square on the 114th Street side is the notable *Monterey* with its handsomely rusticated base, and at 312 Manhattan Avenue, the *Rochambeau*.

Across 114th is an example of the turn-of-the-century grandeur of this area, the *Victor Hugo* at 200.

Adam Clayton Powell, Jr., Boulevard (formerly Seventh Avenue) is a wide street lined with stately apartment houses from West 110th to West 125th streets, built during the Harlem boom of the early years of this century following the building of the IRT Lenox Avenue subway line in 1901: the *Abelard* and the *Arcadia* at 1885 and 1893 (114th to 115th streets) and the *Washington* at 2034–2040 (122nd Street).

At Adam Clayton Powell, Jr., Boulevard and West 116th Street is *Graham Court,* an architecturally important building preserving to a large extent its early-twentieth-century elegance.

One Hundred Twenty-fifth Street is Harlem's main street and has always been more commercial than residential. One block off 125th down Fifth Avenue is Marcus Garvey Park (formerly called Mount Morris Park) which interrupts Fifth Avenue between 120th and 124th streets. It is lined with fine old apartment buildings, among them the *Montana* at 35 Mount Morris Park West and the *Gainsboro* at 2 Mount Morris Park South. The Mount Morris Presbyterian Church built in 1905 is one of Harlem's notable churches.

Public housing projects that may be seen along the route down Fifth Avenue from Marcus Garvey Memorial Park to Central Park North include *Taino Towers* (East 122nd to East 123rd streets, Second to Third avenues), *James Weldon Johnson Houses* (Lexington to Third avenues, East 112th to East 115th streets), *Stephen Foster Houses* (between West 112th and West 115th streets along Fifth Avenue), and Schomburg Plaza (East 110th to 111th streets, Fifth to Madison avenues.)

A right turn off Fifth Avenue to Central Park North leads past two buildings whose names commemorate ancient Near Eastern monarchs: *The Zenobia* at 217 and the *Semiramis* at 137.

END OF TOUR: The Cathedral of St. John the Divine.

TOUR FOUR: WEST
GREENWICH VILLAGE

The first mention of the name "Greenwich Village" is on the Bradford map of New York dated 1734. At that time, it was a suburb of the city extending roughly between Christopher Street and what is now West 21st Street. As is true of so many parts of New York City, its boundaries have always been indistinct. In the early part of the nineteenth century it was the place to which New Yorkers fled when yellow fever struck the city. Many small houses were built there in the 1830s and 1840s, a good number of which survive.

In the late nineteenth and early twentieth centuries the Village, as it has become known, had large communities of blacks, Italians, and "Bohemians," as artists, writers, dancers, and other creative people were popularly known.

The West Village, as this tour shows, presents an extraordinary mixture of small-scale private houses, apartment houses of the 1920s and 1930s, institutional housing, and conversions, dating from the 1970s and 1980s, of all sorts of buildings—from churches to factories—into residential apartments. In no other part of Manhattan can two centuries of the architectural history be so plainly seen in the space of a few blocks' walk.

START OF TOUR: IRT line subway station at Sheridan Square.

At 10 Sheridan Square is *The Shenandoah*. A walk east along Washington Place ends at Washington Square Park, with *Richmond Hall* at the northeast corner of Washington Square North and MacDougal (also known as Washington Square West).

At 33 Washington Square West is *Hayden Hall* (formerly *Holly Chambers*). The street, again known as MacDougal, runs south to Bleecker where on the left at 160 is *The Atrium* (formerly Mills House No. 1).

On Bleecker east between West Broadway and Mercer are *Washington Square Village* on the left and *Silver Towers* on the right, both New York University–sponsored projects.

Left on West Broadway the route leads north to Washington Square Park. See Edmund Wilson's comments in the Introduction (page 22) for an early Village reaction to the huge 1920s buildings in this area, now taken for granted.

North of Washington Square Park is Washington Square Mews. At 8th Street and Fifth Avenue is the old *Marlton Hotel* at 5 West 8th and the *Rhinelander* at 12 Fifth Avenue, across from which is *The Brevoort* at 11 Fifth Avenue with its showy entrance.

Just off Fifth are *The Prasada* at 26 West 9th, the *Portsmouth* at 38–44, and the *Hampshire* at 46–50—old apartment houses, the last with a charming little porter's window by the front door.

Across Fifth Avenue at 20 East 9th, at University Place, is the *Lafayette,* which is on the site of the old Hotel Lafayette, and *The Beaucaire* at 25.

The very successful 1950s *Butterfield House* is at 37 West 12th. A block above and farther west on 13th Street is *Portico Place,* a former church, at 139–145.

South on Avenue of the Americas (Sixth Avenue) at 10th Street, tucked away behind the Jefferson Market Library, is *Patchin Place,* one of several named residential enclaves in Greenwich Village (see page 376).

A walk across West 10th Street to Seventh Avenue leads to Charles Street, with *The Carolus* at 29, *Palazzo Greco* at 115, and *Le Gendarme,* a conversion of a former police station, at 135.

Returning to West 10th Street via Washington Street, at the corner is *Shephard House* (at 277), a former warehouse. From there is visible the enormous pile of the *Archives Building* at 641 Washington Street.

An alternate return would be to walk north up Washington Street from West 10th eight blocks to Horatio Street and down West Street to Christopher. This would include notable buildings converted from commercial to residential use that have changed this part of New York as much as the tearing down of the West Side Highway. Conversions include *West Coast* at 95 Horatio Street, *Waywest* at 380 West 12th, and *Westbeth* at 155 Bank.

END OF TOUR: East across Christopher Street to Sheridan Square and the IRT subway station.

TOUR FIVE: UPPER EAST SIDE

For about a century the Upper East Side has been the most fashionable part of Manhattan, first because of the great mansions that were built along Fifth Avenue from the 1870s to 1890s. Since the mansions were torn down or converted into apartments after World War I, rows of luxury apartment buildings along Fifth and Park avenues, and to some extent along the side streets, have taken their place as the homes of New York's richest and most prominent citizens.

The boundaries of the Upper East Side—unlike those of most neighborhoods in New York—have been pretty clearly understood: from East 59th Street north to East 96th Street, from Fifth Avenue to the East River, although it is only since World War II that luxury apartment houses have been built east of Lexington Avenue.

Very few buildings on Fifth and Park avenues have ever been given names: the street address alone has been a guarantee of fashion and solidity. The modern buildings east of Lexington have been given names, but for the most part, these structures are bland, lacking the style and variety of similar buildings on the West Side.
START OF TOUR: IRT line subway station at East 77th Street and Lexington Avenue.

Going west to Madison Avenue, the walk passes *The Finch* at 61 East 77th Street. At the southeast corner of 77th and Madison Avenue is *The Carlyle.* North up Madison Avenue the first named building is *The Stratford* at 26 East 81st. At 1100 Madison is the enormous *Schermerhorn* with its many galleries and stores at the street level. At 3 East 84th Street, just off Fifth Avenue, is the Art Deco *"Patterson Apartments."*

At the corner of Madison and 86th, is *The Croyden,* and nearby, at the southeast corner of Fifth Avenue at 86th Street is *The Adams*—both 1920s apartment hotels recently renovated.

At 61–69 East 86th, between Madison and Park avenues, is the grand old *Marie.* Up Madison Avenue is *The Graham* at 18 East 89th Street, the Upper East Side's first apartment hotel; *The Ashton* at 26 East 93rd Street; and

The Alamo at 56 East 93rd. The *Wales Hotel* at 1295 Madison Avenue presents a strong contrast to the 1980s *Carnegie Hill Tower* at 40 East 94th Street.

In East 96th Street at Madison Avenue are two fine old apartments: the *Queenston* at 16 and *Woodward Hall* at 50. Equally fine are their neighbors: the *Almscourt* at 1356 Madison Avenue and *Madison Court* at 1361 Madison Avenue.

East on 96th is *The Van Cortlandt* at 1240 Park Avenue, at the northwest corner of 96th.

END OF TOUR: The IRT subway station at 96th Street and Lexington Avenue.

An alternate route is to continue walking south on Lexington Avenue, past the *Paulding* at 1349 Lexington, and the stately *Rhinelander* at 1327–1329. Just one block to the east, at East 90th Street and Third Avenue, is the huge *Ruppert Towers* complex.

END OF TOUR: The IRT subway station at East 86th Street and Lexington Avenue.

VI

Geographical Index

FIRST STREET EAST
          31   Colony, The
          58   Lenmor Apartments
          94   Max Meltzer Tower (NYCHA)
SECOND STREET EAST
          214–216   Henington Hall
THIRD STREET EAST
          130   First Houses (NYCHA)
          141   Azeloff Towers
FOURTH STREET EAST
          66–68   Manhattan Plaza
          First Avenue
          to Avenue A   Village View
          355   Dry Dock
FOURTH STREET WEST
          39½   Washington View
SIXTH STREET EAST
          440   Bierman Court
          at Avenue C   Mascot Flats
SEVENTH STREET EAST
          111   McKinley
EIGHTH STREET EAST
          60   Georgetown Plaza
EIGHTH STREET WEST
          5   Marlton Hotel
NINTH STREET EAST
          20   Brevoort East
          25   Beaucaire, The
          30   Lafayette Apartments

63   Randall House
115   St. Marks
NINTH STREET WEST
26   Prasada, The
38–40 & 42–44   Portsmouth
46–50   Hampshire
61   Windsor Arms
TENTH STREET EAST
15   Mayfield
21   University House
23–25   Albert Hotel and Arbert Chambers
26   Beaucaire, The
28   Devonshire House
39–41   Lancaster
70   Stewart House
321   St. Marie
323   Bonsall
454   Riis Houses (NYCHA)
TENTH STREET WEST
12   Whitney House
44   Alden, John, The
51   Peter Warren House
59   Standish
61   Priscilla
188   Warwick
259   Village Landmark, The
277   Shephard House
ELEVENTH STREET EAST
15   Van Rensselaer
49   [St. George Hotel]
80   [St. Ann's School]
235   [Downtown Community School]
307   Leeds House
ELEVENTH STREET WEST
126–128   Unadilla
328   Washington Arms
TWELFTH STREET EAST
60   Hewlett House
67   Cast Iron Building, The
201–213   [Trow's Directory]
226–230   Virginia
229   Claremont, The
413   C. de Bellis
635   Campos Plaza (NYCHA)
TWELFTH STREET WEST
29   Ardsley House Hotel, The
31–33   Ardea, The
37   Butterfield House
100   Mark Twain

101   John Adams
247   Greenwich House
380   Waywest
THIRTEENTH STREET EAST
27   Van Buren
620   Tanya Towers
THIRTEENTH STREET WEST
25   Montparnasse
105   Greenwich Towers
117   Greenwich Court
139–145   Portico Place
FOURTEENTH STREET EAST
7   Victoria, The
226–228   Navarre, The
230–232   Roosevelt, The
at First Avenue   Stuyvesant Town
FOURTEENTH STREET WEST
7   Parker Gramercy
55   Courtney House
200   Jean——
204   El Greco
315   Victor, The
317   Roslyn, The
FIFTEENTH STREET EAST
145   Gramercy Arms
FIFTEENTH STREET WEST
112   Norma Apartments
117   Marshall
205   Chelsmore Apartments
328   Aurora Apartments
SIXTEENTH STREET EAST
142   Gramercy Spire
145   Washington Irving House
207   [Memorial House]
SIXTEENTH STREET WEST
16   Chelsea Lane
253   Chelsea Hall
SEVENTEENTH STREET EAST
112   Fanwood, The
118   Irving
140   Trevyllian, The
201   Park Towers
210–212   Mon Bijou
SEVENTEENTH STREET WEST
119   Brooks–Van Horn
421   Robert Fulton House (NYCHA)
EIGHTEENTH STREET EAST
130   Gramercy Plaza
150   Gramercy Green

153   Easton
EIGHTEENTH STREET WEST
   12   Chelsea East
   154   Hellmuth Building
NINETEENTH STREET EAST
   151   Gramercy Park Apartments
   222   St. Cabrini Tower
TWENTIETH STREET EAST
   151   Gramercy—Third
   304   [Marion Fahnstock Training School]
   at First Avenue   Peter Cooper Village
TWENTIETH STREET WEST
   200   Kensington House
   237   Premier
   365   Chelsea Court Tower
   402   Donac
TWENTY-FIRST STREET EAST
   201   Quaker Ridge
   301   Petersfield, The
TWENTY-FIRST STREET WEST
   201   Piermont, The
   206   Eldorado
   300   Chelsea
   306   Hoerle Building
   312   Reilly Building
   340   New Chelsea
TWENTY-SECOND STREET EAST
   5   Madison Green
   102   Gramercy Arms
   134   Gramercy Row
   144–146   Lexington
   205   Gramercy Park Habitat
   301   Gramercy East
TWENTY-SECOND STREET WEST
   255   Manhattan
TWENTY-THIRD STREET EAST
   at First Avenue   East Midtown Plaza
TWENTY-THIRD STREET WEST
   148   Chelsea Mews
   208   Carteret
   222   Chelsea Hotel
   262   Swiss House
   300   Chelsea Manor
   312–320   Louis Philippe
   315   Broadmoor, The
   344   Cheyney, The
   442–446   Fitzroy Place
   at Eighth Avenue   Penn Station South
   at Ninth Avenue   London Terrace

TWENTY-FOURTH STREET EAST
    125   Beechwood
    205   Horton Ice Cream Factory
    245   Tracy Towers
    305   New York Towers
TWENTY-FOURTH STREET WEST
    425   Dandrew Lane
    429   Susany Lane
    433   Terry Lane
TWENTY-FIFTH STREET EAST
    160   Carlton Arms Hotel
    201   Peter James
    210–214   Centennial Apartments
    245–251   Spruce Ridge House
    at FDR Drive   Waterside
TWENTY-FIFTH STREET WEST
    107   Johnson Building
    263–265   Tenterden
TWENTY-SIXTH STREET EAST
    137   Hill House
    139   Clementine
TWENTY-SIXTH STREET WEST
    29   Von-Hoffman
    28   Caledonia
    420   Elliott Houses (NYCHA)
    430   Chelsea Houses (NYCHA)
TWENTY-SEVENTH STREET EAST
    240   Parc East Tower
TWENTY-SEVENTH STREET WEST
    26   Greenhouse, The
    39–41   Beverwyck
TWENTY-EIGHTH STREET EAST
    201   Chesapeake House, The
    216   Lo Ruth Terrace
    228   Nathan Straus Houses (NYCHA)
TWENTY-NINTH STREET EAST
    103   Deauville Hotel [Hatfield House]
    154   Habitat
    155   Biltmore Plaza, The
    332   Renwick Gardens Apartments
TWENTY-NINTH STREET WEST
    25   Gilsey House
    321   Chelsea Park House
    357–359   Lamartine
THIRTIETH STREET EAST
    35   Nottingham
    105   Pierrepont, The
    139   Nevada, The
    148   Smithsonian

201   Megantic
245   Leonard, The
at First Avenue   Kips Bay Plaza

THIRTIETH STREET WEST
1   Wilbraham, The
320   Chelsea Town House
327   Herbert Towers
341   Paula House

THIRTY-FIRST STREET EAST
120   Dunsbro
240   Greentree at Murray Hill, The

THIRTY-SECOND STREET EAST
11–13   Stratford House
153   Atrium East, The
165   Byron, The

THIRTY-FOURTH STREET EAST
50   Brookdale Hall
115   Murray Hill, The
155   Warren House
327   Pacifica, The
340   Mayfair South

THIRTY-FIFTH STREET EAST
7   Antoinette
20   Goodhue House
132   Murray Hill House
139   Bromley, The
145   Southfield, The
202–204   St. Gabriel's Court
222   Gregory House
245   Townsley

THIRTY-SIXTH STREET EAST
120   Stimson House
136   Murray Hill
137   Carlton Regency
225   Parker Crescent

THIRTY-SEVENTH STREET EAST
123   Lindley House
201   Wingate, The
207   Murray Hill East
303   Kips Borough House

THIRTY-SEVENTH STREET WEST
448   Glass House Farm

THIRTY-EIGHTH STREET EAST
35   Elizabeth, The
108   Towne House, The
138   Tatham House, The
160   Murray Hill Mews
311   Whitney at Murray Hill, The

THIRTY-NINTH STREET EAST
149   Murray Hill East, The
150   Dryden East
222   Eastgate Tower
330   New York Tower

FORTIETH STREET EAST
144   Seton Hall (Seton Hotel)
245   Marlborough House
300   Churchill, The
305   Parker 40th
at First Avenue   Tudor City

FORTIETH STREET WEST
32   Columns [Engineers Club]

FORTY-FIRST STREET EAST
314   Hatfield House
324   Haddon Hall
325   Essex House
333   Prospect Hill Apartments

FORTY-SECOND STREET EAST
320   Woodstock Tower

FORTY-SECOND STREET WEST
529   Armory, The

FORTY-THIRD STREET EAST
321   Cloister, The
330   Hermitage, The
333   Manor, The

FORTY-THIRD STREET WEST
47   Royalton Hotel
127   Woodstock Hotel
400   Manhattan Plaza
463   Shandon

FORTY-FOURTH STREET EAST
141   Woolsey, The
230   Grand Central Towers
279   Olympia House
307 & 310   Beaux Arts Apartments

FORTY-FOURTH STREET WEST
123   Gerard, The
139   Savoy [Hudson]
401   Lorraine, The
455   Harding

FORTY-FIFTH STREET EAST
333   Lausanne, The

FORTY-FIFTH STREET WEST
301   Camelot
305   Astor Apartments
317   Longacre House
325   Whitby

330   Town House
341   Hildona Court
FORTY-SIXTH STREET EAST
140   Gilford, The
225   Executive House
300   Envoy Towers
310   Turtle Bay Towers
330   Ambassador East
FORTY-SIXTH STREET WEST
352   Lyric, The {Lansdown]
454   Piano Factory
FORTY-SEVENTH STREET EAST
2   L'Ecole
240   Dag Hammarskjold Tower
301   Embassy House
FORTY-SEVENTH STREET WEST
349   Wanaque
401–403   Angela
FORTY-EIGHTH STREET EAST
148   Middletowne, The
160   Buchanan Apartments
249   Turtle Bay House
301   Marlo Towers
321   Continental Apartments
FORTY-EIGHTH STREET WEST
319   Belvedere
FORTY-NINTH STREET EAST
303   Peregrine, The
330   Beekman East
333   Oxford East
FIFTIETH STREET EAST
100   Waldorf-Astoria Towers
135   Randolph, The
155   Plaza 50
230   Beekman Studios
234–236   Roma
317   First Reformed Episcopal Church and
                 Apartments
FIFTIETH STREET WEST
400   Clarice
FIFTY-FIRST STREET EAST
335   Senate East, The
340   Allen House
420   Morad Beekman
425   Beekman Hill House
433   Southgate
439   Beekman Mansion Apartments
455   Beekman Terrace

FIFTY-FIRST STREET WEST

306–310	Lincoln, The
318–322	Washington, The
324–328	Jefferson, The

FIFTY-SECOND STREET EAST

350	Eastgate House
415	Sutton House
427	River Court
435–447	River House
450	Campanile, The

FIFTY-THIRD STREET EAST

211	Hawthorne, The
320	Lyden House Hotel
347	Sutton View

FIFTY-THIRD STREET WEST

15	Museum Tower
159	Tower 53
301	Encore, The

FIFTY-FOURTH STREET EAST

220	Leslie House
245	Brevard, The
300	Connaught Tower
400	Revere, The
415	St. James's Tower
420	River Tower

FIFTY-FOURTH STREET WEST

| 17 | "Rockefeller Apartments" |
| 25 | Regent House |

FIFTY-FIFTH STREET EAST

125	Park Gallery Tower
304	Chart House
412	Sutton Mews
420	Sutton Gardens

FIFTY-FIFTH STREET WEST

77	Gallery House
101	Claridge's
166	Wyoming, The
200	Ontiora
300	Westerly, The
305	Ashfield
321	Stanwood
339–345	Bendor Court
347–355	Cambria
525	Harbor View Terrace (NYCHA)

FIFTY-SIXTH STREET EAST

1	Trump Tower
111	Lombardy
141	Lexington House

300	Bristol
333	Bamford
400	Plaza Four Hundred
430	Sutton Manor
433	Sutton East
440	Sutton Manor East

FIFTY-SIXTH STREET WEST

112	Premier, Le
211	Carnegie Mews
342–344	Summersby, The

FIFTY-SEVENTH STREET EAST

110	Dorchester
117	Galleria
130	Allerton Hotel for Women
153	Gotham Town House
220	Carlton House East
225	Harridge House
301	Excelsior, The
360	Morrison, The
417	New Yorker East, The

FIFTY-SEVENTH STREET WEST

60	Hemisphere House
101	Buckingham Hotel
160	Carnegie Hall Studios
200	Rodin Studios
205	Osborne, The
315	Park Towers South
322	Sheffield, The
330–360	Parc Vendome
333	Westmore, The
347	Colonnade 57, The
435	South Park Apartments
442	Hanover House

FIFTY-EIGHTH STREET EAST

200	Blair House
210	Picasso, The
245	Le Triomphe
320	Caprice
401	York House
425	Sovereign, The

FIFTY-EIGHTH STREET WEST

57	Coronet
134	Wilshire House
180	Alwyn Court
330	Park Towers South
340	Westmore, The
345	Coliseum Park Apartments
444	Blackburn

FIFTY-NINTH STREET EAST

300	Landmark, The

SIXTIETH STREET EAST
14   Bellaire Apartment Hotel [Hotel 14]
118   Plaza Towers
220   Colonnade East
242   Ambassador Terrace
350   Coliseum Park Apartments

SIXTY-FIRST STREET EAST
163   Trump Plaza

SIXTY-FIRST STREET WEST
300   Beaumont, The
205   Amsterdam Houses (NYCHA)

SIXTY-SECOND STREET EAST
30   Cumberland House
175   Victoria
359   Beta II
440   Park Sutton

SIXTY-SECOND STREET WEST
44   Lincoln Plaza Towers
61   Harkness, The

SIXTY-THIRD STREET EAST
26   Leonori, The
28   Lowell, The
140   Barbizon
166   Beekman Townhouse
220   Meyberry House
225   Renoir House
245   Regency Towers
250   Regency South
329   [St. Joseph's Home]
400   Manor
425   Royal York
450   Sutton Terrace

SIXTY-THIRD STREET WEST
235–247   Phipps Houses

SIXTY-FOURTH STREET EAST
2   [Berwind Mansion]
32   Verona
200   Carlton Towers
215   Lyden Gardens
301   Regency East
340   St. Tropez
402   L'Appartement
420   Royal York
at First Avenue   [Model Tenements]

SIXTY-FOURTH STREET WEST
236–248   Phipps Houses

SIXTY-FIFTH STREET EAST
19   Mary Louise, The
30   Colony House
55   Sussex, The

160	Phoenix, The
220	Concorde Apartments
250	[Grace Institute House]
315	Manhattan East
360	Buxley House

SIXTY-FIFTH STREET WEST
| 240 | Amsterdam Houses Addition (NYCHA) |

SIXTY-SIXTH STREET EAST
| 200 | Manhattan House |
| 333 | Bryn Mawr |

SIXTY-SIXTH STREET WEST
| at Amsterdam Avenue | Lincoln Towers |

SIXTY-SEVENTH STREET EAST
136	Gothic House
332–334	Auchmutz
338	Banzer
342	Montreux, The

SIXTY-SEVENTH STREET WEST
1	Hotel des Artistes
15	Central Park Studios
27	Sixty-seventh Street Studios
29–33	Atelier Building

SIXTY-EIGHTH STREET WEST
60	Cambridge
74	Morleigh, The
155	Dorchester Towers

SIXTY-NINTH STREET EAST
150	Imperial House
201	Fairfax, The
301	Mayfair Midtown
321	Atrium, The
333	Premier, The

SIXTY-NINTH STREET WEST
| 140 | Spencer Arms Hotel [Lincoln Plaza] |
| 225–229 | Bachelor Apartments |

SEVENTIETH STREET EAST
| 28 | Hampton House |
| 400 | Kingsley, The |

SEVENTIETH STREET WEST
65	Tuxedo
104	Walton
117	Stratford Arms
135	Pythian Arms
154	Embassy Tower
200	Chalfonte
210	Bradford, The
235	Rose Garden Apartments

315	Presidential Towers
345	Santa Monica, The

SEVENTY-FIRST STREET EAST

110	Viscaya Condominia
114	Lenox Court
176	Townsend House
200	Empire House
311	Diplomat, The
400	Windsor

SEVENTY-FIRST STREET WEST

31	Seventy-first Street Studios
56	Turner House
109	Hotel Margrave
160	Alamac Hotel
171	Dorilton Apartments
228	Parc Coliseum [Robert Fulton Hotel]
342	Riverside Studios
350	Venice

SEVENTY-SECOND STREET EAST

167	Lexington
190	Tower East
200	Wellesley, The
203	Bayard House
220	[Marymount Manhattan Apartments]
325	Walton Hall Apartments
353	Fontaine, The
360	Carroll Tower
520	Parker 72nd
525	[Sokol Hall]
540	Edgewater, The

SEVENTY-SECOND STREET WEST

1	Dakota, The
12	Oliver Cromwell
15	Mayfair Towers
27	Olcott
40	Bancroft, The
49	Parkway
50	Ruxton, The
53	Endicott Apartments
58	Adrian
100	[Park and Tilford Building]
101	St. Charles
110	Hotel Margrave
114–116	Sussex
121	Raleigh
133	Cluny
175	Van Dyck
253	Westover Apartments
301	Hudson Towers

340   Chatsworth Annex
346   Chatsworth
SEVENTY-THIRD STREET EAST
11   [Pulitzer House]
49   James Lenox House
210–235   Mansionettes of 1935, The
301   Domen East
345   Morad Diplomat, The
SEVENTY-THIRD STREET WEST
23   Park Royal
48   Vendome [Westport]
160   Sherman Square Studios
170   Severn Arms
240   Commander Hotel
253   Level Club Condominium [Riverside
                      Plaza]
SEVENTY-FOURTH STREET EAST
23   Volney, The
207   Mayfair—207
340   Avon House
401   Amherst, The
SEVENTY-FOURTH STREET WEST
61   Greylock
100   Graystone
101   Plymouth
201   Lincoln Square
SEVENTY-FIFTH STREET EAST
222   Chateau East
301   Wilshire, The
311   Sandgate, The
444   Larrimore, The
SEVENTY-FIFTH STREET WEST
57   La Rochelle
60   Hartford, The
102   Del Monte
161   Wellston, The
170   Wachusett
245   Astor Apartments
SEVENTY-SIXTH STREET EAST
20   Surrey, The
30   [Madison Avenue Hospital]
32   Gallery Condominium
35   Carlyle, The
55–57   Imperial, The
155   Queen Anne
240   Eastmore House
370   Newport East
SEVENTY-SIXTH STREET WEST
59   Sylvia

60	Aylsmere
100	Viola
242	New Milburn Hotel

SEVENTY-SEVENTH STREET EAST

61	Finch, The
150	Chalk House
176	Lenox Manor
205	Dover House
239	Studio House
249	Hohen-Au
302	Colony, The
400	Emery Towers
401	Beta House
445	Ambassador House
500	Pavilion, The
507–523	Cherokee, The

SEVENTY-SEVENTH STREET WEST

44	Manhattan Square Studios
101	Kenmar
201	Amsterdam Towers
222	Benjamin Franklin [Wellsmore]
250	Belleclair

SEVENTY-EIGHTH STREET EAST

201	Brandon, The
301	Lenox House
508–524	Cherokee, The
555	Riverfront

SEVENTY-EIGHTH STREET WEST

100	Volunteer
101	Evelyn, The
169	Wellesley, The
170	Orchid
200	Rose
202	Cecilia
204	Florence
229	Sanford
250	Curlew

SEVENTY-NINTH STREET EAST

301	Continental Towers
334	[Cherokee Democratic Club]
435	York, The
440	Gregory House
460	Gregory Towers
505	East River House
515	Asten House

SEVENTY-NINTH STREET WEST

112	Hotel Margrave
114	Sussex
117	Indiana

140	Brixford
145	Manchester House
146	Framor
147	Richmond
150	Dorset, The
171	Marboro
200	Gloucester, The
201	Lucerne Hotel
230	Rexford
302–304	Orienta
307	Imperial Court
310	Hereford
316	Kelmscott

EIGHTIETH STREET EAST

40	Charel House
178	Kenilworth, The
222	Kimberly, The
315	Emily Court
345	Eastwinds
401	Gracie Mews
420	London House
445	Clermont South

EIGHTIETH STREET WEST

100	Orleans
101	Warwick Arms
102	Museum Apartments [Anderson]
225	Hadrian

EIGHTY-FIRST STREET EAST

26	Stratford, The
151	Guilford, The
157	Carlton, The
171	Webster, The
215	Duplex 81, The
401	Yorkshire House
520	Salem House, The
529–537	Odhall Courts

EIGHTY-FIRST STREET WEST

1 & 7	Beresford, The [Planetarium]
11	Bownett, The
45	Excelsior Hotel
51	Galaxy [Hotel Colonial]
101	Endicott, The
169	Martha
171	Prague
173	Elliot
175	Amsterdam
202	Albert
204	Hawkins
209	Barrington

251	Forrest, The
265	Beverly

EIGHTY-SECOND STREET EAST

122	Surrey
145	Estelle
200	Wimbledon, The
201	Bremer Buildings
444	Clermont Tower
525	Mansion House

EIGHTY-SECOND STREET WEST

76	Colorado
78	Lyndhurst
80	Nebraska
165	Bedford
176–184	Pontiac, The
202	Ellen Apartments
221	Jerome Palace
250	Saxony
254	De Witt

EIGHTY-THIRD STREET EAST

171	Vondel, The
201	Saxon Towers
301	Camargue, The
353	Continental East
411	Sovereign Apartments

EIGHTY-THIRD STREET WEST

46	Lathrop
71	Dundonald Flats
101	Hilda
215	Surrey, The [Brierfield]
222	Manhill Apartments
233	Amidon
320	Rexton
323	Savage
324	Cayuga

EIGHTY-FOURTH STREET EAST

3	Patterson Apartments
208–214	Virginia, The
213–217	Seneca, The
351	Adam's Tower
444	Claiborne House
530	Chapin, The

EIGHTY-FOURTH STREET WEST

200	Martha
255	Alameda
320	Hyperion
322	Briarton
324	Ransby

EIGHTY-FIFTH STREET EAST
185	Park Lane Tower
324	Harfay
500	Cambridge, The
510	Gracie Mansion

EIGHTY-FIFTH STREET WEST
1	Rossleigh Court
74	Crillon
76–78	Sudeley
77	Carlyle
100	Louise
101	Brockholst, The
170	St. Elmo
175	Sunset
250	Towers, The
328–330	Rexmere
342	Stratton
350	Red House, The
353–355	Lancashire

EIGHTY-SIXTH STREET EAST
2	Adams, The
12	Croyden, The
61–69	Marie
68	Westminster
217	Theodore, The
228	Bettina Towers
230–242	Montgomery
233	East Hill Tower
235	Park East, The
244	Manhattan
305–315	Yorkshire Towers
328	Greenhouse East
355	Garden Gate
401	Fairmount Manor, The
444	Parker 86
511–513	York Row
535	Henderson House

EIGHTY-SIXTH STREET WEST
21	Brewster
27	John Muir, The
41	Parc Cameron
61	Elliott
76	Sterling
100	Amy
101	Ormonde
168	Bedford
200	New Amsterdam
225	Belnord, The
309	Wayne
337	Cambridge House

340	Netherlands
345	Dexter House Hotel

EIGHTY-SEVENTH STREET EAST

56	King, The
115	Carnegie Towers
125	Sherry House, The
201	Claridge House
245	Mayflower
250	Newbury
301	Corniche
409	Colonial House
444	Envoy Apartments
500	Garson Towers
501	River's Bend

EIGHTY-SEVENTH STREET WEST

77	Prague, The
100	Dudley
166–168	Capitol Hall Hotel
247	Montana, The
251	Fife Arms
340	Keith Arms

EIGHTY-EIGHTH STREET EAST

160	Lexington Towers
303–317	Rosewall

EIGHTY-EIGHTH STREET WEST

72	Renaissance
205	Oxford
219	Buchova Apartments
250	Central Condominium
270	Chautauqua, The

EIGHTY-NINTH STREET EAST

18	Graham, The
50	Park Regis
120	Ascot House
171–175	Beta North
346	York Manor
515–525	Gracie Square Gardens

EIGHTY-NINTH STREET WEST

101	Galena
129	Trafalgar Arms
205	Astor Court
210	Wesley Tower
216	Bellguard, The
251	Admaston

NINETIETH STREET EAST

120	Trafalgar House, The
161	Trafalgar Court
174	Hilltop, The
200	Whitney House
321	Gracie Manor

340   David Arms
402   River East Plaza
520–530   Gracie Square Gardens
at Second Avenue   Ruppert Towers and Yorkville Towers
NINETIETH STREET WEST
204–210   Astor Court
215   Haroldon Court
255   Cornwall, The
NINETY-FIRST STREET EAST
114   Lossie
118   Ravenswood
122   Wellswood
124   Trent, The
160   Hillhurst
NINETY-FIRST STREET WEST
5   Town House West
124   Wise Towers (NYCHA)
165   Mirabeau
212   Greystone Apartments
215   De Soto
250   "Versailles"
NINETY-SECOND STREET WEST
71   Raleigh
100   Trinity House Apartments
206–208   Senate Studios
214   St. James Court
NINETY-THIRD STREET EAST
26   Ashton, The
56   Alamo, The
64   Guardsman, The
130   Regency North
175–179   Seward Apartments
340   Plymouth Tower
345   Mill Rock Plaza
403   Stanley Isaacs Houses (NYCHA)
NINETY-THIRD STREET WEST
10   Pembroke
19–35   Nine-G Cooperative
43   Norman
124   Herbert Arms
134   Ralph Arms
175   Westwind, The
201   De Hostos Apartments (NYCHA)
307   Stuart Studio Apartments [Cliffside]
309   Albert Court
312   Clarence
316   Riverview, The
317   Eleanor Court
325   Albea

NINETY-FOURTH STREET EAST
40   Carnegie Hill Tower
NINETY-FOURTH STREET WEST
201   Iroquois
204   Franklin
210   Bonta-Narragansett
215   West Side Studios
261–267   Pomander Walk
306–308   Devon Residence [Earls Court,
                            Norfolk]
310   Fremont
311   Orlando
314   Vancouver, The
315   Georgean Court
316   Beau Rivage
319   St. Louis
NINETY-FIFTH STREET EAST
19   Woodbury, The
182   Highgate
226   Fireside, The
NINETY-FIFTH STREET WEST
200   Sans Souci
206   Camden Residence Hotel
260–266   Pomander Walk
310   Matilda
317   Valencia Court
336   West Point
NINETY-SIXTH STREET EAST
16   Queenston
50   Woodward Hall
306   East River Terrace
NINETY-SIXTH STREET WEST
35   Lucetine
46   Baldwin, The
65   Tower West
104   Enid
111   Harrison
145   Kipling Arms
231   Wollaston
275   Columbia, The
320   Hudson Arms
NINETY-SEVENTH STREET EAST
17   Mannados
51   Chalfonte
53   Farnham
NINETY-SEVENTH STREET WEST
209   Corinseca
221   Powellton
226   Stuart Arms

230	Wilmington
258	Hartcourt
311	Von Colon
316	Piedmont
at Central Park West	Park West Village

NINETY-EIGHTH STREET WEST

203	Evelyn Arms
215	Gramont
220	Borchard
243	William
305	Schuyler Arms
315–317	Holland Court

NINETY-NINTH STREET WEST

200	Norwood
230	La Riviera
233	Trafalgar
244	Clinton Arms Residential Hotel [Navarre]
309	Strand View
315	Paramount
317	Emahrel, The

ONE HUNDREDTH STREET WEST

| 216 | Midway Hotel |
| 318 | Dorlexa, The |

ONE HUNDRED FIRST STREET WEST

20	Manhattan Court
211	Frant Hotel Residence Club
215–217	Chepstow
216	Walter Arms
229	Arlington
230	Broadway, The
241	Ackerly, The

ONE HUNDRED SECOND STREET EAST

| 310 | Metro North Plaza |

ONE HUNDRED SECOND STREET WEST

216	Kent, The
235	Broadmoor, The
240	Magnolia

ONE HUNDRED THIRD STREET WEST

74–78	Northport
205	El Casco Court
235	Friesland
250	Alexandria

ONE HUNDRED FOURTH STREET WEST

111–117	Newport Court
133–135	Iowa
245	Armstead, The

ONE HUNDRED FIFTH STREET EAST

| 418 | East River Houses (NYCHA) |

ONE HUNDRED FIFTH STREET WEST
100	Larchmont
149	Salome
201	Maryland
221–225	Marion
248	Elizabeth
255	Clebourne

ONE HUNDRED SIXTH STREET EAST
at First Avenue	Franklin Plaza

ONE HUNDRED SIXTH STREET WEST
25	Augusta
61–63	Geraldine
111	Rosalind
238	Raymore Court

ONE HUNDRED SEVENTH STREET WEST
200	Packard
201	Chester Hall
235–239	Ostend Court
300	Waumbek

ONE HUNDRED EIGHTH STREET WEST
15	Paula
201	Cornwallis
235–239	Metropolitan
255	Manchester
301	Manhasset, The

ONE HUNDRED NINTH STREET WEST
20–22	Rose
125	Cathedral Parkway Houses
200	Lloyd Court
201	Miller Hall
204–208	Emrose Court
312–316	Ponchartrain, The
535	Cathedral Parkway Apartments

ONE HUNDRED TENTH STREET EAST
at Fifth Avenue	Schomburg Plaza

ONE HUNDRED TENTH STREET WEST
See Cathedral Parkway; Central Park North

ONE HUNDRED ELEVENTH STREET WEST
16–22	Hermal Court
56	Romeyn
108	Westwing
141	Kenosha
143	Manitou
200	Elise
203	Kanawah
213–215	Isabelle
217–219	Mildred
229	Charles, The
257	Raymond

500	St. John Court
503	Clara Court
507	Blennerhassett, The
515	Bertha
518	Trinity Court
521	Kendal Court
526	Criterion Arms
528	Romana
529	De Peyster
532	Charlemagne
535	Mumford
536	Amele Hall
545	Rockfall
603	Antlers, The
610	Cathedral Studios

ONE HUNDRED TWELFTH STREET WEST

48	Franconia
52	De Leon
118	St. Louis
122	Frontenac
200	Langholm
250	Louise
257	Viola
263	Leonora
303	Cedarleigh
306	Stella
511	St. John
521	Summerfeld
524	Van Pradt
526–528	De Boulogne
530–532	Huguenot, The
533	Avalon
539	Phaeton
540	Berkshire
542	Washington Irving
549	Ostend
601	Claremont Hall
605	Clarendon
611–617	Colonial House [Maranamay]
621	Fowler Court
at Lenox Avenue	Stephen Foster Houses

ONE HUNDRED THIRTEENTH STREET WEST

133	LeRoy
203	Sterling
216	Kensington
220	Bellrose
243	Teresa
245	Marjorie
328	Morningside

502–504	Stanford
506–508	Arlington
507	Louisiana
511	Illinois
517	Michigan
526	Quidnet, The
535	Senior Arms
541	Cathedral Court
549	Robert Watt Hall [Claremont Court]
562	Yorkshire
601	Forest Chambers
606	Altamonte Hall
610	Grant Court
614–616	Victoria Hall

ONE HUNDRED FOURTEENTH STREET WEST

100	Arlington
122	Lucille
124	Deshler
200	Victor Hugo
302	Montgomery
306	Ruth
351	Monterey
411	Phillien
520	Santa Maria
609	Heathcote Hall
622	Revere Hall
628	Hudson Hall

ONE HUNDRED FIFTEENTH STREET EAST

300	Jefferson Houses (NYCHA)

ONE HUNDRED FIFTEENTH STREET WEST

83	Lenox Hall
101	Stratford
113	Paragon
357	Douglas
403	Park Court
411	Colonial, The
415	Munroe, The
419	Cragsmoor
600	Luxor, The

ONE HUNDRED SIXTEENTH STREET WEST

117–119	Venice
120	Margaret
122–128	Arcadia
123–125	Berlin
201	Elmore
215	Jerome
315	Grand View
317	Park View
369–373	Stratford

404	Valenciennes, La
438	Fairmont
606	Broadview
616	Fiora-Ville

ONE HUNDRED SEVENTEENTH STREET EAST
| 306 | Corsi Houses (NYCHA) |

ONE HUNDRED SEVENTEENTH STREET WEST
68	American
100	Bernice
342	Endymion
353	Midlothian

ONE HUNDRED EIGHTEENTH STREET EAST
| 426–434 | East River North Apartments |

ONE HUNDRED EIGHTEENTH STREET WEST
101	Lenox
146–148	Porthos, The
152–154	Athos, The
209	Fort Tryon Apartments
350	Claire
352	Rosedale
357–363	Minerva
401	Eastview
405	Terrace, The
421	Elizabeth Court
423	Winthrop

ONE HUNDRED NINETEENTH STREET WEST
23–25	Rappahannock, The
29–31	Arlington, The
95	Century
96	Chester Court
100	Normandie
160	Clifford
435	Laureate Hall

ONE HUNDRED TWENTIETH STREET WEST
| 434 | Poinciana, The |
| at St. Nicholas Avenue | Triangle, The |

ONE HUNDRED TWENTY-FIRST STREET WEST
100	Temple Hall
423–431	Fairfield, The
501	Kings College Apartments
503–507	Fairholm
509	Bancroft Apartments, The
510	Miami.

ONE HUNDRED TWENTY-SECOND STREET EAST
| at Second Avenue | Taino Towers |

ONE HUNDRED TWENTY-SECOND STREET WEST
166	Avon
303	Cedarleigh
416–422	Court Rebelle

500	Reldnas Hall
509–515	Ogontz, The
512	Sarasota, The
514	Grant, The
515	Simna Hall
520	Delaware, The
521	Marimpol Court
540	Castle Court

ONE HUNDRED TWENTY-THIRD STREET WEST

151	Shakespeare
201	Monte Cristo
272	Blitheburn
449–453	Ruth, The

ONE HUNDRED TWENTY-FOURTH STREET EAST

17	Morris Park Homes (NYCHA)

ONE HUNDRED TWENTY-FOURTH STREET WEST

131–133	Sans Souci

ONE HUNDRED TWENTY-FIFTH STREET WEST

16	Bertha

ONE HUNDRED TWENTY-SIXTH STREET WEST

545	Manhattanville Houses (NYCHA)

ONE HUNDRED TWENTY-SEVENTH STREET WEST

14–16	Alvena
40–42	Modern
65	Roxanne
141–143	Viola
145	Rosemere
215	St. Nicholas Houses (NYCHA)

ONE HUNDRED TWENTY-EIGHTH STREET EAST

2	Amity
30–34	Tuxedo Court

ONE HUNDRED TWENTY-EIGHTH STREET WEST

413	St. Lawrence

ONE HUNDRED TWENTY-NINTH STREET WEST

60	Smithsonian
409	St. Elizabeth
419	St. Monica

ONE HUNDRED THIRTIETH STREET WEST

408–410	St. Augusta
418–420	St. Helena
at St. Nicholas Avenue	Lionel Hampton Houses

ONE HUNDRED THIRTY-THIRD STREET WEST

314	Foster
600	Bellmore
501	Sylvia

ONE HUNDRED THIRTY-FIFTH STREET WEST

10	Lenox Terrace Apartments
123	M. Moran Weston Community Apartments

505	Aimée
507	Chalfonte
509	Calumet
511	Helen
513	Ormiston
515	Venice
517	Holland
519	Bertram
521	Corinne
525	Lucille
527	Loraine
531	Milton
601	Kathmere, The
602–616	Riverview Apartments
634	Annapolis

ONE HUNDRED THIRTY-SIXTH STREET WEST

600	William Henry
601	Saxonia, The

ONE HUNDRED THIRTY-SEVENTH STREET WEST

600	Leslie Court
601–609	Cromwell Apartments
606	El Morro
612	Miramar

ONE HUNDRED THIRTY-EIGHTH STREET WEST

600	Royal Arms, The
603–605	Stockbridge
625–627	Jessica
between Adam Clayton Powell, Jr., Boulevard and Frederick Douglass Boulevard	King Model Houses

ONE HUNDRED THIRTY-NINTH STREET WEST

571	Sulgrave, The
601	Palisade Court
602–604	Wiltshire
at Fifth Avenue	Delano Village

ONE HUNDRED FORTIETH STREET WEST

503	Elmhurst
556	Westborne Court
600	Royalty
601	Ellerslie Courts

ONE HUNDRED FORTY-FIRST STREET WEST

462	Grace Apartments
476	Lydia Apartments
505	Sorofeen
552	Laurel-Court
556	Joesam Court
561	Woodmere
572	Highmount
600	Rockclyffe, The

601	Garnet Hall
605	House of York
611	House of Lancaster
630	Greyton Court

ONE HUNDRED FORTY-SECOND STREET WEST

210	Drew-Hamilton Houses (NYCHA)
507–509	Jumel
569	Castleton, The
600	Colonial Court
618	Beacon Hall

ONE HUNDRED FORTY-THIRD STREET WEST

501	Chilmark Hall
505	Lucerne
511	Regent
514–518	Bellefonte, The
515	Bedford
519	Westbourne
523	Opelika
529	Thelma
538	Saguenay
561	Washington Court
601	Greyloch Dwellings

ONE HUNDRED FORTY-FOURTH STREET WEST

477	Northfield
500	Wellington Arms
560	Sylvia
565	Blervie Hall
600	Dallas Court
601	Rafford Hall
605	St. Rita, The

ONE HUNDRED FORTY-FIFTH STREET WEST

520–540	Hudson View
529	Beatrice
531	Ernestine
533	Leondra

ONE HUNDRED FORTY-SIXTH STREET WEST

543–545	St. James Palace
600	Mecklenburg, The

ONE HUNDRED FORTY-SEVENTH STREET WEST

450	Paul Revere
472	Maksen
546	Douglas Court
561	Edwin, The

ONE HUNDRED FORTY-EIGHTH STREET WEST

402–410	Lusitania Court
543	Bernice
557	Abingdon Arms
561	St. Charles
562	Hudson View

ONE HUNDRED FORTY-NINTH STREET WEST

452	Savoy

452	Convent Court
466	Catherine
531	Allston Court
537–541	Plymouth
567	Mansfield
568	Wallace
601	Ethelbert Court

ONE HUNDRED FIFTIETH STREET WEST

400	Belvedere, The
404	Halcyon Hall
500	Alberni
569	Panama

ONE HUNDRED FIFTY-FIRST STREET WEST

221	Harlem River Houses (NYCHA)
400	Navaretto
502	Elsinore
512	Manchester
518	Marlborough
535–537	Sovereign Court
555–557	Kensington Court
601	Washington Irving
628	Rivercliff

ONE HUNDRED FIFTY-SECOND STREET WEST

519	Highland
523	Adriatic
534	Ricacourt, The

ONE HUNDRED FIFTY-THIRD STREET WEST

400	Laonia
445	Aida Arms
550	Trinity Studio

ONE HUNDRED FIFTY-SIXTH STREET WEST

| 559 | Robert Fulton Court |

ONE HUNDRED FIFTY-SEVENTH STREET WEST

| 550 | Columbus |
| 601, 605, & 611 | Beulah |

ONE HUNDRED FIFTY-EIGHTH STREET WEST

| 474–476 | Roger/Morris |
| 558 | Knowlton Court |

ONE HUNDRED FIFTY-NINTH STREET WEST

| 481 | Washington Heights, The |
| 575 | Washington Court |

ONE HUNDRED SIXTIETH STREET WEST

| 555 | Crystal Court |
| 564 | Georgia |

ONE HUNDRED SIXTY-FIRST STREET WEST

| 581 | Alexander Hamilton Apartments |

ONE HUNDRED SIXTY-SECOND STREET WEST

429	Jumel Hall
565	Carolyn Court
602–604	Putnam

| 659 | Peggy, Junior, et al. |
| 666 | Glen Court |

ONE HUNDRED SIXTY-THIRD STREET WEST

560	Rosbert Hall
601	Charleston Court
664–674	Walden Arms

ONE HUNDRED SIXTY-FOURTH STREET WEST

| 545 | Aquitania |
| 601 | Wilton |

ONE HUNDRED SIXTY-FIFTH STREET WEST

| 600 | Hamlet Court |

ONE HUNDRED SIXTY-EIGHTH STREET WEST

| 601 | Carrollton |

ONE HUNDRED SIXTY-NINTH STREET WEST

| 600 | Courtwood |

ONE HUNDRED SEVENTIETH STREET WEST

| 620 | Pocahontas Apartment |

ONE HUNDRED SEVENTY-SECOND STREET WEST

551	Cromartie
601	White House
630	Varona
636	Westport
642	Keyport
650	Onowa

ONE HUNDRED SEVENTY-THIRD STREET WEST

| 501 | Ada |
| 572 | Bella Vista |

ONE HUNDRED SEVENTY-FOURTH STREET WEST

| 551 | Primrose |

ONE HUNDRED SEVENTY-SIXTH STREET WEST

501	Bolton
701	Shirbar Arms
709	Bradshire

ONE HUNDRED SEVENTY-SEVENTH STREET WEST

717	Rotherwood
723	Westland
803	Irving Court
809	Palace

ONE HUNDRED SEVENTY-EIGHTH STREET WEST

598	St. Brendan
610	Cordova Court
718	Inglewood, The
at Wadsworth Avenue	Bridge Apartments

ONE HUNDRED SEVENTY-NINTH STREET WEST

| 661 | Catherwood Court |

ONE HUNDRED EIGHTIETH STREET WEST

502–504	Francis Apartments, The
517–519	Marion, The
521–523	Hennion

541–547	Rockland
600	Hesperion, The
660	Ravenwood
720–722	Ardsleigh

ONE HUNDRED EIGHTY-FIRST STREET WEST

601	St. Benedict
708–714	De Koven
750	Nathan Hale
812–820	Overlook
867	Duncraggan
880	Falkland, The

ONE HUNDRED EIGHTY-THIRD STREET WEST

570	Chestershire
810	Roxbury Terrace

ONE HUNDRED EIGHTY-FOURTH STREET WEST

608–612	Claremont
614	Augher Villa

ONE HUNDRED EIGHTY-EIGHTH STREET WEST

651	Wadsworth Gardens

ONE HUNDRED NINETY-FIRST STREET WEST

601	Bonny Castle

ONE HUNDRED NINETY-SECOND STREET WEST

600	Highland Court
at Wadsworth Avenue	Minerva Court

TWO HUNDRED FIFTEENTH STREET WEST

at East Park Terrace	Park Terrace Gardens

TWO HUNDRED TWENTY-SEVENTH STREET WEST

108	Fort Prince Charles Court

TWO HUNDRED TWENTY-EIGHTH STREET WEST

120	Laura Court
130	Rose Court

NUMBERED AVENUES

FIRST AVENUE

241	G. Wilkens
1780	John Haynes Holmes Towers
2396	Wagner Houses (NYCHA)
2040	Wilson Houses (NYCHA)

SECOND AVENUE

7–9	Germania Flats
57	Victoria
63–65	Majestic
125	Alpine
128	Florence
166	Peter Stuyvesant
193	Onyx Court
223	Temple Courts
231	Evarts, W. M., The
235	U. S. Senate, The

1450	Wagner House
2029	White House (NYCHA)
at East 26th Street	Phipps Plaza

THIRD AVENUE

111	Contempora, The
205	Gramercy Park Towers
364	Elite
382	East View Tower
909	Le Triomphe
1160	Frost House
1474	New Yorker, The
1733	Washington Houses (NYCHA)
1773	Lexington Houses (NYCHA)
2006	Newport

FIFTH AVENUE

11	Brevoort, The
12	Rhinelander Apartments
24	[Fifth Avenue Hotel]
60	Wedgewood House
96	Mayfair Fifth
105	Folio House
641	Olympic Tower
781	Sherry-Netherland
785	Parc–V
1400	Brewster, The
2071	Abingdon
at 61st Street	Pierre, The

SIXTH AVENUE. *See* Avenue of the Americas

SEVENTH AVENUE.

See also Adam Clayton Powell, Jr., Boulevard

77	Vermeer
488	York, The

EIGHTH AVENUE. *See also* Frederick Douglass Boulevard

85	Thomas-Eddy
224–226	Brensonia
228–230	Romanza

NINTH AVENUE

508 & 510	Oregon and Maine

ELEVENTH AVENUE

718	Oengler
724	St. Mary's
790	Clinton Tower

NAMED STREETS, AVENUES, etc.

ADAM CLAYTON POWELL, JR., BOULEVARD (FORMERLY SEVENTH AVENUE)

1845	Versailles
1851	Fontainebleau
1854	Idlewild
1855	Chantilly
1864	Palais Royal

1871–1873	White Hall
1885	Abelard
1893	Arcadia
1923–1937	Graham Court
1961	Lotta
2010	Clifton
2031	Larchmont, The
2034–2040	Washington Apartments
2037	Monmouth, The
2136	Parkhurst
2137	Oakhurst
2139	Greycourt
2228–2230	Majestic
2321–2339	Audubon
2340–2346	Rancley
2588	Dunbar Apartments

ADRIAN AVENUE
9–15	Angela Plaza

ALLEN STREET
189	Hernandez Houses (NYCHA)

AMSTERDAM AVENUE
477	Stella
502–512	Chalfonte, The; Marlborough, The; Clinton, The
852	Bloomingdale
1060	Amsterdam House
1320	Grant Houses (NYCHA)
1785	Josephine
1809–1811	Willa View Apartments
1909	Audubon Apartments (NYCHA)
1920	Dunwell Plaza
1945	Bethune Houses (NYCHA)
2103–2105	McKenna Square Home
2940–2956	Bolton, The

AUDUBON AVENUE
145	Shenandoah
155	Chesapeake
165–175	Algonac Court
185–187	Gertrude, The
188–196	Sun View
214	Herleon Court
215	Brighton
219	Shelburne
220	Edna Court
228	Valentine Court
240	Barney Court
247	Rookville
255	Jeanette Court
274	Merlegh Court
326	Sterling Court
480–490	Arnold Court

AVENUE A
    at 2nd Street   First Houses (NYCHA)
AVENUE B
    131–135   Tompkins Square Apartments
AVENUE D
    54   Wald Houses (NYCHA)
AVENUE OF THE AMERICAS
    241   Breen Towers
BANK STREET
    75   Abingdon Court
    99   Left Bank, The
    155   Westbeth
BARROW STREET
    54   Village Apartments
BEAK STREET
    7–15   Payson House
BEDFORD STREET
    95   J. Goebel & Co.
    102   Twin Peaks
BEEKMAN STREET
    90   Southbridge Towers
    117   Seaport Park Condominium
BENNETT AVENUE
    1   Blue Bell
    31–39   Holmes Court
    41–49   Wendell Hall
    44–54   Bennett Court
    56   Melvin Hall
    165   Champlain Arms
BLEECKER STREET
    77   Bleecker Court
    100–110   Silver Towers
    160   Atrium Apartments, The
    At West Broadway   Washington Square Village
BOWERY, THE
    19   Confucius Plaza
BROADWAY
    366   Collect Pond House [Bernard Semel
                        Building]
    808   Renwick, The
    2020   Seminole
    2107   Ansonia, The
    2109–2119   Apthorp Apartments, The
    2130   Beacon
    2141–2157   Astor Apartments
    2166   Opera, The [Manhattan Towers]
    2349   Euclid Hall
    2350   Bretton Hall
    2612   Marion
    2720   Regent Hotel
    3340   St. Evona
    3542   Hudson

3612–3618	River View
3440	Wingate Hotel
3671	Pavonazza
3675–3677	St. Regis
3679–3681	Halidon Court
3750	Audubon Park Apartments
3900	Medford
3920	Princess Court
4411	Abbey Towers
4761–4779	Broaddyke
4791–4797	George Washington Court
4861–4873	Hawthorne Gardens
4996	Erco Court
5000	Grenville Hall
5009–5021	Isham Park Plaza
5025–5035	Rosewall Court
5220	Marble Hill Houses (NYCHA)

CABRINI BOULEVARD

100	Northern, The
120–200	Castle Village

CARMINE STREET

45	Village Apartments, The
48	Theresia
76–78	Adora

CATHEDRAL PARKWAY (WEST 110TH STREET)

424	Cathedral Parkway Houses
500	Irving Hall
501	Morris Hall
509	Dartmouth
510	Cortland
514	Marc Antony, The
515	St. Albans
520	Prince Humbert
527	Britannia
535	Cathedral Parkway Apartments

CATHERINE STREET

at Monroe Street	Knickerbocker Village

CENTRAL PARK NORTH (WEST 110TH STREET)

137	Semiramis
141	Cambridge Hotel
217	Zenobia, The

CENTRAL PARK SOUTH

120	Berkeley House
160	Essex House
222	Gainsborough, The

CENTRAL PARK WEST

25	Century Apartments
41	Harperly Hall
50	Prasada
88	Brentmore

115	Majestic Apartments, The
135	Langham, The
145–146	San Remo
151	Kenilworth, The
211	Beresford, The
225	Alden, The
230	Bolivar, The
257	Orwell House [Central Park View, Peter Stuyvesant]
262	White House, The
285	St. Urban, The
300	Eldorado
320	Ardsley, The
333	Turin, The
410	Edith
414	Central Park View
415	Parkview Apartments
418	Brander
420	Jadam, The
446	Greenwich
461	Central Park Terrace
477	Loyola
480	Melrose
482–484	Hartley Hall

CHARLES STREET

15	Village Towers
29	Carolus, The
115	Palazzo Greco
129	Thalman, H.
135	Gendarme, Le

CHARLTON STREET

2	Charlton House
112–114	Dunklin Building

CHRISTOPHER STREET

78–80	Nevada, The
87–91	Gessner, The
195	Gansevoort

CLAREMONT AVENUE

3	Paterno
15	Barnard Court
21	Sophomore
25	Peter Minuit
29	Eton Hall
35	Rugby Hall
49	Barieford
175	Fairview Court
189	Medina, The
191	Sonoma, The
195	Crescent Court
200	Garfield

CLINTON STREET
    257   Lands End
COLUMBIA STREET
    81   Masaryk Towers
    100   Baruch Houses (NYCHA)
COLUMBUS AVENUE
    386   Columbus House
    430   Planetarium Apartments
    505   Pomona
    609   Turin House Apartments
    690   Foresters Home
    744   Ninth Avenue Flat
    880   Douglass Houses (NYCHA)
CONVENT AVENUE
    29   St. Veronica
    41   St. Agnes
    110   Convent View
    260   Sound View Court
    310   Hamilton Grange
    435   Emsworth Hall
    462–466   Kenway
    480   Iroquois
    490   Osceola
    492   Fontenoy
COOPER STREET
    10   Cooper Arms
CUMMING STREET
    19   Galsie Garden
DELANCEY STREET
    101   Karg
DIVISION STREET
    2   Confucius Plaza
DUANE STREET
    165   Duane Park
DYCKMAN STREET
    200   Dikewood Arms
EAST END AVENUE
    25   Yorkgate
    180   Gracie Towers
EDGECOMBE AVENUE
    204   Elwood
    267   Florence Mills Apartments
    321   Park Lincoln
    385   Somerset
    393   Vivia
    409–417   Colonial Parkway
ELLWOOD STREET
    111   Renaissance Courts
FAIRVIEW AVENUE
    89–91   Broadway Arms

FORT WASHINGTON AVENUE

15	Rio Grande
21	Rio Vista
25	Rivercrest, The
32–38	Plymouth
46–52	Chateau d'Armes
66–72	Chambold Court
86	Lenathan Hall, The
97	Fairfield
106	Samana Mansion
235	Fortress, The
238	Nassau
245	Court Washington
255	Rock Forest
370	Howard, The
385	Annadale
395	Belle Court
452	Dacorn
453	Hazelhurst
455	Chislehurst
457	Pinehurst, The
536	Shirbar Terrace
609–615	Cloister Arms
720–760	Tryon Gardens

FRANKLIN D. ROOSEVELT DRIVE

at Jackson Street	Gouverneur Gardens

FREDERICK DOUGLASS BOULEVARD (FORMERLY EIGHTH AVENUE)

2338–2348	Shenandoah
2975	Polo Grounds Towers (NYCHA)

FULTON STREET

at Gold Street	Southbridge Towers

GOLD STREET

33	[Excelsior Power Company]

GRAMERCY PARK EAST

34	Gramercy, The

GRAMERCY PARK SOUTH

8	Gramercy House
15	National Arts Club Studios
32	Gramercy Towers

GRAND STREET

500–550	Amalgamated-Hillman Houses

GREENWICH AVENUE

33	St. Germain

GREENWICH STREET

622	Stafford, The
720	Towers, The

GROVE STREET

35	Lyceum
49	Grove Apartments

HAMILTON PLACE
    51   Eufaula
    87   Winslow Court
    115   Washington, The
    135   Park Hill
HAMILTON TERRACE
    19   Ivey Delph Apartments, The
    61   Talladega
HARLEM RIVER DRIVE
    159–16   Ralph J. Rangel Houses (NYCHA)
HAVEN AVENUE
    106   Woodcliff
    112   Haven Cliff
    120   Hudson Cliff
    217–225   Cliffhaven Court
    223–227   Hudson Court
HILLSIDE AVENUE
    25–35   Hillside Court
HORATIO STREET
    14   Van Gogh, The
    26–28   Greenwich.V
    50   Hudson, The
    95   West Coast Apartments, The
HUDSON STREET
    91   [Mercantile Exchange Building]
    105   Powell Building
    181–185   Vestry Place
    421   Printing House
JANE STREET
    31   Rembrandt, The
    61   Cezanne, The
KING STREET
    22–28   Kingston
    29   [P.S. 8]
LAFAYETTE STREET
    226   President Monroe Apartments
    292   Weathering Heights
LENOX AVENUE
    90   Martin Luther King, Jr. Towers
                            (NYCHA)
    135   Graustark
    164–168   Hamilton Court
LEXINGTON AVENUE
    4   Gramercy Towers
    7   Park Gramercy, The
    151   Beta South
    264–266   Sherbrook
    1125   St. George
    1327–1329   Rhinelander, The
    1349   Paulding

1377 & 1379	Weber
1428	Summit
1469	Windsor Court
1744	Clinton Houses (NYCHA)
1844	James Weldon Johnson Houses (NYCHA)
2120	Jackie Robinson Houses (NYCHA)
LIBERTY STREET	
55	Liberty Towers
MACOMBS PLACE	
29–31	Macombs Lane
33–39	Central
MADISON AVENUE	
220	John Murray House
457	Villard Houses
680	Carlton House
1080	La Residence
1100	Schermerhorn, The
1290	Wellington, The
1295	Wales Hotel {Melbourne}
1326	Fairfax, The
1356	Almscourt
1361	Madison Court
1393	Ambassador, The
1475	Carver Houses (NYCHA)
1600	Villahermosa
1605	Lehman Village (NYCHA)
1740	Taft Houses (NYCHA)
2142	Lincoln Houses (NYCHA)
MADISON STREET	
250	La Guardia Houses (NYCHA)
356	Vladeck Houses (NYCHA)
MANHATTAN AVENUE	
2	Sharon
4	Richfield
8	Mont Clemens
10	Cascade
11	Rene
16	Manhattan Court
194–198	Adelaide
272	Golden Gate
312	Rochambeau
320	Lafayette
400	Parthenon, The
408	Hesperus
437	Harold
MARBLE HILL AVENUE	
1	Marble Hill View
2	Marble Hill
70	Fort Charles Court

MITCHELL PLACE
    9   Beekman Tower
    10   Stewart House
MORNINGSIDE AVENUE
    14   Helen Court
    16   Pauline
    18   Vondale
    20–23   Granite, The
MORNINGSIDE DRIVE
    40   East View
    44–47   Cathedral Court
    50   Touraine, La
    54   Mont Cenis
    90   St. Valier, The
    110   Shelburne Hall
    114   Circle, The
MOUNT MORRIS PARK SOUTH
    2   Gainsboro
MOUNT MORRIS PARK WEST
    35   Montana
NAGLE AVENUE
    65–67   Nagle Arms
    140–144   Thayer Court
    165   Nagle Court
    215   Dyckman Houses (NYCHA)
NORFOLK STREET
    65   Seward Park Extension (NYCHA)
PARK AVENUE
    4   [Vanderbilt]
    7   Greenpark, The
    10   [Community Church Apartments]
    23   Advertising Club
    77   Griffon, The
    465   Ritz Tower
    502   Delmonico's
    575   Beekman, The
    610   Mayfair House
    900   Park 900, The
    1065   Carlton Park
    1240   Van Cortlandt, The
    1245   Park House, The
PARK AVENUE SOUTH
    145   Mayfair 14th
PARK ROW
    170   Chatham Towers
    185   Chatham Green
PARK TERRACE EAST
    10   High View Manor
    50   Embassy
    98   Daniel

PEARL STREET
   324   Bindery, The
PERRY STREET
   48   Model, The
   63   McKinley
   80–82   Hampton, The
PIKE STREET
   61   Rutgers Houses (NYCHA)
PINEHURST AVENUE
   10–12   Joan d'Arc
   45   Kenilworth
   91   Palisades Arms
   92–102   Pinehurst Towers
   106–114   Hudson Towers
   116   Hudson View Gardens
   165–171   St. Mihiel
   175   High View Court
   183   Tudor Hall
   187   High View Terrace
   200   Tryon Towers
PITT STREET
   50   Gompers Houses (NYCHA)
POST AVENUE
   66   Irene Hall
   70   Post Hall
   130   Inwood Court
RIVERSIDE DRIVE
   11   Schwab House
   67   Riverdale
   80   Riverside Towers
   125   Turrets, The
   131   Dorchester
   137   Clarendon, The
   140   Normandy, The
   200   St. Denis
   202–208   Terrace Court
   210   Stratford-Avon
   214   Chatillion
   222   Westsider Hotel [Irving Arms]
   223   Estling, The
   227   Avalon Hall
   240   Cliff Dwellers' Apartments
   244   Rhineland, The
   250   Victoria
   252   Peter Stuyvesant
   260   Chesterfield
   265   Clifden
   270   Glen Cairn
   310   Master Apartments, The
   330   Rockledge Hall

337	River Mansion
360	Rutherford
362	Bonavista
380	Hendrik Hudson, The
400	Fowler Court
404	Strathmore
410	Riverside Mansions
420	Hamilton Hall
431	Columbia Court
435	Colosseum
440	Paterno
445	Stadium View
448	Shore View
450	Brookfield
452	Miramar
454	Oxford Hall
460	Aquavista
464	Monte Vista
468	Concord Hall
527	Ardelle, The
528	Ulysses
530	Claremont Court
547	Hague, The
548	Montebello
549	Bordeaux, The
550	Alabama
552	Madrid
575	West Point
583	St. Francis Court
587	Beaconsfield Apartments, The
593	Panmure Arms
596	Haddon Hall
600	Cromwell Apartments
610	Imperial Arms
626	River View Towers
660–666	Elbe, The
668	Norland, The
676	Deerfield
706	Picken Court
720	Andrew Jackson
730	Beaumont
736	Placid Hall
740	Switzerland
747	Onondaga
779	Crillon Court, The
780	Vaux Hall
788	Rhinecliff Court
790	Riviera
800	Grinnell
801	Cragmoor
835	Villa Norma

838–844	Kingsland
870	Armidale
894	Loyal
920–926	Mandel Court
1803	Payson
1825	Dyck Arms
157–10	River Terrace
159–00	River Arts
ST. JAMES PLACE	
21	Smith Houses (NYCHA)
ST. MARK'S PLACE	
10	St. Nicholas
54	Ida
115–119	Tompkins Flats
122–126	St. Mark's Flats
123	L. Schnee Building
ST. NICHOLAS AVENUE	
52–56	St. Nicholas
60	Shoreham
80	Carvel Court
92	Warwick
100	Marion
121	El Nido Apartments
180	Chalmont
182	Grampion Apartments (NYCHA)
188	Capernack
205–207	Triangle, The
337	Dorrence Brooks, The
446	Roscoe
450	Raynor, The
454	Lesster, The
630	College Park Apartments
654	St. Nicholas
680–684	Majestic
695	Sadivian Arms, The
707	Harvard Court
723–727	Montalvo Court
744	Amagansett
795	Plaza, The
801	Leander
930	Victoria Court
936–938	Cliffcrest
961	Franklin Arms
964	Polo
974	Morton Court
1061	Florida
1270	Stratford Avon Hall
1456	Harold Court
ST. NICHOLAS PLACE	
2–4	Audubon Court
18	Juliette

40	Bavaria, The
48	Cedarcliff
52–54	Demaran Court
80	Florida Court
87	Nonpareil
89	Montvale

ST. NICHOLAS TERRACE

41	St. Francis
49	St. Cecilia

SEAMAN AVENUE

1–9	Dyckman Plaza
2–12	Dyckview
35–41	Dyckman Arms
65–71	Milburn Court
100–110	Seaman Towers
222 & 229	Isham Gardens
230–236	Riverview

SHERIDAN SQUARE

3	Parker Town House
10	Shenandoah, The
15	Sheridan Arms

SHERMAN AVENUE

9–21	Sherman Hall
40	Gibraltar Court
31–41	Arden Towers
160	Ruthmore
165–175	Sherman Hall
189–199	Terrace Garden
210	Caroline, The
221	Hazel Court
272–274	Randolpho, The

SICKLES STREET

30–36	Lucille
38–48	Sickles Garden

SOUTH END AVENUE

397	Gateway Plaza

SOUTH HAMILTON PLACE

94	Katterskill North and Katterskill South

SOUTH PINEHURST AVENUE

2	Charlotte Court
4	Emily Court

SOUTH STREET

116–119	Meyers' Hotel

SPRING STREET

21	Little Italy Apartments

SULLIVAN STREET

140	E. H. Friedrichs

SUTTON PLACE SOUTH

45	Cannon Point South

TERRACE VIEW
    110   Katherine Court
TIEMANN PLACE
    31   Edgewood
    45   Whitestone, The
    55   Claremont
TUDOR CITY PLACE
    5   Windsor Tower
    25   Tudor Tower
    45   Prospect Tower
VARICK STREET
    80   Soho Grand, The
VERMILYEA STREET
    72–74   Rexmoore
WADSWORTH AVENUE
    45–49   Wadsworth Manor
    129   Wadsworth Court
    130   Wadsworth Arms
    220   Paul Jones, The
    247   Hedson Apartments
    367   Minerva Court
    374   Traud Hall
    382   Ben Nevis
    390   Grand View
WASHINGTON PLACE
    82–86   Washington Square, The
    119   Lilly, The
WASHINGTON SQUARE NORTH
    27   Richmond Hill, The
WASHINGTON SQUARE WEST
    33   Holly Chambers [Hayden Hall]
WASHINGTON STREET
    641   Archives Building
    at Bank Street   West Village Houses
    at Harrison Street   Independence Plaza
WATER STREET
    130   Seaport South
    245   Ships Chandlery Condominium
WAVERLY PLACE
    123   Van Voorst
WEST BROADWAY
    90–92   Gerken Building
    260   American Thread Building
WEST END AVENUE
    110   Lincoln-Amsterdam House
    225   Collinson
    300   Van Horne
    378   West End Plaza
    401   New Century Apartments
    424   West River House

483	Congressional Hotel
495	Hohenzollern
500	San Jose
666	Windermere Hotel
740	Della Robbia
781	Envoy, The
801	South Pennington and North Pennington
808	Allendale, The
839	Creston
840	West End Hall
924	Clebourne, The
925	Alimar
930	Westbourne
936	Lancaster Apartments
945	Stanley Court
YORK AVENUE	
1161	Sutton Terrace
1175	York River House
1364–1366	Alfredos Casinos
1365	Somerset, The
1385	Stratford, The
1701	Gracie Plaza
1725	East River Tower
at 78th Street	[Model Tenements]

ACKNOWLEDGMENTS

The authors deeply appreciate the help of:

The staffs of the New-York Historical Society, the Museum of the City of New York, and the New York Public Library.

Laurie Beckleman; Albert K. Baragwanath; James F. Carr; Edward Lee Cave; William Doyle; Neysa Furey; Geri Ianuzzi; George Lang; Norbert Machado; Steven Miller; Nancy Phelan; Betsy Pinover; Pamela Pinto; Katherine Richards; Larry Sullivan; Richard Zimmerman.

Thomas A. Stewart of Atheneum Publishers, who was enthusiastic about the project and edited the manuscript with great care.

Every effort has been made to ensure accuracy, but Manhattan is a complex and ever-changing island; any omissions or errors are sincerely regretted.

Born in Maine and brought up in New Jersey, Thomas Norton has lived in Manhattan since finishing a stint in the army in the late fifties. He received a degree in American Studies from Fordham University's College of Arts and Sciences in the Bronx, and upon graduation joined the staff of Parke-Bernet Galleries. He was associated with Sotheby Parke Bernet in every capacity from trainee to cataloguer to expert department head to Senior Vice President for Communications and Marketing until his retirement in 1980. Since then he's appeared in a film, worked as an art consultant and appraiser, moved from a named building to an anonymous building, become a father, and written two books: Living It Up *and* One Hundred Years of Collecting in America: The Story of Sotheby Parke Bernet.

Born in Fort Worth and educated at the University of Texas and Yale, Jerry Patterson became a New Yorker in 1959 when he entered graduate school at Columbia. He has worked as a librarian, editor, and executive at both Sotheby Parke Bernet and Christie's. The author of eight books, including The City of New York: A History Illustrated from the Collections of the Museum of the City of New York.